A PRACTITIONER'S GUIDE TO DIRECTORS' DUTIES AND RESPONSIBILITIES

A PRACTITIONER'S GUIDE TO DIRECTORS' DUTIES AND RESPONSIBILITIES

Consultant Editor
Glen James
Slaughter and May

Second Edition

City & Financial Publishing

City & Financial Publishing
8 Westminster Court, Hipley Street
Old Woking
Surrey GU22 9LG
United Kingdom
Tel: 00 44 (0)1483 720707 Fax: 00 44 (0)1483 727928
Web: www.cityandfinancial.com

This book has been compiled from the contributions of the named authors. The views expressed herein do not necessarily reflect the views of their respective firms. Further, since this book is intended as a general guide only, its application to specific situations will depend upon the particular circumstances involved and it should not be relied upon as a substitute for obtaining appropriate professional advice.

This book is current as at 31 July 2003. Whilst all reasonable care has been taken in the preparation of this book, City & Financial Publishing and the authors do not accept responsibility for any errors it may contain or for any loss sustained by any person placing reliance on its contents.

All rights reserved. Neither the whole nor any part of this publication may be copied or otherwise reproduced without the prior written permission of the copyright holders.

The first edition of this book was published as *A Practitioner's Guide to the Role of Directors and Their Duties and Responsibilities*.

ISBN 1 898830 70 3
© 2003 City & Financial Publishing and the authors.

British Library Cataloguing-in-Publication Data. A catalogue record for this book is available from the British Library.

Typeset by Type Study, Scarborough and printed and bound in Great Britain by Bell & Bain, Glasgow.

Biographies

Glen James is a partner at Slaughter and May. Glen's practice covers all work in the fields of company/corporate finance, including mergers and acquisitions, issues and flotations and corporate restructurings. He has wide experience of these transactions in a number of different industry sectors. He has also advised extensively on the structuring and reconstruction of, and the acquisition and disposal of, insurance and other financial services companies and businesses. He is a member of the Insurance Law Sub-Committee of the City of London Law Society.

Anthony Newhouse is a partner at Slaughter and May. He has worked there after qualifying in the late 1970's having previously worked as a banker. He has a wide commercial and corporate practice, built on lengthy experience in takeover bids, other equity market related work and private company mergers and acquisitions. He has undertaken privatisations, monopolies references and regulatory work and enquiries.

Chris Hale is head of the company department at Travers Smith Braithwaite. He has had 20 years experience in corporate law, principally mergers and acquisitions activity and in particular leveraged buy-outs. He is a member of the editorial board of the Company Lawyer. He is also a member of the Advisory Council of the Institute of Advanced Legal Studies and is treasurer of the Society of Advanced Legal Studies. He writes and lectures regularly on company law matters.

Richard Slynn is a partner in Allen & Overy. He advises on a broad range of corporate finance transactions, including mergers and acquisitions, joint ventures, flotations, demutualisations and other major transactions. He advises the boards of public and private companies, building societies and other corporate bodies on constitutional issues and directors' duties. He has served as a member of the Institute of Directors' Professional Standards Committee and the City of London Law Society Commercial Law Sub-Committee.

Rosalind Nicholson is a Barrister and has practised from 4 Stone Buildings, Lincoln's Inn since 1988. She specialises in company law, corporate reconstruction and corporate insolvency, both advice and litigation in those fields with an emphasis on litigation. She is the author of Table A Articles of Association (Sweet & Maxwell 1997).

Vanessa Knapp has been a partner of Freshfields Bruckhaus Deringer since 1988. She specialises in company law, mergers and acquisitions and financial services regulation. She is chairman of the Law Society Company Law Committee and was a member of two Company Law Review Groups established by the Department of Trade and Industry to review company law. She is the UK representative of the Company Law Committee of the Council of the Bars and Law Societies of the European Union (CCBE).

John Farr is the Head of the Employment Group at Herbert Smith. He has been a partner since 1982.

Andrew Peck has been a partner of Linklaters since 1983. He advises a wide range of industrial, commercial and financial companies on corporate law and corporate governance issues, as well as advising both investment banking and corporate clients on mergers and acquisitions and equity issues.

Caroline Carter is a partner and head of employment at International law firm Ashurst Morris Crisp. She specialises in non-contentious and contentious employment matters advising on all employment aspects of management buy-outs, mergers and acquisitions, flotations and public takeovers. Caroline also has considerable experience of the protection of confidential information and post-termination restrictive covenants, corporate governance issues, senior executive appointments and terminations and workforce restructuring.

Caroline is a member of The Employment Lawyers' Association; The European Lawyers' Association; The City of London Solicitors' Company: Employment Law Sub-Committee and the Institute of Directors.

David Johnson was educated at Trinity Hall, Cambridge and became a partner of Slaughter and May in 2000. He advises on a wide range of corporate and commercial transactions and has particular experience in public and private mergers and acquisitions and equity financings.

Michael Hatchard is practice leader at the London offices of Skadden, Arps, Slate Meagher & Flom LLP. Michael has extensive experience in mergers and other transactions subject to the UK Takeover Code, both hostile and friendly, including the acquisition and disposal of strategic holdings of securities traded in the UK. His practice has also included private M&A, financial restructurings and reorganisations.

Hamish Anderson is a partner in the banking department at Norton Rose, specialising in Insolvency. Hamish qualified as a solicitor in 1973 and has been a licensed insolvency practitioner since 1987. Hamish is a past president and former council member of the Insolvency Lawyers' Association and a serving council member of the Association of Business Recovery Professionals. He is also an active member of the Law Society and City of London Law Society Insolvency Law Sub-committees and the Editorial Board for "Insolvency Law & Practice", as well as serving on the Executive Committee of the Joint Insolvency Examination Board. He is a regular speaker and writer on Insolvency matters.

Angela Hayes is a partner in Lawrence Graham's Financial Services Group. She advises financial services sector clients, listed companies and individual directors on regulatory matters ranging from obtaining Financial Services Authority ("FSA") authorisation for new businesses, through conduct of business, compliance issues and disclosure obligations, to regulatory investigations, market abuse, white collar crime and fraud. During a period of secondment to the FSA in the run up to "N2", she advised the FSA on the implementation of key aspects of the Financial Services and Markets Act 2000.

David Allison is a barrister at 3/4 South Square. His practice encompasses all aspects of company, commercial and financial law, with a particular emphasis on insolvency and restructuring.

Stephen Robins is a barrister at 3/4 South Square in London. His practice encompasses all aspects of commercial litigation and business law, including corporate insolvency, banking law, company law and directors' disqualification.

Foreword

It is a sign of the times that the period that has elapsed since the publication of the first edition of this Guide – just two-and-a-half years – has been one of enormous change in the corporate world. Events in both the UK and the US – regulatory changes; corporate scandals; major insolvencies and the continuing obsession with contracts and remuneration – have conspired to put unprecedented pressure on company directors.

In the UK this state of flux has been most apparent in two key areas: the legislative and regulatory reform of the Enterprise Act 2002, Company Law Review and the implications of Sarbanes-Oxley; and corporate governance reform in the shape of the report bearing my name, which aims to emphasise the role of the non-executive director, and the Smith Report examining the role of the audit committee, amongst other guidance and reports.

The role of the director in helping to promote the success of the company within an ever-increasing legal and corporate governance framework is a challenging one, particularly in today's hostile economic climate.

The need for advice and guidance is probably greater than ever, which is why I can recommend this book. The contributors are leading corporate lawyers whose collective knowledge of the increasingly complicated legal environment within which directors operate is second to none. All of the key developments of the last two years are covered thoroughly to provide an indispensable source of information for directors wanting an informed view of their responsibilities, as well as for those lawyers and others whose role is to advise directors.

Derek Higgs
Chairman, Partnerships UK plc
April 2003

Table of Contents

1	**Introduction** Anthony Newhouse, Partner *Slaughter and May*	1
	1.1 The company's interests	2
	1.2 Duties and responsibilities	4
	1.3 Nature of companies	11
	1.4 Reform	15
2	**Appointment and Vacation of Office** Chris Hale, Partner *Travers Smith Braithwaite*	19
	2.1 Introduction	19
	2.2 Method of appointment of directors	21
	2.3 Qualification	29
	2.4 Vacation of office	38
	2.5 Notification obligations and returns to regulators	48
	2.6 Alternate directors	50
	2.7 Shadow directors and *de facto* directors	53
	2.8 Nominee directors	55
	2.9 Possible future developments and consequences	55
3	**Directors' Duties** Richard Slynn, Partner *Allen & Overy*	65
	3.1 Introduction	65
	3.2 Fiduciary duties	66
	3.3 Care, skill and diligence	84
	3.4 Other duties	90
	3.5 Possible future developments and consequences	99
	3.6 Recent trends and themes concerning directors' duties in other EU countries and the US	102

4	**Potential Liabilities**	**105**
	Rosalind Nicholson, Barrister	
	4 Stone Buildings	
	4.1 Ultra vires acts	105
	4.2 Liability for the acts of the company: crimes	107
	4.3 Liability for the acts of the company: torts	109
	4.4 Liability for the acts of the company: contracts	112
	4.5 Liability for the acts of the company: company debts	116
	4.6 Issues of securities	118
	4.7 Winding up	125
	4.8 Indemnity and insurance against liability	134
	4.9 Statutory relief	135
5	**Fair Dealing and Connected Persons**	**139**
	Vanessa Knapp, Partner	
	Freshfields Bruckhaus Deringer	
	5.1 Introduction	139
	5.2 Loss of office and retirement from office	141
	5.3 Payments which the company has previously agreed to make	143
	5.4 Disclosure of interests in contracts	145
	5.5 Contracts with directors who are sole members	148
	5.6 Substantial property transactions involving directors	149
	5.7 Transactions with related parties	152
	5.8 Loans to directors and related transactions	155
	5.9 Relevant amounts	165
	5.10 Remedies for breach of Section 330	166
	5.11 Liability for transactions involving directors	168
	5.12 Connected persons	169
6	**Service Contracts and Remuneration**	**173**
	John Farr, Partner	
	Herbert Smith	
	6.1 Introduction	173
	6.2 Authorisation of service contracts – compliance with the company's constitution	173
	6.3 Limits on the length of the term of a service contract	176
	6.4 Disclosure of service contracts	178
	6.5 Remuneration of directors	180
	6.6 Other benefits	189
	6.7 Compensation for loss of office	193

7	**Share Dealing by Directors and Connected Persons** Andrew Peck, Partner *Linklaters*		**201**
	7.1 Introduction		201
	7.2 Restrictions on dealing		202
	7.3 The Model Code		211
	7.4 The Takeover Code		216
	7.5 Prohibition on dealing in options		218
	7.6 Disclosure of interests		218
8	**Directors' Powers and Proceedings** Caroline Carter, Partner *Ashurst Morris Crisp*		**225**
	8.1 Powers of companies and their directors		225
	8.2 Delegation		237
	8.3 Access to company books		248
9	**Corporate Governance** David Johnson, Partner *Slaughter and May*		**253**
	9.1 Introduction		253
	9.2 Background		254
	9.3 The Combined Code		258
	9.4 Is the present system of corporate governance adequate?		270
	9.5 Conclusion		284
10	**Directors Facing Disputes** Michael Hatchard, Partner *Skadden, Arps, Slate, Meagher & Flom (UK) LLP*		**287**
	10.1 Disputes within the board		287
	10.2 Disputes between the board and the members		294
	10.3 Derivative actions		301
	10.4 Statutory unfair prejudice remedy (Section 459)		310
	10.5 Proposals for reform		327

11	**Duties of Directors Facing Insolvency** Hamish Anderson, Partner *Norton Rose*	333
	11.1 Introduction	333
	11.2 Statutory duties under the Insolvency Act 1986	333
	11.3 Fiduciary duties of directors	348
	11.4 Public companies and listed companies: duties to shareholders	353
	11.5 Practical matters	355
12	**Regulatory Investigations** Angela Hayes, Partner *Lawrence Graham*	357
	12.1 Introduction	357
	12.2 Scope of the investigation	358
	12.3 The notice of appointment	361
	12.4 Effect of the notice	361
	12.5 Confidentiality of the investigation	363
	12.6 The autonomy of the investigators	364
	12.7 Powers of the investigators	365
	12.8 Sanctions	366
	12.9 Limits on the powers of investigators	367
	12.10 Privilege against self-incrimination	370
	12.11 The product of the investigation	372
	12.12 How may the information be used?	374
	12.13 To whom may the information be disclosed?	376
	12.14 Practical considerations	379
13	**Disqualification of Directors** David Allison and Stephen Robins *3/4 South Square Chambers, Gray's Inn*	391
	13.1 Introduction	391
	13.2 Grounds for disqualification	392
	13.3 The purpose of disqualification	395
	13.4 Territorial limits of CDDA 1986	396
	13.5 Procedure	398
	13.6 Determining unfitness	407
	13.7 Period of disqualification	415
	13.8 Disqualification undertakings	416
	13.9 Discontinuance of proceedings and applications for a stay of the proceedings by the defendant	420

13.10	Appeals	422
13.11	The effect of a disqualification order	422
13.12	Applications for permission to act by a disqualified director	427
13.13	Conclusion	430

Index 431

Chapter 1
Introduction

Anthony Newhouse, Partner
Slaughter and May

This Guide, now in its second edition, is for practitioners – company directors and their professional advisers. They are only too aware that there is no simple model role for the company director; nor has there been, to date, any comprehensive code of their duties and responsibilities. This is partly because of the way that company law and the codes of corporate governance have evolved in the UK; also because of the diverse nature of the purposes and interests which corporate structures serve. Practitioners, however, will want to master all aspects of the regulatory regime, both legal and voluntary, which prescribe the conduct of company directors; the more so, as the consequences of breach are serious. Furthermore, practitioners will wish to be aware of, and be in a position to react to, the changes in the regulatory regime with which they are faced. The roles of directors and their duties and responsibilities will vary according to the type of company they serve, and to some extent to the nature of their position. So too will the level of regulation. But as a preliminary, practitioners may ask whether there is any underlying framework to which they may refer for guidance and from which they may infer what is expected of them.

Since the first edition of this Guide was published, the process of change has moved on. 2002 saw the publication of *Modernising Company Law*,[1] the Government's White Paper, setting out its core proposals in response to the Final Report of the Company Law Steering Group,[2] including proposals for a statement of "General Principles by which Directors are Bound". On the international front, the financial scandals in the US led to the passing in 2002 of Sarbanes-Oxley[3] in response to the perceived lacunae in the American system of corporate governance, which has been

---

[1] See generally: Modernising Company Law: Cm 5553-I; and for the General Principles, Draft Clauses, Schedule 2, Cm 5553-II.
[2] "Modern Company Law for a Competitive Economy: Final Report", the Company Law Review Steering Group, July 2001.
[3] The Sarbanes-Oxley Act of 2002.

of concern to directors of large companies with US listings and which will over time impact on thinking in the UK. 2003 saw the further evolution of the non-statutory framework of corporate governance with the publication of the Higgs Review.[4] Each of these, and others such as the Report of the High Level Group of Company Law Experts,[5] set up by the European Commission in September 2001, highlight the focus of legislators and regulators on the responsibilities and duties of directors. While some of the current debate goes to the role of the directors of large listed companies, all of it is of concern to, and will affect, directors of companies of whatever size and nature.

1.1 The company's interests

As a starting point, company directors need to be clear as to whom they owe their duties. The established rule, that the duties are owed to the company, answers the question of who can enforce those duties: the company, acting through its board or, in limited circumstances, its shareholders. But that begs the question: who is the company? Even if, as some say, the duties of the directors can be reduced to the simple but delphic proposition that the directors must act in good faith in the interests of the company, that does not assist in identifying the constituent interests to which directors must defer.

The interests of the company are normally equated with the interests of shareholders as its founders and as the owners of its equity. The draft General Principles frame the duty as one to act in a way which the directors decide in good faith would be most likely to promote the success of the company for the benefit of its members as a whole. But the formulation is in part prospective. It is to the interests of shareholders, present and future, that directors must look, with the aim of ensuring that the long-term interests of the company are balanced against current interests, rather than that the particular interests of future, unidentified shareholders are taken into account. Even so, specific circumstances qualify a principle such as this. In a takeover offer, the best price available to present shareholders may be the primary concern of target company directors. Although the relationship between director and shareholder

---

[4] Derek Higgs, *Review of the Role and Effectiveness of Non-executive Directors*, January 2003.
[5] "Report of the High Level Group of Company Law Experts on a Modern Regulatory Framework for Company Law in Europe", Brussels, 4 November 2002.

does not of itself give rise to a fiduciary duty, directors may assume a responsibility to shareholders directly when the circumstances require.[6]

At some point, the interests of creditors become paramount as impending insolvency becomes an inevitability. Additionally, the directors must also have regard in the performance of their functions to the interests of the company's employees in general, as well as the interests of its members.[7] This position is recognised in statute and also in the voluntary codes which regulate the affairs of public companies, and it is very different from the position encountered in many continental European jurisdictions, particularly where Works Councils are concerned. As yet, the legal consequences of ignoring the interests of employees have not been fully determined. Thus far, directors will in most situations know or may be advised as to whose interests they must heed when considering the interests of the company.

There are, however, trends evident in the evolution of practice and theory which complicate matters, as the continental European models demonstrated some time since. The relatively recent exposition of the concept of stakeholders' interests, where the interests of shareholders, creditors, employees and the wider community co-exist, has brought into question the pre-eminence of the shareholder interest. This may have come about for a number of reasons: because of developments in the law relating to matters other than shareholder/management issues (on which historically much of the theory was based); and for social and political reasons the values of late nineteenth-century capitalism have been reassessed.

In the 1980s, Sir Hector Laing, a leading company chairman at the time, helped bring to prominence the concept of stakeholders' interests in a series of pamphlets. Drawing comparisons with the Japanese model, he spelled out most clearly the reasons why the company's interests should embrace more than those of shareholders. He argued that: "business cannot isolate itself from the community of which it forms a constituent part, it is an integral part of society: its goals and those of the community are ultimately concurrent."[8] Yet, if the pluralist approach is to be the accepted norm, the responsibilities of the company director become more difficult to discharge, while the position becomes more powerful. It may be argued that the stakeholder concept is merely a different way of

---

[6] *Platt and another v Platt* [1999] 2 BCLC 745.
[7] Section 309 CA 1985, which is proposed to be replaced in the General Principles.
[8] Sir Hector Laing, *Morality and the Distribution of Wealth*, 23 October 1985.

expressing the existing concepts of what are the constituent interests of the company. Sir Hector would say: "this is not just good citizenship, it is good business". But the development of the pluralist approach could result in the notion of the company as an entity having interests of its own gaining ground. It would be for the director of a company to balance the varied interests of those with whom it has relationships in order to carry on its business. If, however, there is any difficulty in resolving a conflict between these interests, the company's interest in its continued commercial viability may take precedence.

The issues were addressed by both the Law Commission[9] and the Company Law Review Steering Group[10] in the context of the debate on reforming this area of the law. The Company Law Review Steering Group thought that: "The overall *objective* should be pluralist in the sense that companies should be run in a way which maximises overall competitiveness and wealth and welfare for all. But the means which company law deploys for achieving this objective must take account of the realities and dynamics which operate in practice in the running of commercial enterprise." That approach has been followed in the White Paper and is reflected in the draft General Principles.

1.2 Duties and responsibilities

It is of little use to directors to know which groups' interests they must have regard to in carrying out their duties if they do not know what those duties are. This area of law has to date been fragmented and difficult, as is typical of law which has evolved in a common law environment.

Currently in the UK a combination of law (statutory and case law) and self-regulation aims to govern the standards of a director's behaviour as an officer of the company. In addition, the legislator and the academic both have recourse to overseas jurisdictions such as the US, Australia and New Zealand in framing directors' duties. While the practitioner will not be familiar with every aspect of these variations, it is important to understand the influence they may have on the development of law in the UK.

---

[9] Law Commission Consultation Paper No. 153 (September 1998) and Law Commission Report No. 261 (September 1999), both entitled "Company Directors: Regulating Conflicts of Interests and Formulating a Statement of Duties".

[10] "Modern Company Law for a Competitive Economy: Developing the Framework", a consultation document from the Company Law Review Steering Group, March 2000.

Introduction

For example, the business judgment rule as adopted in many states of the US protects directors from interference by the courts where certain conditions are fulfilled. The Law Commission has looked to such jurisdictions when considering the desirability of introducing such a rule. Although the Australian Government has proposed the introduction of a similar rule, neither the Law Commission nor the Company Law Review Steering Group has recommended adoption of a statutory business judgment rule. In keeping with the common law background, this is to be left to the courts to develop.

While the common law jurisdictions have been the main influences hitherto, it seems inevitable that the influence of European Union law will be in the ascendant, although there is currently a lack of harmonisation in the area of directors' duties. The report of the High Level Group of Company Law Experts has tackled aspects of corporate governance, but it makes the point that corporate governance has its foundation in company law and partly in the wider laws and practices and market structures which operate in different Member States. While it may not be relevant to all companies, in examining the role of non-executive and supervisory directors, the Report states that a basic financial understanding is a fundamental skill that all board members should possess or acquire upon their appointment. The European perspective will gain increasing importance, but at present progress is slow. The draft fifth directive on company law which contains provisions on the structure and liability of the board of directors is effectively on hold with no current prospect of it being revived. One area of interest may be the adoption of a board structure similar to the two-tier system, with managing directors and a separate supervisory board to replace the unitary board. Such a structure was considered and rejected by the Department of Trade and Industry in the Bullock Report on industrial democracy published in 1977 and has not found favour in the UK since. The report of the High Level Group acknowledges that both systems have their own particular advantages and disadvantages and there is no clear evidence as to which is the more effective monitoring body.

In understanding what is required of a director, it may also be helpful to consider the methodology which has been developed to explain the existing law and how that state has been reached. What is so special about the position of directors? At least part of the answer to this lies in the relationship between directors and the company's shareholders which prima facie is based on the separation of ownership and control. Although the degree of separation varies between types of companies, the values from which this area of law evolved dictate that a basic level of protection must exist for shareholders to ensure that directors do not abuse their position. As is well known, the underlying framework of basic level duties which are common to all directors is founded on loyalty and trust which underpin the fiduciary relationship between a company and its directors. The current approach, however, involves an attempt to determine an economic basis for company law and, more particularly, the fiduciary position of a director.

1.2.1 Economic analysis and company law

Notwithstanding the historical basis of the evolution of the law on directors' duties, it is significant that in their Consultation Paper No. 153, the Law Commission included a report analysing the economic considerations relevant to directors' duties. The discipline of law and economics developed in the US and is reflected in US Corporations Law. It has now spread to the UK and elsewhere in Europe. Its impact is also evident in other jurisdictions including Australia and New Zealand. On an economic analysis, it is argued that the division between ownership and control inherent in the company structure leads to "agency costs" as a result of the "principal" having to monitor the work of the "agent" to whom the principal has delegated management of his/her property, which would be reflected in the price which shareholders would be willing to pay for the shares. The company has an incentive, therefore, to reduce agency costs by encouraging directors to be loyal and to exercise care and skill, thereby increasing the value of the shares. Directors will, however, want to be certain of their duties particularly if they may incur personal liability for breach of such duties[11] or, in extreme cases, criminal sanctions. This means that both directors and shareholders will be looking for a "contract" to regulate their relationship. Although in the case of executive directors there may often be a written contract setting out specific duties of the directors as employees, which will vary from company to company and from director to director, the law can help the parties to reach a sensible bargain in some areas by laying down certain "terms" which apply to all directors. In this way transaction costs can be reduced. The law, therefore, provides a set of rules which can be relied on if the parties choose not to negotiate on an individual basis. This does, however, raise the question of whether or not the parties should be free to amend or exclude these "background rules"

---

[11] *See* as a recent example *Bairstow* v *Queens Moat Houses plc* [2000] BCC 1025 where directors were held liable to repay unlawful dividends plus interest. This point upheld on appeal: *Bairstow* v *Queens Moat Houses plc* [2002] BCC 91, CA.

if they do not think they are appropriate. The answer to this depends on the nature of the rules and what they are aiming to achieve.

The Law Commission paper divided the rules into default rules and mandatory rules. Default rules are those which apply if the parties do not provide to the contrary and can be amended as necessary. Mandatory rules provide limits to the scope of bargaining and provide protection to shareholders where they would be in an unequal bargaining position. They are also necessary in some cases to protect the interests of other stakeholders (as identified above) where those third parties would not have an opportunity to influence the bargain reached. Not all so-called default rules are easy to amend. It may require particular effort and expense on the part of a director in order to prevent their application. Such rules operate effectively as "penalty default rules". The behaviour they are regulating is not so offensive as to be prohibited but should only be allowed if certain conditions are satisfied, for example the provision of information to shareholders. The avoidance of conflicts of interest, at which many of the identified duties of directors are aimed, is just such an example. Often it is not the potential conflict which is the problem, but rather the lack of explanatory information. On an economic analysis, the most efficient way of ensuring the flow of information is to make it a precondition of the relevant director action. An alternative is to require that a rule should be enforced on a "comply or explain basis", which is an approach favoured by the High Level Group of Company Law Experts in certain cases and also by those who frame the voluntary codes of corporate governance.

How does this economic analysis apply to the specific areas of directors' duties, both common law and statutory? Both fiduciary duties and statutory duties (the latter in particular as are currently contained in Part X of the Companies Act 1985 ("CA 1985")) may be seen as promoting the efficient sharing of risk and information, to the extent that duties are enforced by penalty default rules. As a result, agency costs and transaction costs are reduced.

There has been, however, a lack of cohesion in this area, particularly at present in Part X of CA 1985. Certain categories of director actions which are not easy to distinguish in terms of importance come in for different treatment, for example in the satisfying of preconditions such as shareholder approvals and in the imposition of penalties for non-compliance. Economic analysis does not explain these discrepancies. Rather they result from the fact that the role of directors has developed over a lengthy period of time, often leaving the law to catch up later. In considering the origins of the rules, it is evident that they do not come from a coordinated background. As such, it is difficult for the practitioner to predict what the law is or should be in any given situation. Theories of economic efficiency may, however, be of greater use in determining how the law should be shaped to meet the needs of the twenty-first century.

1.2.2 The regulatory background

A helpful approach to analysing the legal and self-regulatory background is that put forward by Lord Hoffman, who identified three layers of regulation which have been built up over the years,[12] namely common law, statute and self-regulation. The General Principles, if enacted, will be a crucially important type of regulation in this area. However, it should be remembered that they will take effect in place of the corresponding equitable and common law rules, and that the stated aim is to do so without changing the essential nature of directors' duties.

The first of these layers consists of the fiduciary duties which directors owe at common law as managers of shareholders' property. The identifiable duties include: a duty of loyalty; a duty to use their powers for a proper purpose; and a duty to show reasonable care and skill. It is the third of these duties which has been the subject of recent development in the courts and it is the subject of keenest debate.

Initially, the duty of care amounted to a very weak duty tested against the director's own knowledge and skill. Given that no qualifications are required in order to be a director, essentially this meant that an unskilled and ignorant director would not have to do any more than his best, which may well amount to incompetent behaviour when judged objectively. This now appears to be unacceptable from the point of view of good management and particularly in larger companies where the directors are not the only shareholders. There have been two discernible approaches to the reformulation of the standard of care: statutory reform, on which the courts have been keen to build; and the development of the concepts of corporate governance.

In this latter case, the result has been that directors, particularly those of public listed companies, are required to adhere to standards of behaviour imposed from outside the law.

---

[12] Lord Hoffmann, "Duties of Company Directors" (1999) European Business Law Review 10(3/4), 78–82.

Introduction

The statutory standard of care and skill set out in Section 214 Insolvency Act 1986 has been applied in cases outside the specific instance of insolvent liquidation (with which the Section deals). Section 214 imposes a dual standard, both objective (by reference to the particular functions which the director in question carries out) and subjective. Directors must now possess an element of professional skill appropriate to the functions they are entrusted to perform. Hoffmann LJ held that the duty of care of a director is set out accurately in Section 214(4) and that it was the conduct of a:

> "reasonably diligent person having both:
> (a) the general knowledge, skill and experience that may reasonably be expected of a person carrying out the same functions as are carried out by that director in relation to the company; and
> (b) the general knowledge, skill and experience that that director has."[13]

This is the approach adopted by the White Paper. This should allow the courts to distinguish between different types of companies and the varied functions performed by different directors in the same company.

Furthermore, the introduction of the Company Directors Disqualification Act 1986 and the cases decided under Section 6 of that Act have also had an impact on the traditional standard of care. A director of a company which has become insolvent may be disqualified under Section 6 if the court believes that his conduct as a director makes him unfit to be concerned in the management of a company by reference to specific matters. These matters include any breach of any of the director's duties to the company. A case worthy of particular note is *Re Continental Assurance Co. of London plc*[14] in which a non-executive director was disqualified even though he did not know of the misconduct in question as it was held that any competent director in his position would have known what was going on and by not knowing he was incompetent. *Re Barings plc (No. 5)*[15] established a continuing duty to acquire and maintain a sufficient knowledge and understanding of the company's business for the proper discharge by the directors of their duties.

---

[13] *Re D'Jan of London Ltd* [1993] BCC 646.
[14] [1996] BCC 888.
[15] [1999] 1 BCLC 433. Appeal dismissed: Re Barings plc (No. 5) [2000] 1 BCLC 523, CA.

Jonathan Parker J referred to the case of *Daniels* v *Anderson*[16] heard by the Supreme Court of New South Wales and adopted the observations made in that case on directors' duties of care, skill and diligence as representing English law. As such, a person who accepts the office of director must ensure awareness of the nature of the duty that he must perform, such duty varying in accordance with the nature of the particular company in question and the experience and skill which the director claims to have.

As a result it would seem that the law is heading towards imposing a more objective standard on directors, although recognising the wide variety of roles adopted by different directors in different companies. This is the approach endorsed by the Law Commission and reflected in the White Paper.

The second layer of regulation consists of the agglomerate of statutory provisions, which have been introduced in part to elucidate the law and in part to attempt to prevent breach of duties rather than simply to provide a mechanism for litigation once they have been breached. A particular example of this statutory layer is Part X of CA 1985 (which it is proposed be reformed), which arguably provides explanatory examples of the common law conflict of duty and interest which have been formulated in response to modern-day problems. There is no consistent scheme to the statutory provisions, either in their scope or in their approach to regulation. While to a certain extent the common law duties of directors may be inferred from an understanding of the social and economic background to their development, there is no alternative for practitioners but to approach the statutory regime section by section.

The third layer of regulation, that of self-regulation, has already been mentioned in the context of the effect it has had on raising the standards of behaviour expected of directors, primarily of listed companies, in the execution of their common law duties. The self-regulatory codes have been the focus of most attention in recent years and, for listed companies, the City Code on Takeovers and Mergers, the FSA Listing Rules of the UK Listing Authority, and the UK Listing Authority's Combined Code of Corporate Governance (which is appended to the FSA Listing Rules) are what directors are most concerned with. The publication of the Higgs Review has brought self-regulation into sharp focus. The general tenet of the report is uncontroversial and commonsensical. Its

---

[16] 1995 16 ACSR 607.

Introduction

recommendations aim to ensure transparency and rigour in the appointment process and to broaden the range of experience within the boardroom. It has provided, however, a degree of controversy, not least in its approach to the role of the chairman and his relationship with the non-executives.

The emphasis of the voluntary codes has been on the need for transparency and accountability and the achievement of the necessary high standards of corporate behaviour. In addition, the development of accounting standards, particularly the requirement for directors to make a statement of responsibility in the annual report and to state whether applicable accounting standards have been followed, has made its contribution to the process. It may be helpful to practitioners assimilating the requirements of the self-regulatory codes that they have been put together and kept up-to-date by leading practitioners of their day. The various codes have not sought to overturn the common law for fiduciary duties of directors but rather to build on them, and in so doing they have acknowledged the flexibility of the common law. As the Hampel Report on Corporate Governance[17] states, and as others have commented to the same effect in the context of the current debate on corporate governance, "box ticking takes no account of the diversity of circumstances and the experiences among companies, and within the same company, over time".

1.2.3 Additional regulation

The State has, for its own purposes, imposed personal sanctions on directors for failure to comply with certain requirements (e.g. relating to the collection of revenues and duties) and imposed "fit and prudent" criteria where the nature of the business so demands. The State insists on certain levels of conduct from directors where consumers may be particularly at risk. For example, the directors of insurance companies, banks and companies providing financial services are subject to additional regimes.

1.3 Nature of companies

General principles and the background to their development provide a framework for practitioners determining the duties and responsibilities

---

[17] Committee on Corporate Governance: Final Report, January 1998.

of directors. But, as can be seen from the way in which the regulatory regime has evolved, in particular the duty of care, the general principles must be applied in the context of the type of company and that of the particular role of the director.

A large proportion of companies in the UK are private limited companies. Many are owner-managed, in some cases effectively housing a sole trader, in others operating more like partnerships. For much of the time there will be little practical need to distinguish between the interests of directors and shareholders. There is a need, however, for legal safeguards to be in place in case things go wrong. The luxury of limited liability enjoyed by "shareholder directors" in such companies calls for at least minimum standards of behaviour for the benefit of third parties. Any other difficulties will generally be of concern to shareholders, in which case Section 459 CA 1985 will be the appropriate procedure to use.

The conduct of private companies has given rise to a lot of case law. This is not so much the case with listed companies as often the additional layer of regulation imposed on them operates by way of default mechanism, filling in any gaps in the law. Although in these smaller private companies the role of directors is easily confused with that of shareholders, the courts have not always recognised this. Decisions have ranged from one where a sole director was required to make a declaration to himself and have a statutory pause for thought (*Neptune (Vehicle Washing Equipment) Limited* v *Fitzgerald*),[18] to those where the courts have recognised the economic reality of the situation. The latter cases are, however, of questionable application to listed public companies because of the differing nature of the director's role. That it is recognised that small private companies should be treated differently is also evident from statute, for example the special provisions relating to the production of accounts of small and medium-sized companies and the relaxation of Section 151 CA 1985 for private companies.[19]

The White Paper acknowledges the differences between small and large companies, however they are defined, taking the former as the fundamental starting point in the reforms it proposes. Additional safeguards and consequently additional burdens are to be added for larger companies, listed or otherwise.

---

[18] [1995] 1 BCLC 352.
[19] Section 155 CA 1985 which is proposed to be repealed for private companies.

Introduction

In the case of larger companies, which will more often than not be public limited companies, there tends to be greater separation between management and ownership. Here the duties and responsibilities of directors are not blurred by the coincidence of ownership, particularly in the case of those companies which are listed or quoted on a recognised stock exchange. Directors will generally have substantial freedom to carry on the business but may find that there are more potholes to fall into, and the consequences which they face in doing so may be more serious for the directors than the shareholders. By way of example, the provisions of CA 1985 and the Financial Services Act 1986 regulating dealings with the public, including those relating to prospectuses and, in the case of listed companies, listing particulars, place onerous requirements on directors, most noticeably, the imposition of personal liability.

It is primarily to listed companies that the most stringent standards (the third layer of regulation) are applied requiring more sophisticated systems of governance, greater disclosure and attention to compliance. For example, the City Code on Takeovers and Mergers demands that documents are produced to prospectus standards. Although breach of one of the self-regulatory provisions does not amount to "breaking the law" and will not, therefore, lead to a criminal conviction or an award for damages by a court, it may be a factor taken into account by a court in deciding whether a director should be disqualified under the provisions of the Company Directors Disqualification Act 1986. However, the influence of self-regulation does not stop with listed companies. The standards set by the various codes on corporate governance are influencing those expected of directors of unlisted companies, whatever their size.

1.3.1 *The particular role of non-executive directors*

The role of non-executive directors, usually of listed public companies, has been brought to the forefront in the context of the corporate governance debate, raising the question of whether prima facie they should owe the same duty of care to the company as the executive directors. It has always been the case that with a single-tier board structure all directors owe an equal duty to the company. CA 1985 makes no distinction. As discussed above, developments in the law, both through statutory reform and through the courts, have underlined the fact that the duties of non-executive directors now go far beyond attending board meetings. The development of concepts of corporate governance, including demands that non-executives sit on board committees, such as the audit committee or the remuneration committee, independent of the executives, has arguably raised to a greater level the duty of care of non-executive directors. Both the Higgs Review in its entirety and the report of the High Level Group in the relevant sections, have concentrated on this subject with differing emphasis, in particular on the questions of the roles of non-executives and their independence.

1.3.2 Group company directors

Directors of companies which are members of groups of companies often find themselves having to consider their position with great care when intra-group transactions or group interests are in issue; the more so where they are directors of more than one of the group companies involved. A director of any company within a group must act in the best interests of each company in which he holds that office, whatever the interests of a subsidiary, parent, group holding company or fellow subsidiary. While in certain circumstances European legislation is framed so as to hold groups as single economic entities in relation to creditors, as well as in the regulation of competition and employment issues, and while the production of consolidated accounts may lead the reader to assume that they are dealing with a single entity, there is no doctrine of English law which permits the directors of one group company to take account of the interests of other group companies as such. Given the advantages conferred on the group by virtue of the limited liability of each company within the group, the courts are keen to ensure that the assets of a company are available only to its creditors and not to those of other group companies. The issue surfaces frequently in two situations: financings, where the lender often seeks to achieve exposure on a group basis for contractual arrangements, the obtaining of cross-guarantees and the like; and in intra-group reorganisations, whether undertaken for taxation or other purposes.

In the latter context, transactions at an undervalue and the practice of transferring assets intra-group for a nominal consideration give rise to particular difficulties. When the directors of a company are in doubt as to their position they may seek direction by resolution of their shareholders. But even in that case, as some acts are not capable of sanction or ratification by shareholders, directors may find themselves faced with hard decisions to make. The position remains that the directors of a subsidiary company (or parent company) owe a duty to that company even if they owe duties to other companies within the group. They may have regard to the interests of the group if, but only if, it is in the interests of the relevant company to do so.

1.4 Reform

With the publication of the White Paper, the path to reform looks set. Further consultations and detailed proposals have yet to be published for large areas of company law which are due to be reformed. But as far as directors' duties are concerned, in publishing the draft General Principles, the White Paper has opted, in line with the Company Law Review, for a partial codification. One difficulty for anyone analysing the law relating to directors' duties is the unpredictability of particular cases. The main problems at present have been perceived to be ones of clarity and access rather than content. Thus the codification of directors' duties as proposed will provide a fixed starting point for those needing to understand and discharge them. It is to be hoped that earlier doubts expressed, that the introduction of a code will inhibit the responsive development of the law, ultimately producing an out-of-date, uncertain, environment in which to conduct business, will prove unfounded. Further, it is to be hoped there will be no increased uncertainty in the gap between the statutory statement and the general law. Codification must prove itself to be both comprehensive and accessible and also sufficiently flexible to accommodate the continuing development of appropriate standards. This is important given the criminal and civil sanctions which can be imposed on directors and ultimately the risk of disqualification. The question remains whether the adoption of the General Principles, notwithstanding the stated aim not to change the law in substance, provides a departure point for the development of the law henceforth in a direction which has not been anticipated; and that the way will remain open for the creation of new uncertainties.

The White Paper also envisages that Part X of CA 1985 will be reformed. It follows the overall approach recommended by the Company Law Review which built on the earlier work of the Law Commission. To some extent the reform of Part X cannot be considered separately from the proposals for adopting the General Principles, as Part X itself can be seen as codifying certain areas of directors' duties. Certainly any clarification, and more importantly, rationalisation of the position in this area is to be welcomed.

The Law Commission has also looked at reforming the law of shareholder remedies (Law Commission Report No. 246). The introduction of a new derivative action with more modern, flexible and accessible criteria is anticipated. This is also to be welcomed but it seems a more distant prospect.

A Practitioner's Guide to Directors' Duties and Responsibilities

While the White Paper takes small companies as a starting point for the regulation of companies and only envisages additional and more burdensome provisions for larger companies where necessary, other pressures for reform, and the acknowledgment of the role of the company as part of the social structure, where cooperatives, collectives and syndicates have failed to fulfil the role, continue to increase the burden on directors. The move to make the offence of corporate manslaughter more effective, in the sense that the crime can be identified and dealt with, is an example; and others can be found in the new rules promulgated by the UK Listing Authority and the publications of institutional investor protection bodies relating to the social and environmental responsibilities.[20] It may be necessary to add to the answer to the question: what is so special about the position of directors? The greater the role undertaken by a company within the structure of society, the greater are the obligations of the directors, which spread beyond shareholders' immediate interests in profitability.

With this in mind it might be optimistic to assume that the General Principles will not be a departure from the current position. The General Principles state that the factors which must be taken into account in fulfilling the directors' obligation to act include the company's need to foster its business relationships, including those with its employees and suppliers and the customer for its products and services; and its need to have regard to the impact of its operations on the communities affected and on the environment. It is in considering these duties that interpreters of the General Principles may focus upon the meaning of the overriding obligation to promote the success of the company and to draw the distinction between success and profitability, so that directors may be permitted to take account of and respond to these pressures.

It seems clear in any case that in relation to the duty of care and skill the objective standard will not be relaxed. By holding a person to the standard expected of a reasonable person in that position, or, if higher, the standard appropriate to his own competence, a director is subject to the same standards as are applied to professional negligence elsewhere. Although in one sense this ensures that a universal standard will be

---

[20] *See* for example the European Commission Green Paper in July 2001 on "Corporate Social Responsibility", and Association of British Insurers: "Investing in Social Responsibility: Risks and Opportunities" and their disclosure guidelines on "Socially Responsible Investment", and note the launch in July 2001 of the FTSE4GOOD index series.

Introduction

applied, regard will be had to the functions of the particular director and the circumstances of the company. A director must, therefore, take into account not only what he considers to be in the best interests of the company in coming to decisions, but what others in the same position would think. An eminent company director was reported in 1995[21] as postulating: "Do your business as if you are going to be examined by a leading QC". That may be a somewhat harsh test to impose on oneself, but such are the demands which law and corporate governance place on those who serve their company.

---

[21] *Sunday Telegraph*, 16 April 1995.

Chapter 2

Appointment and Vacation of Office

Chris Hale, Partner
Travers Smith Braithwaite

2.1 Introduction

British company law distinguishes between the roles of owners/shareholders, who are often not in a position personally to manage the affairs of every company in which they have invested, and managers/directors, even when these two functions are, in many small private companies, performed by the same people. In order to cater for the very wide range of circumstances which arise in practice, the Companies Act 1985 ("CA 1985") is largely silent on the issue of how directors are to be appointed and removed, leaving the shareholders to define their preferred procedures in the company's articles of association ("the articles") and/or in a shareholders' agreement.

In most companies, decisions relating to the appointment of new directors (after incorporation) will be a matter primarily for the directors themselves. In this way the directors, acting properly, are able to identify the skills required within the boardroom and the individuals who will provide those skills in a manner harmonious to the other personalities within the boardroom. The shareholders' role in the appointment of directors will often be limited in practice to voting on their re-election at the first annual general meeting ("AGM") after their appointment and, commonly, when they retire by rotation every three years or so thereafter. In some circumstances, however, the shareholders may take a more active role in the appointment of directors. For example, one or more shareholders may wish to take part in the management of the company either by being a director personally or through the appointment of specified individuals to the board. So, where the company is the wholly-owned subsidiary of another company, the parent company will usually control appointments to the board of that company and any other subsidiaries. A private company with institutional shareholders, such as a private equity-backed company, will usually have one or more nominees on the board who are appointed by the institutional shareholders or, more unusually, lenders. Such directors fall into the subcategory known as "nominee directors" (*see* 2.8 below).

Shareholders will wish to monitor the performance of the directors after their appointment. As mentioned above, the articles may require directors, for example, to seek re-election from time to time. Where the shareholders become dissatisfied with the performance of a director, CA 1985 reserves the right for shareholders (regardless of any provision in the articles or in any other agreement between the company and the director) to remove the director and to elect their own replacement.

Recent changes in the sphere of corporate governance (*see* Chapters 6 and 9) have meant that directors, particularly those of listed companies, are more accountable to shareholders than ever before. For example, the Directors' Remuneration Report Regulations 2002 (SI 2002/1986) entitle shareholders of listed companies to vote on the company's remuneration policy towards its directors. In addition, the Institutional Shareholders' Committee, a body which represents institutional shareholders in listed companies (and comprises the Association of British Insurers, the National Association of Pension Funds, the Investment Management Association and the Association of Investment Trust Companies), has responded to the Government's drive for increased monitoring and scrutiny of company performance by institutional shareholders by publishing a memorandum on shareholder activism. That memorandum (*The Responsibilities of Institutional Shareholders and Agents – Statement of Principles*, ISC, October 2002) states that institutional shareholders should monitor the performance of their investee companies and intervene where necessary. Such intervention could in some cases involve pressing for changes to the board (*see* also 2.4.2 below). These measures have already resulted in some directors of listed companies experiencing shareholder opposition to their re-election, often as a result of opposition to over-generous remuneration and severance arrangements. Further reforms in this area are likely to increase directors' accountability to shareholders, for example the Higgs proposals in relation to non-executive directors (*see* 2.9.2 below) and the DTI consultation on severance pay for directors (*see* Chapter 6). CA 1985 imposes obligations in relation to the disclosure and publication of the identity of directors and certain personal details.

CA 1985 contains no clear definition of the term "director", merely stating (Section 741(1)) that for the purposes of the Act a "director" includes any person occupying the position of director, by whatever name called. This means that for the purposes of the Act, a person may be treated as a director even though their appointment proves to be invalid. Equally, someone who acts as a director, even though they have never been appointed as such, may be deemed to be a "director" for the purposes of CA 1985 (i.e., a *de facto* director – *see* 2.7 below). Modern business practice has given rise to a number of sub-categories of director, not all of which are formally recognised in CA 1985. For example, directors may be executive or non-executive, or they may be acting as nominee or *de facto* director, shadow director or alternate. As outlined in 2.6, 2.7 and 2.8 below, only the term "shadow director" is defined in CA 1985. Alternates are usually dealt with only in a company's articles.

In spite of the multiplication of roles and titles at board level, the unitary board is, and looks set to continue to be, a feature of English companies which sets them apart from some of their European counterparts. It seems likely that whilst the new Companies Bill will continue to recognise the concept of shadow directors (and, in whatever replaces Table A, alternate directors æ *see* 2.9.1 below), for most purposes under the Bill, a "director" will continue to be any person occupying the position of director, by whatever name called.

2.2 Method of appointment of directors

2.2.1 *The first director(s)*

In order to effect registration of a new company, subject to what is said below, a number of documents need to be delivered to the Registrar of Companies. These include a statement in the prescribed form (Form 10) containing the name(s) and certain required particulars of the person or persons who is/are to be the company's first director(s). These particulars include, in the case of an individual, his present and former names, usual residential address, nationality, business occupation (if any), particulars of other directorships held by him (and certain past directorships) and his date of birth. This statement must be signed by or on behalf of the subscriber(s) to the proposed company's memorandum and it must also be signed by each of the persons named as a director so as to signify their consent to act (Section 10 and Schedule 1 CA 1985). When the Registrar of Companies issues a certificate that the company has been incorporated, those persons named in Form 10 as directors are deemed to have been appointed as the first directors of the new company (*see* Section 13(5) CA 1985). Companies can now be incorporated electronically, that is to say that certain of the documents required to be sent to the Registrar of Companies on incorporation may be submitted electronically, and Companies House has arrangements in place to "verify the authenticity" of the signatures on such documents. *See* 2.5.2 below for further details.

Following a number of much-publicised cases of harassment of directors of companies involved in particular sectors of commerce or industry (for example Huntingdon Life Sciences), directors may now apply for a confidentiality order whereby their usual residential address is kept on a confidential register and the public register contains details of a service address only. At present, these provisions (inserted into CA 1985 by the Companies (Particulars of Usual Residential Address) (Confidentiality Orders) Regulations 2002 (SI 2002/912)) apply only to directors who are threatened with violence or intimidation, although there have been suggestions that it should be open to all directors to apply for such an order if they consider themselves to be at risk. It remains to be seen whether the Government will respond to this proposal.

Following incorporation of the company, CA 1985 is silent on the procedures for the appointment of further directors (other than in certain specific circumstances, such as the appointment of a director to replace one removed by the shareholders under Section 303 CA 1985), such provisions being left as a matter for shareholders to determine in the company's articles. Frequently, a company will include in its articles many of the provisions of Table A to the Companies Act 1985 (SI 1985/805 as amended by SI 1985/1052) ("Table A"). It is possible for a company limited by shares to be incorporated without having its own set of articles, in which event Table A will apply in its entirety to the company. In every instance when considering the appointment (or removal – *see* 2.4 below) of a new director it is, therefore, necessary to check that company's specific articles (and any relevant shareholders' agreement). For the purposes of this Chapter it is assumed (unless the contrary is stated) that Table A applies. References to "Regulations" are to the Regulations contained in Table A.

2.2.2 *Appointment by directors*

The most common method of appointment of a director after the company's incorporation (whether as an additional director or as a director appointed to fill a casual vacancy) is by resolution of the board itself. Table A, for example, confirms this power in Regulation 79, provided that the person to be appointed is willing to act and that his appointment does not cause the number of directors to exceed any number fixed as the maximum permitted by or in accordance with the company's articles. As the appointment is by resolution of the directors, normal rules apply for the passing of that resolution, as set out in the company's articles. Accordingly (where Table A applies), notice of the board meeting at which the resolution is to be proposed must be given to the directors properly, the meeting must be quorate and the resolution must be passed by a majority of the votes cast (Regulation 88). Special provisions apply where the number of directors has fallen below the requisite quorum in that the continuing director(s) may still act for the purposes of filling vacancies by appointing additional directors (Regulation 90). Written resolutions may also be used where permitted by the company's articles (e.g. Regulation 93). A new director must signify his consent to act by signing the declaration of consent on Form 288a. Form 288a can now be submitted to the Registrar of Companies in electronic form (*see* 2.5.2 below for further details).

In order to provide the shareholders with some protection against the appointment by the board of unsuitable candidates as directors, many companies' articles contain provisions, similar to those set out in Regulation 79 of Table A, which require a director so appointed to retire at the next following the AGM[1] and to seek reappointment at that meeting by the shareholders (*see* 2.4.2 below). Limited protection for shareholders is also provided by the fact that, in exercising their powers of appointment, the directors must have regard to their general fiduciary duties. These duties will apply to all aspects of the appointment of a new director, including the timing of the appointment, the selection of the candidate and the resulting balance of power which they seek to create within the boardroom.

Public companies whose securities have been admitted to the Official List ("listed companies") are required by the Listing Rules to state in their Annual Report and Accounts how they have applied the principles set out in Section 1 of the Combined Code of Corporate Governance and appended to the Listing Rules ("the Combined Code") and they must also state whether or not they have complied throughout their relevant accounting period with the more detailed "Code provisions" set out in the Combined Code and specify any areas of non-compliance, giving reasons. The Combined Code was published by the Committee on

---

[1] The Companies Bill proposes that private companies will not be obliged to hold AGMs unless they have elected to do so. Clearly this will have an impact on the appointment of directors. *See* 2.9.1 for further details.

Corporate Governance chaired by Sir Ronald Hampel in June 1998 and underwent substantial revision in July 2003 following publication of the Higgs Review of non-executive directors (*see* 2.9.2 below). Principle A.4 of the July 2003 Combined Code already states that "there should be a formal, rigorous and transparent procedure for the appointment of new directors to the board". A majority of the members of this committee should be non-executive directors, and the chairman should be either the chairman of the board or a non-executive director. The chairman and members of the nomination committee should be identified in the annual report. Accordingly, for listed companies seeking to comply with the Combined Code, the appointment of a new director by the board involves first a recommendation of a particular candidate by the nomination committee and second (unless, unusually, the power of appointment has been delegated to the nomination committee) a resolution of the board itself.

2.2.3 Appointment by shareholders

The shareholders as a whole have an inherent power to appoint directors, whether in addition to those already in office or to fill casual vacancies, unless this power has been restricted in its articles. Regulation 78 of Table A, for example, confirms this power, stating that the company may, by ordinary resolution, appoint a person who is willing to act as a director, either to fill a casual vacancy or as an additional director.

However, Regulation 76 lays down strict formal arrangements which must be observed in the exercise of this power by shareholders, so that no person other than a director retiring by rotation shall be appointed or reappointed as a director at any general meeting unless he is either recommended by the directors or, no fewer than 14 nor more than 35 clear days before the date appointed for the meeting, notice executed by a member qualified to vote at the meeting has been given to the company of the intention to propose that person for appointment or reappointment. Such a notice to the company must also state the particulars which would, if the person proposed were so appointed or reappointed, be required to be included in the company's register of directors (pursuant to Section 289 CA 1985) and must be accompanied by a notice executed by that person confirming his willingness to be appointed or reappointed. In addition, Regulation 77 states that, not less than seven nor more than 28 clear days before the date appointed for holding the relevant general meeting, notice must be given to all who are entitled to receive notice of that meeting of any person (other than a director who is merely coming up for re-election as a result of retiring by rotation – *see*

2.4.2 below), who is either recommended by the directors for appointment or reappointment as a director at the meeting or in respect of whom notice has been duly given to the company of the intention to propose him at the meeting for appointment or reappointment as a director. Any such notice must give the particulars of the proposed director which would, if he was so appointed or reappointed, be required to be included in the company's register of directors.

Where the shareholders consider that their proposed appointment of a new director cannot wait until the next AGM they may, notwithstanding anything in the company's articles, requisition an extraordinary general meeting for the purpose (provided that they are able to comply with the requirements as to procedure and the level of support set out in Section 368 CA 1985). The requisition route is rarely used because of the level of formality involved, but it is a useful power, particularly for a controlling shareholder which does not control the board (and which may wish to secure control by appointing additional directors). If there are no surviving directors or if there are not sufficient directors in the UK to convene a general meeting, then the company's articles may enable any director or any member to convene the necessary general meeting (e.g. Regulation 37 of Table A). If these provisions are not available, or if for any other reason it is impractical to call or hold the necessary general meeting, any director or member entitled to vote may apply to the court pursuant to Section 371 CA 1985 for it to order a meeting to be called, held and conducted in the manner the court sees fit. There have been several recent cases considering the extent to which Section 371 can be relied upon in circumstances in which a director or shareholder or body of shareholders is using his or its position to frustrate the holding of a general meeting in order to effect changes at board level. In *Re Woven Rugs Limited* [2002] 1 BCLC 324, a director threatened with dismissal refused to attend board meetings convened to call an EGM to table a resolution to remove him as a director. His presence was required at the meeting to make up a quorum. It was held that a meeting could be ordered under Section 371 despite submissions of unfairness by the director.[2]

In view of the cumbersome nature of the procedures under Sections 368 and 371 CA 1985, a company's articles (or a shareholders' agreement) may contain provisions granting certain shareholders special rights to appoint directors to the company's board. Such provisions are common

---

[2] *See* also *Union Music Limited* v *Watson* [2003] All ER(D) 238.

where the structure of the board or the identity of the directors is important to certain shareholders and where it may be important to such shareholders to effect board changes quickly to enable those shareholders to take control to protect their investment in the company. Examples would be where the company is private-equity backed or is the vehicle for a joint venture or a wholly-owned subsidiary of another company.[3] In such circumstances, the articles will also usually specify a simple procedure for the appointment without the need for a general meeting, such as the deposit at the registered office of the company of a written notice of appointment and consent to act. Care is required when drafting or interpreting such provisions in order to distinguish between a power to appoint and a power to nominate a candidate to be considered by the directors or by the company in general meeting. If the latter, the candidate may be voted down by the directors or shareholders.

A public company in general meeting may not consider a single motion for the appointment of two or more directors unless it has first been agreed by the meeting, without any vote being cast against the proposal, that a single resolution is acceptable (Section 292 CA 1985). In the absence of such unanimous agreement, a separate resolution must be proposed for the appointment of each candidate. Any resolution moved in contravention of the requirement is void, whether or not any objection was raised at the time. Section 292 is designed to ensure that shareholders are given a genuine choice as to the composition of the board.[4]

Although a resolution moved in contravention of Section 292 is void, it may still have some consequences, namely:

(a) Section 285 CA 1985 states that the acts of a director are valid notwithstanding any defect that may be discovered in his appointment afterwards;[5] and
(b) it will prevent the application of any provision (such as Regulation 75 of Table A) which states that, if at the meeting at which a director retires by rotation the company does not fill the vacancy, the retiring director shall (if willing to act) be deemed to have been reappointed (*see* Section 292(2) CA 1985).

---

[3] *See* 2.8 on nominee directors.
[4] The requirements of Section 292 were considered in *PNC Telecom plc* v *Thomas* [2002] All ER(D) 315.
[5] *See* 2.3.9 on the effect of invalid appointments.

It should be noted that nothing in Section 292 prevents a resolution altering the company's articles (*see* Section 292(4)). Accordingly, it would be possible, although highly unusual, for the general meeting to pass a special resolution adopting an article providing that two or more named persons be directors of the company without first obtaining uncontested consent to the proposing of such a resolution.

Where any resolution for the appointment of a director is proposed by the board, as with any other resolution proposed by the directors, it will be necessary for the directors to include with the notice of that resolution sufficient information to enable shareholders to make a proper judgement as to whether and, if so, how they wish to vote. The nature and amount of information required to discharge this duty will depend upon the circumstances and particular provisions apply for listed companies (*see* paragraph A.7.1 of the Combined Code). It would also be a breach of the directors' fiduciary duties to propose a candidate for improper purposes.

Where a director is appointed by the company in general meeting, the moment at which he assumes office is determined by the time at which the resolution appointing him is passed. Where the resolution is to be determined by a poll, it will be effective not from the moment that the poll is taken but from the moment that the result of a poll is declared or ascertained.

It is not unusual for resolutions appointing directors to specify that the appointment will take effect at a particular date and time or upon the happening of a specified event (for example, completion of a transaction whereupon new directors are to be appointed). In an acquisition context, if two parties have entered into a conditional agreement for the sale and purchase of a company, it would not be unusual for the purchaser to request the right to appoint someone to the board of the target company during the period between exchange of contracts and completion of the sale in order to give the purchaser some control over the business it has contracted to acquire. For reasons of commercial sensitivity and confidentiality, the vendor may object to such a request.

2.2.4 Appointment by third parties

Directors cannot usually be appointed by third parties (i.e. other than by the board or the company in general meeting), although the board or a nomination committee of the board may, in practice, seek assistance from third parties in identifying potential candidates. However, it is possible for the company to adopt articles which confer the power to appoint directors on a third party, although Table A contains no such provisions. Such delegation through the articles does not have to be in favour of a shareholder and could be in favour of any third party. A further example of where such a power may be granted in practice, in addition to private equity-backed companies and joint ventures where this approach is common and which have been referred to earlier, is a power in favour of a vendor of a company who is to receive consideration based upon the performance of the business after the completion of the sale to appoint a director of the company during the period of the "earn-out" so as to monitor and/or control the company during that period.

A third party to whom the articles give a right to appoint and remove directors should, however, be aware that he cannot enforce that right against the company. Whilst the memorandum and articles of a company bind the company and its members to the same extent as if they were deeds by each member containing covenants to observe all the provisions of the memorandum and articles (see Section 14 CA 1985), they do not have the effect of conferring rights on third parties. This is confirmed by Section 6(2) of the Contracts (Rights of Third Parties) Act 1999 which specifically excludes memorandum and articles from the scope of that Act. If a third party wishes to ensure that his right to appoint or remove a director is always implemented, that party should seek a direct contractual undertaking from the shareholders in the company to implement his wishes. The third party should also be aware that the shareholders of a company have a statutory right (in Section 303 CA 1985) to remove a director by ordinary resolution and that right cannot be overridden by the articles or any agreement between the company and the director. Again, the third party should consider seeking an undertaking from the shareholders of the company not to exercise their rights to remove a director nominated by the third party unless the third party has requested or agrees to his removal (*see* also 2.2.6 and 2.4.5 below).

2.2.5 *Appointment by the court*

Theoretically it is possible, on application by a member to the court pursuant to Section 459 CA 1985 (unfair prejudice), that the court may exercise the extremely wide powers granted to it by Section 461 to make "such order as it thinks fit" for giving relief in respect of the matters complained of, and order the appointment of one or more directors. In practice, however, even in extreme cases, the courts have been reluctant to interfere in the management of a company's affairs in this way, preferring instead to order the acquisition of one party's shares by another and for the resulting shareholders to appoint whomsoever they wish to act as the ongoing directors.

2.2.6 Entrenchment

It is relatively difficult under English law to entrench the appointment of a director, largely in view of the provisions of Section 303(1) CA 1985, which provides that the shareholders' right to remove a director by ordinary resolution cannot be overridden by anything in the articles or any agreement between the company and the director in question. As noted in 2.2.4 above, this restriction does not appear to extend to an agreement between shareholders outside the articles of association whereby they agree not to exercise their rights to remove a director nominated by a particular shareholder or class of shareholders or indeed a third party, unless the appointor has requested or agreed to his removal. Such an agreement could not bind the company without falling foul of the principle outlined in the case of *Russell* v *Northern Bank Development Corporation Ltd* [1992] 3 All ER 161, namely that it would be unlawful to place any fetter on the company's statutory powers, whether in the articles of association or in a shareholders' agreement. The agreement will, though, bind shareholders. In *Thomas and others* v *York Trustees Limited* [2001] ERD 179 it was held that a special resolution to remove directors under Section 303 CA 1985, which would be in breach of a provision of a shareholders' agreement providing for a shareholder with the right to appoint a director at all times and until expiry of the agreement, could not be put to shareholders. *See* also *Criterion Properties plc* v *Stratford UK Properties LLC and others* [2002] EWCA Civ 1783, in which a company sought to entrench the appointment of two directors as a poison pill to deter a hostile takeover offer.

2.3 Qualification

As we have seen, the Act defines a "director" as including any "person" occupying the position of director, by whatever name called. Schedule 1 to the Interpretation Act 1978 states that a "person" includes a body of persons corporate or unincorporated. Accordingly, any individual or corporation is currently eligible to be a director.[6]

---

[6] The Companies Bill proposes that corporate directors will be phased out. This proposal is described more fully in 2.9.1.

Although the position of director is one of considerable importance to the effective management of the company, there is no statutory requirement that a director should hold any form of qualification or take any examination in order to enable him to take up his office. Nevertheless there are certain safeguards designed to reduce the risk that inappropriate persons become directors or, if they do, to ensure that on the occurrence of certain events they should vacate their office automatically or shareholders should have the opportunity to remove them. Apart from those safeguards inherent in the mechanism for appointment, for example:

(a) references above to the duties of directors when exercising their powers to appoint additional or replacement directors;
(b) the requirement that a separate resolution is required for the appointment of each director of a public company in general meeting;
(c) the general duty of directors who propose a resolution at a general meeting to provide sufficient information to shareholders to enable them to make an informed decision; and
(d) for listed companies, the nomination committee procedure set out in the Combined Code,

there are a number of additional relevant provisions, as follows.

2.3.1 Age limit

Where the company is a public company (or, being a private company, it is a subsidiary of a public company or of a body corporate registered under the law relating to companies for the time being in force in Northern Ireland as a public company), no person is capable of being appointed a director if, at the time of his appointment, he has attained the age of 70. Further, any director of such a company is required to vacate his office at the conclusion of the AGM following his 70th birthday and is not then eligible for automatic reappointment in default of another director being appointed in his place (Section 293 CA 1985).[7]

These provisions of CA 1985 may be overridden if the relevant director's appointment or reappointment is approved by the company in general meeting after special notice (Section 379 CA 1985) has been given of the

---

[7] The Company Law Review has proposed that the age requirement for directors of public companies be abolished. See 2.9.1.

Appointment and Vacation of Office

relevant resolution to appoint him; also the notice of the resolution given to the company, and the notice by the company to its members, must state the age of the person to whom it relates (Section 293(5) CA 1985). Any person reappointed as a director following retirement under the requirements of Section 293, or appointed in place of a director so retiring, is to be treated for the purposes of determining the time at which he or any other director is to retire under any usual rotation provisions in the company's articles, as if he had become a director on the day on which the retiring director was last appointed before his retirement (Section 293(6) CA 1985). Accordingly, special care is required when considering the rotation provisions under a company's articles when the provisions of Section 293 have operated. A company can, in its articles, exclude or amend the provisions of Section 293.

CA 1985 does not make any provision for retirement due to age in relation to directors of private companies which are not subsidiaries of public companies. However, any company can in its articles set out specific age limitations for directors. Although such provisions are not common, the particular company's articles should be consulted in all cases.

There is no minimum age for a director set out in CA 1985. Under Scottish law, however, where Section 1 of the Age of Legal Capacity (Scotland) Act 1991 states that a person under the age of 16 years shall have no capacity to enter into any transaction and the expression "transaction" includes "the giving by a person of any consent having legal effect", it is possible that a person under the age of 16 is incapable of consenting to be appointed a director.

2.3.2 *Number of directors*

The Act does not prescribe the maximum number of directors that a company may have and Regulation 64 of Table A states that, unless otherwise determined by an ordinary resolution of the company in general meeting, the number of directors (other than alternate directors) shall not be subject to any maximum. A company's articles may contain some provision on this, even if only a default provision. When considering any appointment of a new director it is therefore necessary to check if there is any maximum fixed by or under the authority of the relevant articles and, if so, that it will not thereby be exceeded.

In order for a company to maintain maximum flexibility in respect of board appointments, a specified maximum number of directors is relatively unusual in private companies. For example, a private equity-backed company will rarely have a maximum limit on the number of directors, so that the private equity house can "flood" the board by appointing such number of additional directors as would give it control of the board in order to safeguard its investment if, for example, the company is under performing. By contrast, in August 1993, the Institutional Shareholders' Committee recommended, in a Statement of Best Practice ("The Role and Duties of Directors – A Statement of Best Practice" available from www.ivis.co.uk), that the articles of listed companies should provide for a maximum as well as a minimum number of directors.

More commonly, a company's articles may set a minimum number of directors, as is the case with Table A, which states in Regulation 64 that, unless otherwise determined by ordinary resolution, the number of directors shall not be less than two. The Act requires that every public company registered on or after 1 November 1929 must have at least two directors. Every public company registered before that date and every private company must have at least one director. Where the company has only one director, that individual cannot also be the company secretary (Sections 282 and 283(2) CA 1985).

If for any reason a company which should have more than one director ends up with a sole director, the company's articles will usually determine what the sole director can and cannot do until such point as a new director is appointed to comply with the minimum requirement. For example, Regulation 90 of Table A provides that a sole director may act only for the purpose of filling vacancies or of calling a general meeting (for example, at which a resolution to appoint new directors is to be proposed).

2.3.3 Qualifications specific to certain types of company

In some instances, legislation specific to particular types of company may contain provisions affecting whether a particular individual is capable of being appointed a director or whether the appointment of a particular individual may result in the company ceasing to have ability to conduct certain types of business. For example, before an investment company with variable capital (otherwise known as an open-ended investment company) can be formed, the Financial Services Authority ("the FSA") must be satisfied that the proposed directors are fit and proper persons to act as directors of it and, if there are two or more directors, that the combination of their experience and expertise is such as is appropriate

Appointment and Vacation of Office

for the purposes of carrying on the business of the company. These are ongoing requirements, failure to comply with which is a ground for revocation of its authorisation by the FSA and so liquidation.

2.3.4 Shareholding qualification

Neither the Act nor Table A requires a director to hold any shares in "his" company. Many years ago it was common for a company's Articles to provide that to hold office a director should have a shareholding qualification. The rationale behind this requirement was to ensure that the director had a personal financial interest in the success of the company beyond his salary. Today this sort of provision is extremely rare. In those rare cases where a company's articles do contain a requirement that a director hold a specified minimum number of shares ("qualification shares") the provisions of Section 291 CA 1985 will apply and the director concerned will be required to obtain his qualification shares within two months after his appointment (or such shorter time as may be fixed by the relevant articles). As stated in 2.2.3 above, the date of appointment of a director – where he is appointed by the company in general meeting by a resolution which is passed on a poll – is not the date of the meeting but the date of declaration of the result of the poll. This will be relevant for the purposes of calculating the two-month (or other) period during which any qualification shares must be acquired. If the articles require the director merely to "hold" the qualification shares, this is satisfied by the director being the registered holder and he does not also have to own the shares beneficially. However, the precise wording of the relevant article must be considered carefully.

The director will cease to hold office automatically if he does not, within the required period, obtain his qualification shares. He will also cease to be a director automatically if at any subsequent date he ceases to hold his qualification shares and will be incapable of being reappointed as a director of that company until he has reacquired the necessary qualification shares. If any person acts as a director whilst disqualified under Section 291 he is liable to a fine. As CA 1985 allows companies, in their articles, to state a period shorter than two months within which a director must acquire his qualification shares, it is possible for articles to place, effectively, a condition precedent upon the appointment of any person as a director, by stating that he shall not be eligible as a director unless he has already acquired a particular shareholding.

Unless the articles state that a director is required to obtain his qualification shares in the form of new shares issued by the company, he would usually be free to acquire them from any source and on any terms. For the purposes of Section 291 CA 1985, the bearer of a share warrant is not considered to be the holder of the shares specified in the warrant. While not stated in the Section, this provision will also apply to share options.

If a third party is seeking to acquire a company whose articles contain a requirement for directors to hold qualification shares, the acquisitor should take care to ensure that the articles of the company are changed (so as to remove the share qualification requirement) before it acquires all of the company's shares – otherwise the acquisitor will find that it has a company without any directors.

2.3.5 Other qualifications contained within the company's articles

It is possible for companies to place further qualifications within their articles, although care needs to be taken to ensure that any such provisions do not contravene any rules against discrimination contained within UK or European Community law (e.g. if qualification was on the grounds of race or religion). Such provisions are not common.

2.3.6 Disqualification

It is possible that an individual may, from time to time, be disqualified from being appointed as a director. Such disqualification may arise by virtue of provisions in the relevant company's articles. In such cases, great care needs to be taken as to the interpretation of the relevant provision to ensure that it is effective. For example, many provisions in articles are designed to ensure the removal of an existing director who commits some act or suffers some event.

Disqualification may also arise, and this is the sense in which the term "disqualification" is usually employed, as a result of an order made under the Company Directors' Disqualification Act 1986 ("CDDA 1986"). Following amendments made to CDDA 1986 by the Insolvency Act 2000, the Secretary of State may now accept a disqualification undertaking from a director, rather than making a disqualification order. The new provisions came into effect from 2 April 2001, and such an undertaking will usually have the same effect as a disqualification order (Section 1A CDDA 1986).

Any person against whom the court has made a disqualification order or from whom a disqualification undertaking has been accepted under CDDA 1986 shall not, without the leave of the court, be a director, liquidator, administrator, receiver or manager of a company's property or in any way, whether directly or indirectly, be concerned or take part in the promotion, formation or management of a company for the period specified within the relevant order or undertaking (*see* 2.4.4 below). The court does have a discretion to permit a person to continue as a director of a specified company notwithstanding the grant of a disqualification order or acceptance of a disqualification undertaking if it is satisfied that the circumstances do not require disqualification from acting as a director of that particular company and the interests of third parties, such as creditors, are adequately protected. The use of disqualification orders and undertakings is increasing in an attempt to reduce the number of dishonest and/or incompetent persons holding the office of director within the UK.

Directors may also be disqualified for breaches of competition law pursuant to the provisions of the Enterprise Act 2002. The Enterprise Act 2002 received Royal Assent in November 2002 and the provisions relating to directors' disqualification came into force on 20 June 2003. Under the new provisions, a disqualification order may be made or a disqualification undertaking accepted in respect of a director who is in breach of competition law and whose conduct as a director is considered to make him unfit to be a director of a company. The effect of Competition Disqualification Orders and Competition Disqualification Undertakings will be broadly similar to a disqualification order or undertaking made or accepted under the existing provisions of CDDA 1986. On 1 May 2003 the OFT published guidance on the new disqualification provisions, which can be obtained from the OFT at www.oft.gov.uk/enterpriseact.htm.

2.3.7 Listed companies

For listed companies, further provisions apply, driven by the need to ensure that high standards of corporate governance and management suitability and competence are imposed upon the directors of companies, including many of Britain's largest and most economically significant, using the country's principal stock market. First, the Combined Code contains the principle (Principle A.1) that every company should be headed by an effective board, which is collectively responsible for the success of the company.

Code provisions A.1.5 and A.1.6 of the Combined Code state that all directors should bring an independent judgement to bear on issues of strategy, performance, resources (including key appointments) and standards of conduct, and that every director should receive appropriate training on the first occasion that he is appointed to the board of a listed company and subsequently as necessary.

In addition, Principle A.3 of the Combined Code requires that boards should include a balance of executive and non-executive directors (including independent non-executives), such that no individual or small group of individuals can dominate the board's decision taking. Code provisions A.3.1 and A.3.2 then state that:

(a) the board should include non-executive directors of sufficient calibre and number for their views to carry significant weight in the board's decisions;
(b) non-executive directors should comprise not less than one-third of the board;
(c) the majority of non-executive directors should be independent of management and free from any business or other relationship which could materially interfere with the exercise of their independent judgement; and
(d) non-executive directors considered by the board to be independent in this sense should be identified in the Annual Report.

Pressure from institutional shareholders and from the press for listed companies to observe these provisions has become even more intense following the highly-publicised corporate failures such as Enron and the spotlight now on corporate governance. There is also pressure to strengthen these provisions – hence the Higgs Review. The focus on these requirements is likely to spread from listed companies to companies with securities traded on other markets and to some private companies, particularly those with large numbers of shareholders and those with institutional shareholders keen to promote best practice.

A listed company's sponsor must be satisfied, before any application for listing is made which requires the production of listing particulars, that the directors of the issuer have had explained to them by the sponsor, or other appropriate professional adviser, the nature of their responsibilities and obligations as directors of a listed company under the Listing Rules (Listing Rule 2.13). If so requested, the sponsor must confirm in writing that it is satisfied about the matters described in Listing Rule 2.13 on the appointment of a new director in respect of that director only, or on the appointment of a new sponsor (Listing Rule 2.14).

It is a condition for the admission of a company to listing that the directors and senior management of an applicant must have, collectively, appropriate expertise and experience for the management of the group's businesses. Details of such expertise and experience must be disclosed in any listing particulars prepared by the company (Listing Rule 3.8). An applicant for listing must ensure that each of its directors is free of conflicts between duties to the company and private interests and other duties unless the applicant can demonstrate that arrangements are in place to avoid detriment to its interests (*see* Listing Rule 3.9 and also Listing Rule 3.12 where the company has a controlling shareholder).

In addition, when a company issues listing particulars the Listing Rules require disclosure of certain information about its directors, their interests, remuneration, management expertise and experience, other directorships and details of any personal bankruptcy or convictions, and of receiverships, liquidations or administrations of any company of which the individual has been a director (paragraph 6F of the Listing Rules). There are similar rules in relation to prospectuses issued under the POS Regulations and the AIM Rules.

2.3.8 *Training for directors*

In response to a desire by some of its members to improve their skills and to provide a solution for outside observers seeking to ensure the presence of certain skills at board level, the Institute of Directors has introduced a voluntary training and assessment programme leading to qualification as a chartered director. Those who attain the qualification must also undertake continuing training so as to maintain and develop their knowledge and skills.

The chartered director qualification was introduced in 1999. Since then, as at 1 May 2003, 164 directors have been chartered. Several hundred directors are currently taking the courses required for qualification and it seems likely that the use of the qualification will increase.

One of the recommendations of the Higgs Report was that non-executive directors should receive a comprehensive, formal and tailored induction. Higgs also suggested the introduction of performance evaluation for all board members and that, as part of the evaluation process, directors should regularly appraise their individual skills, knowledge and expertise, and determine whether further professional development would help them develop their expertise and fulfil their obligations (*see* 2.9.2 below and *see* also 2.9.1 below on Company Law Review proposals in relation to disclosure of directors' training and experience). Both suggestions have been incorporated into the Combined Code as good practice.

2.3.9 Effect of invalid appointment

Section 285 CA 1985 provides that the acts of a director or manager are valid, notwithstanding any defect that afterwards may be discovered in his appointment or qualification. This would be so even if the appointment had been void under Section 292(2). A similar provision is contained in Table A at Regulation 92 and this provision, or something similar, will be incorporated into the articles of most companies. However, it is likely that the provisions of Section 285 and equivalent provisions in a company's articles offer only limited protection to a person dealing with the company because its application appears to be restricted to a procedural defect in the appointment only. *See Morris* v *Kanssen* [1946] 1 All ER 586 [HL] 459, 471, which is authority for a number of propositions:

(a) that neither Section 143 Companies Act 1929 (and therefore its successors, Section 180 Companies Act 1948 and Section 285 CA 1985) nor Article 88 Companies Act 1929 Table A (or its successors, Regulation 105 Companies Act 1948 Table A or Regulation 92 of Table A) validate an appointment which is contrary to the Companies Acts or the articles of association of the relevant company;
(b) that neither the Section nor the article can assist a party if that party had knowledge of the facts giving rise to the invalidity;
(c) it cannot assist the party if that party is put on enquiry and does not enquire;
(d) it cannot avail anyone where there is no appointment at all.[8]

2.4 Vacation of office

Once appointed, there are then a number of ways in which a director's term of office may be brought to an end.

2.4.1 Voluntary resignation

A director may resign his office at any time, despite the fact that he may also be employed by the company and have a service agreement with it which requires him to serve for a fixed term or to give a period of notice of resignation. The director's service agreement may continue notwithstanding his resignation from the office of director. If the director

---

[8] *See* also *Re: New Cedos* [1994] 1 BCLC 797.

terminates his service agreement at the same time and without giving the notice required by the service agreement he may be liable to the company in damages for breach of contract. Sometimes a company's articles will specify a procedure to be followed for giving effect to a resignation from the office of director. Table A, for example, provides (*see* Regulation 81(d)) that the office of a director shall be vacated if he resigns by giving notice to the company, and Regulation 111 states that any notice to be given by any person pursuant to those Regulations shall be in writing. In addition to any such procedural measures in the articles, Section 725 CA 1985 enables a notice of resignation to be served on the company by leaving it at, or sending it by post to, the company's registered office. A resignation once made cannot be withdrawn except with the consent of the company.

In circumstances where a share qualification exists (*see* 2.3.4 above), a director may resign voluntarily simply by disposing of his qualification shares.

2.4.2 Retirement by rotation and potential re-election

Many companies have provisions in their articles requiring a proportion of the directors to retire at each AGM. The rationale behind retirement by rotation provisions is to ensure that an individual director's appointment as a director is not wholly entrenched and shareholders have an opportunity to review that appointment periodically. Many private companies disapply the retirement by rotation provisions because they are considered unnecessary and cumbersome for a small, closely held company and where there may be a shareholders' or other agreement giving shareholders the right to review directors' appointments.[9]

By way of example of the way retirement by rotation works, Table A contains provisions (Regulation 73) to the effect that at a company's first AGM all of the directors shall retire from office and, at every subsequent AGM, one-third of the directors who are subject to retirement by rotation (or, if their number is not three or a multiple of three, the number nearest to one-third) shall retire from office; but, if there is only one director who is subject to retirement by rotation, he shall retire. In order to determine which of the directors are to retire at any particular AGM from amongst those eligible, it is normal (and Table A, subject to any provisions in CA

---

[9] The Company Law Review has recommended that the retirement by rotation provisions of Table A should be removed for private companies. *See* 2.9.1.

A Practitioner's Guide to Directors' Duties and Responsibilities

1985, so requires) for companies to select for retirement those directors who have been in office longest since their last appointment or reappointment (but *see* 2.3.1 above where a director has been appointed to replace another director who is retiring due to age). Where more than the required number were last appointed or reappointed at the same time, then those to retire are to be determined by lot, unless they agree amongst themselves who is to stand for re-election in that year (Regulation 74). A director who retires by rotation is normally eligible for reappointment and would, until the recent focus on corporate governance, be re-elected as a matter of formality. Indeed, under Table A (Regulation 75), if the retiring director is willing to continue, he is deemed to have been reappointed unless, at the meeting, it is resolved not to fill the vacancy, or unless a resolution for his reappointment is put to the meeting and lost. If the director is not reappointed then he continues to hold office until either the appointment of a replacement at the meeting at which he retires or, if no replacement is appointed, until the end of the meeting. For details about persons eligible for appointment in his place *see* 2.2.3 above.

For listed companies, Principle A.7 of the Combined Code requires all directors to submit themselves for re-election at regular intervals and at least every three years. Best practice provision A.7.1 then states that all directors should be subject to election by shareholders at the first opportunity after their appointment, and to re-election thereafter at intervals of no more than three years. Accordingly, companies to which the Combined Code applies have either changed their articles so as to ensure that all directors do submit themselves for re-election within three years after their last appointment or reappointment, or, if retaining "traditional" rotation arrangements, they may be required from time to time (where a director does not come up for re-election within three years either because of the timing of the AGM or because of the dynamics of the board itself) to highlight the derogation from the Combined Code in the next following annual report and accounts, as required under Listing Rule 12.43A.[10]

---

[10] This area is also the subject of likely reform. New Code Provision E.2.1 annexed to the Higgs Review provides that institutional shareholders should apply the principles set out in the ISC's Statement of Principles on shareholder activism (*see* 2.9.2). The Government's White Paper on the Companies Bill (*see* 2.9.1) states, at paragraph 2.44, that the Government is considering how to ensure that institutional investors intervene actively to protect and enhance the value of their investment where companies are being managed ineffectively, or even dishonestly, as part of its response to the Myners Report on institutional investment ("Institutional Investment in the UK, a Review", Paul Myners, March 2001).

Appointment and Vacation of Office

For listed companies, the corporate governance climate has evolved such that nowadays directors can no longer assume that their re-election is a formality. Since the introduction of the Directors' Remuneration Report Regulations 2002, which made changes to CA 1985 to provide that submission of the directors' remuneration report to a shareholder vote is now mandatory (it was previously only advisory under the terms of the Listing Rules and Combined Code), directors are more accountable than ever to shareholders for their performance. Whilst a negative vote in respect of the directors' remuneration report will not affect the appointment or terms of appointment of individual directors (other than by exerting moral pressure and to avoid the risk of adverse publicity and "blacklisting" by the major institutional shareholders), one of the ways in which institutional shareholders can actively express their disapproval is by voting down the re-election of directors retiring by rotation.

It should be borne in mind that institutional shareholders are already under a positive obligation to monitor the performance of their investee companies and their directors and senior management. The ultimate weapon for institutional shareholders would be to requisition an EGM to change the composition of the board (see Institutional Shareholders' Committee "Statement of Principles on the Responsibilities of Institutional Shareholders and Agents" (October 2002), available from www.ivis.co.uk). *See* also Principle E.3 of the Combined Code, which requires institutional shareholders to make considered use of their votes.

It is common for a company's articles to require that a director appointed initially by the board must retire at the first AGM following his appointment (e.g. Regulation 79 of Table A). This provision can, at times, create practical difficulties. For example, if the board appoints a new director after the dispatch of notice of the company's AGM but before the meeting itself takes place, many companies' articles would require (as in the case of Regulation 79) that the director concerned must, nevertheless, still retire at the AGM and, if not reappointed at that meeting, vacate office at the end of it. In these circumstances the board will need to consider carefully the other provisions of the company's articles and the precise wording of the notice convening the meeting. Possible courses of action may include:

(a) proposing a resolution at the AGM to reappoint the relevant director under a provision in the company's articles if they enable such a resolution to be included within the "ordinary business" of the AGM, for which no specific notice is required in the notice of the meeting;[11]

(b) sending a further notice to shareholders including details of the additional resolution and, if necessary, adjourning the AGM to enable the necessary notice period to elapse; or

(c) allowing the new director's appointment to lapse at the end of the AGM and then reappointing him immediately by further resolution of the board.

In this last situation, the director will have to retire again at the next AGM and proper notice of his proposed re-election should be given.

A further possible solution would be for the director to retire at the AGM and for the board to then recommend his appointment to the AGM, thus taking advantage of the provisions of Regulations 76(a) and 78 of Table A (if they apply). Not less than seven days' notice must be given to all who are entitled to receive notice of the meeting of the intention so to recommend and including details of the relevant director, all as required by Regulation 77 of Table A (if it applies). Further, as well as considering carefully the provisions of the relevant company's articles, if the company is a listed company, attention will be required to the provisions of best practice statement A.7.1 which states that the names of all directors subject to election or re-election should be accompanied by sufficient biographical details to enable shareholders to make an informed decision as to their election.

2.4.3 Age

The provisions of Section 293 referred to in 2.3.1 above may apply to terminate a director's period of office.

2.4.4 Vacation of office pursuant to the company's articles

Most companies' articles contain some provisions pursuant to which directors must vacate office automatically. The most common provisions

---

[11] If, as is common, the notice of AGM contains full particulars of the directors retiring by rotation and submitting themselves for reappointment, it is doubtful whether the company could rely on the ordinary business provisions to table the resolution for the reappointment of a director who had not been named in the notice.

Appointment and Vacation of Office

are similar to those contained within Regulation 81 of Table A, which states that the office of a director shall be vacated if:

(a) he ceases to be a director by virtue of any provision of CA 1985 or he becomes prohibited by law from being a director;
(b) he becomes bankrupt or makes any arrangement or composition with his creditors generally;
(c) he is, or may be, suffering from mental disorder and either:
   (i) he is admitted to hospital in pursuance of an application for admission for treatment under the Mental Health Act 1983 or, in Scotland, an application for admission under the Mental Health (Scotland) Act 1960, or
   (ii) an order is made by a court having jurisdiction (whether in the UK or elsewhere) in matters concerning mental disorder for his detention or for the appointment of a receiver, *curator bonis* or other person to exercise powers with respect to his property or affairs;
(d) he resigns his office by notice to the company; or
(e) for more than six consecutive months he shall have been absent without the permission of the directors from meetings of directors held during that period and the directors resolve that his office be vacated.

These provisions incorporate the consequences of the CDDA 1986, pursuant to which a director may be prohibited by court order or pursuant to a disqualification undertaking from being a director for a specified period, unless he first obtains leave of the court. Such orders may be granted (or undertakings given) following general misconduct in connection with companies (such as conviction of indictable offences, persistent breaches of companies legislation or fraud); or for reasons of unfitness to hold the office of director (if the court is satisfied that the individual has been a director of a company which has, at any time, become insolvent and his conduct as a director of that company makes him unfit to be concerned in the management of a company). (*See* also Chapter 13.)

In addition to these "normal" provisions, specific provisions may be found in a company's articles or in a shareholders' agreement. For example, where a director has been appointed by a particular interest group, the company's articles may provide for his appointor to remove the director in a similar manner to which the appointment was made (for example a private equity investor may be entitled to appoint and/or remove a specified number of directors, or sometimes any and all directors, by depositing a notice to that effect at the company's registered office). Similarly a director's period of office may terminate on some event specified in the articles (e.g. the end of an earn-out period where a particular director was appointed by the vendor to the company and where such vendor had the right to appoint a director until the earn-out period had terminated). There are also, occasionally, provisions in a company's articles enabling termination of a director's office by resolution of a particular majority (or by unanimous) resolution of the directors (excluding the director concerned).[12] Such provisions are usually designed to enable the board to procure the removal of a disruptive director without the publicity and procedural difficulties of Section 303 CA 1985 referred to below in circumstances where a director, who no longer has the support of his fellow directors, refuses to resign.

2.4.5 Removal pursuant to Section 303 CA 1985

As a safeguard for shareholders (notwithstanding any provision in the company's articles) a company may, pursuant to Section 303 CA 1985, by ordinary resolution remove a director before the expiration of his period of office. This provision also overrides any agreement or arrangement between the company and the director, although it does not prevent the director from seeking compensation for breach (by reason of the operation of the Section) of any contractual rights which he may hold. This provision is not used very frequently in practice but can be helpful if the board is unwilling to operate the provisions (if any) contained in the company's articles (*see* 2.4.4 above) or in the relevant director's service agreement (*see* 2.4.6 below) entitling them to remove a director and the director to be removed controls less than 50 per cent of the voting rights in issue.

The provisions of Section 303(1) should not prevent there being an agreement between a company's shareholders (outside the articles of association) which contains an undertaking, enforceable as between shareholders, that they will not exercise their rights under Section 303 to

---

[12] An August 1993 Statement of Principles from the Institutional Shareholders' Committee ("Role and Duties of Directors – A Statement of Best Practice", available from www.ivis.co.uk) suggests that listed companies' articles should provide that a director should only be dismissed by written resolution (unanimous) of the board or, at the very least, a majority of 75 per cent of co-directors. The Statement also suggests that the articles should provide that a director may be dismissed from office by his fellow directors for failing to attend a specified number of board meetings or board meetings held in a specified period.

Appointment and Vacation of Office

remove a particular director provided the agreement is not binding on the director or the company (*see* also 2.2.6 above). This might be useful to secure the position of a director appointed by a particular shareholder or class of shareholder, e.g. a private equity investor. In private equity-backed companies, the appointment and removal of nominee directors of such investors is usually, as mentioned above, within the power of the private equity investor itself acting on its own (*see* also 2.8 below).

Special notice of a Section 303 resolution is required. Pursuant to Section 379 CA 1985, a Section 303 resolution is not effective unless notice of the intention to table it has been given to the company at least 28 days before the meeting at which it is to be considered and the company has given its members notice of any such resolution at the same time and in the same manner as it gives notice of the meeting. If that is not practicable, the company must give members notice, either by advertisement in a newspaper having an appropriate circulation or by any other mode allowed by the company's articles, at least 21 days before the meeting at which the resolution is to be considered. If, after notice of the intention to table such a resolution has been given to the company, a meeting is called for a date 28 days or less after the notice has been given to the company, the notice is deemed properly given, even though the notice was not actually given within the time required.[13]

On receipt of the notice of an intended resolution to remove a director under Section 303 the company must, forthwith, send a copy of the notice to the director concerned. The director is entitled to be heard on the resolution at the meeting at which it is put, whether he is a member of the company or not. The director is also entitled to make written representations to the company (not exceeding a reasonable length) and to request that they be notified to members. The company must then (unless the representations are received by it too late for it to do so):

(a) in any notice of the resolution given to members of the company, state the fact that the representations have been made; and
(b) send a copy of the representations to every member of the company to whom notice of the meeting is sent (whether the notice is sent to members before or after the company receives the director's representations).

---

[13] In view of the special arrangements for notice of a resolution to remove a director, the written resolution procedure available to private companies under Section 381A CA 1985 does not apply to Section 303 resolutions.

If a copy of the representations is not sent as required above because they were received too late or because the company failed to do so, the director may, in addition to being able to speak at the meeting, require that his written representations be read out at the meeting. Copies of the director's representations need not be sent out and they need not be read out at the meeting if, on the application of either the company or any other person who claims to be aggrieved, the court is satisfied that the director's rights to have his statement circulated are being abused to secure needless publicity for defamatory matters. Even if the director is not a party to such an application, the court may order the company's costs on the application to be paid by him.

Any person appointed as a director in place of a person removed from office under Section 303 is treated, for the purposes of determining the time at which he or any other director is to retire, as if he had become a director on the day on which the person in whose place he is appointed was last appointed a director.

There are some restrictions on the extremely wide application of Section 303. For example, nothing in the Act prevents the operation of any provision in the articles of the company, pursuant to which the director concerned (or any other person) is granted enhanced voting rights entitling him to defeat any resolution proposed pursuant to Section 303 (*Bushell* v *Faith* [1970] AC 1099).[14] However, such provisions do need to be drafted carefully if they are to provide effective protection for the director concerned and if they are not to be circumvented. For example, the provisions need to create enhanced voting rights not only in respect of the Section 303 resolution itself but also any resolution which may first be proposed to change the articles in order to remove or dilute the article by which his voting rights are enhanced.

There have been several recent cases considering a petition for relief under Sections 459–461 CA 1985 as a result of allegations of unfair prejudice in relation to the removal of directors under Section 303. It appears that the circumstances in which a Section 459 petition would be most likely to succeed are where the director is a "founder", or the company is a family company, where the individual would have some

---

[14] There is some doubt as to whether *Bushell* v *Faith* provisions would be upheld in the articles of association of a public company, as a result of *obiter dicta* in the judgment of the House of Lords in the *Bushell* v *Faith* case which indicate that the principle is most appropriate to small, family-owned private companies.

reasonable expectation of involvement in management. *See* for example *Brownlow* v *GH Marshall* [2001] BCC 152 and *Parkinson* v *Euro Finance Group Limited & Ors.* [2001] 1 BCLC 720. Conversely, in the case of *Re Astec (BSR) Plc* (unreported) May 1998, Chancery Division, it was held that unfair prejudice could not be established simply because there was no reason for the removal of directors, nor were "legitimate expectations" relevant.[15]

2.4.6 Vacation of office pursuant to a provision in a service contract

Provisions are often contained within a director's service contract with the company which require, as a matter of contract, a director to resign his office as director of the company if his employment with the company is terminated. Such provisions would usually also grant a power of attorney[16] in favour of one or more of the remaining directors, enabling such other directors to sign his letter of resignation on his behalf should he fail to do so as required by the terms of the service contract. Care needs to be taken when operating such provisions in a service contract to ensure that the service contract is terminated lawfully and that the events which give rise to the requirement for the director to resign have arisen.

In the case of many private equity-backed companies, it would not be unusual to find provisions in the service contract providing for termination of the director's employment (and therefore triggering dismissal as a director) for breach of the director's undertakings (or covenants or warranties), *qua* shareholder, in any shareholders' agreement or the company's articles of association.

2.4.7 Vacation by order of the court

As noted in 2.2.6 above, the court's powers on an application under Section 459 CA 1985 (unfair prejudice) are, in theory, wide enough for the court to order that a director cease to hold office. In practice, however, the courts are extremely reluctant to interfere in the direct management of a company in this way.

---

[15] *See* also *Woolwich* v *Twenty Twenty Productions Limited* [2003] All ER(D) 211.
[16] To be valid the power of attorney must be properly executed as a deed in accordance with the Law of Property (Miscellaneous Provisions) Act 1986. So, either the power of attorney should be contained in a separate document or the service contract should be executed as a deed.

2.5 Notification obligations and returns to regulators

On any change in the identity or details of a director of a company, in addition to any requirements specific to a particular type of company (*see* 2.3.3 above), a number of notifications must be made and returns filed with regulators, as follows.

2.5.1 Notifications to the company

On the appointment of any director, he is required (pursuant to Section 324 CA 1985) to notify his interests (and those of certain connected persons) in the share capital of, and any debentures issued by, the company and any other body corporate being the company's subsidiary or holding company or a subsidiary of the company's holding company. The interests to be notified are those referred to in Schedule 13 CA 1985. Thereafter, while he remains a director he is required (pursuant to Section 324(2) CA 1985) to notify any changes to such interests.

In addition, on the appointment of any director, the company must record certain details of the director in the register of directors maintained pursuant to Section 288(1) CA 1985.

Pursuant to Section 318 CA 1985 the company must keep, at an appropriate place, a copy of any written service contract between the director and the company (or a subsidiary) or, where it is not in writing, a written memorandum setting out its terms. The appropriate place includes the company's registered office, the place where its register of members is kept and its principal place of business; such documents are open to inspection by any member of the company without charge (*see* also Listing Rules 16.9–16.11).

2.5.2 Registrar of companies

As mentioned in 2.2.1 above, on the application for the incorporation of a new company, a statement of its first directors (Form 10) is required to be signed by those first directors and duly filed with the Registrar of Companies to enable incorporation to take place. Thereafter, any new appointment must be notified to the Registrar of Companies on Form 288a, any vacation of office must be notified on Form 288b, and any change in the notifiable particulars of a director must be notified on Form 288c. All such notifications must be filed with the Registrar of Companies

Appointment and Vacation of Office

within 14 days after the relevant event. In addition, care must be taken to ensure that any changes are properly recorded in any subsequent annual return filed on Form 363a.

As is also mentioned in 2.2.1 above, since the introduction of changes to CA 1985 by the Companies Act 1985 (Electronic Communications) Order 2000 (SI 2000/3373), certain documents can be submitted to Companies House in electronic form. These include Forms 288a, 288b and 288c, and the Annual Return Form 363a. Advice on how documents can be filed electronically with Companies House can be found on the Companies House website at www.wf6.companies-house.gov.uk/services.

2.5.3 *The UK Listing Authority*

Where the company is a listed company, Listing Rules 16.7, 16.8 and 16.8A require that the company notify the Regulatory Information Service[17] of any change to the board without delay and no later than by the end of the business day following the decision or receipt of notice about the change by the company. No such notification is required where a director retires and is reappointed at a general meeting. The notification must state the effective date of change if it is not with immediate effect. If the effective date is not known at the time of the announcement, or has not been determined, the announcement should state that fact and the company must notify the Regulatory Information Service when the effective date has been decided. In the case of the appointment of an additional director, the company's notification must state whether the position is executive or non-executive and the nature of any specific function or responsibility to be undertaken by the director.

In addition, Listing Rule 16.4 requires listed companies to notify to the Regulatory Information Service the following information in respect of any new director appointed to the board, unless such details have already been disclosed in listing particulars or some other circular published by the company:

---

[17] Following the recent deregulation of the system for listed company announcements, changes were made to the Listing Rules so that references to the "Company Announcements Office" have been replaced by references to a "Regulatory Information Service", now defined under the Listing Rules as a service listed in Schedule 12 to the Listing Rules. Schedule 12 contains a list of the names of the various commercial operations set up in competition with the Regulatory News Service of the London Stock Exchange following deregulation. The Regulatory News Service is one of the approved services.

(a) the details of all directorships held by such director in any other publicly quoted company at any time in the previous five years, indicating whether or not the individual is still a director; and
(b) the details of any unspent convictions or relevant insolvencies or public criticisms (all as detailed in Listing Rule 6F.2 (b) to (g))

or, if there are no such details to be disclosed, that fact.

The information required must be notified either:

(a) in the notification made regarding the appointment of the relevant director; or
(b) within 14 days of the appointment of the relevant director becoming effective.

Listing Rule 16.6 obliges a listed company to require each of its directors to disclose to it all information which the company needs in order to comply with these obligations. A company is not required to notify the Regulatory Information Service of information which the company does not have.

Sometimes a company will receive notification of a matter by a director in consequence of his fulfilling his obligations under Sections 324 or 328 CA 1985 (interests in shares and debentures). If that company's shares or debentures are listed on a recognised investment exchange (such as the London Stock Exchange) and if the matter relates to the shares or debentures so listed, that company must notify that investment exchange of the matter concerned in the director's notification before the end of the next day following that on which the obligation arises (Section 329 CA 1985).

2.5.4 Information on company stationery

If any director's name is included on its business letters (other than in the text or as a signatory), then the names of all directors must be stated. Therefore, any change in the identity of the directors of the company will also need to be reflected in the company's notepaper as required by Section 305 CA 1985 if the notepaper sets out the names of the directors.

2.6 Alternate directors

There is nothing in CA 1985 in relation to alternate directors. However, it is very common for companies, in their articles, to make provision for a director to appoint an alternate to stand in his place as a director of the company when he is not available. As the principal director continues in office at all times, the appointment of an alternate does not constitute an "assignment" of his office under Section 308 CA 1985 and, therefore, does not require approval by a special resolution of the company.

It is necessary to look carefully at the wording of the particular company's articles to identify the precise detail of any procedures to be followed for the appointment and removal of an alternate, and to establish the nature and extent of his duties whilst the appointment continues.

Where Table A applies, Regulations 65 to 69 state that any director may appoint any other director, or any other person approved by a resolution of the directors and willing to act, to be his alternate, and may remove his alternate from office at any time. Appointment and removal are by notice to the company, signed by the director, or by any other manner approved by the board. Under Table A, the board retains control over the identity of the alternate.

Regulation 66 goes on to detail certain administrative provisions. For example, an alternate is entitled to:

(a) receive notice of all meetings of directors and all meetings of committees of directors of which his appointor is a member;
(b) attend and vote at any such meetings at which his appointor is not personally present; and
(c) generally perform all of the functions of the appointor as a director, in his absence.

The alternate is not entitled to receive any remuneration from the company for his services as an alternate and it is not necessary to give notice of any meeting to an alternate who is absent from the UK.

Regulation 67 provides that a person shall automatically cease to be an alternate if his appointor ceases to be a director. If his appointor retires by rotation or otherwise but is reappointed or deemed to have been reappointed at the meeting at which he retires, any appointment of an alternate made by him which was in force immediately before the retirement of the director continues after his reappointment.

Apart from administrative arrangements, the actual status of the alternate is also governed by the company's articles. In the case of Table

A (Regulation 69) an alternate is deemed for all purposes to be a director of the company and shall alone be responsible for his own acts and defaults. However, an alternate is not deemed to be the agent of his appointor.

Given that the position of an alternate is defined by the articles of the particular company, great care needs to be taken in drafting and in interpreting the relevant regulations to identify the precise boundaries of an alternate's powers and the nature of his responsibilities. As a general rule, it is likely that an alternate will be treated as a director for the purposes of CA 1985[18] and would, therefore, have to complete and file Form 288a on his appointment. In those circumstances, his details should also be entered into the Register of Directors and he will be subject to all of the usual rules relating to disclosure of interests in shares and transactions and the rules relating to conflicts of interest set out in Part X CA 1985.

As far as an alternate signing documents is concerned, Regulation 93 of Table A expressly contemplates signature of a directors' written resolution by an alternate, and states that if a resolution has been signed by the alternate, it need not be signed also by the appointor and vice versa.

By contrast, CA 1985 does not expressly address the powers of alternates in respect of statutory declarations required of directors under the Act. The accepted view is that an alternate can swear a statutory declaration in place of (but not in addition to) his appointor. This is consistent with the status of the alternate as a director in his own right under Regulation 69 of Table A and Section 741(1) CA 1985. As such, an alternate could also act as a director for the purposes of signing contracts on behalf of the company, and witness the company seal if the company's articles provide that documents to which the company seal is affixed are to be signed by one or more directors (as is the case with Regulation 101 of Table A). However, in respect of documents executed as a deed without the company seal, under Section 36A(4) CA 1985, it is less certain that an alternate is entitled to sign as a director because the Section seems to envisage personal signature by the directors and/or secretary in question.

This issue was not addressed by the Law Commission in its report, *The Execution of Deeds and Documents by or on behalf of Bodies Corporate*

---

[18] This is supported by the definition of director in Section 741(1) CA 1985.

Appointment and Vacation of Office

published in August 1998 (available from the Law Commission's website at www.lawcom.gov.uk (Report reference 253)). In September 2002 the Lord Chancellor's Department announced that it is to press ahead with the reforms proposed in the Law Commission's Report and it is possible that the uncertainty in relation to alternates will be clarified by the new provisions. The current thinking is that the new provisions will be wrapped up in the Companies Bill process.

In the meantime, if a director is not available to execute a document as a deed under Section 36A(4) CA 1985, rather than the director appointing an alternate to execute the document in place of the director, the better route (on current thinking) would be for the company to appoint an attorney to execute the document as a deed on its behalf. Following the recommendations of the Law Commission in its report, it is clear that the appointment of either a corporate or individual attorney to act on behalf of the company would be valid, provided the power of attorney itself was validly executed by the company as a deed.

2.7 Shadow directors and *de facto* directors

Where a person exerts control over a board of directors to the extent that the directors (as a whole) are accustomed to acting in accordance with his directions or instructions then (unless the directors are merely acting on advice given by him in a professional capacity) Section 741(2) CA 1985 states that he will be treated as a "shadow director" of the company.

The purpose of the shadow director provisions is to ensure that those persons who seek to control the affairs of a company without accepting a formal appointment as a director of it are, nevertheless, caught by the relevant parts of the legislation.

Those Sections of CA 1985 which expressly apply to shadow directors include Section 323 (prohibition on directors dealing in share options), Section 317 (the duty of directors to disclose interest in contracts) and Section 324 (duty to disclose shareholdings).

Further Sections of CA 1985 are also expressed to apply to shadow directors, but Section 741(3) CA 1985 states that, in relation to these Sections, a body corporate is not to be treated as a shadow director of any of its subsidiary companies by reason only that the directors of the subsidiary are accustomed to acting in accordance with its directions or instructions. These include:

(a) Section 309 (directors' duty to have regard to the interests of employees), 319 (directors' long-term contracts of employment);
(b) Sections 320–322 (substantial property transactions involving directors);
(c) Section 322B (contracts with sole members who are directors); and
(d) Sections 330–346 (general restrictions on power of companies to make loans etc. to directors and others connected with them).

In addition, some provisions of other legislation are expressly stated to apply to shadow directors. *See* Sections 6–9 CDDA 1986 (in relation to disqualification for unfitness) and the wrongful trading provisions of Section 214 Insolvency Act 1986.

Whether or not a particular person is held to be a shadow director will depend on the precise nature of the relationship and the facts of each individual case.[19] Because of the very nature of the position, there is no formal appointment or removal process and, therefore, it will be necessary for any person engaged in a relationship with the board of directors of a company to consider very carefully whether he is likely to fall within the definition, and to act accordingly.

As directors' non-statutory duties are established and developed by the courts, the courts are free to apply them to any person whom they consider, on the facts of the particular case, to have performed the duties or functions of a director, including shadow directors and *de facto* directors, as well as those who have been formally appointed to office.

In the case of *Re Kaytech International plc, Secretary of State* v *Kaczer* [1998] All ER (D) 655, the Court of Appeal adopted a flexible and practical approach to the determination of whether a person is a *de facto* director. A *de facto* director is a person who acts as a director without having been duly appointed as such, or who continues so to act after his formal appointment has been terminated or expired. There is no definition of *de facto* director in CA 1985, but in the case of *Re Kaytech International plc*, the Court of Appeal stated that the crucial issue in determining *de facto* directorship was whether the individual in question had assumed the

---

[19] In the case of *Secretary of State for Trade and Industry* v *Deverell* [2000] 2 All ER 365, the Court of Appeal gave a broad definition to the term "shadow director". The judgment in that case stressed that the primary purpose of including the concept of shadow directors in legislation is to protect the public and therefore the term should be construed broadly.

status and functions of a company director so as to make himself responsible as if he had been formally appointed as a director. Some sections of CA 1985 apply to *de facto* directors, such as Section 317 (disclosure of directors' interests in contracts), as well as the provisions of CDDA 1986 and the Insolvency Act 1986. The extent of the Companies Acts provisions which apply to *de facto* directors looks set to be clarified by the statutory statement of directors' duties to be introduced by the Companies Bill (*see* 2.9.1 below and Chapter 3).

2.8 Nominee directors

The term "nominee director" generally means a director appointed by one of the shareholders or a lender to look after the interests of the appointor or some other third party. A nominee director may be executive or non-executive. The role of the nominee director is potentially complex. He represents the interests of his appointor and reports to him on the activities of the company, but he may also be required to act as an "independent" director or as adviser to the board, and he must also bear in mind his general fiduciary duties to the company itself as a director, which will be paramount. Except where the interests of his appointor and the company coincide, the nominee director should not identify the interests of the company with those of his appointor (*see Scottish Co-operative Wholesale Society Limited* v *Meyer* [1999] BCLC 351.) However, this does not mean that the nominee may not pay any attention to the concerns and interests of his appointor, or that he should not, in appropriate cases, have special regard to such interests. What he must not do is subordinate the company's interests to those of his appointor.

It is possible that the new Companies Bill will contain additional requirements on companies to disclose in the company's annual report relationships of influence over individual directors, although the precise nature of the sort of relationship which should justify disclosure has yet to be finally determined (*see* 2.9.1 below).

2.9 Possible future developments and consequences

We are in the midst of a period of major reform in the sphere of company law and regulation. Most importantly, the Government is consulting on proposals for a new Companies Act, which is the culmination of a lengthy review of company law carried out by the Company Law Review Steering Group set up by the Government in 1998. The new Companies Act is intended to replace altogether the existing Companies Act 1985 and 1989 (*see* 2.9.1 below).

The European Union is also consulting on changes to the framework Directives on EU company law and some of those changes will impact upon directors (*see* 2.9.3 below).

In the UK, EU and in the US, the recent high-profile corporate failures such as Enron have placed corporate governance and company reporting and accountability to shareholders under intense scrutiny. In the US this has resulted in the far-reaching provisions of the Sarbanes-Oxley Act of 2002, whose provisions may also apply to UK companies with securities registered with the SEC or who are otherwise required to file reports with the SEC.

In the UK, the Government is conducting a far-reaching review of the arrangements governing the independence of a company's auditors and, most significantly for directors, the Government commissioned Derek Higgs to conduct a review of the role and effectiveness of non-executive directors (*see* 2.9.2 below).

Some of the changes (for example, the recommendations of the Higgs Report) have come into effect during 2003; others, such as the Companies Bill, are moving to a longer timetable. It should be borne in mind that a large part of the law and regulation upon which this Chapter is based is set to change.

2.9.1 Companies Bill

In July 2002 the Government published a White Paper entitled "Modernising Company Law" (available from the DTI website at www.dti.gov.uk/companiesbill/index.htm). The White Paper was the first step in the process of implementing the recommendations of the Company Law Review launched in 1998. The Steering Group of the Company Law Review published its final report in July 2001 and made far-reaching recommendations for reform of company law, to result in a new Companies Act. Alongside the White Paper, the Government published the first 220 or so draft clauses of the Companies Bill for consultation. Consultation on that initial drafting closed in November 2002 and the responses to the consultation were published in April 2003.

Appointment and Vacation of Office

At the time of writing (May 2003), the Government's own conclusions on the outcome of the initial consultation have not yet been published. The current thinking is that further clauses of the draft Bill will be published in chunks over the coming months. The Government has stated its intention to present the Bill to Parliament during the current Parliamentary session, but it seems unlikely that the Bill will become law much before the end of the current session, which is due to end in 2006 at the latest.

As set out in the White Paper, the Government's core proposals are to simplify and modernise company law, which has not had a thorough overhaul since the nineteenth century. In relation to directors, the White Paper contains a much-publicised, fairly radical proposal to codify directors' duties. However, in the sphere of the appointment and removal of directors, relatively little has been said so far, and, other than as summarised below, in relation to the appointment and removal of directors, there is little of direct significance in the draft clauses of the Bill published so far. However, it should be remembered that the Government intends to re-enact even unchanged provisions of the existing Companies Acts in "simple" language. It may be, therefore, that changes come about as a result of the revised drafting, whether or not any substantive change was intended.

The changes to be made in the Companies Bill which will impact on directors' appointment and removal, which have already been announced in the July 2002 White Paper, are summarised below. More will follow when the remainder of the draft Companies Bill is published in the coming months.

2.9.1.1 *Single constitutional document to replace memorandum and articles*

The Government has concluded that the objects clause in a company's memorandum serves no useful purpose and should be removed, and that a company's constitution should be contained in a single document (paragraph 2.2 of the White Paper). The Government is also proposing to provide new model constitutions (to replace the existing Tables A to F), and there will be a separate model for private and public companies. Neither has yet been published (and the White Paper states that they will not be published until the Companies Bill has been fully prepared – *see* paragraph 2.5 of the White Paper) but, to the extent that the current Table A (and Tables B to F in respect of other types of company) deals with matters relating to the appointment and removal of directors, the new model forms may change the current position.

The White Paper (at para. 6.2) states that it will be possible under the Companies Bill to "entrench" certain provisions of a company's constitution so that they may not be altered except:

(a) by a resolution passed by a specified majority of more than 75 per cent; *and/or*
(b) where other specified conditions are met.

(*Note*: It is not clear from the draft Bill whether these provisions will be cumulative (i.e. linked by "and") or alternative (i.e. linked by "or"). The distinction could be important for the purposes of entrenching the appointment of a director as only part (b) will normally be of any use in this respect.)

The draft Bill contains a provision on entrenchment at clause 21. It will not be entirely clear until the rest of the Bill is published and, in particular, whatever is to replace Section 303(1), whether this power will be capable of being used to entrench the position of particular directors on the board. (*Note*: the replacement for Section 391, which is the equivalent of Section 303 in relation to the removal of auditors, has been drafted (*see* clause 119 of the draft Bill) and preserves the principle that an auditor can be removed notwithstanding any agreement between the company and the auditor. This may (or may not) be taken to suggest that the replacement for Section 303 will preserve the same principle.)

2.9.1.2   Private companies to opt in (not opt out) of the requirement to hold an AGM

The current elective regime for private companies pursuant to Section 379A CA 1985 is to be reversed so that they will opt in rather than opt out. The default position will be that a private company is not obliged to hold an AGM (or lay its accounts before shareholders or reappoint the auditors annually) unless it has positively elected to do so by ordinary resolution or unless requested by an individual shareholder. This will mean that private companies may have to make other arrangements for certain decisions relating to the appointment of directors, for example the confirmation, by shareholders' resolution, of appointments of directors made by the board to fill casual vacancies.

The Company Law Review recommended that the retirement by rotation provisions of Table A should be abolished for private companies. It also recommended that companies which do not hold an AGM should be able to make decisions which the current Companies Acts require to be taken in general meeting either by written resolution or by unanimous consent.

Appointment and Vacation of Office

The Review also recommended that companies which dispense with an AGM should be obliged to comply with rules to be developed in relation to those matters which would normally be decided in general meeting and which meet public policy concerns, such as the exercise of the rights of members and enforcing the accountability of directors. Whether or not the Government acts on these recommendations and, if so, whether they will be the subject of statutory provision or will be dealt with in the new model constitution or elsewhere, remains to be seen. The White Paper (paragraph 2.15) states that the Government is considering the Review's recommendations in this respect.

Public companies will continue to be required to hold an AGM unless their shareholders agree unanimously to dispense with the AGM. The requirement for unanimity for such a decision is likely to deter most public companies from taking advantage of this facility, so there is unlikely to be much change as regards directors' appointments at AGM for public companies.

2.9.1.3 *Shareholders' resolutions*
The Government is also proposing to simplify the procedures for shareholders' resolutions by reducing the minimum notice period for a special resolution from 21 days to 14 days, and by providing a procedure whereby private companies may pass a "written ordinary resolution" with a simple majority of eligible votes, and a "written special resolution" with 75 per cent of the eligible votes.

However, the White Paper specifically states (at paragraph 2.23) that the Government proposes to retain the special (extended) notice provisions for resolutions to remove a director under what is now Section 303 CA 1985 (or removal or non-reappointment of the company's auditors under the current Section 391 CA 1985). Whilst the White Paper does not expressly confirm that the new written resolution procedure will not be extended to include resolutions to remove a director or auditor (which are currently excluded from the regime under Section 381A CA 1985), the Company Law Review recommended that the current exceptions for such resolutions be preserved.

2.9.1.4 *Corporate directors*
The Government proposes to phase out corporate directors altogether, although this proposal is still the subject of some lobbying by, amongst others, company formation agents. Companies incorporated under the new Companies Act will not be permitted to have any director which is another company, LLP, local authority or other corporate entity.

A Practitioner's Guide to Directors' Duties and Responsibilities

Companies incorporated under the existing Companies Acts will not be allowed to appoint any more once the Bill becomes law, and companies with existing corporate directors will have to replace them with individuals by the end of a transitional period (to be finally decided).

2.9.1.5 Shadow and de facto *directors/disclosure of relationships of influence*
The Company Law Review recommended that the present definition of "shadow director" should be retained, and that *de facto* directors should be subject to the same rules as *de jure* directors.

The Review also recommended that information about more limited relationships of influence over individual directors should be disclosed in the annual report, which, if implemented, could impact on nominee directors. However, this was one of a number of recommendations made by the Review, designed to improve the transparency of the voting process, which are still under consideration by the Government.

2.9.1.6 Directors' service contracts
The Company Law Review made various recommendations on directors' service contracts which were not specifically addressed in the White Paper and have yet to be reflected in the draft Companies Bill. The Review suggested an extension of Section 318 CA 1985, which requires directors' service contracts to be open to inspection by members, so that the new provision would require disclosure of ancillary provisions (subject to a confidentiality exception, the invocation of which would be subject to scrutiny by the auditors). Both the Company Law Review and the Higgs Review (*see* 2.9.2 below) recommended that non-executive directors' terms of engagement should also be open to inspection.

The Company Law Review also suggested that directors' service contracts should have a maximum fixed term of one year, with flexibility to contract for three years on first employment, subject to shareholder approval. For listed companies, this is currently the subject of a Combined Code provision recommending notice or contract periods of one year or less (Combined Code provision B.1.7), and this provision is supported by the Higgs Review. The White Paper was silent on this issue, but in April 2003 the Government announced a separate consultation on severance pay for directors, which is the main concern underlying lengthy notice periods or fixed terms in directors' service contracts (*see* Chapter 6).

2.9.1.7 Directors' training, qualification and age requirements

The Company Law Review proposed that public companies should be required to disclose the training and experience of directors, and that the provisions of Section 293 in relation to the appointment of directors over 70 by public companies should be replaced by a requirement simply to state the age of a proposed director in the biographical details to be given in the notice of meeting. These proposals have yet to be addressed in the drafting of the Companies Bill.

2.9.1.8 Information on company stationery

As part of the Company Law Review, the Government has consulted on changes to the disclosure regime which currently imposes various requirements on companies to disclose the company name and, in some cases, the directors' names and other particulars in correspondence and at business premises. The main focus of the consultation was to update the current regime to take account of the prevalence of electronic communications. It is not clear whether there will be any changes in respect of disclosure of directors' details, although the consultation asked whether certain types of company should be exempt from the requirements relating to the publication of its name and other particulars, including directors' names. The consultation closed on 12 April 2001. The revised provisions will probably be included in the draft Companies Bill, but no draft clauses in this respect have yet been published.

2.9.2 Higgs Review

The Higgs Review on the role and effectiveness of non-executive directors was published in January 2003 and its recommendations for a revised Combined Code were due to be implemented with effect from 1 July 2003. However, the Review attracted a great deal of criticism, particularly from chairmen of FTSE 100 companies and, to a more limited extent, from bodies such as the CBI and London Stock Exchange and shareholder representative bodies such as the ABI. As a result, the Financial Reporting Council ("FRC"), which is charged with implementing Higgs' recommendations in a revised Combined Code, delayed the implementation of the proposals pending further consultation on the principles and drafting of the revised Combined Code. At the time of writing the new Combined Code had indeed been published and was due to take effect in for financial years beginning on or after 1 November 2003.

The main proposals in the original Review which impact on the appointment and removal of directors generally are summarised below. Where codified in the new Combined Code, references have been given.

2.9.2.1 The role of the board

The Higgs Review recommended that the Combined Code should include more detailed provision on the role of the board, building on the principle contained in the White Paper on the Companies Bill, whereby the board is obliged, in the draft statutory Statement of Directors' Duties, to promote the success of the company for the benefit of its shareholders as a whole (suggested Code provision A.1 and implemented as A.1).

2.9.2.2 Size and composition of the board

Higgs proposed that the board should not be so large as to become unwieldy (Supporting Principles to Code provision A.3). Notwithstanding this, the cumulative effect of various proposals in the Higgs Review is thought likely to result in larger boards for listed companies than the current average of seven (12 for FTSE 100 companies). For example, Higgs proposed that:

(a) the roles of chairman and chief executive should be separated (Code provision A.2);
(b) there should be strong executive representation on the board (Code provision A.3);
(c) at least half of the members of the board, excluding the chairman, should be independent non-executive directors (Code provision A.3.3); and
(d) no single individual should serve on all three principal board committees (remuneration, audit and nomination) at the same time (Supporting Principle to Code provision A.3.7).

2.9.2.3 Board appointments

Higgs recommended that all listed companies should have a nomination committee which should lead the process for board appointments and make recommendations to the board. The nomination committee should consist of a majority of independent non-executive directors and should be chaired by the Chairman or an independent non-executive director (Code provision A.4.1).

One of the tasks of the nomination committee will be to ensure that the company carries out adequate succession and planning for appointments to the board and to senior management. Chairmen and chief executives will be expected to consider implementing executive development programmes to train and develop suitable individuals for future director roles.

Appointment and Vacation of Office

2.9.2.4   *Role of non-executive directors*
Higgs suggested that the revised Code should set out a description of the role of the non-executive director and the Related Guidance to the Code contains a sample letter of a non-executive director appointment. Higgs also recommended that the terms of engagement of non-executive directors should be publicly available (Code provision A.4.4). Chapter 6 deals with remuneration of non-executive directors.

2.9.2.5   *Training and performance evaluation for directors*
The Higgs Report recommended a "step change" in training and development provision for directors. Code provision A.5.1 will require that all new directors receive a comprehensive, formal and tailored induction on joining the board. In addition, the Code provides that the performance of the board as a whole, of its committees, and of its members, is evaluated annually, and the annual report should state whether such performance evaluation has taken place and how it is conducted (Code provision A.6.1).

2.9.2.6   *Shareholder activism*
Higgs endorsed the Government's aim to encourage more active engagement by institutional shareholders and proposes that the ISC Code of Shareholder Activism (*see* 2.4.2 above) should be endorsed by specific reference in the Combined Code (Supporting Principles of Code provision E. 1).

2.9.3   *European Company Law Reform*

In November 2002 a report on proposed reform of company law in Europe was published by the High Level Group of Company Law Experts, chaired by Jaap Winter. The report follows a request by the European Commission for a fundamental review of company law in Europe, with a view to updating the framework Directives upon which national company law in the European Union is based. Part of the brief of the High Level Group was to review corporate governance structures in Europe.

The recommendations of the High Level Group in relation to corporate governance include recommendations on the composition and role of the board, its committees and members, and proposals to encourage shareholder activism and greater accountability of the board to shareholders in relation to performance and remuneration. Many of the recommendations made in the Report of the High Level Group reflect requirements which either already exist in the UK corporate governance framework or

A Practitioner's Guide to Directors' Duties and Responsibilities

are the subject of ongoing consultation. In any event, the UK Government is committed to ensuring that the recommendations of the High Level Group on reform of company law at EU level are reflected in the drafting of the Companies Bill.

Chapter 3

Directors' Duties

Richard Slynn, Partner
Allen & Overy

3.1 Introduction

In the case of *Re Continental Assurance Co of London Plc (In Liquidation)* [2001] BPIR 733, Mr Justice Park remarked:

> "I do not base my decision on what I say now, but I cannot refrain from remarking that, if the non-executive directors were liable to pay millions of pounds to the liquidators in this case, it is hard to imagine any well-advised person ever agreeing to accept appointment as a non-executive director of any company. I would not on that account shrink from deciding this case in favour of the liquidators if I thought that they had established what they needed in order to succeed. However, I readily acknowledge that it is a source of some relief to me that, in my judgment, the liquidators have not done that."

It can sometimes be a fine line when determining whether a director has complied with the duties that are placed upon him at law, and the consequences of being on the wrong side of the line can be severe. This Chapter examines the current status of the law on directors' duties as follows:

(a) it considers fiduciary duties (what they are, to whom they are owed and the circumstances in which the court will interfere with decisions taken by the board);
(b) it examines the common law duties of care, skill and diligence that must be exercised by directors and highlights certain recent developments both in case law and the growing impact of the recent corporate governance reviews;
(c) it assesses the developments in the sphere of responsibilities for financial statements in the light of recent corporate scandals and looks at how the impact is driven not only by domestic changes but also developments in the US and Europe;
(d) it touches on certain recent legislative developments which can have profound and direct consequences for directors; and

(e) it looks to the future by reference to the recent White Paper "Modernising Company Law".

The Chapter concludes with a brief analysis of certain recent trends and themes concerning directors' duties in other EU countries and the US to give a flavour of the significance of this area of the law in a more global context.

The duties and liabilities imposed upon directors under the Listing Rules, the Public Offers of Securities Regulations, the Takeover Code, the insolvency legislation and directors' potential liabilities generally are dealt with in Chapter 4.

3.2 Fiduciary duties

3.2.1 General

A director is a fiduciary. That is, he is subject to fiduciary duties by reason of his relationship to the company and the "stakeholders" in that company. A director is not strictly a trustee but he may be subject to very similar obligations to a trustee, for example in respect of the company's property.[1] The position of a fiduciary has been well described by Millett LJ in *Bristol and West Building Society v Mothew* [1998] Ch 1 at page 18:

> "A fiduciary is someone who has undertaken to act for or on behalf of another in a particular matter in circumstances which give rise to a relationship of trust and confidence. The distinguishing obligation of a fiduciary is the obligation of loyalty. The principal is entitled to the single-minded loyalty of his fiduciary. This core liability has several facets. A fiduciary must act in good faith; he must not make a profit out of his trust; he must not place himself in a position where his duty and his interest may conflict; he may not act for his own benefit or the benefit of a third person without the informed consent of his principal. This is not intended to be an exhaustive list, but it is sufficient to indicate the nature of fiduciary obligations. They are the defining characteristics of the fiduciary. As Dr. Finn pointed out in his classic work *Fiduciary Obligations* (1977) p. 2, he is not subject

---

[1] *Re Lands Allotment Co.* [1894] 1 Ch 616 at page 631 per Lindley LJ: "Although directors are not properly speaking trustees, yet they have always been considered and treated as trustees of money which comes into their hands or which is under their control".

Directors' Duties

to fiduciary obligations because he is a fiduciary; it is because he is subject to them that he is a fiduciary."

The fiduciary duties described below are all owed to the company (*see* 3.4.1 below for duties owed direct to shareholders). As the duties are owed to the company, it is the company that can enforce the duties. Directors may be tempted to adopt the attitude that their company will never sue them for breach of their fiduciary (or other) duties as they control the company. Before they succumb to that temptation, directors should remember:

(a) if their company is a public company, it could be taken over by new owners – hostile offers can succeed;
(b) there could be a management coup or other change of directors, perhaps instigated by institutional shareholders if they become dissatisfied – shareholder activism has come under the spotlight recently (*see* below);
(c) insolvency could strike the company (and it can come about by reason of matters over which the management may have no control, such as a collapse in the economy or in the market for their products, or the failure of a major customer or of a provider of crucial services or supplies). In that event the receiver, administrator or liquidator is likely to pursue every course open to him to recover funds for the company and its creditors. The receiver, administrator or liquidator is also bound to report to the Department of Trade and Industry ("the DTI") if he considers that any director's conduct makes him unfit to be concerned in the management of a company;
(d) disgruntled shareholders (or even employees) could take steps which lead to the DTI instigating an investigation into the company's affairs or some other regulatory review being carried out (e.g. by the Listing Authority where the company's shares are listed); and
(e) possibly, proceedings could be started under Section 459 of the Companies Act 1985 ("CA 1985") (conduct unfairly prejudicial to certain shareholders) or as a derivative action.

So, directors and their advisers ignore directors' duties at their peril.

In addition, the directors of UK listed companies have to take account not only of the recent developments in corporate governance (such as the Higgs Review and the Smith Report, which are touched on later in this Chapter) but also of the fact that shareholder activism is on the increase.

In October 2002 the Institutional Shareholders' Committee ("ISC"), which represents almost all UK institutional investors (including pension funds, insurance companies and investment trusts), published a statement of principles setting out best practice for institutional shareholders in relation to their responsibilities with respect to UK listed investee companies. The points covered by the statement of principles include:

(a) setting out the policy of how institutional shareholders propose to discharge their responsibility;
(b) monitoring the performance and establishing as necessary a regular dialogue with UK listed investee companies;
(c) intervening where necessary; and
(d) evaluating the impact of their activism and reporting back to clients/beneficial owners.

The aim is "to ensure that shareholders derive value from their investments by dealing effectively with concerns over under-performance".

Similarly, Hermes, which manages funds for UK corporate and pension funds, has sent its latest statement of principles to the boards of all UK listed companies stating generally that it wants to resurrect the idea that business is a joint enterprise between the boards and employees of the company and its owners represented by their agents, the investment managers, to create shareholder value.

3.2.2 Loyalty – acting in the best interests of the company

As stated by Millett LJ in *Bristol and West Building Society v Mothew* (above): "The principal is entitled to the single-minded loyalty of his fiduciary". Directors, as fiduciaries, must act in good faith in the best interests of the company (*Re Smith & Fawcett* [1942] Ch 304 at page 306). The best interests of the company are generally accepted as being ascertained by reference to the interests of shareholders in the company (present and future), balancing their short-term interests and their long-term interests.[2]

---

[2] In certain takeover situations, for example where it is clear that a takeover will happen but where there are competing bids, the courts have indicated that the interests of the target company are to be judged by reference to the interests of the current shareholders and that the duty of the directors is to obtain the best price. See *Heron International Ltd. v Lord Grade* [1983] BCLC 244 supported by Hoffmann J at first instance in *Morgan Crucible Co. plc v Hill Samuel Bank Ltd* [1991] CH 295, but c.f. *Dawson International plc v Coats Patons plc* [1991] BCC 276 which emphasised that directors' duties are to the company and not current shareholders.

Directors' Duties

However, this test is subject to the following qualifications.

3.2.2.1 Creditors' interests
If the company is insolvent or nearing insolvency, the interests of the creditors will prevail (*West Mercia Safetywear* v *Dodd* [1988] BCLC 250) – in any insolvency, the liabilities to creditors must, of course, be discharged before shareholders benefit; indeed, a deliberate policy not to pay creditors until pressed for payment has been held to be misconduct sufficient to render a director liable to disqualification (*Secretary of State for Trade & Industry* v *McTighe & Another (No. 2)* [1996] 2 BCLC at page 477).

In the recent case of *Colin Gwyer & Associates Ltd* v *London Wharf (Limehouse) Ltd* [2002] All ER (D) 226 (Dec) it was stated that:

> "where a company is insolvent or of doubtful solvency or on the verge of insolvency and it is the creditors' money which is at risk the directors, when carrying out their duty to the company, must consider the interests of the creditors as paramount and take those into account when exercising their discretion."

In that case, Mr Leslie Kosmin QC (sitting as a Deputy Judge of the Chancery Division) held that a board decision was invalid in the situation where both directors at the meeting knew the company was insolvent and failed to consider properly the interests of the creditors. Each director was therefore in breach of his fiduciary duty in voting on the resolution in question and, in consequence, should be treated as incapable of voting on the business before the board.

3.2.2.2 Employees' interests
Section 309(1) CA 1985 states that:

> "the matters to which the directors of a company are to have regard in the performance of their functions include the interests of the company's employees in general, as well as the interests of its members."

To make it clear that this provision does not confer rights which enable any employee (or even the employees generally) to bring an action directly against the directors, subsection (2) states that the duty "is owed by them to the company (and the company alone) and is enforceable in the same way as any other fiduciary duty owed to a company by its directors". Section 309 (or its statutory predecessor) was introduced at the same time as Section 719 CA 1985 (or, rather, its predecessor) which reversed the decision in *Parke* v *Daily News* [1962] Ch 927. In that case, the court held that ex gratia payments to employees on the closing down of the company which published the *News Chronicle* were contrary to the directors' fiduciary duties as the shareholders had no continuing interest in maintaining good relations with employees (since it was going out of business). Since the 1880s it has been established that directors may give benefits to employees as, without their goodwill, a company would soon find itself deserted of employees.

> "The law does not say that there are to be no cakes and ale, but there are to be no cakes and ale except such as are required for the benefit of the company." (*Hutton* v *West Cork Railway Co.* [1883] 23 Ch D 654 at page 673)

Section 719 states that a company has power to make provision for employees (or former employees) of the company or any of its subsidiaries in connection with the cessation of the company or such subsidiary. This power is expressed to be exercisable notwithstanding that its exercise is not in the best interests of the company – thus reinforcing the principle that having regard to the interests of employees under Section 309 is not (or is not necessarily) of itself in the company's interests. It should also be noted that the power to pay benefits under Section 719 may be exercised by the directors only if so authorised by the company's memorandum or articles or by a shareholders' resolution.

3.2.2.3 Not-for-profit companies

A large number of charities take the form of companies – usually companies limited by guarantee (rather than companies with a share capital), with members of the board or other governing body being the members of the company who "guarantee", usually to a very limited extent, its liabilities. There are special statutory provisions relating to directors and other aspects of charitable companies.[3] The question of how the best interests of such a company are determined will differ from normal companies. The best interests are most unlikely to be determined by what will enhance the position of the members; they are likely to be determined by reference to the interests of the charitable objects, having regard in particular to the company's memorandum of association. Companies that are not charitable but whose constitutions provide that they are established for some benevolent or philanthropic purpose (i.e.

---

[3] For example Charities Acts 1992 and 1993 and Sections 35 and 35A CA 1985.

Directors' Duties

they are what is commonly referred to as "not-for-profit" companies) are likely to be treated in the same way when determining the best interests of the company. Although it is outside the scope of this Guide to consider the law relating to directors of such companies or the directors of other entities, such as building societies, it is of interest to note that the leading textbook[4] on building societies addresses the question of the best interests of a building society (whose members are its savers and its borrowers) and expresses the view that the society's directors can properly take the view that the interests which they are primarily concerned to promote are:

(a) the saving member's interest in having a safe home for his money with attractive rates of interest;
(b) the borrowing member's interest in having a long-term mortgage loan with affordable interest rates; and
(c) the interest of both classes of members in receiving good service from the society's staff.

Returning to the case of a normal company, the question often arises: when considering the company's best interests, how far can a director take into account:

(a) the interests of other stakeholders (e.g. the local community, the environment, third world economies);
(b) the interests of other companies in the same group of companies to which the company belongs;
(c) a particular shareholder, especially where the director has been appointed by that shareholder and is capable of being removed by the shareholder?

3.2.2.4 *Other stakeholders*

The interests of the company are assessed by reference to the interests of its shareholders (present and future). Directors are not entitled to put the interests of other stakeholders (such as the local community, the environment or third world economies) ahead of shareholders' interests. However, this does not require directors to take a short-term or unduly narrow view of shareholders' interests. Indeed, having regard only to the immediate profit of the company may fail to take account of the interests of future shareholders as well as present shareholders. Furthermore, to

---

[4] *Wurtzburg and Mills: Building Society Law*, 15th edition (London, Stevens & Sons, 1989), Chapter 16.01.

take account of other stakeholders' interests (such as local community, environment etc.) may well promote the interests of the company, particularly its longer-term interests, and failure to take account of such factors may amount to not acting in the company's best interests. Thus, directors are entitled (and, to a certain degree, are obliged) to take an enlightened approach to the company's best interests to ensure that there is a proper balance between short-term and long-term interests.

The so-called "Long Term" issue emerged as a factor of great significance in the Company Law Review Steering Group's consultation papers.[5] In the February 1999 document it stated that there is "considerable evidence that the effect of the law is not well recognised and understood". In the draft statutory statement of general principles contained in the White Paper "Modernising Company Law", there is express reference to the need to take account of "the likely consequences (short and long term) of the actions open to the director, so far as a person of care and skill would consider them relevant".

3.2.2.5 *Other companies in the same group*
A director may take into account the interests of other companies in the group (or the interests of the group as a whole) only to the extent that it is in the company's best interests to do so.

If the other group company is a subsidiary of the company, it may well be in the best interests of a company to take action which promotes that subsidiary's interests (e.g. by guaranteeing its bank account) if that action will enhance the value of the company's investment in the subsidiary. Support of the company's parent company may quite possibly be in the company's interests, especially if the company is dependent on the parent for finance or services. Support of a fellow subsidiary may be less likely to be in the company's interests. Thus, to avoid possible breaches of the directors' fiduciary duties, it is normal, where a company is proposing to take action which primarily benefits a parent company or a fellow subsidiary (e.g. guaranteeing that other company's bank borrowings), for the company's shareholders to pass a resolution authorising the directors' actions; it is usual to pass such a resolution as a special resolution. If, as a general body, the shareholders authorise or ratify a particular course of action there can be no challenge by the

---

[5] The Company Law Review Steering Group's Consultation Document: The Strategic Framework (February 1999) Chapter 5.1.20 at page 40, and *see* also the Group's Consultation Document: Developing the Framework (March 2000) Chapter 3.54 to 3.56 at page 35.

shareholders as to whether the directors acted in the company's best interests. However, where the company is insolvent (or near insolvency) the interests of the creditors intrude and a shareholders' resolution is not effective to sanction the directors' actions. Accordingly, when members of a group of companies give cross-guarantees in relation to each other's borrowings or other obligations (or in relation to those of the principal company in the group), insolvent (or near insolvent) companies are excluded from giving such guarantees.

In practice, directors may be inclined to act in a particular way having regard to the group's best interests rather than the best interests of their particular company. Failure to consider separately what is actually in their company's interests may not, however, be fatal to the fulfilment of their fiduciary duties. It has been held that the directors of a subsidiary will not be in breach of their fiduciary duties provided that an intelligent and honest man in the same position could reasonably have come to the conclusion that their actions were for the benefit of the subsidiary (*Charterbridge Corporation Ltd* v *Lloyds Bank* [1970] Ch 62).

Where the director is also a director of one or more other companies in the same group, he may also have to consider the question of his conflict of interest (*see* 3.2.6 below).

3.2.2.6 *Appointing shareholder*

Occasionally a company's memorandum or articles may specify that a third party (often, but not always, a significant shareholder) has the right to appoint and remove one or more directors. A person who is appointed as a director of a company by such a person may consider that, when acting as a director of the company, he is obliged to promote the interests of his appointer. However, to do so could be a breach of his fiduciary duties – directors may not act as representatives of particular interests (*see* further below). Each director owes the same duty to act in the best interests of the company and may not exercise his powers so as to favour one particular shareholder or sectional interest. This does not of course preclude him from drawing his fellow directors' attention to the particular benefits or disadvantages for the company of any particular course of action (especially where these benefits or disadvantages are known to him and are unlikely to be known to his fellow directors, e.g. because he is aware of them by virtue of some outside experience), but any decision must be taken by the directors purely by reference to the company's best interests.

When acting as a director of a company, a director has a duty to that company and not to his appointer. This includes his duties of confidentiality – thus he may not pass confidential information relating to the company to the person who appointed him unless the consent of the company has been properly obtained. In *Harkness v CBA* (1993) 12 ACSR 165 (an Australian case), the question arose as to whether a company's bank knew that the company was insolvent when the company made a payment to the bank. One of the bank's senior managers was a director of another company (a clearing house) and, in that capacity, knew that the company was insolvent at the time of its payment to the bank. The court held that his knowledge, gained in that capacity, was not attributable to the bank. Whilst ordinarily there is a duty to communicate knowledge received, the "duty of confidentiality to that other organisation will subsume any duty he might otherwise owe to the company which appointed him to that organisation".

3.2.2.7 "Business judgment" rule applied by the Court

Finally, the test of whether the directors are acting in the best interests is a subjective one. In other words, the courts will not hold that there has been a breach of a fiduciary duty if the directors acted bona fide in what they considered to be in the best interests of the company. The court will not substitute its own judgment of what is in the company's best interests (even if it would have reached a different conclusion from that of the directors) nor will it question the correctness of the management's decision if arrived at bona fide. Thus, the English courts apply a type of "business judgment" rule.

It is unlikely, however, that a court would still accept the directors' view of a company's best interests (even if claimed to be arrived at bona fide) if that view was so extreme that no reasonable directors would hold it. The courts have applied the Wednesbury principles[6] to decisions of directors. The Wednesbury principles, in relation to governmental authorities, provide that a decision may be set aside on two grounds:

(a) if those making the decision had taken into account factors that they should not have considered or had failed to take into account factors that they should have considered;

(b) if, having considered all the right factors, they had come to a conclusion so unreasonable that no reasonable authority could have come to it.

---

[6] *Associated Provincial Picture Houses Limited* v *Wednesbury Corporation* [1948] 1 KB 223.

Directors' Duties

In the reported cases on companies[7] the courts have set aside decisions on the first basis, but there appears to be no decided case relying on the second basis (unreasonableness) (*re a Company, ex parte Glossop* [1988] BCLC 570 is the nearest).

Nonetheless, a director would be unwise to test the issue and, certainly, any person advising a director would be foolish not to warn the director in strong terms that he may incur liability if his intended action appears not to meet the test of reasonableness.

3.2.3 *Obedience – acting for proper purposes only*

This duty falls into two parts:

(a) a director must act in accordance with the company's constitution; and
(b) a director must exercise his powers only for the purposes allowed by law.

3.2.3.1 Compliance with constitution
A director must not cause the company to undertake activities outside what is permitted by the objects clause in the company's memorandum of association. As a result of changes in the law over the last few decades, the effect of the ultra vires rule (under which acts of a company outside its objects were void) has been substantially mitigated – at least for bona fide outsiders dealing with the company. However, the company's directors are still obliged to comply with the constraints imposed by the objects clause and may be liable if the company exceeds its powers (*see* Section 35(3) CA 1985). Furthermore, transactions outside a company's powers which are entered into with a director of the company or of its holding company (or with a person connected with such a director or with a company with whom such a director is associated) will be voidable at the request of the company.

A director will also be obliged to comply with the procedural and other requirements imposed by the company's articles of association ("the articles").

---

[7] *Byng* v *London Life Association* [1989] 1 All ER 560, *Re a Company, ex parte Glossop* [1988] BCLC 570 at page 577(i), and *Heron International Ltd* v *Lord Grade* [1983] BCLC 244.

3.2.3.2 *Acting for proper purpose only*

Directors must exercise their powers only for the purpose for which those powers are conferred. For instance, they must not exercise their powers to protect their own positions or to make life difficult for particular shareholders or potential shareholders. This is the case even if the manner in which they exercise their powers happens to be in the best interests of the company. The authoritative case on the issue is *Howard Smith v Ampol Petroleum*,[8] in which a company (Millers) had two shareholders together holding 55 per cent of the shares. A third shareholder (Howard Smith) announced its intention to make an offer which the board of Millers wanted to succeed but which the two principal shareholders opposed. The board allotted additional shares to Howard Smith which diluted the two principal shareholders' interest to a minority interest. The court held that, although the board acted bona fide and it was in the best interests of Howard Smith to raise funds by the issue of shares, the substantial purpose of the allotment was to favour one shareholder over others. The allotment was therefore set aside. It was not necessary for the plaintiffs to prove that the directors acted out of self interest or to preserve their own control of the management. It was sufficient that the directors had exercised their powers for an improper purpose. The court set out the judicial approach as follows:

> "Having ascertained, on a fair view, the nature of this power, and having defined, as can best be done in the light of modern conditions, the, or some, limits within which it may be exercised, it is then necessary for the court, if a particular exercise of it is challenged, to examine the substantial purpose for which it was exercised and to reach a conclusion whether that purpose was proper or not. In doing so it will necessarily give credit to the bona fide opinion of the directors, if such is found to exist, and will respect their judgment as to matters of management; having done this, the ultimate conclusion has to be as to the side of a fairly broad line on which the case falls."

The real issue, therefore, relates to the directors' substantial purpose. It does not matter if a consequence of a particular course of action by the directors is that their own interests are advanced if that was not their principal or substantial purpose (*Hirsche v Sims* [1894] AC 654 at page 660).

---

[8] *Howard Smith Ltd v Ampol Petroleum Ltd* [1974] AC 821 at page 835. *See* also *Punt v Symons & Co Ltd* [1903] 2 Ch 506 and *Hogg v Cramphorn Ltd* [1967] Ch 254.

Directors' Duties

The principle can be invoked in relation to any power whose purpose can be clearly discerned from the articles. For example, in *re a Company ex parte Glossop* [1988] BCLC 570, the principle was applied to the directors' power to recommend dividends.

3.2.4 No secret (i.e. unauthorised) profits or misapplication of property

It is a well-established principle that a fiduciary may not benefit from the "trust" property or the opportunities which come to him by virtue of his position as a fiduciary unless he has the informed consent of the persons to whom he owes his fiduciary duties. In the case of a director of a company, this consent may come in the form of provisions in the company's articles or a resolution of the shareholders (*Aberdeen Railway Co. v Blaikie Brothers* (1854) 2 Eq. Reg. 128, [1843-60] All ER 249). Most companies' articles relax the full rigour of the fiduciary's duty to account for benefits he receives. In fact, directors are not allowed any fees or remuneration even for the performance of executive functions except to the extent expressly permitted in their company's articles. For this reason, directors will normally want to ensure that their companies' articles contain adequate provision allowing them to receive fees, expenses and (where relevant) remuneration, and (subject to certain limitations) relieving them of their duty to account where they have an interest (directly or indirectly) in contracts or arrangements to which the company is a party (*see* further below and Chapter 5).

The duty to account is such that a director may be liable to the company for any profit he has made by virtue of his position even if the company could not itself have made a profit.

The duty not to make a secret (or, rather, unauthorised) profit can be illustrated best by the following two cases.

In *Regal (Hastings) Ltd v Gulliver* [1942] 1 All ER 378, four directors and Regal's solicitor subscribed for shares in a subsidiary of Regal to give it sufficient additional funds to acquire extra cinema leases. Regal did not have sufficient resources itself to provide the funds to the subsidiary. When the shares in the subsidiary were sold at a profit, Regal (controlled by new owners) claimed the profits from the directors and the solicitor. The court held that, as fiduciaries, the directors were liable to account to the company for the profit they had made (in fact, the solicitor was held not to be liable). It was held in the House of Lords that:

> "The rule of equity which insists on those who by the use of a fiduciary position make a profit, being liable to account for that profit, in no way depends on fraud or absence of bona fides; or upon such questions or considerations as whether the profit would or should otherwise have gone to the plaintiff, or whether he took a risk or acted as he did for the benefit of the plaintiff, or whether the plaintiff has in fact been damaged or benefited from his action."

The directors were liable even though Regal could not have made the profit itself (because of lack of resources) and even though they had acted in the best interests of the company and had not caused it loss. However, the directors could have kept the profit if they had obtained the approval of the company's shareholders in general meeting. If the circumstances were repeated now and Regal were a listed company, the transaction would in any event have needed shareholders' approval as a "related party transaction". But it is important to remember in the case of non-listed companies (including private companies), shareholder approval may be needed if the directors are to be entitled to retain any profit which they have derived by virtue of their position.

A more recent case illustrating the point is *Guinness* v *Saunders and Another* [1990] 1 All ER 652. Guinness was in the process of making a contested takeover bid for another company. The conduct of the bid was left in the hands of a committee, comprising three directors, one of whom was a US lawyer. The committee approved the payment of a fee of £5.2 million to an offshore company controlled by the lawyer/director for services rendered by him. Subsequently, the company succeeded in its claim for the recovery of the £5.2 million. The director acknowledged that he had not declared his interest in the contract with the offshore company in accordance with Section 317 CA 1985. The House of Lords held that the fee had not been paid in accordance with the company's articles (which allowed remuneration and special fees to be paid to directors where approved by the board) as approval by a committee was not sufficient; there was, therefore, no contract (and technically no need for disclosure under Section 317). The director's claim for payment on the basis of quantum meruit was also rejected as the court would not exercise its discretion to allow remuneration on a quantum meruit basis where the articles conferred power on the board of directors to approve any remuneration.

The duty not to make an unauthorised profit from opportunities which arise by virtue of holding the position of a director applies even where the profit arises after the individual has ceased to be a director (e.g. where a customer placed a contract with the director rather than with the company but the director resigned before the profit from the contract was realised). The duty also applies where the opportunity to profit (e.g. the contract) arises after the director's resignation, for example where the business opportunity was maturing while the individual was a director and his resignation was influenced by a wish to take advantage of the business opportunity for himself.[9]

As mentioned above, most companies' articles allow directors to retain any benefits derived by the director from a contract or other arrangement entered into by the company where the director has an interest. The director will, of course, have to declare any interest in accordance with Section 317 CA 1985. If the contract is sufficiently large, it may also be necessary to obtain shareholders' approval under Section 320 CA 1985.

In addition to the director's duty to account for any personal profit, he is also under an obligation not to misapply the company's property, even though he may not obtain any personal benefit from such misapplication. For example, a director must not authorise the sale of an asset at a value lower than its true value unless it is in the best interests of the company to do so or the gratuitous element of the transfer is made up of distributable profits with the approval of its shareholders. Similarly, a director who authorises unlawful dividends (e.g. dividends in excess of distributable profits) may be liable for such dividends. He will be liable if he knew (or ought, as a reasonably competent and diligent director, to have known) that the payments were unlawful or if he knew (or should be taken to have known) the facts which established the impropriety of the payments.

Passing on confidential information without authority (e.g. not in the proper course of business) will be a misapplication of the company's property. This may be particularly relevant where the director has a position with another entity which may be interested in such information. Similarly, failure to direct to the company business opportunities which come to the director may be a breach of duty by the director. The Court of Appeal's judgment in *Bhullar and others* v *Bhullar and another* [2003] EWCA Civ 424 (concerning the diversion by a director of a business opportunity to himself) considered the test for determining

---

[9] *Industrial Development Consultants Ltd* v *Cooley* [1972] 2 All ER 162 (*see also CMS Dolphin Ltd* v *Simonet* [2002] BCC 600.) – the position in these cases is to be contrasted with a case where a former director derived a business opportunity by virtue of knowledge gained whilst he was a director but where there was no maturing opportunity at that time – *see Island Export Finance Ltd* v *Umunna* [1986] BCLC 460 at pages 480 to 483.

what constitutes an opportunity for the company. The court affirmed that the test would be satisfied if a reasonable man looking at the facts would think there was a real, sensible possibility of conflict between the director's personal interest and the interests of the company.

3.2.5 Independence

This duty is described as a duty on a director not to agree to restrict his power to exercise an independent judgment. It is also referred to as a duty on a director not to fetter his discretion. In practice, it means that a director may not bind himself to vote on board resolutions (or to fulfil other functions as a director) in a particular predetermined way – when voting (or fulfilling such other functions) he must consider all the circumstances at the time and decide then what is in the best interests of the company. If he were to agree in advance how to exercise his votes (or fulfil other functions), he would have deprived himself of the ability to exercise proper judgment.

Thus it is not open for a director (even one who has been appointed by a shareholder or other third party under a special power in the company's constitution) to agree to vote etc. in accordance with the directions of another person. Shareholders may insert into a company's memorandum or articles provisions limiting the matters on which the directors may reach decisions or take actions (or on which directors may do so without shareholders' approval) but any restrictions on the directors' powers agreed by directors outside the company's constitution will be in breach of their fiduciary duties and unenforceable.

However, this does not prevent the directors from causing their company to enter into a contract and undertaking to exercise their powers in such a way as to ensure the proper fulfilment of the contract. If it is in the best interests of the company to enter into the contract, it is open to the directors to agree to exercise their powers to ensure that the contract is carried out. This was decided in *Fulham Football Club Ltd* v *Cabra Estates plc* [1994] 1 BCLC 363 at page 392, where the Court of Appeal approved a rule established in an Australian case (*Thorby* v *Goldberg* (1964) 112 CLR 597):

> "If, when a contract is negotiated on behalf of a company, the directors bona fide think it in the best interests of the company as a whole that the transaction should be entered into and carried into effect, they may bind themselves by the contract to do whatever is necessary to effectuate it."

Two earlier cases[10] held (at first instance) that undertakings by directors to recommend proposed transactions to shareholders for their approval were unenforceable. The court in the *Fulham Football Club* case stated that, whilst these cases may be justified on their particular facts, they should not be read as laying down a general proposition that directors can never bind themselves as to the future exercise of their powers. Each of these cases involved an agreement by a company to sell a subsidiary to a purchaser with the agreement being conditional on the approval of the shareholders; in one case these were the seller's shareholders and in the other case they were the purchaser's shareholders. The directors of the relevant companies agreed with the other side to recommend the transactions to their shareholders, or to use their best endeavours to procure the fulfilment of the condition. Before the meeting of the shareholders other events occurred which caused the sale/purchase to be seriously disadvantageous to the relevant companies, and the directors refused to recommend the relevant transaction to their shareholders. The courts held that the directors were under a fiduciary duty to make full and honest disclosure to their shareholders and not to give bad advice. The courts upheld the directors' actions in each case.

These cases, it seems, still support the principle that directors should not give an unqualified undertaking in advance to recommend a course of action to shareholders in case, at the time of the recommendation, the directors are no longer of the view that the proposed course of action is in the best interests of the company; the recommendation could not then be made honestly. Nor should the directors give an unqualified undertaking to make statements to shareholders in the future which might amount to a misrepresentation, for example as to the supposed merits of a proposal compared with the merits of any available alternative. If pressed to give such undertakings, directors should make it clear that their obligations are subject to the proper fulfilment of their duties to the company and to its shareholders.

3.2.6 Conflict of interest

The Law Commission has described this duty by saying that, if there is a conflict between an interest of the company and another interest (or a duty) of the director in any transaction, the director must account to the company for any benefit he receives from the transaction (unless, by

---

[10] *Rackham v Peek Foods Ltd* (1977)[1990] BCLC 895 (decided in 1977) and *John Crowther Group plc v Carpets International plc* [1990] BCLC 460.

reason of the company's constitution or an informed approval given by the shareholders, he is permitted to retain the benefit).

In the recent case of *JJ Harrison (Properties) Ltd v Harrison* [2002] 1 BCLC 162 a director of a company acquired some land from the company at a price which reflected the fact that planning permission had been refused to develop the land. At the time of the acquisition the director was aware that, for various reasons, the prospect of planning permission being granted had improved. This fact was not disclosed to the board at the meeting to approve the transaction. The court found that the director was in breach of his fiduciary duties to the company and held the property upon trust for the company. Accordingly, he was liable to account for the profits he made from the subsequent sale by him of the land.

The duty in fact goes further than this. For instance, if the company suffers a loss by virtue of the conflict (e.g. because the director directed a benefit to go to another entity rather than to the company), the director will be liable to account for the loss. This is so even though the director did not derive any benefit personally and was under a duty to that other entity to promote its interests.

For example, in *Scottish Co-operative Wholesale Society Ltd v Meyer* [1959] AC 324, directors of a partly owned subsidiary acquiesced in a policy of its holding company to deprive the subsidiary of business contracts, which were diverted to the parent company. In an action by minority shareholders in the subsidiary, those directors of the subsidiary who were "nominees" of the holding company (and also directors of the holding company) were held to be in breach of their duties to the subsidiary by their inaction in failing to protect that company from the loss of business.

It has been held that it is permissible for a director to hold a directorship with another company which is a competitor (*Bell v Lever Bros. Ltd* [1932] AC 161 at page 195). This case is also authority for the proposition that there is no duty on a director to disclose his own misconduct. There are, however, exceptions to this principle. In *Item Software (UK) Ltd v Fassihi & Others* [2003] All ER (D) 68 (Jan) a sales and marketing director who sabotaged the negotiation of a distribution agreement so that another company which he owned and controlled could enter into the agreement instead was held to have breached his duties. The director's misconduct gave rise to a "super added" duty of disclosure because of the relevance to the ongoing negotiations. In addition, the non-disclosure of his own misconduct amounted to fraudulent concealment which made it a breach of duty and distinguishable from *Bell v Lever Brothers* (above).

In practice it is unlikely that a director (especially where he has any business-acquiring role) will be in office very long before finding that he is faced with a conflict of duties with regard to any competitor company of which he is also a director – when the first business opportunity emerges, to which company should he refer it? When that stage arises, it may be too late for the director to avoid a breach of duty by resigning from one company. It can still be a breach of fiduciary duty if a person resigns as a director to enable him to pursue with another company a business opportunity which he should have directed to the company from which he resigned.

One solution for a person considering taking directorships with two companies which are competitors may be for him to get the informed approval of the shareholders of at least one of the companies that, where there is any conflict, his duties to the other company and his interests in it will prevail over his duties to the first company. Whilst it might be possible to obtain that approval where the shares in the first company are closely held, great care would have to be taken to ensure that sufficient information is given to the shareholders to enable them to make an informed decision. A preferable solution may be to make a change in the company's constitution to relieve the director of his duty not to divert away business opportunities. Even if shareholders are happy with the concept, great care would have to be taken with the wording of any such provision. If the company were to become insolvent, the liquidator or receiver would, no doubt, seek to give the contract as narrow an interpretation as possible. Other difficulties may face an individual with directorships with competing companies, such as the inability to act on information which he has learnt in confidence in his capacity as a director of one company which may be highly relevant to the other company. He may also find himself (unjustly) suspected of having leaked information to the other company. Probably the most practical solution is to refrain from taking on one of the directorships.

3.2.7 *Fairness between shareholders*

Directors must act fairly as between different shareholders. This is not a requirement to give equal treatment to all shareholders, only that the treatment should be fair. The duty was spelt out in *Mutual Life Insurance v Rank Organisation Ltd* [1985] BCLC 11 where US shareholders of Rank brought an action on the grounds that the directors had excluded them from participating in a rights issue by Rank. The directors justified the exclusion on the grounds of the cost and effort which would be incurred in meeting US registration requirements if the offer had been extended to all shareholders. The action failed as the court held that the directors had exercised their powers in good faith in the interests of the company and that they had in fact exercised them fairly as between the different shareholders. The principle of fair treatment between shareholders has been upheld in later cases, although limited in number.[11]

The concept of fair, albeit different, treatment of shareholders is echoed in Section 459 CA 1985, which allows a member to apply for a court order where the company's affairs are being conducted "in a manner which is unfairly prejudicial to the interests of" members or some part of its members. A member can also apply where an actual or proposed act or omission of the company would be unfairly prejudicial.

3.3 Care, skill and diligence

The duties of directors as regards the level of care, skill and diligence they must exercise have developed considerably over recent years. Gone are the days when, for example, the Marquis of Bute could, with impunity, be absent from all but one board meeting during 39 years (*Re Cardiff Savings Bank* [1892] 2 Ch 100), or the court could hold that a director is "not bound to bring any special qualifications to his office. He may undertake the management of a rubber company in complete ignorance of everything connected with rubber, without incurring responsibility for the mistakes which may result from such ignorance" (*Re Brazilian Rubber Plantation and Estates Limited* [1911] 1 Ch 425); or when the court could hold that a director's "duties are of an intermittent nature to be performed at periodical board meetings" (*Re City Equitable Fire Insurance Co.* [1925] Ch 407).

The change has come about partly as a result of a change in the approach to directors of insolvent companies, including the increasing numbers of directors who face disqualification for failure to perform the function properly,[12] partly as a result of a less lenient approach by the courts and

---

[11] *See* for example *Re BSB Holdings Ltd (No.2)* [1996] 1 BCLC 155.
[12] Section 214 Insolvency Act 1986 (wrongful trading); Section 9 Company Directors Disqualification Act 1986 including Schedule 1. *See* also *Re Landhurst Leasing plc* [1999] 1 BCLC 286.

Directors' Duties

partly by a great public concern with corporate governance. The issue of various codes of conduct and guidance, such as the Cadbury Report, the Combined Code, the Turnbull Guidance and, more recently, the Higgs Review of the role and effectiveness of non-executive directors (which is considered in more detail below) and the Smith Report on audit committees, is having the effect of increasing the standards of care generally expected of directors.[13]

The standard of care expected of directors is now regarded as that set down by Hoffmann LJ (as he then was) in *Re D'Jan of London Limited* [1993] BCC 646 when it was held that a director must satisfy the higher of a subjective test and an objective test. A director must take such actions as would be taken by:

> "a reasonably diligent person, having both:
> (a) the general knowledge, skill and experience that may reasonably be expected of a person carrying out the same functions as are carried out by that director in relation to the company; and
> (b) the general knowledge, skill and experience that that director has".

The effect of this test (which is based on Section 214(4) of the Insolvency Act 1986 – wrongful trading) is that it is dangerous for a person to accept a directorship when he is not sufficiently qualified or experienced to be able to fulfil the functions he is expected to carry out. A director of a rubber company is unlikely to be able to claim as a defence his complete ignorance of the rubber industry, nor will a finance director of a FTSE 100 company be able to claim as a defence the fact that he is innumerate. On the other hand, whilst a director of a small building firm may not normally be expected to have a sophisticated grasp of the foreign exchange markets, he would be expected to have such knowledge (and to have exercised it) if he was also a senior employee of a bank engaged in that sphere of activity. This is illustrated by *Re Continental Assurance Co. of London plc (In Liquidation) (No. 1)* [1997] 1 BCLC 48 where a senior executive of a bank was appointed a non-executive director of the company and its subsidiary. In breach of Section 151 CA 1985, the subsidiary made a loan to the holding company to enable it to service its bank loans. When the subsidiary became insolvent, the director was

---

[13] *See* Chapter 9 on Corporate Governance; for judicial application of codes, *see Re Marco (Ipswich) Ltd* [1994] 2 BCLC 354, *Re Chez Nico (Restaurants) Ltd* [1992] BCLC 192 and *Re Astec (BSR) plc* [1998] 2 BCLC 556.

disqualified – his ignorance about the purpose of the upstream loan was held not to be a defence but evidence of his failure to exercise the appropriate degree of competence, especially in the light of his experience as a banker and his ability to understand the accounts of the holding company. The moral of the cases is that a person should not accept a directorship where he is out of his depth and, further, that a highly qualified person should remember to continue to exercise his skills even when he is acting as a director in a role where the exercise of such skills would not normally be expected. Once appointed, a director cannot discharge himself from his responsibilities by maintaining a negligible actual involvement in the affairs of the company. For example, in *Re Galeforce Pleating Co Ltd* [1999] 2 BCLC 704 it was held that, for as long as an individual continued to hold office as a director, and in particular to receive remuneration from it, it was incumbent on that person to inform himself as to the financial affairs of the company and to play an appropriate role in the management of its business.

In *Bairstow v Queens Moat Houses plc and others* [2000] 1 BCLC 549 the court held that an executive director who is paid substantial remuneration is expected to know the requirements that must be satisfied before a payment of dividends may be made.

However, a director is entitled, in the absence of suspicious circumstances, to rely on the experience and expertise of his co-directors and other officers of the company. Directors may also rely on the opinions of outside experts and, indeed, they may be negligent if they do not obtain an outside opinion in appropriate circumstances (*Re Duomatic Ltd* [1969] 2 Ch 365).

Directors cannot absolve themselves entirely of responsibility by delegation to others. In *Re Bradcrown Ltd* [2001] 1 BCLC 547 a finance director who relied solely on professional advice received without making his own independent judgment was found to be unfit. Lawrence Collins J stated that a director is obviously entitled to rely on legal advice, but in this case he had asked no questions and sought no advice while approving transactions that removed substantially all of the assets from the company. The director had simply done what he was told and abdicated all responsibility. "In these circumstances he cannot seek refuge in the fact that professional advisers were involved in the transactions."

By contrast, in *Re Stephenson Cobbold Ltd (In Liquidation), Secretary of State for Trade and Industry v Stephenson and others* [2000] 2 BCLC 614 the court refused to disqualify a non-executive director as, although he was a

Directors' Duties

cheque signatory, he was not involved in deciding which creditors should be paid where preferential treatment had been given. On the evidence, the defendant, an experienced business man, was not a party to any policy of non-payment of Crown debts as he relied on professional accountants. The fact that he was a cheque signatory did not make him a party. Again, on the facts, his being a signatory did not amount to permitting a breach of fiduciary duties by the managing director in relation to the misuse of the company's funds. He had queried the payment and received assurances from the auditors. He was not disqualified.

The extent to which non-executive directors could be liable for failures within the company will depend on the circumstances, including the part which the director could be reasonably expected to play. There is no difference between the tests to be applied to non-executives and those applied to executives; the difference will lie in the functions they fulfil and the extent of the care and diligence that they can be reasonably expected to exercise. For instance, failure to ensure that proper controls are exercised over management (and by management) could be evidence of breach of duty, though the extent to which directors are expected to investigate whether proper controls are exercised will vary in the circumstances.

Re Continental Assurance Co of London plc (In Liquidation) [2001] BPIR 733 (also referred to as *Singer* v *Beckett* [2001] BPIR 733) involved a trial of an application made by the liquidators against eight former directors (two executive and six non-executive) alleging wrongful trading and misfeasance. The liquidators' case with respect to the misfeasance was that the non-executive directors had failed to exercise the requisite skill and care as directors in relying on the management accounts and other financial information as presented to them from time to time. It was held in this case that the non-executive directors had not followed blindly the advice of the finance director and auditors but had been in the habit of probing and testing the financial information provided from time to time, and it had been reasonable and proper for them to have relied on such financial information.

In *Re Barings plc and others (No. 5)* [1999] 1 BCLC 433 the chief executive of a bank faced disqualification proceedings following the insolvency of the bank caused by unauthorised securities trading of an individual employee. The executive chairman sought (unsuccessfully) to defend himself by claiming that his expertise was in the corporate finance side of the business, that he had very little understanding of the activities in which the trader was involved (despite its representing a significant proportion of the bank's reported profits) and that he relied on the internal audit department and external auditors. The judge's summary of the duties of directors includes the following (at page 489):

> "(i) Directors have, both collectively and individually, a continuing duty to acquire and maintain a sufficient knowledge and understanding of the company's business to enable them properly to discharge their duties as directors.
> (ii) Whilst directors are entitled (subject to the articles of association of the company) to delegate particular functions to those below them in the management chain, and to trust their competence and integrity to a reasonable extent, the exercise of the power of delegation does not absolve a director from the duty to supervise the discharge of the delegated functions.
> (iii) No rule of universal application can be formulated as to the duty referred to in (ii) above. The extent of the duty, and the question whether it has been discharged, must depend on the facts of each particular case, including the director's role in the management of the company."

The judge also stated (at page 488):

> "Where there is an issue as to the extent of a director's duties and responsibilities in any particular case, the level of reward which he is entitled to receive or which he may reasonably have expected to receive from the company may be a relevant factor in resolving that issue."

Although the decision in the Barings case was on the question of disqualification, it does not require much imagination to conclude that, if a director has conducted himself in a manner which renders him unfit to be a director, the company may have a claim against him for not exercising proper skill, care or diligence if it has suffered a loss as a result.

3.3.1 The chairman

It is also worthy of mention that in a recent Australian case the court had to consider whether there are any special duties required of a director who holds the office of non-executive chairman.

In the case of *ASIC v Rich* [2003] NSWSC 85, which concerned an application by a director of a company (who was also the non-executive chairman of the board) to strike out a statement of claim against him, the Australian Securities & Investments Commission sought to demonstrate that it is the usual practice in listed companies for the chairman to be responsible to a greater extent than any other director for ensuring that the board is familiar with the financial circumstances, position and performance of the company and for ensuring the performance by the board of its supervisory duties. The court considered the flow of corporate governance literature, including the Higgs Review (and, in particular, Annex D to the review headed "Guidance for the Chairman"). Austin J agreed that there was a reasonably arguable case that the director did have the enhanced responsibilities pleaded by the Commission by virtue of being the chairman. The director's application for summary dismissal of the statement of claim was dismissed. This case will be of persuasive authority if the question of the chairman's duties is argued before the English courts.

3.3.2 Higgs Review

As mentioned above, the development of the standards of skill and care required of directors is also influenced (particularly in the case of listed companies) by the various reviews of certain aspects of corporate governance. The most recent and significant of these insofar as directors' duties are concerned was the *Review of the Role and Effectiveness of Non-Executive Directors* published by Derek Higgs on 20 January 2003 ("the Higgs Review"). The main recommendations proposed significant changes to the Combined Code on Corporate Governance ("the Combined Code"). The use of the Combined Code to clarify and expand the duties of directors of listed companies is sometimes referred to as the "soft law" approach to legal development, as opposed to the "hard law" of legislative reform (as contemplated by the White Paper "Modernising Company Law"). The philosophy is one of "comply or explain", in that listed companies have to report how they apply the principles of the Combined Code and state whether they comply with the detailed provisions and, if not, why not. The ultimate sanction for failure to comply is delisting. Insofar as directors' duties are concerned, the Higgs Review recommended that the Combined Code should include more detailed provision of the board's role. It aims to build on directors' duties in relation to care, skill and diligence and makes it clear that although non-executive directors and executive directors have the same legal duties and objectives as board members, their involvement is likely to be different. Thus, for non-executive directors, it recommended provisions to be included in the Combined Code to the effect that:

"Non-executive directors should constructively challenge and contribute to the development of strategy. Non-executive directors should scrutinise the performance of management in meeting agreed goals and objectives and monitor the reporting of performance. They should satisfy themselves that financial information is accurate and that financial controls and systems of risk management are robust and defensible. They are responsible for determining appropriate levels of executive remuneration and have a prime role in appointing, and where necessary removing, senior management and in succession planning."

The effect of this "soft law" approach to developing directors' duties is to set a level of best practice against which a particular director can be judged if there is any question as to whether he acted with the required level of skill and care. Many recommendations of the Higgs Review were incorporated by the Financial Reporting Council and the Financial Services Authority in the revised Combined Code published in July 2003.

3.4 Other duties

3.4.1 Direct duties to shareholders

There will be occasions when directors, particularly of public companies, will be communicating with their shareholders. They owe a general duty to those shareholders to be honest and not to mislead (*Gething* v *Kilner* [1972] 1 WLR 337) or (when seeking their approval of transactions or recommending particular courses of action) to make full (as well as honest) disclosure (*Normandy* v *Ind Coope & Co.* [1908] 1 Ch 84). In addition, quite apart from the liability that can arise in respect of the general duty of disclosure in relation to prospectuses and listing particulars,[14] directors could be personally liable for the tort of negligent misstatement, that is, if shareholders were to suffer loss by relying on negligent misstatements made by the directors (*Re Chez Nico (Restaurants) Ltd* [1992] BCLC 192). Such statements do not necessarily have to be made in writing (as in circulars); they can be made orally, as may be more likely in the case of dealings with shareholders in private companies with few shareholders (*see* below).

---

[14] Sections 86 and 90 FSMA 2000 and Regulation 14 Public Offers of Securities Regulations 1995.

It has long been considered that directors owed no direct fiduciary duty to shareholders, as opposed to their company. This has stemmed from the decision in *Percival v Wright* [1902] 2 Ch 421 where the headnote states that, "The directors of a company are not trustees for individual shareholders, and may purchase their shares without disclosing pending negotiations for the sale of the company's undertaking". This case has been quoted as the reason why insider dealing was thought not to give rise to direct liability to shareholders who were not "in the know". In the case of *Percival v Wright*, the plaintiffs wished to sell their shares and approached the board. The shares were eventually sold to three directors. The plaintiffs later learned that the directors had been negotiating to sell the company at a much higher price than was paid for the plaintiffs' shares and the plaintiffs sought to have the sale of their shares set aside. In fact, critical points were conceded by the plaintiffs (e.g. that there was no unfair dealing or purchase at an undervalue) which meant that the decision does not justify the general statement of law set out in the headnote.

The decision has been doubted in a number of recent cases both in the UK and elsewhere where it has been held that, in certain special circumstances, directors can be placed under fiduciary duties, including a duty of disclosure, *vis-à-vis* shareholders individually. In *Re Chez Nico (Restaurants) Ltd*, Nico Ladenis (a somewhat high-profile restaurateur) had sought to exercise powers of compulsory acquisition of minority shares under Section 429 CA 1985. A minority of shareholders objected and the court decided that, as a matter of law, the powers were not in fact exercisable in the light of the particular events. However, the court noted with disapproval the failure of Mr Ladenis to give the minority shareholders sufficient or accurate information, but commented that, as the powers of compulsory acquisition were not exercisable, it was unnecessary to hold whether Mr Ladenis was, under the general law, under a fiduciary duty to disclose the true position to the minority shareholders; *obiter*, however, it confirmed its approval of the decision of the New Zealand Court in *Coleman v Myers* [1997] 2 NZLR 225, in which directors were held to be under such a duty to shareholders.

More recently, in *Platt v Platt* [1999] 2 BCLC 745 a director has been held liable for negligent misrepresentation and breach of his fiduciary duties owed directly to his fellow shareholders. In that case, a director persuaded his brothers to transfer their shares to him for £1 to enable the business to be sold to the main supplier – the alternative, the director said, was to call in the receivers. When the sale to the supplier failed to materialise and no receivers were appointed, the brothers called for their shares to be returned to them. The director refused and subsequently sold all of the shares at a profit. The director had failed to give his brothers adequate or up-to-date financial or trading information about the company and had made it difficult for his brothers to check the facts with the supplier. It was held that in the circumstances the director was under a fiduciary duty to disclose matters which he knew or had reason to believe would be material to his brothers' decision to transfer their shares. The director was held liable for the loss of value of the brothers' shares.

In *Peskin and another* v *Anderson and others* [2001] 1 BCLC 372, former members of the RAC Club, who did not benefit from payments made on the disposal of a motoring services business, unsuccessfully alleged that the directors were in breach of fiduciary duty in not informing them of the proposed sale and thereby deprived them of the opportunity to be re-admitted as members in order to be eligible for the windfall. The Court of Appeal examined the duties owed to shareholders. Mummery LJ stated:

> "The fiduciary duties owed to the company arise from the legal relationship between the directors and the company directed and controlled by them. The fiduciary duties owed to the shareholders do not arise from that legal relationship. They are dependent on establishing a special factual relationship between the directors and the shareholders in the particular case. Events may take place which bring the directors of the company into direct and close contact with the shareholders in a manner capable of generating fiduciary obligations, such as a duty of disclosure of material facts to the shareholders, or an obligation to use confidential information and valuable commercial and financial opportunities, which have been acquired by the directors in that office for the benefit of the shareholders, and not to prefer and promote their own interests at the expense of the shareholders ... There are, for example, instances of the directors of a company making direct approaches to, and dealing with, the shareholders in relation to a specific transaction and holding themselves out as agents for them in connection with the acquisition or disposal of shares; or making material representations to them; or failing to make material disclosure to them of insider information in the context of negotiations for a take-over of the company's business; or supplying to them specific information and advice on which they have relied. These events are capable of constituting special circumstances and of generating fiduciary obligations, especially in those cases in which the directors, for their own benefit,

Directors' Duties

seek to use their position and special inside knowledge acquired by them to take improper or unfair advantage of the shareholders."

Whilst these decisions show that English law recognises the duties of directors to shareholders in certain circumstances, it does not mean directors must at all times reveal all they know to shareholders or risk incurring liability. Frequently, directors will be under duties (e.g. regulatory duties or duties of confidentiality, whether owed to third parties or to the company itself) not to reveal information prematurely nor to reveal it selectively. The courts will respect the bona fide views of directors as to the best interests of the company (as long as they are not unreasonably held) and will not seek to substitute their own views. But the courts are increasingly reluctant to allow companies (and their shareholders or creditors) to suffer as a result of directors failing to conduct themselves in accordance with others' reasonable expectations of them or as a result of directors putting their own interests or other outside interests ahead of the company's interests.

3.4.2 Recent developments relating to financial statements

3.4.2.1 Responsibility for financial statements
In the light of recent corporate collapses, the responsibility of directors for financial statements has been the subject of much scrutiny in the US and Europe. In July 2002 the Sarbanes-Oxley Act was passed in the US (*see* below) introducing changes to financial reporting which extends in part to UK companies with secondary listings in the US. In the EU this area was considered in the Winter Report (*see* below). In the UK the Co-ordinating Group on Audit and Accounting Issues was set up by the Government to oversee and coordinate the response to the major corporate failures in the US. As part of this response a group appointed by the Financial Reporting Council and chaired by Sir Robert Smith produced further guidance for Audit Committees in relation to the provisions of the Combined Code in its report published in January 2003.

In addition, the White Paper "Modernising Company Law" contains provisions for the directors' report to be replaced either by a short supplementary statement for smaller companies or by an Operating and Financial Review ("OFR") for larger companies. The OFR would report on a wider range of factors and would be forward looking. The expectation is that this will impose an additional burden on the companies concerned. It will be for the directors to decide precisely what information is material to their particular business and they will be responsible for how these factors are covered in the OFR.

3.4.2.2 Sarbanes-Oxley

The Sarbanes-Oxley Act of 2002 was enacted in July 2002 as a swift response to the high-profile corporate scandals in the US. The legislation codifies a broad range of corporate reforms regarding:

(a) corporate governance practices;
(b) certification of periodic reports;
(c) additional disclosure;
(d) oversight of the accounting profession;
(e) securities analysts' conflicts of interest;
(f) criminal acts; and
(g) corporate fraud liability.

Certain of the provisions came into effect immediately, but many others only become operative when implementing regulations are adopted by the Securities and Exchange Commission or other relevant entity. The legislation applies to all "issuers" which have securities listed on a US Stock Exchange or have securities registered with the SEC or are otherwise required to "file" reports with the SEC or have filed a registration statement with the SEC and not withdrawn it. This covers approximately 140 UK listed companies which have a secondary US listing. In terms of directors' duties, the certification requirements of Sections 302 and 906 of the Sarbanes-Oxley Act are particularly relevant. This requires that principal executive officers and principal financial officers (or persons serving a similar function) of public companies which are subject to SEC reporting requirements provide a certificate in relation to certain periodic reports filed with the SEC. Under Section 906 of the Sarbanes-Oxley Act each of these persons must certify that the report complies with applicable reporting requirements of the Securities Exchange Act of 1934 and fairly presents in all material respects the financial condition and results of operations of the issuer. This subjects certifying officers to criminal liability. Under Section 302, the chief executive officer and chief financial officer must include a further certificate in relation to certain reports filed with the SEC as to the fact that they have reviewed the report; the accuracy of the financial and non-financial information contained in the report; the effectiveness of the internal controls and as to disclosure controls and procedures. This subjects certifying officers to civil liability.

3.4.2.3 European Company Law Reform: the Winter Report

On 4 November 2002 the High Level Group of Company Law Experts (chaired by Jaap Winter) published its final report which contains recommendations for a fundamental overhaul of European Company

Directors' Duties

Law. Although directors' duties do not feature prominently among the company law issues upon which the report focuses, it does address two areas of directors' responsibility in a European context. One area is wrongful trading. The other is the responsibility for financial statements and certain non-financial data in the light of recent corporate scandals. The report advocates that the collective responsibility of the board for these matters should be confirmed as a matter of EU law. It is recommended that this would extend not only to annual and consolidated accounts, but to all statements regarding the financial position of the company save in exceptional cases of mandatory disclosure where it will not be practical to get full board consideration. Insofar as key non-financial data is concerned, it is recommended that collective responsibility of the full board would extend to areas such as information on:

(a) the company's risk management system;
(b) its business prospects and investment plans;
(c) its strategies in technical, organisational and human resources areas; and
(d) in relation to the accuracy of the annual statement relating to the company's corporate governance structuring and practices.

In response to the Winter Report, on 21 May 2003 the European Commission published for public consultation its Action Plan on Modernising Company Law and Enhancing Corporate Governance in the EU. The Commission has also published 10 priorities for action aimed at improving and harmonising the quality of statutory audit in the EU.

3.4.3 *Criminal liability*

By accepting office as a director, a person puts himself in a position where he could incur criminal liability for a large number of offences if appropriate steps are not taken. Three main areas are relevant:

(a) requirements arising under the Companies Act 1985 and related legislation;
(b) requirements arising under general legislation;
(c) liability in relation to corporate manslaughter.

3.4.3.1 *Companies Act requirements*
The Companies Act 1985 imposes a number of requirements directly on directors, failure to comply with which constitutes a criminal offence. The most well-known example is probably Section 242 – directors to deliver to the registrar of companies copies of their company's annual

accounts.[15] Other obligations are imposed directly on the company but, if that obligation is not fulfilled, an offence will be committed not only by the company but also by every "officer who is in default"; the latter expression is defined[16] as meaning "any officer of the company who knowingly and wilfully authorises or permits the default, refusal or contravention". Directors should assume that, wherever their company can commit an offence under the Companies Act 1985 and there is not a direct obligation on them personally as described above, they could be liable as "officers in default".[17] Schedule 24 CA 1985 sets out details of the offences which can be committed under that Act; these total over 150 in number.

Discretionary relief from liability by the court is available in certain circumstances under Section 727 CA 1985.

3.4.3.2 General legislation
Nearly all UK legislation introduced in the last few decades has adopted a common provision for imposing criminal liability on directors where their company could be guilty of an offence under that legislation.

Examples of where this provision may be of particular interest to directors are environmental and health and safety legislation. However, the provision is widespread in all legislation where a company could be liable itself for an offence. Under the provision, if a company is guilty of an offence and it is proved that the offence occurred "with the consent or connivance of, or was attributable to any neglect on the part of any director, manager, secretary or other similar officer of the company", that officer, as well as the company, will be guilty of that offence and will be liable accordingly.

---

[15] Other sections imposing direct obligations on directors include Section 80(9) (directors allotting shares without authority); Section 142(2) (directors not convening a shareholders' meeting following a serious loss of capital); Sections 156(7) and 173(6) (directors making a statutory declaration without having reasonable grounds); Sections 232(4), 294(4), 314(3), 317(7), 324(7) etc. (directors failing to notify the company of their personal details or interests); Section 234B(3) (failures regarding the preparation of a directors' remuneration report for quoted companies); Section 347F(2) (failure to comply with the rules on donations and political expenditure by companies) and many other Sections.

[16] Section 730(5) CA 1985.

[17] Section 733 sets out a different test (the "consent, connivance or attribution test" described under "general legislation") for offences under certain specified Sections CA 1985.

Directors' Duties

It is also worthy of note that there has recently been a significant amount of new legislation which may, depending on the circumstances, have profound effects on directors. Three examples of this are set out below.

Financial Services and Markets Act 2000 ("FSMA 2000")
It is important that directors do not put themselves, or allow employees of the company to be put, into a position where liability under FSMA 2000 could be incurred. In addition to the potential liabilities relating to the publication of prospectuses, directors must, in particular, be very familiar with the provisions in FSMA 2000 (and with the related statutory instruments and guidance) dealing with:

(a) misleading statements and practices (Section 397);
(b) market abuse relating to qualifying investments traded on prescribed markets – which carries criminal penalties but with the less onerous civil burden of proof (Section 118); and
(c) financial promotion, which catches a wide variety of communications containing an invitation or inducement to engage in investment activity – which is a criminal offence and can also result in the unenforceability of contracts and money or property being repayable to the other party (Section 21).

Anti-Terrorism, Crime and Security Act 2001 ("ATCSA 2001")
ATCSA 2001 received Royal Assent on 14 December 2001 in reaction to the terrorist attacks on New York and Washington on 11 September 2001. Part 12 ATCSA 2001 brings in provisions to strengthen the law on international corruption. Directors should be aware that Britain now has one of the most stringent sets of anti-bribery rules which extends to "facilitation payments" (bribes aimed at saving time rather than influencing decisions). This is a criminal offence with unlimited fines and up to seven years' imprisonment, and the courts are given extraterritorial jurisdiction over such offences committed abroad by UK nationals and bodies incorporated in the UK.

Enterprise Act 2002
The Enterprise Act, which amends the competition and insolvency regimes, received Royal Assent on 7 November 2002. The majority of competition provisions of the Enterprise Act came into force on 20 June 2003. The new law makes it a criminal offence punishable by up to five years' imprisonment for individuals to participate dishonestly in cartel activity (market sharing, price fixing and bid rigging between competing companies). Another feature of the Enterprise Act is that company directors who have been involved in a breach of UK or EC competition

A Practitioner's Guide to Directors' Duties and Responsibilities

law (for example where they have contributed to the company's actions, where they have not stopped the company's actions, or where they ought to have known about the company's actions) may face disqualification if they are considered by the court to be unfit for office. The maximum period for disqualification is 15 years.

3.4.3.3 Corporate manslaughter

There has been considerable public comment in recent years about the liability (or otherwise) of companies and their officers where the acts or omissions of the companies have resulted in deaths. This has arisen partially as a result of a number of disasters where people have been killed and the companies have subsequently been held to have operated dangerous practices or to have had serious lapses in their controls, but no prosecutions were brought or, if they were, no convictions resulted.[18] The reason for the absence of prosecutions or convictions was normally that there was insufficient evidence to convict any individual of the crime of manslaughter and, without such an individual, there could be no conviction of the company itself. To gain a conviction of a company, the prosecutor must show that the relevant acts amounting to manslaughter have been committed by an individual or individuals who are "identified as the embodiment of the company itself" or are "the directing mind and will of the company".[19] In fact, there have been very few successful prosecutions for corporate manslaughter; each of these concerned small companies where the directors were involved in the day-to-day activities of the business.[20]

In May 2000 the UK Government announced proposals for changes in the law. These included the proposed introduction of two new offences capable of being committed by individuals: reckless killing and killing by gross carelessness. In addition, there would be a separate offence of corporate killing where a business undertaking's conduct in causing a death fell far below what could reasonably be expected. However, following consultation, it was announced on 21 May 2003 that the

---

[18] *See The Law Commission's Report Legislating the Criminal Code: Involuntary Manslaughter* (Law Com. No. 237) published in March 1996, for an excellent discussion of the subject; also *see Reforming the Law on Involuntary Manslaughter: The Government's Proposals* published by the Home Office in May 2000.

[19] *Tesco Supermarkets Ltd v Nattrass* [1972] AC 153 at pages 170 and 171 and *R v HM Coroner for East Kent ex parte Spooner* [1989] 88 Cr App R10 at page 16.

[20] *R v Kite and OLL Ltd* (1994) unreported (school children canoeists lost in Lyme Bay); *R v Jackson Transport (Ossett) Ltd* (1996) unreported; and *R v Roy Bowles Transport Ltd* (1999) unreported.

Directors' Duties

legislation will be targeted at companies themselves and not the criminal liability of directors. An announcement concerning the timetable for this legislation is likely to be made in the autumn of 2003. By way of a separate development, the Company Directors' (Health and Safety) Bill received its first reading in the Commons on 25 March 2003. This Bill proposes to amend the CA 1985 by requiring public companies to appoint a health and safety director and by imposing duties on this director. The Bill also imposes duties on all other directors of companies in relation to health and safety.

Implementation of these proposals would emphasise further the desirability of boards of directors implementing proper risk control systems. However, as yet nothing has come of the proposals.

3.5 Possible future developments and consequences

3.5.1 White Paper "Modernising Company Law"

In July 2002 the White Paper (Cm 5553) entitled "Modernising Company Law" was published. This set out the Government's response to the independent Company Law Review's *Final Report* which was published in July 2001 (Modern Company Law for Competitive Economy: Final Report, URN 01/942, 01/943). The White Paper highlights the concerns that, under the current law, the general rules relating to directors' propriety of conduct and standards of skill and care are laid down by "complex and inaccessible case law". The Government is of the view that:

> "the basic goal for directors should be the success of the company in the collective best interests of shareholders, but that directors should also recognise, as the circumstances require, the company's need to foster relations with its employees, customers and suppliers, its need to maintain its business reputation, and its need to consider the company's impact on the community and the working environment."

The White Paper states that the general duties of directors to the company should be "codified in statute", replacing the corresponding common law and equitable rules and the statutory duty to have regard to the interests of employees contained in Section 309 CA 1985. A summary of the proposed statutory statement of general principles is set out below, although the Government is consulting on the drafting.

Concerns have been expressed in response to the White Paper's proposals in this area. These include fears as to the loss of flexibility which arises when enshrining the duties in statute coupled with the likelihood that the advantage of having a clear set of principles will be short-lived once they are overlaid by case law which interprets and develops them. Clarification is also needed as to the nature of each of the duties (for example, whether they are fiduciary or not, since the principles are to replace both the existing common law and equitable rules) and the remedies available for breach. The Government stated that due to the complexity of this area, it would only publish draft clauses for consultation if a workable scheme can be devised. Also, to the extent that any areas of existing common law are omitted from the statutory statement, it is presumed that existing common law will apply.

On 13 May 2003 the House of Commons Trade and Industry select committee published its report on the Government's White Paper and, insofar as directors' duties are concerned, gave general approval to the proposed definition of directors' duties.

3.5.2 *Summary of proposed statutory statement of general principles*

3.5.2.1 *Obeying the constitution and other lawful decisions*
A director must act in accordance with the company's constitution and decisions taken under the constitution or other lawful means of taking company decisions and must exercise his powers for their proper purpose.

3.5.2.2 *Promotion of company's objectives*
A director must act in the way that he decides, in good faith, would be most likely to promote the success of the company for the benefit of its members as a whole taking account of all the material factors that it is practicable in the circumstances for him to identify. These factors include, as far as a person of care and skill would consider them relevant:

(a) the likely consequences (short and long term) of the actions open to the director;
(b) the company's need to foster its business relationships (for example, with its employees, suppliers and customers);
(c) the impact of its operations on the communities affected and on the environment;
(d) the need to maintain a reputation for high standards of business conduct; and
(e) the need to achieve outcomes that are fair as between its members.

3.5.2.3 Delegation and independence of judgement
A director must not, except where authorised to do so, delegate any of his powers or fail to exercise his independent judgement in relation to any exercise of his powers. It is recognised that, in certain circumstances, a director may enter an agreement which effectively restricts his power to exercise independent judgement at a later date.

3.5.2.4 Care, skill and diligence
A director must exercise the care, skill and diligence which would be exercised by a reasonably diligent person with both the knowledge, skill and experience which may reasonably be expected of a director in his position and any additional knowledge, skill and experience which he has.

3.5.2.5 Transactions involving conflict of interest
A director must not permit the company to enter into a transaction, or enter into a transaction with the company himself, if he has an interest in the transaction which he has not disclosed in accordance with the relevant provisions of the Companies Act 1985.

3.5.2.6 Personal use of the company's property, information or opportunity
A director or former director must not use for his own or anyone else's benefit any property, information or opportunity of the company unless duly authorised to do so.

3.5.2.7 Benefits from third parties
A director or former director must not accept any benefit which is conferred because of the powers he has as a director or by way of reward for any exercise of his powers unless the benefit is conferred by the company or duly authorised or is incidental to the performance of his functions as a director.

The White Paper asked for comments as to whether the proposed statutory statement of general principles provides clear and authoritative guidance and strikes the right balance between modern business needs and the wider expectations of responsible business behaviour. The response of the Law Society's Company Law Committee of November 2002 expressed major concerns on both these issues and drew attention to a significant number of drafting concerns relating to the language used which give rise to difficulties of interpretation.

The Government decided not to include any duties of directors in relation to creditors in the statutory statement. It considered that it would be unhelpful to conflate company and insolvency law and it was felt that a statutory statement of the duties of directors at a time when a company was likely to become insolvent will lead (as highlighted by the independent Company Law Review) to a "chilling effect" leading to the running down or abandonment of going concerns at the first hint of insolvency. This runs counter to the "rescue culture" which the Government is fostering through the Insolvency Act 2000 and the Enterprise Act 2002. In the White Paper the Government seeks comments as to whether mention of creditors should be made in the statutory statement.

The White Paper also addressed the question as to the best way to ensure the directors are made aware of their duties. It proposed that all new directors would receive from Companies House plain-language guidance summarising the main legal requirements placed on directors by company and insolvency legislation.

3.6 Recent trends and themes concerning directors' duties in other EU countries and the US

To conclude this Chapter, it may be of interest to note some of the themes, similarities and differences in relation to directors' duties in certain other jurisdictions by way of comparison with the UK. In EU countries which operate under civil law, the main duties of directors are set out in civil codes the principles of which are interpreted under case law. The civil codes, like UK legislation, are not easy to change rapidly and so the same issues regarding a lack of flexibility of the law apply.

It is common ground in EU countries that there is generally no distinction between executive and non-executive directors regarding the basic duties, although certain countries such as Germany and the Netherlands have two-tier boards (i.e. a supervisory board and a managing board) and the duties of the directors differ in relation to the tasks they perform.

It is generally the case in EU countries and the US that directors owe their duties to the company on whose board they sit. There is not a general concept of owing duties to the group to which a particular company belongs although in Germany, for example, if there is a domination agreement ("Beherrschungsvertrag") under the codified law of corporate groups ("Konzernrecht") between a parent and a subsidiary, the members of the management board of the subsidiary are required to follow binding instructions given by the parent. In Italy, recent reforms provide that subsidiaries may be managed under group instructions

Directors' Duties

insofar as such management does not result in damage to the company, its shareholders or creditors.

In a number of EU countries, new laws have been passed recently which impact on directors' duties. Examples include the following:

(a) In Italy the Parliament has recently enacted the reform of Italian Company Law (which comes into effect in January 2004). This will impose higher standards of diligence on directors as well as more responsibilities regarding the evaluation of general management of the company and reviewing the company's strategic and financial plans.

(b) Recent changes to the Belgian Companies Code include a change to authorise the board of directors to delegate to a management committee ("comité de direction/directiecomité") all its power except in relation to certain matters of a strategic nature and duties reserved for the board of directors by law (such as the drawing up of the annual accounts and report). The members of such a committee may be appointed from outside the members of the board. The management committee members are, within their delegated powers, liable in the same way as the directors. The directors owe to the company a duty of supervising the management committee.

(c) In Germany the German Government has published proposals for the reform of company legislation which, among other things, will increase the personal liability of board members for breaches of their duties.

The US has, of course, also seen many recent changes introduced through the Sarbanes-Oxley Act. One example is that, with effect from 27 January 2003, directors are required to disclose the adoption of a "code of ethics" or to specifically state reasons for failing to adopt such a code or for waiving any of its provisions in respect of any of its principal officers.

It is generally the case in EU countries that directors are not required to sign any statement to the effect that they have read and understood their duties. However, in the light of recent developments in the corporate and securities world concerning director liability, it is fair to say that directors are probably becoming increasingly aware of the duties that they owe to their company and the ways in which they can attract liability. The above demonstrates that it is not just the UK where the law relating to directors' duties is in a state of flux.

Chapter 4
Potential Liabilities

Rosalind Nicholson, Barrister
4 Stone Buildings

This Chapter deals with certain liabilities to third parties which a director may attract, with the questions of his entitlement to be indemnified by the company and relief by statute.

4.1 Ultra vires acts

4.1.1 Acts ultra vires the company

The objects for the purposes of which a company is incorporated must be stated in its memorandum of association ("memorandum").[1] A company only has the capacity to do those acts that fall within its objects as set out in its memorandum or are reasonably incidental to the attainment or pursuit of those objects.[2] Acts outside the capacity of the company are referred to as "ultra vires". As the agents of the company, the directors' powers to transact on its behalf cannot exceed those of the principal. It follows that the powers of the directors of a company to transact on its behalf are limited to transactions that are within the company's capacity.

The stringency of the ultra vires doctrine has been mitigated by Section 35(1) Companies Act 1985("CA")[3] which provides that the validity of an act done by a company shall not be called into question on the ground of lack of capacity by reason of anything in the company's memorandum.[4] However, it remains the duty of the directors to observe any limitation on their powers flowing from the company's memorandum. This duty is a fiduciary duty owed to the company and is expressly

---

[1] Section 2(1)(c) CA.
[2] *Rolled Steel Products (Holdings) Ltd* v *British Steel Corporation & Others* [1986] Ch 246 at 295 per Slade LJ.
[3] Substituted by Section 108(1) Companies Act 1989.
[4] Section 35(1) CA.

preserved by Section 35(3) CA. Accordingly, a director who causes the company to enter into an ultra vires transaction is in breach of his fiduciary duty to the company[5] and is liable to indemnify the company against any loss incurred by it in consequence.[6]

The company may determine to relieve the director from such liability. Such relief may be granted by special resolution. Such a resolution is distinct from, and must be resolved separately from, any resolution ratifying the action.[7]

4.1.2 Acts beyond the directors' authority

In practice, the scope of the actual authority which a director has to commit the company is defined by the contractual terms, express or implied, which govern his appointment as the company's agent. Those terms may be found in the memorandum or, more usually, the Articles of Association ("Articles"), in shareholders' agreements, or in resolutions of the company or of a particular class of shareholders. Whilst the terms of a company's Articles are a statutory contract between a company and its members and are not automatically binding between a company and its officers as such, the Articles may be incorporated into the contract between the company and a director expressly or impliedly if the director accepted his appointment "on the footing of the articles". In the usual case, relatively little will be required to incorporate the Articles into such a contract by implication.[8] They may also be implied by the particular office or job to which the person is appointed.[9]

If an agent purports to commit his principal to a transaction which is beyond the actual authority that he has on its behalf, then, unless the principal chooses to adopt (ratify) the transaction, it will not be bound thereby. In the corporate context, a transaction in excess of authority is sometimes also referred to as "ultra vires".[10] This principle has been relaxed in the case of companies by Section 35A CA which operates in

---

[5] *Re Sharpe* [1892] 1 Ch 154.
[6] *Re Lands Allotment Co. Ltd* [1894] Ch 616.
[7] Section 35(3) CA.
[8] *Globallink Telecommunications Ltd* v *Wilmbury and others* [2002] 1 BCLC 145.
[9] *Hely Hutchinson* v *Brayhead Ltd* [1968] 1 QB 549.
[10] Or "ultra vires in the wider sense" as opposed to the narrow or "proper sense" (*Rolled Steel Ltd* v *British Steel Corporation*) [1986] 1 Ch at 297 per Slade LJ. Following the direction of Slade LJ, in this Chapter the term "ultra vires" is used only to describe acts outside of the company's corporate capacity.

Potential Liabilities

favour of persons dealing in good faith with a company and provides that "the power of the board of directors to bind the company, or authorise others to do so, shall be deemed to be free of any limitation under the company's constitution".[11] The effect of this provision is to prevent the company from relying on the directors' want of authority to repudiate the transaction. However, this provision does not affect any liability incurred by the directors, or any other person, by reason of the directors exceeding their powers.[12]

(a) A director may be liable to the company for breach of his fiduciary duty. He may be required to indemnify the company against any loss incurred by it in consequence of the transaction.
(b) If the parties to the transaction include a director of the company or of its holding company or a person connected with such a director or a company with whom such a director is associated, Section 322A(3) CA exposes to liability any director who has authorised the transaction and renders him liable to account to the company for any gain which he has made directly or indirectly as a result of the transaction and to indemnify the company for any loss or damage resulting from the transaction. A company may ratify the act by an ordinary resolution which has the effect of retrospectively supplying the wanting authority and relieving the directors from liability.[13]
(c) A director may be liable in damages to the third party for breach of the implied warranty of his authority to enter the transaction on the company's behalf. The practical effect of Section 35A CA is likely to mean that such cases are limited in future.

4.2 Liability for the acts of the company: crimes

In certain circumstances, the officers of a company may attract criminal liability in respect of criminal acts committed by a company in the course of its business. However, in every case, specific culpability must be proved against the individual concerned and is not to be inferred from the fact that he holds office as a director of the company: there is no concept of guilt by association. So, for example, a director may be guilty

---

[11] Section 35A(1) CA.
[12] Section 35A(5) CA; for a discussion as to the limits on this provision *see Smith* v *Hennicker Major & Co* (a firm) [2002] EWCA Civ 762, [2002] 1 BCLC.
[13] *Grant* v *United Kingdom Switchback Railways Co.* (1888) 40 ChD 135; *Irvine* v *Union Bank of Australia* (1877) 2 App Cas 366.

of conspiring with a company to commit a wrong, or of aiding or abetting the commission of a criminal offence by the company provided that the requisite elements of the offence including *mens rea* can be proven against him.

4.2.1 Offences of "consent or connivance"

A director may also be liable where statute attaches liability to persons who "caused or knowingly permitted" the commission by a company of an offence. In more recent statutes, the practice has been to provide that an offence is committed by: "any director, manager, secretary or other similar officer ... or any person purporting to act in any such capacity" if the offence "occurred with the consent or connivance of, or was attributable to any neglect" on his part. Examples of offences of "consent or connivance" include certain offences under the Unsolicited Goods and Services Act 1971 (by Section 5 of the Act), under Sections 210, 216, 394A(1), and 447 to 451 CA (by Section 733 of that Act), under Section 157(1) of the Environmental Protection Act 1990, under the Banking and Financial Dealings Act 1971 (by Section 2(5)), under the Health and Safety at Work Act 1974 (by Section 37) and under the Competition Act 1998 (by Section 72 of that Act). In each of these cases, the director's guilt depends on there having been an offence committed by the company but his personal guilt, in terms of his knowledge, consent, connivance or neglect, must be independently proven against him.

4.2.2 Contempt of court and breaches of injunctions and undertakings

A judgment or order of the court requiring a company to do an act within a specified time or to abstain from doing an act may be enforced, with the leave of the court, by writ of sequestration against the property of any director or other officer of the company or, subject to the provisions of the Debtors Act 1869 and 1878, by an order of committal against such an officer (RSC Order 45 Rule 5).

However, in spite of the broad words of the Rule, a director is not liable to be committed for contempt or to have his property sequestrated merely by virtue of his office. An order for committal can only be made against an officer of a company where he himself can be shown to be in contempt (*Director General of Fair Trading* v *Buckland*)[14] or where he is responsible for the company's breach of the order or judgment whether

---

[14] [1990] 1 WLR 920.

Potential Liabilities

by his actions or by his wilful failure to ensure the company's compliance with its obligations (*Re British Concrete Pipe Association's Agreement*).[15] In this context, it is clear that where a company has been restrained by order from doing certain acts, or has given an undertaking to the same effect, a director or other officer of the company who is aware of its terms is under a duty to take reasonable care to secure the company's compliance with it. If such an officer wilfully fails to take adequate and continuing steps to ensure that those to whom the relevant matters had been delegated have not misunderstood or overlooked the obligations imposed, and the company breaches the order or undertaking, then he is liable to be punished for contempt of court, notwithstanding that he has not actively participated in the breach (*A.G. for Tuvalu* v *Philatelic Distribution Corp*).[16]

4.3 Liability for the acts of the company: torts

4.3.1 Negligent acts and omissions

The fact that a director holds office as such does not, without more, render him liable for torts committed by the company.[17] The doctrine of separate corporate personality means that a director is not automatically to be identified with his company, however small the company and however powerful that director's control over its affairs.[18] However, there are, broadly, two situations where a director may be jointly liable with the company in respect of the same wrong even though he was not personally involved in the commission of the tort. First, if a director authorises, directs and/or procures the commission of a tort by his company, he may attract personal liability even though he is not personally involved in the commission of the tort.[19] It will be a question of fact in every case whether the director has authorised the act or acts complained of and will require analysis of the part he played personally in regard to those acts.[20] For example, in *Mancetter Developments Ltd* v *Garmanson Ltd*,[21] industrial premises were leased by the claimants to a

---

[15] [1982] ICR 182 at 195.
[16] [1990] 1 WLR 926.
[17] *Rainham Chemical Works Ltd* v *Belvedere Fish Guano Co. Ltd* [1921] 2 AC 465 at 476.
[18] *Evans (C.) and Sons Ltd* v *Spritebrand Ltd* [1985] 1 WLR 317 per Slade LJ at 329.
[19] *Evans (C.) and Sons Ltd* v *Spritebrand Ltd* [1985] 1 WLR 317; *PLG Research Ltd* v *Ardon International Ltd* [1993] FSR 197, 238 to 239.
[20] *Evans (C.) and Sons Ltd* v *Spritebrand Ltd* [1985] 1 WLR 317, 329.
[21] *Mancetter Developments Ltd* v *Garmanson Ltd* [1986] 1 All ER 449.

chemical manufacturing company which cut holes in the outside walls of the building in order to install pipes and extractor fans. Five years later that company's assets, including the lease and tenant's fixtures, were transferred to Garmanson Ltd ("the company"), the first defendant. Mr Givertz, the second defendant, was the only active director of the company. The company soon decided that it was not viable to continue trading in the premises and delivered up possession. However, before delivering up possession the company removed all of the tenant's fixtures installed by its predecessor, and in particular the pipes and extractor fans, which involved reopening the holes in the brickwork. No attempt was made to fill up those holes. The claimants sued the company and its director for, *inter alia*, the damage caused by the removal of the tenant's fixtures without making good the walls. It was held (and confirmed by the Court of Appeal) that the defendant company had committed tortious acts of waste and that the second defendant was personally liable to the claimants as he had himself directed or procured such acts. Dillon LJ stated the proposition as follows:

> "It does not of course follow, because the claimants have suffered damage, that the second defendant is personally liable. There are, however, cases which establish that if a director of a company gives instructions for the commission of a tort by the company, the director may be personally liable in damages to the injured party for the tort although the tort was the act of the company."

Similarly, in *A.P. Besson Ltd* v *Fulleon Ltd*[22] a director of a company was held jointly liable with the company as he had been personally involved in the actual ordering or commission of the tort.

Second, a director will be liable jointly with the company where he has expressly or by implication assumed responsibility to the victim for the act or omission.[23] The test is an objective one: whether, objectively assessed, the acts and speech of the defendant were such as to lead the claimant to believe that the director was assuming responsibility towards the claimant instead of (or, more likely, in addition to) the responsibility of the company.

---

[22] [1986] FSR 319.
[23] *Fairline Shipping Corporation* v *Adamson* [1975] QB 180; *Yuille* v *B&B Fisheries (Leigh) Ltd, The Radiant* [1958] 2 Lloyd's Rep 596.

4.3.2 Negligent misrepresentations

In *Williams v Natural Life Health Foods*[24] the House of Lords considered the circumstances in which a director of a company may be liable for negligently made misrepresentations in the context of a single member company. Lord Steyn reminded the House of Lords that:

> "The trader who incorporates a company to which he transfers his business creates a legal person on whose behalf he may afterwards act as director. For present purposes, his position is the same as if he had sold his business to another individual and agreed to act on his behalf."

For an individual director to attract personal liability in those circumstances, in accordance with the principles established in *Hedley Byrne & Co Ltd v Heller & Partners*,[25] there must be a special relationship between the director and the claimant (it is not sufficient that there should have been a special relationship between the claimant and the company). Further, there must have been an assumption of responsibility such as to create a special relationship with the director or employee himself: this issue is to be resolved objectively against the matrix of fact by reference to things said or done by the director or on his behalf in dealings with the claimant and primarily on statements and conduct which cross the line between them to ascertain whether the director, or anybody on his behalf, conveyed directly or indirectly to the claimant that he assumed personal responsibility towards them. On the facts of the case, the House of Lords concluded that there were no exchanges or conduct crossing the line which could have conveyed to the claimants that the director was willing to assume personal responsibility to them. Of course, a claimant must also demonstrate that he relied on the assumption of personal responsibility in order to establish that the misrepresentation was causative of the loss. The test here is not merely a question of fact, but involves the question whether the claimant could reasonably rely on an assumption of personal responsibility by the individual who performed the services on behalf of the company. Although each case will clearly turn on its particular facts, it appears from *Williams v Natural Life Health Foods* that the courts will be reluctant to readily infer an assumption of responsibility by a director.

---

[24] [1998]1 WLR 830.
[25] [1964] AC 465.

4.4 Liability for the acts of the company: contracts

A director is not generally personally liable for his company's contracts even where he has signed on the company's behalf. However, there are certain circumstances in which a director may be liable on contracts made in the company's name.

4.4.1 Pre-incorporation contracts

A company does not exist prior to its incorporation.[26] As a non-existent entity, it has no capacity to transact business or to instruct agents to transact business on its behalf. It follows that a contract purportedly executed by a company prior to its incorporation or by agents purportedly on its behalf – whether they style themselves as its directors or otherwise – is null and void and unenforceable by or against the company.[27] It also follows that a company cannot "ratify" a pre-incorporation contract following its incorporation as there is nothing for it to ratify.[28]

Where a contract is purportedly entered into by, or on behalf of, a company prior to its incorporation, then those who entered into the transaction purportedly on its behalf are potentially exposed to personal liability on the contract. At common law, if the other party to the contract could show that, though ostensibly contracting as agents, the representatives in fact contracted as principals, then those representatives were themselves liable on the contract.[29] Although the court scrutinises the words and manner of execution of the particular contract in order to ascertain whether the representatives are to be regarded as contracting as principals, it will be keen to impute such a liability as the only means whereby the agreement could be given effect.[30] Section 36(C) CA[31] now expressly provides that, subject to any agreement to the contrary, the person purporting to act for the company or as agent for it is personally liable on a contract which purports to be made by, or on behalf of, a

---

[26] The formalities required before the registrar will issue a certificate of incorporation under Section 13(1) CA are contained in Sections 10 to 12 inclusive.
[27] *Newborne v Sensolid (GB) Ltd* [1954] 1 QB 45.
[28] *Kelner v Baxter* (1867) LR 2 CP 174; *Natal Land and Colonisation Co. v Pauline Syndicate* [1904] AC 120.
[29] *Kelner v Baxter* (1867) LR 2 CP 174.
[30] *Newborne v Sensolid (GB) Ltd* [1954] 1 QB 45.
[31] Substituted for Section 36(4) by Section 130 CA 1989 implementing Article 7 of the EC First Company Law Directive (68/151/EEC).

company at a time when the company has not been formed. Such a contract has effect as one made with the agent with the result that not only is he personally liable thereunder but he is also entitled to sue on the contract on his own account.[32]

4.4.2 Business transacted by a public company prior to the issue of a Section 117 certificate

A company registered as a public company on its original incorporation must not do business or exercise any borrowing powers unless the registrar has issued it with a certificate under Section 117 CA or the company is re-registered as a private company.[33] Executing a contract will plainly constitute "doing business" for the purposes of this prohibition.

Two consequences follow from a breach of the Section:

(a) if such a company does business or exercises borrowing powers without first securing a certificate under Section 117 CA then the company and any officer of it who is in default is liable to a fine (Section 117(7) CA);
(b) although a transaction entered into by a company in contravention of the provisions of Section 117 CA is not rendered invalid by the breach,[34] if the company fails to comply with its obligations in respect of such a transaction within 21 days from being called upon to do so, then the directors of the company are jointly and severally liable to indemnify the other party to the transaction in respect of any loss or damage suffered by him by reason of the company's failure to comply with those obligations.

4.4.3 Non-disclosure of company details: Sections 349 to 351 CA

Section 349 CA requires a company to have its name mentioned in legible characters in all:

---

[32] *Braymist Ltd and others* v *Wise Finance Co Ltd* [2002] EWCA Civ 127 [2002] 1 BCLC 415.
[33] The conditions to be satisfied before the registrar issues a certificate under Section 117 CA are set out in Section 117(2) to (6).
[34] This is expressly provided by Section 117(8) CA. At common law, a contract entered into in such a case where the trading certificate was never granted did not bind the company and was unenforceable against it (*Re Otto Electrical Manufacturing Company (1905) Limited., Jenkins's Claim* [1906] 2 Ch 390).

(a) business letters of the company;
(b) its notices and other official publications;
(c) bills of exchange, promissory notes, endorsements, cheques and orders for money or goods purporting to be signed by or on behalf of the company; and
(d) its bills of parcels, invoices, receipts and letters of credit.

Section 349(4) CA imposes personal liability on an officer of a company or other person on its behalf who signs or authorises to be signed on behalf of the company any bill of exchange, promissory note, endorsement, cheque or order for money or goods[35] in which the company's name is not mentioned as required by Section 349(1) CA. In such a case, unless it is duly paid by the company, the officer concerned is personally liable to the holder of the bill of exchange, promissory note, cheque or order for money or goods for the amount of it.

Historically, this provision has been strictly enforced by the courts. Its object is to protect persons who deal with the company in ignorance of the fact that they are dealing with an entity with limited liability.[36] However, its scope has been extended by the courts to include not only those cases in which the words indicating the company's limited liability status are omitted but to cases where the word "limited" appeared but the company's name has been misstated by the omission of a word,[37] where the words in the company's name are transposed[38] and where

---

[35] Services do not fall within the scope of this provision and electricity is not "goods" (*East Midlands Electricity Board* v *Grantham* [1980] CLY 271).

[36] *Penrose* v *Martyr* (1858) ElBl & El 499; *Atkin* v *Wardle* (1889) 5 TLR 734; *British Airways Board* v *Parish* [1979] 2 Lloyds Rep 361; *Blum* v *OCP Repartition SA* [1988] BCLC 170.

[37] *Hendon* v *Adelman* (1973) 117 SJ 631, LR Agencies Ltd rather than L & R Agencies Ltd; *Barber and Nicholls Ltd* v *R and G Associates Ltd* (1981) 132 NLJ 1076, "(London)" omitted from the company name R and G Associates (London) Limited. The abbreviations "Co" and "Ltd" are acceptable substitutes for company and limited respectively (*Banque de l'Indochine et de Suez* v *Euroseas Group Finance Co. Limited* [1981] 3 All ER 198 and *Stacey & Co. Ltd* v *Wallis* (1912) 106 LT 544). Other abbreviations may be accepted where the abbreviation is one generally accepted and where no other word is similarly abbreviated – not, for example, where "M" was substituted for "Michael" in the name Michael Jackson (Fancy Goods) Limited (*Durham Fancy Goods Ltd* v *Michael Jackson (Fancy Goods) Limited* [1968] 2 QB 839).

[38] *Atkins* v *Wardle* (1889) 61 LT 23 (the company name, South Shields Salt Water Baths Company Limited, misstated as Salt Water Baths Company Limited, South Shields and South Shields Water Baths Company).

Potential Liabilities

additional words have been added to the name.[39] By contrast, misspelling a company's name will not amount to a breach of the Section provided that no danger of confusion arises therefrom.[40] The officers' liability arises only if the company itself defaults on payment.

4.4.4 Bills of Exchange Act 1882

Clearly a company does not have a signature of its own and can only execute documents through human agency. A document is signed by a company if it is signed on behalf of the company by an authorised human agent or officer, signing his own name, acting within the scope of his authority in the course of the company's business.[41] An individual signing a company document as agent for the company in such circumstances will not incur personal liability. However, where a bill of exchange is concerned (and for this purpose a cheque is a bill of exchange)[42] Section 26(1) of the Bills of Exchange Act 1882 provides:

> "Where a person signs a bill as drawer, indorser, or acceptor, and adds words to his signature, indicating that he signs for or on behalf of a principal, or in a representative character, he is not personally liable thereon; but the mere addition to his signature of words describing his as agent, or as filling a representative character, does not exempt him from personal liability. In determining whether a signature on a bill is that of the principal or that of the agent by whose hand it is written, the construction most favourable to the validity of the instrument shall be adopted."

In practice, a cheque expressed to be drawn on the company's account at its bank will suffice to avoid the signatory being personally liable on it.[43] However, in the case of other bills of exchange, prudence would suggest that to ensure no liability attaches to him, the signatory should include words expressly stating that he signs as a director of the company for and on its behalf.

---

[39] *Nassau Steam Press* v *Tyler* (1894) 70 LT 376, "Old Paris and Bastille Syndicate Ltd" rather than "Bastille Syndicate Ltd".
[40] For example "Primkeen" rather than Primekeen (*Jenice Ltd* v *Dan* [1994] BCC 43).
[41] *UBAF Ltd* v *European American Banking Corporation* [1984] QB 713.
[42] Section 73 Bills of Exchange Act 1882.
[43] *Bondina Ltd* v *Rollaway Shower Blinds Ltd* [1986] 1 WLR 517.

4.5 Liability for the acts of the company: company debts

4.5.1 Crown debts

4.5.1.1 Social security contributions
Non-payment by an employer of social security contributions is a criminal offence (Section 114 Social Security Administration Act 1992). If the employer is a body corporate, then any director, manager, secretary or other similar officer commits a summary criminal offence if the non-payment is due to his consent, connivance or neglect (Section 115). The offence constituted by Section 114 is one in relation to which the magistrates have power to make a confiscation order under the Criminal Justice Act 1988 and the personal assets of the directors could be forfeited (Criminal Justice Act 1988 (Confiscation Orders) Order 1996, SI 1996/1716).

4.5.1.2 Betting duty
Under the Betting and Gaming Duties Act 1981, a director is jointly and severally liable with his company for general betting duty, pool betting duty or bingo duty due to be paid (Sections 5(3), 8(2) and 18(2)) and sums due may be recovered directly from the Director. The director is liable under this Act whether or not he knew or might have known of the company's failure to pay, and Section 727 CA does not apply to liability under this Act (*Customs and Excise Commissioners v Hedon Alpha Ltd*).[44]

4.5.1.3 VAT
Where a company has been held liable to pay a penalty on grounds of fraudulent concealment of its liability to pay VAT, any director who has dishonestly contributed to the conduct which has led to the company's liability may become personally liable to pay the penalty in question (Value Added Tax Act 1994 Section 61). The required standard of proof was to be established on the balance of probabilities (and not beyond reasonable doubt) as this penalty was civil in nature (*1st Indian Cavalry Club Ltd and Chowdhury v Customs and Excise*).[45]

4.5.1.4 National Insurance
Where a company collapses owing sums to the Contributions Agency in respect of National Insurance contributions the directors can be held

---

[44] [1981] QB 818.
[45] [1998] Simon's Tax Cases 293.

personally accountable for any shortfall to the extent that the company's failure to pay is attributable to their fraud or neglect (Social Security Act 1998).

4.5.2 *Disqualified directors and those acting on their instructions*

A person will be personally responsible for all the relevant debts of a company if he is involved in the management of the company in contravention of a disqualification order or of Section 11 of the Company Directors Disqualification Act 1986 ("CDDA 1986") (Section 15(1)(a) CDDA 1986). A person is "involved in the management of a company" if he is a director of the company or if he is concerned directly or indirectly with, or takes part in, the management of the company (Section 15(4) CDDA 1986). Further, a person who is involved in the management of the company will be personally responsible for all of the relevant debts of a company if he acts or is willing to act on instructions given without the leave of the court by a person whom he knows at that time to be the subject of a disqualification order or to be an undischarged bankrupt (Section15 (1)(b) CDDA 1986). The "relevant debts" of a company for this purpose are, in the first instance, such debts and other liabilities of the company as are incurred at a time when that person was involved in the management of the company, and in the second instance such debts and other liabilities of the company as are incurred at a time when that person was acting or was willing to act on instructions so given (Section 15(3) CDDA 1986). Liability is joint and several with that of the company and with any other person liable (Section 15(2) CDDA 1986). Where a person has at any time acted on instructions given without the leave of the court by a person whom he knew at that time to be the subject of a disqualification order or to be an undischarged bankrupt he will be presumed, unless the contrary is shown, to have been willing at any time thereafter to act on any instructions given by that person (Section 15(5) CDDA 1986).

4.5.3 *Costs of unsuccessful litigation*

The principle of limited liability will usually protect shareholders and directors from liability for the costs of unsuccessful litigation carried on in the company's name.[46] However, the court has a discretion to award costs against non-parties to the action under Section 51 of the Supreme

---

[46] *Taylor* v *Pace Developments Ltd* [1991] BCC 406 at 409.

A Practitioner's Guide to Directors' Duties and Responsibilities

Court Act 1981[47] and may exercise its discretion to award costs against directors who have caused a company improperly to prosecute or defend proceedings,[48] or where the directors have pursued litigation for their own private ends rather than for a proper corporate purpose,[49] particularly where the company is insolvent and so unable to meet any costs order itself.[50]

4.6 Issues of securities

4.6.1 The Listing Rules and the Financial Services Authority

Issues of listed securities are governed by the Financial Services and Markets Act 2000 ("FSMA 2000") together with the Listing Rules of the UK Listing Authority ("the UKLA").

Paragraph 5.2 of the Listing Rules requires the listing particulars and any supplementary listing particulars to include a statement by the directors of the issuer in the prescribed form or in such other form as may be permitted by the UKLA accepting responsibility for the information contained in the document. For this purpose, "directors of the issuer" includes any person who has authorised himself to be made, and is named, in the listing particulars or supplementary listing particulars as a person:

(a) who has agreed to become a director of the issuer;
(b) who has been, or will be invited to become, a director of the issuer; or
(c) whose appointment as a director of the issuer is otherwise in contemplation other than a person exempted or excused by the UKLA.

In addition, Listing Rule 5.5 requires the issuer to provide the UKLA with a letter signed by every director of the issuer (or by his agent or attorney, with a copy of the authority to any such agent or attorney) confirming that the listing particulars include all such information within their knowledge (or which it would be reasonable for them to obtain by

---

[47] *Aidan Shipping Co. Ltd* v *Interbulk Ltd* [1986] AC 965.
[48] *Symphony Group plc* v *Hodgson* [1994] 1 QB 179.
[49] *Re Tajik Air Ltd* [1996] 1 BCLC 317.
[50] *Re Land & Property Trust Co. plc* [1991] BCC 459, in *Re Records Tennis Centres* [1991] BCC 509, *Gamelsstaden plc* v *Brackland Magazines Ltd* [1993] BCC 194.

Potential Liabilities

making enquiries) as investors and their professional advisers would reasonably require and reasonably expect to find (regard being had to the matters mentioned in Section 80(4) FSMA 2000), for the purpose of making an informed assessment of the assets and liabilities, financial position, profits and losses and prospects of the issuer and of the rights attaching to the securities to which the listing particulars relate.

Section 90(1) FSMA 2000 renders "any person responsible" for any listing particulars or supplementary listing particulars liable to pay compensation to any person who has acquired any of the securities in question and suffered loss in respect of them as a result of any untrue or misleading statement in the prospectus or supplementary prospectus or the omission from it of any matter required by Section 80 or 81 FSMA 2000 to be included. Financial Services and Markets Act 2000 (Official Listing of Securities) Regulations 2001 (SI 2001/2956) as amended by SI 2001/3439 Part 3 para 6(1) defines the class of "persons responsible" for the purposes of Part VI FSMA 2000 and they include, where the issuer is a body corporate:

(a) each person who is a director of that body at the time when the particulars are submitted to the competent authority; and
(b) each person who has authorised himself to be named, and is named, in the particulars as a director or as having agreed to become a director of that body either immediately or at a future time.

However, a person will not be responsible for particulars if they are published without his knowledge or consent and on becoming aware of their publication he forthwith gives reasonable public notice that they were published without his knowledge or consent (FSMA Part VI para 6(2)). Where a person has accepted responsibility for, or authorised only part of, the contents of any particulars, he is responsible for only that part and only if it is included in (or substantially in) the form and context to which he has agreed (FSMA Part VI para 6(3)).

FSMA 2000 Schedule 10 para 1 exempts a responsible person from liability for loss under Section 90(1) where he is able to satisfy the court that, at the time when the particulars were submitted to the competent authority he reasonably believed, having made such enquiries (if any) as were reasonable, the statement was true and not misleading or that the matter whose omission caused the loss was properly omitted and that:

(a) he continued in that belief until the time when the securities were acquired;

(b) they were acquired before it was reasonably practicable to bring a correction to the attention of persons likely to acquire the securities in question;
(c) before the securities were acquired he had taken all such steps as it was reasonable for him to have taken to secure that a correction was brought to the attention of those persons; or
(d) he continued in that belief until after the commencement of dealings in the securities following their admission to the Official List and that the securities were acquired after such a lapse of time that he ought in the circumstances to be reasonably excused.

Where the loss was caused by a statement purporting to be made by or on the authority of another person as an expert which is, and is stated to be, included in the particulars with that other person's consent, then a responsible person will be exempted from liability if he can show that at the time when the particulars were submitted to the competent authority he believed on reasonable grounds that the other person was competent to make or authorise the statement and had consented to its inclusion in the form and context in which it was included and that:

(a) he continued in that belief until the time when the securities were acquired;
(b) they were acquired before it was reasonably practicable to bring a correction to the attention of persons likely to acquire the securities in question;
(c) before the securities were acquired he had taken all such steps as it was reasonable for him to have taken to secure that a correction was brought to the attention of those persons; or
(d) he continued in that belief until after the commencement of dealings in the securities following their admission to the Official List and that the securities were acquired after such a lapse of time that he ought in the circumstances to be reasonably excused (Schedule 10 para 2 FSMA 2000).

For this purpose, "expert" includes any engineer, valuer, accountant or other person whose profession, qualifications or experience give authority to a statement made by him (Schedule 10 para 8 FSMA 2000).

Such a person may also be exempted in such circumstances where:

(a) before the securities were acquired a correction, or the fact that the expert was not competent or had not consented, had been

published in a manner calculated to bring it to the attention of persons likely to acquire the securities in question; or
(b) the responsible person can show that he took all such steps as it was reasonable for him to take to secure such publication and reasonably believed that it had taken place before the securities were acquired (Schedule 10 paras 3 and 4 FSMA 2000).

Where loss results from a statement made by an official person or contained in a public official document which is included in the particulars, if the responsible person satisfies the court that the statement is accurately and fairly reproduced he may also be exempted from liability under Schedule 10 para 5 FSMA 2000. A person may also be exempted if he satisfies the court that the person suffering the loss acquired the securities in question with knowledge that the statement was false or misleading, of the omitted matter or of the change or new matter, as the case may be (Schedule 10 para 6 FSMA 2000).

If there is a significant change affecting any matter contained in listing particulars or a significant new matter arises which would have had to be included in the listing particulars had it arisen when they were prepared, Section 81 FSMA 2000 requires supplementary listing particulars to be submitted and published. A responsible person is exempted from liability in respect of a failure to deliver supplementary listing particulars where he is able to satisfy the court that either:

(a) the person suffering the loss acquired the securities in question with knowledge that the statement was false or misleading, of the omitted matter or of the change or new matter, as the case may be (Schedule 10 para 6 FSMA 2000); or
(b) he, as a responsible person, reasonably believed that the change or new matter in question was not such as to call for supplementary listing particulars (Schedule 10 para 7 FSMA 2000).

Where listing particulars relate to securities to be issued in connection with an offer by (or by a wholly owned subsidiary of) the issuer for securities issued by another entity, or in connection with a takeover offer, a director will not be liable for any part of the particulars relating to that other entity unless he has accepted and is stated in the particulars as having accepted responsibility for that part of the particulars. This exemption only applies where the other entity and, where it is a body corporate, its directors at the time when the particulars are submitted and other persons who have authorised themselves to be named as its directors have themselves accepted and are stated in the particulars as

A Practitioner's Guide to Directors' Duties and Responsibilities

accepting responsibility for that part of the particulars. (Financial Services and Markets Act 2000 (Official Listing of Securities) Regulations 2001(SI 2001/2956) part 3 para 7).

4.6.2 Public Offers of Securities Regulations 1995 (the "POS Regs")

Offers of unlisted securities are governed by the POS Regs. The regime is very similar to that affecting issues of listed securities.

Schedule 1 Part III of the POS Regs requires a prospectus to state the names, home or business addresses and functions of those persons responsible for the prospectus or any part of the prospectus, specifying such part and a statement by any person who accepts responsibility for the prospectus, or any part of it, that he does so.

Regulation 13 defines the class of persons responsible for a prospectus or supplementary prospectus and includes, where the issuer is a body corporate:

(a) each person who is a director of that body corporate at the time when the prospectus or supplementary prospectus is published;
(b) each person who has authorised himself to be named, and is named, in the prospectus or supplementary prospectus as a director or as having agreed to become a director of that body either immediately or at a future time;
(c) where the offeror is a body corporate but is not the issuer and is not making the offer in association with the issuer, each person who is a director of that body corporate at the time when the prospectus or supplementary prospectus is published.

In addition, a prospectus must contain a declaration by the directors of the issuer (or, if the offeror is not the issuer, by the directors of the offeror) that to the best of their knowledge the information contained in the prospectus is in accordance with the facts and that the prospectus makes no omission likely to affect the import of such information (Schedule 1, Part III, paragraph 10).

Regulation 14(1) renders the person or persons responsible for a prospectus or supplementary prospectus liable to pay compensation to any person who has acquired the securities to which the prospectus relates and suffered loss in respect of them as a result of any untrue or misleading statement in the prospectus or supplementary prospectus or the omission from it of any matter required by Regulations 9 or 10 to be

Potential Liabilities

included. This liability is expressly in addition to any other liability which may be incurred in the same circumstances. Regulation 14(3) imposes similar liability for loss arising from a failure to deliver a supplementary prospectus in circumstances where Regulation 10 requires one. Further, Regulation 16 renders certain contraventions of the Regulations governing the registration and publication of a prospectus (Regulations 4(1) and (2)) and advertisements etc. in connection with offers of securities (Regulation 12) actionable at the suit of a person who suffers loss as a result of such contravention. Regulation 15 affords certain exemptions from liability in circumstances equivalent to those prescribed by Schedule 10 to FSMA 2000 in the case of listed securities.

4.6.3 The Takeover Code

The City Code on Takeovers and Mergers ("the Code") applies to offers for all listed and unlisted public companies (other than open-ended investment companies) considered by the Panel on Takeovers and Mergers ("the Panel") to be resident in the UK, the Channel Islands or the Isle of Man and to private companies so resident where (in broad terms) their equity share capital has been made available to the public during the 10 years prior to the relevant offer. Rule 19.2 of the Code provides that:

> "Each document issued to shareholders or advertisement published in connection with an offer must state that the directors of the offeror and/or, where appropriate, the offeree company accept responsibility for the information contained in the document or advertisement and that, to the best of their knowledge and belief (having taken all reasonable care to ensure that such is the case), the information contained in the document or advertisement is in accordance with the facts and, where appropriate, that it does not omit anything likely to affect the import of such information...."

The inclusion of the specific responsibility statement in accordance with Rule 19.2 is sufficient to give rise to a common law duty of care owed by each individual director to persons relying on the information contained in the document or advertisement.[51] A director is potentially liable in damages to such persons if the document contains material misstatements which occasion loss to individuals who rely on it.

---

[51] Under the principles established in *Hedley Byrne & Co. Limited* v *Heller* [1964] AC 465.

Rule 19.1 expressly states that anyone issuing a circular to shareholders in connection with takeovers is expected to use the highest standards of care and accuracy whether they are involved as directors, offerors or their advisers (paragraph 5 of the General Principles and Rule 19.1 of the Code). In certain circumstances, the Panel will consider permitting the directors to take responsibility for less than the whole of the document. For example, an offer may contain details about both the target and the predator and the Panel may be prepared to allow the directors to confine their statements of responsibility to information relating to the particular company of which they are a director. It may also be possible for directors to limit their responsibility for the contents of a document or advertisement containing information about another company derived from published sources. Provided that the document makes clear the source of the information, the directors of the issuing company need only take responsibility for the correctness and fairness of the reproduction or presentation of that information.

4.6.4 *Fraudulent misrepresentation*

Where a person makes a false representation of fact, either knowing it to be false or recklessly not caring whether it is true or false,[52] intending that it should be acted upon by a class of which the claimant is a member, he is exposed to liability in damages for deceit if that claimant, influenced by the representation, acts on it and suffers loss as a result. So if a person is induced by a fraudulently made representation to subscribe for or purchase shares, the director(s) responsible for making that statement may be liable to compensate him for any loss which he sustains in consequence.[53]

Where the intention of the issuer and other parties to a prospectus extends to informing and encouraging aftermarket purchasers, the directors may also be liable to a person purchasing shares on the market (as opposed to subscribing on the strength of a circular or prospectus) who acquires the shares on the strength of the fraudulent statement. In *Possfund Custodian Trustee Ltd* v *Victor Derek Diamond*[54] Lightman J took the view that market practice supports the existence of such an extended purpose with the consequence that, at least arguably, the liability of the

---

[52] *See per Lord Herschell Derry* v *Peek* (1889) 14 App Cas. 337.
[53] *Andrew* v *Mockford* [1896] 1 QB 372, cf. *Peek* v *Gurney* (1873) LR 6 HL 377; also *Al-Nakib Investments (Jersey) Ltd* v *Longcroft* [1990] 3 All ER 321.
[54] [1996] 2 All ER 774.

directors will extend to such a class. Whether such an intention exists will be a matter of fact. If it is intended only to invite subscribers and not subsequent purchasers, a purchaser who buys shares on the market will have no claim in respect of his loss even though he may have been induced to make his investment by the statement in the fraudulent prospectus (*Peek* v *Gurney*).[55]

The award of damages payable to a victim of a fraudulent misrepresentation will be directed to put the injured party in the same position as if the wrong had not been sustained (*Smith New Court Securities Ltd* v *Scrimgeour Vickers (Asset management) Ltd*).[56]

4.7 Winding up

4.7.1 Section 212: misfeasance

Section 212 of the Insolvency Act 1986 ("IA 1986") affords a summary remedy to a liquidator where in the course of the winding up of a company it appears that a person who:

(a) is or has been an officer of the company;
(b) has acted as liquidator, administrator or administrative receiver of the company;
(c) not being a person falling within (a) or (b) above, is or has been concerned, or has taken part in, the promotion, formation or management of the company,

has misapplied or retained, or become accountable for, any money or other property of the company, or been guilty of any misfeasance or breach of any fiduciary or other duty in relation to the company (Section 212(1) IA 1986).

A director of a company qualifies as an "officer" by virtue of Section 744 CA. On an application by the official receiver or the liquidator, or of any creditor or contributory, the court may examine the conduct of the person falling within subsection (1) and compel him:

---

[55] [1873] LR 6 HL 377.
[56] [1996] 4 All ER 769, 774, per Lord Browne-Wilkinson.

A Practitioner's Guide to Directors' Duties and Responsibilities

(a) to repay, restore or account for the money or property or any part of it, with interest at such rate as the court thinks just; or
(b) to contribute such sum to the company's assets by way of compensation in respect of the misfeasance or breach of fiduciary or other duty as the court thinks just (Section 212(3) IA 1986).

Although the power of the court under Section 212 IA 1986 may be exercised at the behest of a creditor or contributory as well as the official receiver or liquidator, the power of a contributory to make an application under subsection (3) is not exercisable except with the leave of the court, but is exercisable notwithstanding that he will not benefit from any order that the court may make on the application.

Section 212 IA 1986 does not create any new liability but merely provides a summary procedure which will allow for speedier relief in a liquidation without the need to resort to a full-scale trial. The words of the Section are not confined to breaches of fiduciary duty but are wide enough to extend to liability for negligence (e.g. *Re D'Jan of London Ltd*).[57] However, the Section does not extend to the recovery of a contractual debt (*Re Etic Ltd*).[58]

When assessing compensation or damages under Section 212 IA 1986, the court is not confined to cases of misfeasance involving moral turpitude but may consider the whole spectrum of directors' duties including the duty of care owed to a company at common law.[59]

When exercising the power conferred by Section 212(3)(b) of the Insolvency Act 1986 to compel a delinquent director "to contribute such sum to the company's assets by way of compensation in respect of ... the breach of ... other duty" in a case where the breach of duty complained of is a breach of the common-law duty to take care, the court has to be satisfied that the negligence has caused a loss in respect of which compensation can be awarded. The position, in this respect, is the same as it would be if the company brought an action in its own name.[60]

---

[57] [1993] BCC 646, approved and applied in *Re Simmon Box (Diamonds) Ltd* [2000] BCC 275.
[58] [1928] 1 Ch 861.
[59] *Re Westlowe Storage and Distribution Ltd (In liquidation)* [2000] 2 BCLC 590.
[60] *Cohen v Selby* [2001] 1 BCLC 176.

4.7.2 Fraudulent trading

4.7.2.1 Criminal liability
Section 458 CA renders it a criminal offence knowingly to be a party to the carrying on of the business of a company with intent to defraud creditors of the company or creditors of any other person, or for any fraudulent purpose. The Section applies whether or not the company has been or is in the course of being wound up. The Section does not just cover fraudulent trading as it affects creditors; the words "or for any fraudulent purpose" are wide enough to permit a conviction where the company is merely the setting or vehicle for a fraud (*R v Kemp*).[61] Dishonesty is an essential ingredient of the offence[62] and the same standard of dishonesty applies to "commercial fraud" as it does in any other crime of dishonesty.[63]

4.7.2.2 Civil liability
Section 213 IA 1986 provides:

> "(1) If in the course of the winding up of a company it appears that any business of the company has been carried on with intent to defraud creditors of the company or creditors of any other person, or for any fraudulent purpose, the following has effect.
> (2) The court, on the application of the liquidator may declare that any persons who were knowingly parties to the carrying on of the business in the manner above-mentioned are to be liable to make such contribution (if any) to the company's assets as the court thinks proper."

(*See* also Chapter 11.2.2.) A number of elements need to be established in order for liability under Section 213 to be established: First, the liquidator must establish that the business of the company has been carried on with intent to defraud creditors; where no fraudulent intent was alleged against the board which had carried on the company's business, other persons could not be "party to" the offending conduct. In *Re Augustus Barnett & Son Ltd* Hoffmann J put it as follows:[64]

---

[61] [1988] QB 645; (1988) 4 BCC 203 CA. *See* also *R v Philippou* (1989) 5 BCC 665.
[62] *R v Cox and Hodges* (1982) 75 Cr App R 291.
[63] *R v Lockwood* (1986) 2 BCC 99, 333.
[64] (1986) 2 BCC 98,904 at p. 98, 907.

> "It is a necessary condition of the court's power to make an order under this section that it appears that 'any business of the company has been carried on with intent to defraud'. Transferring the passive to the active voice, this in my judgment involves a finding that someone has done an act which can be described as carrying on some business of the company and that in doing so he had an intent to defraud. Equally, the words 'any business of the company has been carried on ... for any fraudulent purpose' must mean that someone carrying on the business had a fraudulent purpose in doing so. Once this condition has been satisfied, the court may impose personal liability on any persons who were knowingly 'party to' the carrying on of the business 'in manner aforesaid'."

Section 213 IA 1986 expressly requires an intention to defraud. This must be proved by showing that the person had the requisite knowledge to found such an intention. This must be properly averred in the pleading, for the court cannot convert acts which were not pleaded as fraudulent into a course of conduct which was (*Rossleigh Ltd* v *Carlaw & Carlaw*[65]). The required intent to defraud is subjective rather than objective and it is necessary to show either an intent or a reckless indifference whether creditors were defrauded (*Bernasconi* v *Nicholas Bennett & Co (a firm)* [2000] BCC 921).

Second, the person in respect of whom a declaration is sought must be "party to" the fraudulent trading. When a liquidator of a company claims relief against a person under Section 213, any fraudulent acts which were done by or on behalf of the company, but to which that person was not "knowingly a party" are wholly irrelevant to the liquidator's claim.[66]

Hoffman J in *Re Augustus Barnett & Son Ltd* considered the words "persons ... party to" to be wide enough to cover "outsiders who could not be said to have carried on or even assisted the carrying on of the company's business but who nevertheless in some way participated in the fraudulent acts". So a creditor may be party to fraudulent trading if he accepts sums which he knows were obtained in such a transaction (*Re Gerald Cooper Chemicals Ltd*).[67] Contrast, however, *Re Maidstone Buildings Provisions Ltd*[68] where the court considered that an employee who is not

---

[65] (1985) 1 BCC 99, 537.
[66] *Re Bank of Credit and Commerce International SA & Anor. Morris & Others* v *State Bank of India* [1999] BCC 943.
[67] [1978] Ch 262.
[68] [1971] 1 WLR 1085.

Potential Liabilities

a member of the board of a company with which the decision whether or not to continue to trade rests is not a "party" to the fraudulent trading even where he is aware of the financial position.

The words "business ... carried on" have been widely construed. The scale of the fraud is irrelevant. In *Re L Todd (Swanscombe) Ltd*[69] only one creditor was defrauded and in *Re Gerald Cooper Chemicals Ltd*[70] only one transaction was alleged. "Carrying on business" for Section 213 IA 1986 purposes is wider than carrying on trade and includes collection and realisation of assets for distribution to creditors in discharge of their debts (*Re Sarflax Ltd*).[71]

> "Prima facie the appropriate amount that a director is declared to be liable to contribute is the amount by which the company's assets can be discerned to have been depleted by the director's conduct which caused the discretion under Section 214(1) to arise."[72]

However, Section 213 also contains a punitive element[73] and the declared sum may be, or include, a punitive as well as a compensatory element.[74] As far as the sum for which the person in question is declared to be responsible is compensatory, then the better approach is to limit the sum to the amount of the debts of the creditors proved to have been defrauded by the fraudulent trading.[75] In addition to the personal liability to contribute under Section 213 IA 1986, the court may, if it thinks fit, also make a disqualification order against the person concerned from being involved in the management of a company (Sections 4 and 10 CDDA 1986).

4.7.3 Section 214: wrongful trading

Section 214 IA 1986 was introduced on the recommendation of the Cork Committee (Cm 8558, 1982) in order to create a civil liability on a director

---

[69] [1990] BCC 125.
[70] [1978] Ch 262.
[71] [1979] Ch 592.
[72] Knox J in *Re Produce Marketing Consortium Ltd* (1989) 5 BCC 569 at p. 597G adopted for the purposes of determining the appropriate relief under Section 213 IA 1986 by Leonard Bromley QC in *Re a Company (No. 001418 of 1988)* [1990] BCC 526.
[73] *Re William C Leitch Bros Ltd* [1932] 2 Ch 71 at p. 80 per Maugham J.
[74] Per Lord Denning MR in *Re Cyona Distributors Ltd* [1967] Ch 889, at p. 902.
[75] *Re a Company (No. 001418 of 1988)* [1990] BCC 526, His Honour Judge Bromley QC at 523E approved by Neuberger J. *Re Bank of Credit and Commerce International SA & Anor. Morris & Others* v *State Bank of India* [1999] BCC 943.

to pay compensation where loss was suffered as a result of conduct that, whilst "unreasonable", falls short of the dishonesty necessary to establish liability for fraudulent trading. The provision on wrongful trading is supplementary to any possible liability for fraudulent trading.

Section 214(1) and (2) provides as follows:

> "if in the course of the winding up of a company it appears that subsection (2) of this Section applies in relation to a person who is or has been a director of the company, the court, on the application of the liquidator, may declare that that person is to be liable to make such contribution (if any) to the company's assets as the court thinks proper."

This subsection applies in relation to a person if:

(a) the company has gone into insolvent liquidation;
(b) at some time before the commencement of the winding up of the company, that person knew or ought to have concluded that there was no reasonable prospect that the company would avoid going into insolvent liquidation;
(c) that person was a director of the company at that time,

but the court shall not make a declaration under this Section in any case where the time mentioned in (b) above was before 28 April 1986.

The Section only applies to a company which is in insolvent liquidation. A company goes into insolvent liquidation if it goes into liquidation at a time when its assets are insufficient for the payment of its debts and other liabilities and the expenses of the winding up (Section 214(6)). Proceedings under Section 214 IA 1986 may only be brought by the liquidator. The Section is directed at persons who have been directors of the company. It extends to shadow directors as much as to directors (Section 214(7)). It almost certainly applies to *de facto* directors[76] and to foreign directors, resident abroad, of a foreign company being wound up in England and Wales under the Insolvency Act 1986 (*Re Howard Holdings Ltd*).[77] A claim may be made against the estate of a deceased director.[78]

---

[76] Millet J accepted counsel's concession to this effect as correct in *Re Hydrodan (Corby) Ltd* [1994] BCC 161.
[77] [1998] BCC 549.
[78] *Re Sherborne Associates Ltd* [1995] BCC 40.

Potential Liabilities

In determining whether or not a person "knew or ought to have concluded that there was no reasonable prospect that the company would avoid going into insolvent liquidation" the court applies the semi-objective standard prescribed by Section 214(4) which provides:

> "(4) the facts which a director of a company ought to know or ascertain, the conclusions which he ought to reach and the steps which he ought to take are those which would be known or ascertained, or reached or taken, by a reasonably diligent person having both –
> (a) the general knowledge, skill and experience that may reasonably be expected of a person carrying out the same functions as are carried out by that director in relation to the company, and
> (b) the general knowledge, skill and experience that that director has."

It is not sufficient for a director to plead that his general knowledge, skill and experience did not equip him to form a realistic judgment as to the company's prospects (*Re Purpoint Ltd*).[79] The court expects a minimum standard – that of a reasonably diligent person who has taken on the office of director – from persons acting as directors which will not be reduced because of the personal inadequacy of the particular director in question (*Re Brian D Pierson (Contractors) Ltd*).[80] The knowledge to be imputed to a director in testing whether or not directors knew or ought to have concluded that there was no reasonable prospect of the company avoiding insolvent liquidation is not limited to the documentary material actually available at the given time. The words "ought to know or ascertain" indicates that facts which given reasonable diligence and an appropriate level of general knowledge, skill and experience, are capable of being ascertained must be included (*Re Produce Marketing Consortium Ltd*).[81]

A director has a defence to a claim under Section 214 if he is able to satisfy the court that after the time at which he first knew or ought to have concluded that there was no reasonable prospect that the company would avoid going into insolvent liquidation he "took every step with a view to minimising the potential loss to the company's creditors as (assuming him to have known that there was no reasonable prospect that

---

[79] [1991] BCC 121.
[80] [1999] BCC 26.
[81] [1989] 5 BCC 569.

A Practitioner's Guide to Directors' Duties and Responsibilities

the company would avoid going into insolvent liquidation) he ought to have taken" (Section 214(3)). The provisions of Section 214(4) apply equally to the consideration of the steps which a director "ought to have taken" as they do to the knowledge which he ought to have had. Note that the requirement is for the director to have taken "every step". This provision is intended to apply to cases where directors take specific steps with a view to preserving or realising assets or claims for the benefit of creditors, even if they fail to achieve that result, and was not satisfied merely by continuing to trade just because this was done in the hope of trying to make a profit – that is, the very act of wrongful trading (*Re Brian D Pierson (Contractors) Ltd*).[82]

The court may declare that the person is to be liable to make such contribution (if any) to the company's assets as the court thinks proper (Section 214(1)). The jurisdiction under Section 214 is primarily compensatory and prima facie the appropriate amount that a director is declared to be liable to contribute is the amount by which the company's assets can be discerned to have been depleted by the director's conduct which caused the discretion under Section 214(1) to arise.[83] However, the court has a discretion to award a larger, punitive or exemplary sum (*Re Produce Marketing Consortium Ltd*).[84] The liquidator may accept property other than money to satisfy the liability of a director under an order under Section 214 (*Re Farmizer (Products) Ltd Moore v Gadd*).[85]

Where the court makes a declaration against a director under Section 214, it may make a disqualification order in relation to that person either on application or of its own volition (Section 10 CDDA 1986). There is no minimum period of disqualification under Section 10, but the maximum period is 15 years (Section 10(2) CDDA 1986). The defence under Section 727(1) CA, that the director has acted honestly and reasonably and ought fairly to be excused, does not apply to a wrongful trading claim (*Re Produce Marketing Consortium Ltd Halls v David*).

---

[82] [1999] BCC 26.
[83] *See Re Purpoint Ltd* [1991] BCC 121 and *Re DKG Contractors Ltd* [1990] BCC 903 where this was the approach adopted.
[84] [1989] BCC 569 at 597.
[85] [1997] BCC 655 applied in *Re Brian D Pierson (Contractors) Ltd* [1999] BCC 26.

Potential Liabilities

4.7.4 Sections 216 and 217: "phoenix companies"

IA 1986 Section 216 targets the so-called "phoenix syndrome": the practice whereby directors of insolvent companies simply roll over the business into a new company with the same or a similar name. Section 216 applies where a company (the "liquidating company") has gone into insolvent liquidation (Section 216(1)) – that is, it goes into liquidation at a time when its assets are insufficient for the payment of its debts and other liabilities and the expenses of the winding up (Section 216(7)). It prohibits any person who was a director or shadow director of the liquidating company at any time in the period of 12 months ending with the day before it went into liquidation from being a director of, or in any way, whether directly or indirectly, being concerned or taking part in the promotion, formation or management of any other company that is known by a "prohibited name", or in any way, whether directly or indirectly, being concerned or taking part in the carrying on of a business carried on (otherwise than by a company) under a "prohibited name" except with the leave of the court,[86] or in certain prescribed cases[87] (Section 216(3)). The prohibition endures for the period of five years

---

[86] "The court" means any court having jurisdiction to wind up companies; and on an application for leave under that subsection, the Secretary of State or the official receiver may appear and call the attention of the court to any matters which seem to him to be relevant (Section 216(5) IA 1986).

[87] Three cases have been prescribed in which a person may use a prohibited name without leave of the court:

(a) where the successor company has acquired the whole or substantially the whole of the business of the insolvent company under arrangements made by an insolvency practitioner and the successor company has, within 28 days of completion of this arrangement, given notice in prescribed terms to all the creditors of the insolvent company of which it is aware in Insolvency Rule ("IR") 4.228. A person named in that notice may act without the leave of the court (IR 4.228(3) and (4));

(b) if a person subject to Section 216 IA 1986 applies for leave not later than seven days from the date on which the liquidating company went into liquidation, he is exempt during the period of six weeks after that date or the day on which the court disposes of the application for leave under Section 216 whichever of those dates first occurs (IR 4.229);

(c) the court's leave under Section 216(3) is not required where, though a company is known by a prohibited name, it has been known by that name for the whole of the 12 months ending with the day before the liquidating company went into liquidation and has not at any time during those 12 months been dormant within the meaning of Section 252(5) CA (IR 4.230) (IR 4.230).

beginning with the day on which the liquidating company went into liquidation (Section 216(3)). A "prohibited name" is a name by which the liquidating company was known at any time in the period of 12 months ending with the day before it went into liquidation or which is so similar to that name as to suggest an association with the liquidating company (Section 216(2)). Section 216(4) renders a breach of the Section a criminal offence punishable by imprisonment or a fine, or both. References to a name by which a company is known are to the name of the company at that time or to any name under which the company carries on business at that time (Section 216(6)).

Section 217(1) IA 1986 renders a person personally responsible for all the relevant debts of a company, if he is involved in the management of the company in contravention of Section 216 IA 1986 at any time or if he is involved in the management of a company and he acts or is willing to act on instructions given (without the leave of the court) by a person whom he knows at that time to be in contravention of Section 216 in relation to the company. A person is "involved in management" if he is a director of the company or if he is takes part or is concerned directly or indirectly in the management of the company (Section 217(4)). The "relevant debts" of a company for this purpose are, in the first instance, such debts and other liabilities of the company as are incurred at a time when that person was involved in the management of the company, and in the second instance such debts and other liabilities of the company as are incurred at a time when that person was acting or was willing to act on instructions so given (Section 217(3)). Liability is joint and several with that of the company and with any other person liable (Section 217(2)). In the second case, where such a person has at any time acted on instructions given without the leave of the court by a person whom he knew at that time to be in contravention in relation to Section 216, he will be presumed, unless the contrary is shown, to have been willing at any time thereafter to act on any instructions given by that person (Section 217(5)).

4.8 Indemnity and insurance against liability

Section 310 CA renders void (save to the extent expressly permitted by Section 310(3)):

> "any provision, whether contained in a company's articles or in any contract with the company or otherwise, for exempting any officer of the company or any person (whether an officer or not) employed

by the company as auditor from, or indemnifying him against, any liability which by virtue of any rule of law would otherwise attach to him in respect of any negligence, default, breach of duty or breach of trust of which he may be guilty in relation to the company."

It follows that a provision purporting to exempt directors and auditors from liability for losses to the company in respect of negligence, default, breach of duty or breach of trust will be void even where the indemnity is restricted to case of "wilful default" or save in the case of dishonesty.[88]

However, Section 310(3)(b)[89] does allow a company lawfully to indemnify an officer or auditor against any liability incurred by him in defending any proceedings (whether civil or criminal) in which judgment is given in his favour or he is acquitted, or in connection with any application under Section 144(3) or (4) CA (acquisition of shares by innocent nominee) or Section 727 CA (general power to grant relief in case of honest and reasonable conduct) in which relief is granted to him by the court. Regulation 118 of Table A mirrors the permitted indemnity.

Articles which disapply the rules against profiting and against conflicts of interest and duty (e.g. Regulations 85 and 94 of Table A) do not breach Section 310 CA because they do not exempt a director from the consequence of a breach of a "duty" owed to the company.[90]

Further, Section 310(3)(a) CA[91] expressly permits a company to purchase and maintain for any officer of the company insurance against any liability attaching to him in respect of any negligence, default, breach of duty or breach of trust in relation to the company.

4.9 Statutory relief

Section 727 CA permits the court hearing proceedings against a director for negligence, default, breach of duty or breach of trust in which he is or may be liable, to relieve him, either wholly or partly, from his liability.

---

[88] Prior to the enactment of the predecessor of Section 310 in the Companies Act 1929, such a clause was held to be valid (*Re Brazilian Rubber Estates Ltd* [1911] 1 Ch 425 and *Re City Equitable Fire Insurance Co.* [1925] Ch 407).

[89] Inserted by Section 137 CA 1989.

[90] *Movitex Limited* v *Bulfield & Others* (1988) BCLC 104.

[91] Inserted by Section 137 CA 1989.

The Section applies whether the relief sought is damages or an account of profits.[92]

The court may grant such relief providing it is satisfied that:

(a) the director concerned has acted honestly and reasonably; and
(b) having regard to all the circumstances of the case (including those connected with his appointment), he ought fairly to be excused for the negligence, default, breach of duty or breach of trust.

When exercising its discretion under Section 727, all three requirements of subsection (1) must be satisfied.[93] If a director apprehends that any claim will or might be made against him in respect of any negligence, default, breach of duty or breach of trust, he may apply to the court for relief and, on such an application, the court has the same power to relieve him as it would have under Section 727(1) (Section 727(2)). However, once proceedings are actually commenced, the only court which can give relief under Section 727 in respect of those matters is the court before which proceedings are pending.[94]

Where a case to which subsection (1) applies is tried by a judge with a jury, the judge may withdraw the case in whole or in part from the jury and forthwith direct judgment to be entered for the defendant or defender if, having heard evidence, the judge is satisfied that the defendant or defender ought to be relieved in whole or in part from the liability sought to be enforced against him in accordance with the terms of Section 727(1) (Section 727(3)).

Section 727 is restricted to claims by or on behalf of a company or its liquidator against the officer concerned for their personal breach of duty and to penal proceedings for the enforcement of specific duties imposed by the Companies Acts on the company's officers.[95]

The test imposed by Section 727 is an essentially subjective one, requiring an examination of all the circumstances of the case to ascertain whether the director concerned has acted honestly and reasonably and deciding

---

[92] *Coleman Taymar Ltd* v *Oakes* [2001] 2 BCLC 749: liability to account being just as much a liability for this purpose as liability to pay damages, per Judge Robert Reid QC at 770.
[93] *Coleman Taymar Ltd* v *Oakes* [2001] 2 BCLC 749.
[94] *Re Gilt Edge Safety Glass Ltd* [1940] Ch 495.
[95] *Customs and Excise Commrs.* v *Hedon Alpha Ltd* [1981] QB 818.

Potential Liabilities

whether on those grounds he ought to be excused. It follows that the court has no jurisdiction to grant relief from liability under Section 727 where the claim made against the officer involves the application of an objective standard to his behaviour.[96] The standard of reasonableness to be satisfied in the context of Section 727 is that of "a man of affairs dealing with his own affairs with reasonable care and circumspection" in such a case.[97]

---

[96] *Re Produce Marketing Consortium* [1989] 1 WLR 745.
[97] *Re Duomatic Ltd* [1969] 2 Ch 365, 377, per Buckley J.

Chapter 5

Fair Dealing and Connected Persons

Vanessa Knapp, Partner
Freshfields Bruckhaus Deringer

5.1 Introduction

This Chapter looks at some of the provisions in Part X of the Companies Act 1985 which deal with fair dealings between a director and his company (or another company in the same group) and between such companies and anyone connected with a director. It does not deal with the various obligations to disclose details of certain transactions or arrangements in the company's accounts.

This area of law was reviewed by the Law Commission in 1998 (*see* Law Commission Consultation Paper No. 153) at the request of the Department of Trade and Industry ("the DTI") in connection with the review of company law. The Law Commission said that many of the provisions represented a "hasty legislative response" to a number of financial scandals in the 1970s. It identified the many inconsistencies between the various provisions – for example whether a particular act is prohibited absolutely, is not prohibited provided disclosure has taken place or is not prohibited provided consent is given, and whether approval must be given beforehand or may be given afterwards.

In September 1999 the Law Commission published a report (Law Commission No. 261) which considered the responses it had received to the earlier Consultation Paper. This recommended that most of the provisions of Part X should be retained as a supplement to the protection provided by the general law. It also recommended some specific changes to some of the provisions and the introduction of a coherent code of civil remedies. The Consultation Document on Modern Company Law published by the Company Law Review Steering Group in March 2000 accepted most of these proposals. The *Final Report on Modern Company Law* published by the The Company Law Review Steering Group in June 2001 did not propose any further major changes to the existing regime.

However, for the time being directors and companies have to live with the current law. A review of the following provisions may, however, encourage companies and directors to lobby the DTI for a change which would introduce a more rational and practicable regime.

Before looking at various provisions in Part X, it is helpful to understand some of the defined terms which are used in those provisions. All of the provisions of Part X apply to a "company". This means a company formed and registered under the Companies Act 1985, the Companies Acts 1948 to 1983 or under certain earlier Acts (*see* Section 735).[1] It includes unlimited companies. In contrast, "body corporate" includes companies incorporated outside Great Britain, but not a corporation sole (*see* Section 740).

The Part X provisions apply to a "director". This is defined (*see* Section 741) to include any person who occupies the position of director, "by whatever name called". This means that someone whom a company thinks it has appointed as a director is a director even if the appointment proves to be invalid. It also includes someone who acts as a director, even though the company has never appointed them as such. In some cases it can also include an alternate director. Some of the provisions also apply to a person connected with a director. Those who come within this category are set out in Section 346. As this is a fairly complicated provision, it is dealt with separately at the end of this Chapter in 5.12. For the purposes of the various provisions dealt with in this Chapter, it does not matter what law governs the transaction or arrangement in question (*see* Section 347).

Some of the provisions in Part X also relate to subsidiaries, holding companies and subsidiaries of holding companies. Section 736 sets out the definition of "subsidiary", "holding company" and "wholly-owned subsidiary". In each case the definition extends to bodies corporate as well as Companies Act companies and to sub-subsidiaries and holding companies of a holding company. A company is a subsidiary of another (which is therefore the holding company of that subsidiary) if one of three tests is satisfied. The first is if the holding company holds a majority of the voting rights in the subsidiary. The second is if the holding company is a member of the subsidiary and has the right to appoint or remove a majority of the directors. The third test is if the holding

---

[1] In this Chapter all Section references are to the Companies Act 1985 unless otherwise stated.

company is a member of the subsidiary and controls alone a majority of the voting rights, pursuant to an agreement with other shareholders or members. Section 736A sets out further provisions to explain and supplement these tests.

5.2 Loss of office and retirement from office

The Companies Act 1985 requires companies to disclose payments to directors for loss of office or as consideration for retiring from office or in connection with their retirement from office. Such payments are unlawful unless they have been disclosed and approved by shareholders. For Section 312 of the Companies Act 1985 to apply, the payments must relate specifically to the office of director. If the payments relate to some other position within the company, such as an honorary life presidency, then the payments will not be caught.[2]

(a) Section 312 deals with payments by the company to its directors but not payments by a subsidiary to directors of its holding company or by a holding company to a director of a subsidiary.
(b) Section 313 deals with payments in connection with the transfer of all or any part of the company's undertaking or property and prohibits any payments (i.e. not just those made by the company), unless details of the proposed payment (including its amount) are disclosed to members of the company and the proposal is approved.
(c) Section 314 deals with any payments (again, not just those made by the company) made in connection with certain transfers of shares. It applies where all or any shares in a company are transferred to one or more persons as a result of an offer which is either:
   (i) made to all the target shareholders;
   (ii) made by or on behalf of a body corporate with a view to the target becoming its subsidiary or a sister company (i.e. a subsidiary of the offeror's holding company);
   (iii) made by or on behalf of an individual with a view to his being able to exercise at least one-third of the voting power at any target general meeting (or control the exercise of that voting power); or
   (iv) conditional on receiving a certain number or percentage of acceptances.

---

[2] *See Mercer v Heart of Midlothian Plc* 2001 SLT 945.

Section 314 applies as much to offers for private companies as to offers for public companies which are subject to the City Code on Takeovers and Mergers. If the City Code applies, the company will also need to consider Rules 21 and 24.5, as well as any Listing Rule requirements (*see* 5.7 below).

In *Mercer* v *Heart of Midlothian Plc* 2001 SLT 945, Lord Macfadyen considered what sorts of payments are caught by Section 312. He held that it is important to bear in mind the whole language of the section and to have regard to the "nature and circumstances" of the payment in order to determine its true character. Whilst the primary meaning of payment is a transfer of money, Lord Macfadyen thought that in some contexts payments in a form other than money can amount to a "payment" for the purposes of Section 312. While the receipt of benefits over a period of time might make valuation difficult, this would not preclude them from being regarded as payments. In the case of payments subject to Section 312 or 313, the proposals must be disclosed to all members of the company (whether or not they hold voting shares) and must be approved by the company. In *Mercer* v *Heart of Midlothian Plc* Lord Macfadyen rejected a submission that the effect of Section 232, which requires directors' emoluments and benefits to be disclosed in the notes to the company's accounts, was to give approval to the benefits as required by Section 312. He said that Section 312 required disclosure and approval to happen before the payment is made. He also suggested that in determining what is meant by "payments", it is the cost to the company rather than the benefit received by the retiring director that is relevant. Therefore, where the provision of benefits would not cost the company anything, Section 312 does not apply.[3] For payments subject to Section 314 the director has a duty to take all reasonable steps to make sure the document offering to acquire the shares contains details of the proposed payment (including the amount). However, any "bona fide payment by way of damages for breach of contract or by way of pension for past services" is excluded from the requirements of all three Sections (*see* Section 316(3)). In practice, companies usually rely on this exclusion to avoid having to disclose payments and seek shareholder approval. Companies are increasingly frequently criticised for taking a generous view of what constitutes a bona fide payment by way of damages. In December 2002 the Association of British Insurers ("ABI") and National Association of Pension Funds ("NAPF") issued a joint statement on Best Practice on Executive Contracts and Severance. It can often be difficult

---

[3] ibid, 2.

to agree what reduction is appropriate to reflect the director's chance of finding another directorship. The Law Commission has suggested (*see* Law Commission Consultation Paper No. 153) that directors will have the protection of Section 316(3) if they rely on proper legal advice, even if it is wrong.

5.3 Payments which the company has previously agreed to make

One of the problems with Sections 312 to 316 is establishing whether they apply to payments which a company has agreed to make to a director when he retires or loses office, before the retirement or loss of office occurs. The leading case is *Taupo Totara Timber* v *Rowe*,[4] an appeal to the Privy Council from the New Zealand Court of Appeal. Section 191 of the New Zealand Companies Act 1955, which the Privy Council had to consider, is identical to Section 312 of the Companies Act 1985. The question in that case was whether a provision in the service contract of a managing director, which required the company to pay an amount of money to the director on resignation or dismissal, had to be approved by the company under Section 191. The agreement did not fix the amount of the payment and the amount would only be ascertained when the resignation or dismissal happened. The Privy Council held that Section 191 only applied to payments which the company had not previously agreed to pay or which the company did not have a legal obligation to make. Accordingly, no disclosure to members or approval was needed.

The *Taupo Totara* case was followed in a case before the Outer House of the Court of Session, *Lander* v *Premier Pict Petroleum Ltd*.[5] In that case, Mr Lander, who was a company director, became entitled to a golden parachute payment under the terms of his service agreement if there was a change of control of the company and he gave notice to terminate his employment. He resigned in the circumstances envisaged by the contract but the company refused to make the payment and argued that the payment was unlawful as it had not been disclosed and approved under Section 312. Lord Osborne rejected the company's argument. Following the Privy Council decision, he decided that the Sections only apply to proposed payments, that is, that payments which the company was already legally obliged to pay were not covered by the Sections.

---

[4] [1978] AC 537, PC.
[5] [1997] SLT 1361.

However, while contractual payments agreed when a director was appointed are now, as a result of the *Taupo Totara* and *Lander* cases, clearly outside the scope of Section 312, in *Mercer v Heart of Midlothian Plc* Lord Macfadyen's statements suggest that this is not the case where a contractual payment is agreed just before resignation in order to ensure that Section 312 will not apply. Lord Macfadyen thought it was likely that an agreement which is entered into on the basis that there will be a further period of continuing office would fall to be treated as a covenanted payment and so would fall outside the scope of the Section.

The consequences of breaching Sections 312 to 316 vary. If Section 312 or 313 is breached the payment is unlawful. However, under Section 314 the payment is not unlawful, so an agreement to make the payment will be enforceable. Section 315 sets out the position of a director who receives a payment in breach of his duty under Section 314 or where the proposed payment is not approved by the holders of the target shares to which the offer relates (whether or not the particular shareholder's shares are included in the offer) before shares are transferred pursuant to the offer. The director holds any amount received in trust for shareholders who have sold shares as a result of the offer. A director who receives a payment in breach of Section 313(2) also receives the amount in trust for the company.

Section 316 contains some anti-avoidance provisions. Sections 313 and 314 are deemed to apply (unless the contrary is shown) if a payment is made in pursuance of any arrangement entered into as part of an agreement for the relevant transfer (or within one year before or two years after the agreement or offer leading to it) provided the company or the person to whom the transfer was made was privy to the arrangement. If a director is paid more per share than other shareholders or is given any valuable consideration in either case in connection with a transfer subject to Section 313 or 314, the excess price or the money value of the consideration is deemed to be a payment by way of compensation for loss of office or as consideration for or in connection with his retirement from office.

The relationship between Sections 312 to 314 and Section 320 (*see* 5.6 below) is not entirely clear. Lord Osborne in the *Lander* case considered that Section 320 did not apply to such cases as the right to payment could not be valued when it was created and, because it was a right to a payment in cash, it was not a non-cash asset for the purposes of Section 320. *Gooding v Cater* (unreported) 13 March 1989 came to the same conclusion. In principle these decisions seem correct, although doubt is sometimes still expressed about the position. In *Mercer v Heart of Midlothian Plc* Lord Macfadyen rejected the submission that the scope of Section 312 is restricted by the scope of Section 320.

5.4 Disclosure of interests in contracts

A director who is in any way, whether directly or indirectly, interested in a contract or a proposed contract with the company has a duty under Section 317(1) to declare the nature of that interest at a meeting of the directors of the company. A director who breaches Section 317 is liable to a fine. It is not enough to declare an interest to a committee of the board (*Guinness plc v Saunders and another*[6]).

In the case of a proposed contract, the declaration must be made at the directors' meeting at which the proposed contract is first considered or, if the director is not interested in the proposed contract at that meeting but later becomes so, at the next directors' meeting after he becomes interested in the proposed contract. Where a director becomes interested in a contract after it has been made, the declaration must be made at the first directors' meeting held after the director becomes interested.

A director can declare an interest by giving a general notice to the directors that he is a member of a specified company or firm and is to be regarded as interested in any contract which is made with that company or firm after the date of the notice. A director can also give a general notice that he is to be regarded as interested in any contract made with a specified person who is connected with him (within the meaning of Section 346) after the date of the notice (*see* 5.12 below). However, to be effective, a general notice must either be given at a directors' meeting or the director must take reasonable steps to secure that the notice is brought up and read at the next directors' meeting after the notice is given. All the provisions of Section 317 relating to contracts also apply to transactions and arrangements (whether or not they constitute a contract). A director is deemed to be interested in a transaction or arrangement of the kind described in Section 330 (*see* 5.8 below) between the company and the director or between the company and a person connected with the director. This is the case even if the transaction or arrangement is prohibited by Section 330.

---

[6] [1988] 1 WLR 863.

Section 317(9) makes it clear that the director's obligation to disclose interests to the board does not alter the general law, which prevents a director voting on any matter in which they are interested, or receiving any benefit unless they have the informed consent of shareholders. A company's articles of association ("the articles") often contain a provision allowing a director to vote or receive a benefit provided the director has met his obligations under Section 317 (e.g. Regulations 85 and 86 of Table A Statutory Instrument 1985/805).

The Section also applies to shadow directors (Section 317(8)). "Shadow director" is defined in Section 741(2) as any person in accordance with whose directions or instructions the directors of the company are accustomed to act. However, there is an exception for someone who gives advice in a professional capacity, such as a solicitor or accountant, provided the only reason that person would be treated as a shadow director is because of that advice. There is another exception for the purposes of some Sections in the Companies Act 1985 (including Sections 320 to 322 and Sections 330 to 346). Under this exception a body corporate is not treated as a shadow director of any of its subsidiaries only because the directors of the subsidiary are accustomed to act in accordance with the holding company's directions or instructions.

Shadow directors can only declare their interests in a contract by a notice in writing to the directors. This notice must be given before the date of the meeting at which a declaration would have had to be made if the shadow director were a director. Alternatively a shadow director can give a general notice. However, a shadow director does not have to take steps to secure that the notice is brought up and read at the next directors' meeting. Where a notice is given, the shadow director is deemed to have declared his interests at the meeting at which the contract is first considered or, as appropriate, at the first board meeting after the notice is given. The making of the declaration is deemed to form part of the proceedings of the meeting (Section 382(3)).

The director's duty is not merely to disclose that he has an interest: he must disclose "the nature of his interest". His declaration must make his colleagues "fully informed of the real state of things" (*see Imperial Mercantile Credit Assn v Coleman*[7]). The fact that the interest is the same as other employees' or that it is an interest in another group company does not

---

[7] [1873] LR 6 (HL) 189 at 201 per Lord Chelmsford.

mean that it does not have to be disclosed. The Section even requires disclosure of interests which the director does not know about, and disclosure of interests which the board already knows about (although *see* the *Runciman* case referred to below).

Section 317 has been held to apply even where a company has only one director. In *Neptune (Vehicle Washing Equipment) Ltd v Fitzgerald*[8] Lightman J held that a sole director must make a declaration to himself and must allow a statutory pause for thought, although the declaration does not have to be out loud unless the meeting is attended by someone else (e.g. the company secretary). The declaration must be recorded in the minutes. Lightman J also thought that the obligation to disclose an interest at a directors' meeting applied even where a contract had been (or was proposed to be) entered into without being considered or approved at a directors' meeting.

If a director fails to comply with Section 317 this does not make the contract in which the director is interested unenforceable. In *Hely Hutchinson v Brayhead*[9] Lord Pearson said that the Section merely created a statutory duty of disclosure and imposed a fine for non-compliance. This approach was approved, obiter, in *Guinness Plc v Saunders*.[10] Harman J also took this view in *Lee Panavision Ltd v Lee Lighting Ltd*,[11] concluding that remarks by Lord Templeman in the *Hely Hutchinson* case that suggested a contract was voidable where there was a breach of contract were incorrect.

In *Craven Textile Engineers Limited v Batley Football Club Limited*[12] the Court of Appeal held that the court did not have a general discretion to do what seemed "fair and just" if a director was in breach of Section 317. In that case, a director claimed payment for work done and goods supplied to the company. He had failed to disclose his interest in the contract to the company. The Court of Appeal said it was impossible to restore the parties to their original positions and so rescission of the contract was not possible. The director was entitled to payment of his invoices notwithstanding the breach of Section 317.

---

[8] [1995] 1 BCLC 352.
[9] [1968] 1 QB 549.
[10] [1990] 2 AC 633.
[11] [1991] BCC 620.
[12] 7 July 2000 (unreported).

In *Runciman* v *Walter Runciman plc*,[13] a question arose as to the position where a director failed to disclose an interest in a contract and a variation to that contract, but all the affected parties were aware of the director's interest in the contract. In that case, the director failed to disclose his interest in his own service contract in accordance with Section 199 Companies Act 1948 (now Section 317). The director was wrongfully dismissed. The company conceded the claim but argued it was not bound by the contract because of the breach of Section 199. Simon Brown J held that there was no suggestion that the director or his fellow directors had abused their position. Even if the Section had not been complied with, the contract was not automatically invalid. The decision in this case was that the balance of justice did not require a "technical breach" of the Section to render the variation unenforceable. This case shows that the courts are not necessarily sympathetic to companies seeking to avoid obligations as a result of a technical breach of Section 317. However, it may not be safe to assume the case means a company cannot ever avoid a contract where an interest has not been properly disclosed.

5.5 Contracts with directors who are sole members

If a private company which has only one member enters into a contract with that member, there are particular requirements that the company must follow if the sole member is a director or shadow director of the company (*see* Section 322B). Section 322B applies to private companies limited by shares or by guarantee, but not to unlimited or public companies. It does not apply to contracts entered into in the ordinary course of the company's business. There is no case law on what is the ordinary course of business in the context of Section 322B. However, in other contexts it has been held to mean "part of the undistinguished common flow of business done . . . calling for no remark and arising out of no special or particular situation" (*Broome* v *Speak*[14]). The question will be one of fact which will depend on what the company does.

Unless the contract is in writing (in which case, the company need do nothing more), the company must ensure that the terms of the contract are either set out in a written memorandum or are recorded in the minutes of the first meeting of the directors of the company after the contract is made (*see* Section 322B(1)). If the company fails to meet this

---

[13] [1992] BCLC 1085.
[14] [1903] 1 Ch 586.

requirement, the company and every officer who is in default is liable to a fine (*see* Section 322B(4)), but the validity of the contract is not affected (*see* Section 322B(6)). These requirements are in addition to any other statutory or other requirement which may apply to the contract (*see* Section 322B(5)).

5.6 Substantial property transactions involving directors

Companies are prohibited from entering into certain transactions to transfer non-cash assets above a certain value to or from directors (or people connected with them) unless certain approvals have first been obtained. Section 320 applies to transfers to a director of the company or to a director of any holding company of the company or to any person connected with such a director. Shadow directors are treated as directors for the purposes of the Section (Section 320(3)).

"Non-cash asset" is defined in Section 739(1) as "any property or interest in property other than cash". For this purpose, cash includes foreign currency. Section 739(2) extends the meaning of transfer or acquisition of a non-cash asset to include creating or extinguishing an estate or interest in any property or a right over property. It also includes the discharge of any person's liability other than a liability for a liquidated sum.

In *Re Duckwari plc (No. 1)*,[15] a company acquired either the benefit of a contract or a beneficial interest in the property which was the subject of the contract. The Court of Appeal held that the asset acquired was a non-cash asset for the purpose of Section 739(2). However, where a company discharges its own liability for damages for breach of a director's service contract, it does not have to obtain prior approval under Section 320.[16] Also, Section 320 does not apply to covenanted payments under a director's service agreement.[17] In *Mercer v Heart of Midlothian Plc* Lord Macfadyen thought it was "questionable" whether the benefits received by the former director (including seats in the director's box at Tynecastle Stadium on match days, access to the boardroom and a car park pass) amounted to a non-cash asset as they were a personal right against Heart of Midlothian rather than a right over property.

---

[15] [1997] 2 BCLC 713.
[16] *See Gooding v Cater* (unreported) 13 March 1989 Chancery Division.
[17] *See Lander v Premier Pict Petroleum Ltd* 1997 SLT 1361.

Transfers of non-cash assets only need to be approved if the value of the asset exceeds £100,000 or (if less) it exceeds 10 per cent of the company's asset value (although transfers of assets valued at less than £2,000 do not need to be approved). The company's asset value is determined by reference to the accounts prepared and laid under Part VII Companies Act 1985 for the last preceding financial year in respect of which accounts were laid. Where no accounts have been laid before the arrangement is entered into, the company's asset value is treated as being the amount of the company's called-up share capital. The non-cash asset must be valued when the arrangement in question is entered into. In *Micro Leisure Ltd* v *County Properties and Developments Limited*,[18] the Scottish Court of Session held that the value of the asset can be the special value of the asset to the director and not the objective market value of the asset.

There are various exceptions from the requirement to obtain approval. Section 320 only applies to companies within the meaning of the Companies Acts (*see* Section 735). If the company is a wholly-owned subsidiary (as defined in Section 736(2)), no approval is needed wherever its holding company is incorporated (*see* Section 321(1)). No approval is needed for transfers between members of the same wholly-owned group: that is, from a holding company to a wholly-owned subsidiary or vice versa, or from one wholly-owned subsidiary to another wholly-owned subsidiary in the same group. This exception is necessary because the holding company may be a person connected with the director (*see* 5.12 below).

Approval is required if an arrangement is entered into when the company is in a members' voluntary winding up but not otherwise if the company is being wound up (Section 321(2)(b)). It is also required if administrative receivers enter into a transaction with a director or a connected person (*see Demite Limited* v *Protec Health Limited*[19]). Approval is not required if the director acquires the non-cash asset in his capacity as a member, for example where a director receives bonus shares in common with other members or shares under a scrip dividend arrangement. Finally, no approval is needed if the director or a connected person effects a transaction on a recognised Stock Exchange through an independent broker as defined in Section 321(4). Where approval is required, it must be obtained before the company enters into the relevant arrangement. The company cannot enter into a contract conditional upon

---

[18] *The Times* January 12, 2000.
[19] [1998] BCC 638.

obtaining shareholder approval (unlike the Listing Rule requirements). This can make it difficult for companies to structure deals.

Section 320(1) provides that where approval is needed the arrangement must be approved "by a resolution of the company in general meeting". This requirement has been held to be satisfied where all the shareholders of a company had unanimously agreed, at a meeting, to the transfer of company property to certain of those shareholders and directors, even though the meeting was described as a "board meeting" and no shareholders' resolution giving prior approval was passed.[20] If the arrangement is with a director of a holding company (or a connected person of such a director) it must also be approved "by a resolution in general meeting of the holding company".

The consequences of entering into an arrangement in breach of Section 320 are set out in Section 322. The company can avoid the arrangement and any transaction entered into in pursuance of the arrangement, unless one of a number of conditions has been satisfied. These are:

(a) that it is no longer possible to return the money or asset which was the subject of the arrangement or transaction;
(b) the company has been indemnified by some other person for the loss or damage it has suffered;
(c) a person who is not a party to the arrangement or transaction has acquired any rights bona fide for value and without actual notice that Section 320 had been breached, and those rights would be affected if the arrangement or transaction were avoided; or
(d) the company in general meeting affirms the arrangement within a reasonable period and, if the arrangement involves a transfer of an asset to or by a director of its holding company (or someone connected with that director), the arrangement is also affirmed by a resolution in general meeting of the holding company.

A transaction is not illegal just because Section 320 has been breached (see *Niltan Carson Ltd* v *Hawthorne*).[21] Also the transaction is not void *ab initio*. However, directors (both the director who enters into the arrangement or transaction and the directors who authorise it) and connected persons of the director who enter into the transaction or arrangement are

---

[20] See *In the Matter of Conegrade Limited* (unreported), 4 November 2002 Chancery Division.
[21] [1988] BCLC 298, 322.

liable to account to the company for any direct or indirect gains made as a result and to indemnify the company for any resulting loss or damage (Section 322(3)). The liability to indemnify is a joint and several liability with anyone else who is liable under Section 322. The liability arises whether or not the company avoids the arrangement or transaction and is in addition to any other liability. However, a director can avoid liability for an arrangement between the company and a person connected with him if he can show that he took "all reasonable steps" to secure the company's compliance with Section 320. A person connected with a director and a director who authorised the arrangement or transaction can avoid liability if he can show that he did not know the relevant circumstances constituting the contravention when the relevant arrangement was entered into. In *Duckwari plc* v *Offerventure Ltd*,[22] it was held that the liability to indemnify the company extends to a decline in the market value of an asset after it has been acquired.

5.7 Transactions with related parties

Companies whose securities are listed by the UK Listing Authority ("UKLA") and are therefore subject to the Listing Rules are also subject to restrictions on transactions between the listed company or any of its subsidiary undertakings and certain group directors or an associate of such a director. Under Chapter 11 of the Listing Rules, if a listed company (or any of its subsidiary undertakings as defined in Section 258 Companies Act 1985) wishes to enter into a transaction with a director or his associate, broadly speaking it must meet certain disclosure requirements and obtain shareholder approval for the transaction, unless an exception applies. The company must ensure that the director does not vote on the resolution to approve the transaction and that the director takes all reasonable steps to ensure his associates do not vote. The requirements do not apply to transactions of a revenue nature in the ordinary course of business or to listed companies who do not have listed equity shares or listed securities convertible into equity shares. However, they do extend to any arrangements under which the listed company or any of its subsidiary undertakings and the director or his associate each invest in, or provide finance to, another undertaking or asset.

The directors who are subject to the Listing Rules requirements are the directors and shadow directors of the company, any of its subsidiary

---

[22] *The Times* May 18, 1998.

undertakings, any parent undertaking or any subsidiary undertaking of a parent undertaking (*see* Section 258). Anyone who was a director of a group company in the 12 months before the date of the transaction is also caught by the requirements. "Associate" is widely defined to mean:

(a) that individual's spouse or child under the age of 18 (who together are referred to as "the individual's family");
(b) the trustees (acting as such) of any trust of which the individual or any of the individual's family is a beneficiary or discretionary object. There are exceptions for a trust which is an occupational pension scheme, as defined in Regulation 3 of The Financial Services and Markets Act 2000 (Regulated Activities) Order 2001, or an employees' share scheme provided, in each case, the trust does not have the effect of conferring benefits on persons all or most of whom are related parties;
(c) any company if the individual or any member or members (taken together) of the individual's family, or the individual and any such member or members (taken together), are directly or indirectly interested in the company's equity shares (or have a conditional or contingent entitlement to become interested) so that they are (or would be if the condition were met or the contingent interest became an interest) able:
  (i) to exercise or control the exercise of 30 per cent or more of the votes able to be cast at general meetings on all, or substantially all, matters, or
  (ii) to appoint or remove directors holding a majority of voting rights at board meetings on all, or substantially all, matters.

For the purpose of (c), where more than one director of the listed company, its parent undertaking or any of its subsidiary undertakings is interested in the equity shares of another company, then the interests of those directors and their associates will be aggregated when determining whether that company is an associate of the director. If a listed company (or any of its subsidiary undertakings) proposes to enter into a transaction which might be a related party transaction, the company must consult the UKLA at an early stage. The draft contract must be provided to the UKLA if it so requests.

The usual requirement is that the company must make an announcement if it would otherwise be required to do so by Chapter 10 of the Listing Rules. That Chapter contains separate rules dealing with transactions by listed companies where the requirements depend upon the size of the transaction. Where an announcement is required, it must include certain details including the name of the related party (i.e. the director or associate) and details of the nature and extent of the related party's interest in the transaction. The listed company must send a circular to shareholders containing certain prescribed information (*see* paragraph 11.10 of the Listing Rules). This includes full particulars of the transaction together with the related party's name and the nature and extent of his interest in the transaction. Where an asset is being acquired or disposed of under a "related party" transaction which would have to be approved by shareholders because it is a Class 1 transaction for the purpose of Chapter 10 of the Listing Rules, there must be an independent valuation of the asset if "appropriate" financial information is not available. The directors of the listed company must state in the circular that the transaction is fair and reasonable as far as the shareholders of the company are concerned, and that the directors have been advised that this is the case by an independent adviser acceptable to the UKLA. The director who is a party to the related transaction (or whose associate is a party to the related transaction) does not have to make this statement.

If a company (or any of its subsidiary undertakings) varies or novates an existing agreement with a director or associate, the variation or novation is caught whether or not the original agreement was made when the director or associate was a related party. There are various exceptions to the requirements, which are set out in paragraph 11.7 of the Listing Rules. These include:

(a) exceptions for certain benefits in accordance with the terms of an employees' share scheme or a long-term incentive scheme;

(b) granting credit on normal commercial terms or of an amount and on terms no more favourable than those offered generally to group employees;

(c) granting an indemnity to a director to the extent not prohibited by Section 310 or maintaining an insurance contract for a director to the extent allowed by that Section;

(d) small transactions – this is defined by reference to various percentage ratios used for classifying transactions. Where all of these do not exceed 0.25 per cent the exception applies. If one or more ratio exceeds 0.25 per cent but is less than 5 per cent, the UKLA will allow the company not to seek shareholder approval provided the company provides the UKLA with written details of the proposed transaction and provides a written confirmation from an independent adviser acceptable to the UKLA that the proposed terms are fair and reasonable as far as the company's shareholders are

Fair Dealing and Connected Persons

concerned. The company must undertake to include details of the transaction in its next published annual accounts. These details must include, where relevant, the identity of the related party, the value of the consideration for the transaction and all other relevant circumstances. If a company enters into more than one related party transaction with the same director (or any of his associates) in a 12-month period, the transactions must be aggregated unless a transaction has been approved by shareholders. If the transactions in aggregate would be treated as a Class 2 or Class 1 transaction, the UKLA may require the company to follow the usual requirements for the latest transaction and give details of all the transactions being aggregated in the circular to shareholders;

(e) where the related party is (or was within the 12 months preceding the transaction) a director (or shadow director) of an insignificant subsidiary or is (or was within the 12 months preceding the transaction) a substantial shareholder in an insignificant subsidiary. This is a subsidiary undertaking which has contributed less than 10 per cent of the turnover or profit of the listed company and has represented less than 10 per cent of the assets of the listed company in each of the three financial years preceding the date of the transaction for which accounts have been published. In exceptional circumstances, the UKLA may agree a shorter period than three years. It is not possible to average out the turnover, profits and assets tests over the three-year period (although the UKLA does have a discretion as to how it applies its rules).

Where the transaction involves property or an unlisted property company, an investment entity or a venture capital trust, there are other Listing Rule requirements which may also be relevant.

If a director of a listed company is knowingly concerned in a breach of the Listing Rule requirements, the UKLA can impose a fine on him or publish a statement censuring the director.

5.8 Loans to directors and related transactions

5.8.1 *Loans*

Subject to various exceptions, companies are prohibited from making loans to directors and persons connected with them and entering into similar transactions. The provisions are very detailed and quite complex; they contain various anti-avoidance provisions. The requirements vary

A Practitioner's Guide to Directors' Duties and Responsibilities

depending, broadly, on whether or not there is a public company in the company's group.

The basic prohibition (*see* Section 330(2) applies to all companies. A company must not:

(a) make a loan to a director or to a director of its holding company; or
(b) enter into a guarantee (which includes an indemnity – *see* Section 331(2)) or provide any security in connection with a loan made by anyone to a director of the company or its holding company).

For the purposes of Sections 330 to 346 a director includes a shadow director (*see* Section 330(5)) but, for these purposes, a body corporate is not treated as a shadow director of any of its subsidiaries only because the directors of the subsidiary are accustomed to act in accordance with the holding company's directions or instructions (*see* Section 741(3)). It appears from the Section that it does not matter whether the director is entering into the loan in another capacity, for example as a trustee of an employee share trust.

A "loan" is not defined. Generally, this involves a payment of money to or for someone on condition that it will be repaid in money or money's worth. It is not essential for interest to be paid on the money lent. In *Currencies Direct Limited* v *Peter Simon Ellis*[23] there was a dispute as to whether moneys paid by the company to a director were a loan or remuneration for work and services. At first instance Gage J found, on the facts, that most amounts were remuneration but that some amounts were loans. In the case of the amounts which were loans there was an express written acceptance by the director of his liability to pay the sum on demand whereas there was no evidence that the other amounts were paid to the director as advances, subject to an express or implied term that they be repaid. The Court of Appeal upheld this approach. *In the Matter of Ciro Citterio Menswear PLC sub nom (1) Ciro Citterio Menswear PLC (in Administration) (2) Johal (3) Freakley* v *Thakrar and Others*[24] the Court found that there was a loan of company funds where it was only evidenced by a debit entry in the company's computerised nominal ledger. The case considered an arrangement between the directors of the

---

[23] [2002] EWCA Civ 779.
[24] *See In the Matter of Ciro Citterio Menswear PLC sub nom (1) Ciro Citterio Menswear PLC (in Administration) (2) Johal (3) Freakley* v *Thakrar and Others* [2002] All ER 717.

company to make unused credit balances on the directors' accounts available to other directors. However, on the facts, the Court held that the arrangements between the directors had not created a loan by the directors in favour of the director in question. It was the company which had partly funded the transfer of property. Agreeing to make money available probably does not, of itself, amount to making a loan until the money is actually advanced. In *Champagne Perrier – Jouet SA v Finch*[25] the court held that a company which had paid a director's bills and supplied goods to a company he controlled, on credit, had not made a loan to him. However, such an arrangement would fall within the definition of a quasi-loan (*see* 5.8.2 below). Providing security is also not defined. However, it seems fairly clear that the Section would catch a situation, for example, where a bank or other third party lends money to a director and the company enters into an agreement where, if the loan or interest is not repaid, the lender has rights against some or all of the company's assets or undertaking to recover the amount not paid.

Companies which are part of a group which includes a public company are subject to further restrictions. Such companies are called "relevant companies". A relevant company is defined in Section 331(6) as a company which:

(a) is a public company;
(b) is a subsidiary of a public company;
(c) is a subsidiary of a company which has a public company as another of its subsidiaries; or
(d) has a subsidiary which is a public company.

5.8.2 *Quasi-loans*

A relevant company cannot:

(a) make a quasi-loan to a director of the company or a director of its holding company or to a person connected with such a director;
(b) enter into a guarantee or provide any security in connection with a quasi-loan or loan made by anyone for such a director or a person connected with him (*see* Section 330(3)).

Also, it must not make a loan to a person connected with such a director.

---

[25] [1982] 1 WLR 1359.

A quasi-loan is defined in Section 331(3). It is a transaction under which one party (the creditor) agrees to pay a sum for another (the borrower) or in fact pays a sum for the borrower other than under an agreement. It also includes situations where the creditor agrees to reimburse expenditure incurred by a third party for the borrower or in fact reimburses such expenditure other than under an agreement. The terms of the transaction must include that the borrower (or a person on his behalf) will reimburse the creditor or that the borrower incurs a liability to reimburse the creditor. Examples of quasi-loans include a relevant company paying for goods on behalf of a director, even if the director subsequently reimburses the company, and a relevant company allowing a director to use a company credit card for private expenditure.

5.8.3 Credit transactions

A relevant company is also prohibited from entering into a credit transaction as a creditor for a director or a director of its holding company or a person connected with such a director (*see* Section 330(4)(a)). Also, it cannot enter into any guarantee or provide any security in connection with a credit transaction made by anyone for such a director or a person connected with him (*see* Section 330 (4)(b)). Credit transaction is defined in Section 331(7). It is a transaction under which one party (the creditor):

(a) supplies any goods or sells any land under a hire-purchase agreement or a conditional sale agreement (defined in the Consumer Credit Act 1974 – *see* Section 331(10) and Section 744 Companies Act 1985); or
(b) leases or hires any land or goods in return for periodical payments.

It also includes transactions where the creditor otherwise disposes of land or supplies goods or services on the understanding that payment is to be deferred. For this purpose, services means anything other than land or goods, and it does not matter whether payment is made in a lump sum, instalments, periodical payments or in any other way.

5.8.4 Transactions or arrangements on behalf of another

Section 331(9) sets out when a transaction or arrangement is made "for" a person. In the case of a loan or a quasi-loan, it is made for him if it is made to him. In the case of a credit transaction, it is made for him if he is the person to whom goods or services are supplied or the land is sold or otherwise disposed of under the transaction. A guarantee or security is made for a person if it is entered into or provided in connection with

Fair Dealing and Connected Persons

a loan or quasi-loan made to him or a credit transaction made for him. In the case of any other transaction or arrangement for the supply or transfer of goods, land or services (or the supply or transfer of any interest in goods, land or services), it is made for him if he is the person to whom the goods, land, services (or interest in them) is supplied or transferred.

5.8.5 Anti-avoidance provisions

Section 330(6) and (7) contains some anti-avoidance provisions which are relevant to the transactions and arrangements which are prohibited for both private companies and relevant companies. Section 330(6) prohibits a company from assuming any rights, obligations or liabilities under a transaction which it would have been prevented from entering into itself under Section 330. So, for example, a private company cannot take an assignment of a loan made by a third party to one of its directors and a relevant company cannot assume obligations under a guarantee made in connection with a quasi-loan to a person connected with one of its directors or a director of one of its holding companies. In such cases, the transaction is treated as being entered into on the date the arrangement is made for the company to assume the rights, liabilities or obligations. This is relevant when looking at some of the exceptions dealt with below.

Section 330(7) deals with more complicated avoidance techniques. It prohibits a company taking part in any arrangement under which someone else (A) enters into a transaction which the company itself would have been prohibited from entering into by Section 330 and that person (A) has obtained any benefit or is to obtain a benefit under the arrangement. It does not matter whether it is the company, one of its subsidiaries or holding companies or a subsidiary of any of the company's holding companies which provides the benefit. This Section would stop a company entering into a "back-to-back" arrangement with a totally unconnected company to make loans to that company's directors in return for that company making loans to its directors or directors of its holding company. It would also stop an arrangement under which a third party provides a guarantee or security for a loan to a company's director under an arrangement for another group company to place business with that third party.

"Arrangement" is not defined (in contrast, for example, to Section 204(5) and (6) Companies Act 1985). Arguably it is intended to catch something which is not a legally binding agreement, although the Law Commission has said that it is thought it must be legally enforceable and refers to *Re*

British Basic Slag Ltd's Application[26] (*see* paragraph 6.11 of Law Commission Consultation Paper No. 153). In the parliamentary debates on what is now Section 330(7) the Government stated that the Section was intended to apply only where the benefit provided by the company or another group company was the quid pro quo for the transaction entered into by the third party. This makes it clear that if there is a usual course of dealing between the company and the third party, unconnected to the transaction between the third party and the director, this is not prohibited by the Section. According to the parliamentary debates the burden of proof of an arrangement is on the person who alleges it exists.

5.8.6 Exceptions to the prohibitions

Given the breadth of the prohibitions in Section 330, it is not surprising that there are a large number of exceptions to the prohibitions. Some of the exceptions apply to all companies, while others are only appropriate to relevant companies. The exceptions are as follows.

5.8.6.1 Short-term quasi-loan

Relevant companies are not prohibited from making short-term quasi-loans to their directors or directors of their holding companies provided two conditions are met (*see* Section 332). The first condition is that the quasi-loan must contain a term requiring the director (or a person on the director's behalf) to reimburse the company's expenditure within two months of its being incurred. The second condition is that the aggregate amount of the quasi-loan and the amount outstanding under any other relevant quasi-loan does not exceed £5,000. A quasi-loan is a relevant quasi-loan for this purpose if the loan was made to the director by the company or any of its subsidiaries or, where the quasi-loan is being made to a director of a holding company, if the loan is made by any subsidiary of that holding company. The amount outstanding is the amount of the outstanding liabilities of the director to whom the quasi-loan was made. This test is different from the relevant amount test in Section 339 which is used for other exceptions.

The exception only applies to quasi-loans and not to guarantees or security. It also does not apply where the quasi-loan is made to a person connected with a director. However, where the exception does apply, Sections 330(6) and (7) will not be relevant. Because of the relatively small amount and the short time period set out in the exception, it is likely to

---

[26] [1963] 1 WLR 727.

Fair Dealing and Connected Persons

be useful mainly where a relevant company provides a credit card for a director.

5.8.6.2 Intra-group loans
Because the provisions of Section 330(3) are widely drawn, they could prohibit one company in a group making a loan or quasi-loan to another company in the same group or entering into a guarantee or providing security in connection with a loan or quasi-loan by a third party to another group member. This could arise because a director of one group company is associated with another group company – for example, because the director holds 20 per cent of its equity share capital (*see* 5.12 below). If the only reason the company is prohibited from making the loan is because a director is associated with the other group company, the prohibition in Section 330(3)(b) and (c) does not apply (*see* Section 333). The exception does not extend to credit transactions. Where the exception does apply, the anti-avoidance provisions of Section 330(6) and (7) will not be relevant. However loans and quasi-loans by a company to its holding company, credit transactions for a holding company, and guarantees and security in connection with a credit transaction for a holding company may be exempt under Section 336 (*see* 5.8.6.4 below).

5.8.6.3 Small loans
A company can make a loan to a director or a director of its holding company if the aggregate of the "relevant amounts" is £5,000 or less (*see* Section 334). Section 339 sets out how the relevant amount is determined (*see* 5.9 below). The idea of the relevant amount concept is to aggregate certain transactions, so that the exception cannot be used as a way of avoiding the basic prohibition – for example, by having a number of group companies making small loans to a director. This exception does not allow a company to guarantee loans of £5,000 or less or give indemnities or provide security for such loans, but it does mean that the anti-avoidance provisions in Sections 330(6) and (7) do not apply where the exception applies.

5.8.6.4 Minor/business transactions
A relevant company can enter into a credit transaction or enter into a guarantee or provide security in connection with a credit transaction which would otherwise be prohibited by Section 330(4) if the aggregate of the relevant amounts is £10,000 or less (*see* Section 335(1)). Again, Section 339 sets out how to determine the relevant amounts. Where the exception applies, the anti-avoidance provisions in Sections 330(6) and (7) do not apply (*see* Section 330(1)) . If the relevant amounts are £10,000 or more, the exception can still apply if:

(a) the company enters into the transaction in the ordinary course of its business; and
(b) the value of the transaction is no greater than the value it is reasonable to expect the company to have offered to someone unconnected with the company and of the same financial standing, and the terms of the transaction are no more favourable than it is reasonable to expect the company to have offered to such a person (*see* Section 335(2)).

5.8.6.5 *Transactions for holding companies*

Section 336 provides a helpful exception for loans and other transactions by a company to or for one of its holding companies. It allows a company to make a loan or quasi-loan to a holding company and allows it to enter into a guarantee or provide security in connection with a loan or quasi-loan made to its holding company. It also allows a company to enter into a credit transaction for its holding company or enter into a guarantee or provide security for a credit transaction between a third party and its holding company. When the exception applies, the anti-avoidance provisions in Section 330(6) and (7) do not apply.

5.8.6.6 *Funding directors' expenditure*

Difficult questions can arise as to whether a company makes a loan to a director if it advances money to him to allow him to meet his business expenses. Although the better view is probably that normally there is not a loan to the director where money is provided in advance to meet expenses, it may be harder to reach this view if, for example, a director is advanced a large amount for a long period and can use this to meet personal expenditure, even if he subsequently repays his personal expenditure and any unused amounts. Section 337 provides an exception from the prohibitions in Section 330 as long as certain conditions are met. Where the conditions are met, the company can do anything to provide a director with funds to meet expenditure he has incurred or will incur or to enable the director to avoid incurring such expenditure. This means, for example, that the company can arrange for goods or services to be available to the director so that he does not have to arrange and pay for these himself. The conditions are as follows:

(a) the company must provide the director with funds to meet expenditure he has already incurred or is to incur;
(b) the expenditure must be incurred "for the purposes of the company" or "for the purpose of enabling him to perform his duties

as an officer of the company". Following *Brady v Brady*,[27] there is a risk that the courts would adopt a narrow construction of what "for the purposes of the company" means;

(c) either the company in general meeting must approve the company's proposed action, or it is a condition that the loan will be repaid or any other liability arising under the transaction will be discharged within six months of the next annual general meeting unless the action taken is approved at or before that annual general meeting;

(d) certain prescribed disclosures must be made at the general meeting (as set out below);

(e) if the company is a relevant company, the aggregate of the relevant amounts (calculated in accordance with Section 339) must not exceed £20,000.

The disclosures referred to in (d) above are:

(a) the purpose of the expenditure incurred, or to be incurred, or which would otherwise be incurred, by the director;

(b) the amount of the funds the company is to provide; and

(c) the extent of the company's liability under any transaction which is, or is connected with, the proposed action.

If the company uses a written resolution under Section 381A to give an approval under Section 337(3)(a), these matters must be disclosed to each relevant member no later than the time he is given the written resolution to sign (*see* paragraph 8 of Schedule 15A to the Companies Act 1985). In practice, this exception is not widely used, possibly because the disclosure requirements make it unattractive.

5.8.6.7 *Money-lending companies*

Section 338 provides an exception from the prohibitions in Section 330 for "money-lending companies". A money-lending company is a company whose ordinary business includes making loans or quasi-loans or giving guarantees or indemnities in connection with loans or quasi-loans. Provided certain conditions are met, a money-lending company can make a loan or quasi-loan to anyone or enter into a guarantee or indemnity in connection with a loan or quasi-loan without breaching Section 330. The exception does not, however, extend to credit transactions or providing security. Where the conditions are met, the anti-avoidance provisions in

---

[27] [1989] AC 755.

A Practitioner's Guide to Directors' Duties and Responsibilities

Section 330(6) and (7) do not apply in relation to loans, quasi-loans, guarantees or indemnities. The conditions are as follows:

(a) the company must make the loan or quasi-loan or give the guarantee or indemnity in the ordinary course of its business;
(b) the terms of the loan, quasi-loan, guarantee or indemnity must not be any more favourable than the company could reasonably be expected to have offered to a person of the same financial standing who was unconnected with the company and the amount lent or guaranteed must not be greater than could reasonably have been expected to be offered to such a person;
(c) if the company is a relevant company, the aggregate of the relevant amounts (calculated in accordance with Section 339) must not exceed £100,000 unless the relevant company is a banking company. "Banking company" is defined in Section 744 as a company authorised under the Banking Act 1987.

The Section does not define what constitutes the "ordinary course of the company's business". It is generally thought that this means that the loan or guarantee must be consistent with the normal course of the company's business and of a kind and on a scale normal for the company. It does not matter that the company's normal practice differs from the normal practice of other similar companies.[28] A decision as to whether the conditions are met in any case will therefore involve some research into the company's usual approach. In calculating whether a relevant company will exceed the £100,000 limit a company will be deemed not to be connected with a director unless the director controls it (*see* 5.12 below as to when this will be the case).

There are special provisions which allow money-lending companies to give house purchase loans to their directors or a director of one of their holding companies on favourable terms or for a larger amount than would normally be the case (*see* Section 338(6)). The conditions to be satisfied are:

(a) the loan must be made to facilitate the purchase or improvement of all or part of any dwelling-house together with land occupied and enjoyed with that house or to replace a loan made by a third party which meets these requirements;

---

[28] *See Steen* v *Law* [1964] AC 303 and, in contrast, *Countrywide Banking Corporation Ltd* v *Dean* [1998] 2 WLR 441.

Fair Dealing and Connected Persons

(b) the house must be the director's only or main residence;
(c) the company ordinarily makes loans to its employees on terms no less favourable than those on which the loan to the director is made; and
(d) the aggregate of the relevant amounts (calculated in accordance with Section 339) does not exceed £100,000.

The exception does not allow a money-lending company to enter into a quasi-loan or guarantee or indemnity even if the conditions are met. The conditions mean that a company can lend a director a larger amount than it would lend to a comparable third party provided the terms of the loan are no better than are ordinarily made available to the company's employees. Note that the company must, in fact, ordinarily make loans to its employees for the exception to apply. However, the amount must not be so large as to fall outside the company's ordinary course of business.

5.9 Relevant amounts

Sections 339 and 340 set out how "relevant amounts" are to be calculated for the purpose of the various exceptions from Section 330. To calculate the relevant amount, the company must first identify all the transactions for the director or for one of his connected persons which the company or one of its subsidiaries has entered into relying on the particular exception it proposes to rely on for the proposed transaction or arrangement. So, for example, if the company proposes to rely on the exception in Section 334 for loans up to £5,000 to make a loan to a director it must identify any other loans under £5,000 that it has already made to the director or a connected person and any such loans made by a subsidiary. It must also identify any existing arrangement which falls within Section 330(6) or (7) which the company or a subsidiary entered into for the director or a connected person, relying on the relevant exception. If the proposed transaction or arrangement is to be made for a director of a holding company or a connected person, the company must identify all the transactions for that director or a connected person entered into by the holding company or any of its subsidiaries. If any of the earlier transactions were made by a company which was a subsidiary when the transaction was made but is no longer a subsidiary when the relevant amount is being calculated, those transactions can be ignored.

If the proposed transaction is a loan for a house purchase which will fall within the exception in Section 338(6), the company only has to identify transactions that it or another group company has entered into in reliance on the Section 338(6) exception when calculating whether the £100,000 limit is exceeded.

Once all of the relevant transactions or arrangements have been identified, the value of each must be determined in accordance with Section 340 and aggregated with the value of the proposed transaction or arrangement to see if the limit for the proposed transaction is exceeded. For loans, the value is the amount of its principal less any amount by which the principal has been reduced. Where a guarantee or security is to be given (or has been given) it is the amount guaranteed or secured. Where there is a Section 330(6) or (7) arrangement, the value is the value of the transaction to which the arrangement relates after deducting any reduction in the liabilities of the person for whom the arrangement was made. In any other case, the value is the price which could reasonably be expected to be obtained for the goods, land or services to which the transaction or arrangement relates if they had been supplied in the ordinary course of business and on the same terms (other than price) as the terms on which they were in fact supplied. If it is impossible to ascertain a monetary amount, the value is deemed to exceed £100,000, which means that the proposed transaction will not fall within any of the exemptions.

5.10 Remedies for breach of Section 330

There are both civil and criminal penalties if a company breaches Section 330. Under Section 341 a transaction or arrangement is voidable at the company's instance except in two cases. The first is where the money or asset which is the subject of the transaction or arrangement can no longer be restored, or the company has been indemnified for the loss or damage it suffers pursuant to Section 341(2)(b). The second case is where a third party has acquired any rights bona fide for value and without actual notice of the breach of Section 330 and those rights would be affected if the transaction or arrangement were avoided.

As the terms of Section 341 provide that a transaction made in contravention of Section 330 is voidable at the instance of the company (unless the provisions of Section 341(a) or Section 341(b) apply), it follows that neither Section 341 nor public policy prevent a company from recovering a loan made to a director in breach of Section 330.[29]

If a transaction or arrangement is made for a director of the company or a director of a holding company, the director incurs liabilities. If the

---

[29] *See Currencies Direct Limited* v *Peter Simon Ellis* [2002] EWCA Civ 779, Court of Appeal.

transaction or arrangement is made for a person connected with a director of the company or a holding company, both the person connected with the director and the director concerned are liable under Section 341, although the director can escape liability in this case if he shows that he took all reasonable steps to make sure the company complied with Section 330. In either case, any director of the company who authorised the transaction or arrangement is also liable and the liability is incurred even if the transaction or arrangement is avoided.

The liability in each case is twofold. First, it is to account to the company for any gain the director or connected person has made directly or indirectly by the transaction or arrangement. Second, it is to indemnify the company for any loss or damage which results from the transaction or arrangement. The liability to indemnify is a joint and several liability with anyone else liable under Section 341. The liability does not prejudice any other liability a director or person connected with a director may incur. It is a defence if a person connected with a director or a director who authorised the transaction or arrangement can show that he did not know the relevant circumstances which constituted the breach of Section 330 when the transaction or arrangement was entered into.

Criminal liability can be incurred only if the company entering into the transaction or arrangement is a relevant company. A director of a relevant company who authorises or permits a relevant company to enter into a transaction or arrangement in breach of Section 330 is guilty of an offence if he knows, or has reasonable cause to believe, that the company was breaching Section 330. The company itself is also guilty of an offence if it enters into a transaction or arrangement for a director or a director of one of its holding companies, unless it can show that it did not know "the relevant circumstances" when the transaction or arrangement was entered into. Criminal liability does not attach where the transaction or arrangement is for a person connected with a director. Anyone else who procures a relevant company to enter into a transaction or arrangement, knowing or having reasonable cause to believe it will breach Section 330, is also guilty of any offence. The penalty in each case is imprisonment or a fine or both.

In the case of *Ciro Citterio Menswear Plc*[30] the High Court held that in some cases breach of Section 330 could give rise to a constructive trust

---

[30] *See In the Matter of Ciro Citterio Menswear PLC sub nom (1) Ciro Citterio Menswear PLC (in Administration) (2) Johal (3) Freakley v Thakrar and Others* [2002] All ER 717.

even though neither Section 330 nor Section 341 mention this. However, in that case the High Court held that a constructive trust had not arisen. The director was not in breach of his fiduciary duties and there was no straightforward misappropriation of the company's property.

5.11 Liability for transactions involving directors

Directors, their connected persons and companies associated with them can incur liabilities where the board of directors exceed any limit on their powers under the company's constitution (Section 322(A)). For liability to be incurred there must be a transaction (which includes any act) between the company and:

(a) one of its directors;
(b) a director of any of its holding companies;
(c) a person connected with one of the directors or a director of a holding company; or
(d) a company associated with one of the directors or a director of a holding company.

References to a board of directors exceeding any limitation on their powers under the company's constitution include limits which arise as a result of a shareholders' resolution or any shareholders' agreement (*see* Section 322A(8)).

In such cases, any party to the transaction and any director of the company who authorised the transaction is liable to account to the company for any gain he has made directly or indirectly by the transaction and also to indemnify the company for any loss or damage resulting from the transaction. This is in addition to any other liability that the director or other person may have to the company (*see* Section 322A(4)). It does not matter whether the company avoids the transaction or not (*see* Section 322A(3)). It is a defence for a person other than a director of the company to show that he did not know that the directors were exceeding their powers when the transaction was entered into (*see* Section 322A(6)). The court also has a discretion (under Section 322A(7)) to affirm, sever or set aside a transaction on such terms as appear to it to be just if a transaction is voidable under Section 322A but is valid by virtue of Section 35A. Section 35A provides that, if a person deals with a company in good faith, any limitation under the company's constitution on the directors' powers to bind the company or authorise others to do so can be ignored. It is not a defence for a person to show that he did not know that a "connected person" or "associate company" was in fact connected or associated, even though it is often quite difficult to establish whether or not such connection or association exists.

In *Re Torvale Group Ltd*,[31] Torvale Group Limited granted three debentures. Two were granted to trustees of the Torvale Retirement Benefits Scheme and the third to Captain Hazelhurst, a director and major shareholder of the company. One of the five trustees was a director of the company when the debentures were granted to the trustees. The company had a provision in its articles which required the holders of preferred ordinary shares in the company to sanction the creation of any mortgage or charge by passing an extraordinary resolution at a separate class meeting of those shareholders. Administrative receivers of Torvale were appointed the year after the debentures were created. They could not find any record of any extraordinary resolution of the preferred ordinary shareholders or any other consent sanctioning the creation of the debentures and applied to the court for directions as to whether the debentures were voidable under Section 322A. The court found that this was a case which could have fallen within Section 322A(1), that is, that the requirement for a sanction was a limit on the board of directors' powers under the company's constitution. It decided further cross-examination of the witnesses was needed before a decision could be made about whether consent had, in fact, been given. However, on the facts, it found that even if the debentures granted to the trustees had been voidable it was appropriate to validate them under Section 322A(7) because four of the five trustees could have relied on Section 35A. The question of the validity of the debenture in favour of Captain Hazelhurst was stood over, pending further examination of the evidence.

5.12 Connected persons

Section 346 sets out when a person is connected with a director for the purposes of Part X of the Companies Act 1985. A person (A) is connected with a director of a company (B) if (but only if) A is:

(a) B's spouse, child under 18 or step-child under 18 (whether or not the child is legitimate);
(b) a body corporate with whom B is associated (*see* below) – but not "where the context otherwise requires". As explained below, in two

---

[31] [1999] (2) BCLC 605.

situations a body corporate associated with a director will not be treated as a connected person of that director;

(c) a person acting as a trustee of a trust if the beneficiaries of the trust include B, anyone in (a) above or a body corporate with which B is associated (*see* below) or if the trustees have a power under the trust that can be exercised for the benefit of any of those people or bodies. However, trustees acting as trustees of an employees' share scheme (as defined in Section 743) or as trustees of a pension scheme will not be connected with a director merely because he is a beneficiary or potential object of the trust;
(d) acting as B's partner or acting as a partner of anyone in (a), (b) or (c);
(e) a Scottish firm in which B is a partner;
(f) a Scottish firm, if one of the partners of that Scottish firm is connected with B as set out in (a), (b) or (c) above;
(g) a Scottish firm (X), if B is a partner in another Scottish firm which is a partner of X, or a person connected with B as set out in (a), (b) or (c) is a partner in another Scottish firm which is a partner of X.

Put more simply, (e), (f) and (g) mean that if a director is a partner in a Scottish firm, that Scottish firm and any other Scottish firm which the first firm is in partnership with are each connected with the director. Similarly, if a person connected with a director is a partner in a Scottish firm, that Scottish firm and any other Scottish firm which the first firm is in partnership with are each connected with that director.

Section 346(4) sets out when a director is associated with a body corporate. There are two situations where this is the case. The first is if the director and persons connected with him are together interested in at least 20 per cent of the nominal value of the equity share capital of the body corporate. Equity share capital means the issued share capital but not share capital which only has a limited right to participate in a distribution for both dividends and capital (*see* Section 744). So, for example, preference shares with a fixed right to a dividend and a right only to the return of a fixed amount of capital, such as the amount paid on subscription of the shares, and no further right to participate in any surplus would not be equity shares. The second case where a director is associated with a body corporate is where he and the persons connected with him are together entitled to exercise more than 20 per cent of the voting power at any general meeting of that body corporate or control the exercise of such voting power.

A director is deemed to control a body corporate if (but only if) he is interested in any part of that body's equity share capital (as defined in

Fair Dealing and Connected Persons

Section 744 – *see* above) or any person connected with him has such an interest and the director, his connected persons and any other directors of the relevant company together are interested in more than half of the equity share capital or can exercise (or control the exercise of) more than half the voting power at general meetings of the body corporate. If a director controls a body corporate (A) which can control the exercise of voting power at a general meeting of another body corporate (B), the director is treated as being able to exercise control over that voting power at B's general meetings (*see* Section 346(8)). When working out whether a director is associated with a body corporate or is deemed to control it, there are special rules where a person connected with a director is:

(a) a body corporate with which the director is associated; or
(b) a trustee.

In the first case the interests in shares or votes held by the body corporate are ignored unless the body corporate is also a connected person by virtue of being a trustee or a partner of the director or someone else connected with him (*see* Section 346(6)(a)). The interests of shares or votes held by a trustee of a trust are ignored provided the only reason the trustee would be treated as a connected person is because the beneficiaries of the trust include (or may include) a body corporate which is associated with the director (*see* Section 346(6)(b)).

As will be seen from the above, the definition of connected person is extremely wide and catches people and companies (including those incorporated overseas) which would not, ordinarily, be thought of as being connected with a director. The definition is further broadened by the rules set out in the Companies Act 1985 Part I of Schedule 13 which apply when determining whether a director is associated with a body corporate or is deemed to control a body corporate. Under this, any restrictions or restraints on the exercise of any right attached to an interest in shares are ignored, and a director will be treated as being interested in shares when he has agreed to buy them or has a right or obligation under which he can become entitled to exercise a right conferred by them (e.g. he has a call option or is subject to a put option). The provisions of Schedule 13 should be considered carefully in each case to see whether the director has an interest.

Most of those who responded to the Law Commission's Consultation Paper on Part X thought that the definition of "connected persons" caused difficulties in practice and should be amended. The Law

A Practitioner's Guide to Directors' Duties and Responsibilities

Commission thinks that they are justified in their concerns, particularly as to when a body corporate is treated as a connected person and the Company Law Review Steering Group agrees with this (*see* the Consultation Document on Modern Company Law published in March 2000).

Chapter 6

Service Contracts and Remuneration

John Farr, Partner
Herbert Smith

6.1 Introduction

This Chapter considers the legal issues relevant to directors' service contracts and remuneration and what may be considered best practice in this area. Proposed reforms relevant to this area of law are considered at 6.7.5.1–6.7.5.3 below.

The following issues are examined in the light of the Companies Act 1985 ("CA 1985"), the Combined Code issued by the Committee on Corporate Governance, the Listing Rules issued by the UK Listing Authority ("UKLA"), the City Code on Takeovers and Mergers ("the Takeover Code") issued by the Panel on Takeovers and Mergers, the Guidelines on Executive Remuneration published by the Association of British Insurers ("the ABI Guidelines") and relevant case law:

(a) authorisation by the board of the company's entry into service contracts with directors (and changes to their terms);
(b) limits on the length of the term of a director's service contract;
(c) disclosure of service contracts, both to shareholders and the wider public;
(d) remuneration of directors;
(e) other benefits accorded to directors, for example pension arrangements and share option schemes; and
(f) compensation payable to directors for loss of office.

6.2 Authorisation of service contracts – compliance with the company's constitution

Any service contract with a director must be authorised in accordance with the company's articles of association ("the articles"), within which the directors are legally required to act. The articles usually prescribe that vacancies may be filled or additional directors may be appointed by the board of directors (subject to the articles' maximum number of directors) and will state the quorum required in order for a board meeting to take place. In complying with the articles, the directors are under an overriding duty to act bona fide in the best interests of the company. The consequence of a failure to follow the articles is that any purported agreement will be void. These principles apply equally to any changes to the terms of directors' service contracts.

The cases of *Guinness PLC v Saunders*[1] and *Runciman v Walter Runciman plc*[2] illustrate the importance of the directors complying with the company's articles in deciding issues relating to directors' terms. Both cases also examine the nature of a director's duty under Section 317 CA 1985 to disclose personal interests in contracts entered into with the company (i.e. in this instance, the service contracts) and the directors' duty to act bona fide in the best interests of the company.

6.2.1 Guinness PLC *v* Saunders

In *Guinness PLC v Saunders* the issue was whether a committee of the board was properly authorised under the company's articles to agree that a director, Mr Ward (who was a member of that committee), would be entitled to a £5.2 million payment for his services in connection with the takeover bid made by Guinness of the Distillers Company Plc.

After the bid was complete and the payment made, Guinness claimed recovery of the payment on the basis that the payment had been received in breach of Mr Ward's fiduciary duty as a director in that he had not disclosed the payment as required under Section 317 CA 1985 or the company's articles. (It was assumed that Mr Ward had acted throughout in good faith and that he had in fact rendered valuable services to Guinness.) The House of Lords examined the issue of authority to enter into such arrangements in the light of Guinness' articles. The board had appointed the committee of directors to settle the terms of the offer for Distillers and take the necessary additional steps to implement the proposals. Guinness' articles provided that "special remuneration" was to be authorised only by the board, but the definitions section of the articles provided that "the board" included a committee authorised by

---

[1] [1990] 2 AC 663.
[2] [1992] BCLC 1084.

the board. The House of Lords considered, however, that this definition of "the board" did not apply in the context of the express provision requiring full board approval for special remuneration. For the same reason there was no basis for a payment to be due to Mr Ward on a quantum merit basis as there had been no implied contract to make such a payment unless the contract was entered into in accordance with the articles. The House of Lords emphasised that shareholders were entitled to compliance with the articles.

6.2.2 Runciman *v* Walter Runciman plc

In *Runciman* v *Walter Runciman plc* the High Court examined the position where the articles were silent as to how and when the board could determine issues relating to directors' service contracts, but merely stated that the board's approval was required.

Lord Runciman was executive chairman of the company and his notice period had been increased, by way of a letter from the company's deputy chairman, from the original three years in his service contract to five years. The increase had arisen at a time of a possible takeover where it was felt that two key executive directors might be tempted to move elsewhere and their notice periods were increased to five years to secure their loyalty. Three other directors' notice periods (including Lord Runciman's) were also increased to five years in line with this. The change to Lord Runciman's service contract had not been decided upon at a board meeting, nor even discussed at a board meeting, but had been implemented after a process of consultation. Lord Runciman was subsequently dismissed following a takeover (by a different bidder) and he claimed damages for wrongful dismissal on the basis that his contractual notice period was five years. The company argued that the increase to the notice period was not a legally binding agreement as it had not been properly authorised in accordance with the company's articles. The relevant article provided that the terms of an office holder were to be "as the directors may determine". The change to Lord Runciman's notice period had not been decided by the directors at a board meeting so the critical question was whether it was sufficient that the directors as a body, that is all of them, had decided that Lord Runciman's notice period should be increased. The court considered that if the directors had agreed the change, albeit informally, then the change was made in accordance with the articles in a situation where the articles were silent as to how the directors were to decide the issue. The crucial fact was that all the directors who would have been party to any formal resolution had been involved in the process and had therefore in effect participated in the eventual decision.

The court further considered that there had been no failure by the directors to act bona fide in the best interests of the company. The company argued that the only reason for amending the contract was that of symmetry within the board and that this was not a sufficient or proper purpose. The court rejected this and relied on the principle that it was for the directors to decide what was in the company's best interests – the court's only role was to decide whether a decision was made in good faith and with the correct motivation. The court further held that any failure by Lord Runciman to declare to the directors his interest in the new terms to his contract had been merely technical and did not breach Section 317 CA 1985 – to have disclosed his interest would have served no purpose and would have been "mere incantation".

Although the lack of a formal procedure in Runciman did not prove fatal, clearly it is not a course to be recommended. The board should formally approve service contracts and changes to their terms, strictly complying with Section 317 and the articles and after a proper consideration of the company's best interests. The minutes of the board meeting should confirm compliance with these formalities and a copy of the minutes, signed by the chairman of the meeting, should be kept as evidence that the proper procedure has been followed.

6.3 Limits on the length of the term of a service contract

6.3.1 Statutory limits – Section 319 CA 1985

Section 319 provides that in the absence of a shareholder resolution approving the term, a company cannot enter into a service contract (or a contract for services) for a period of more than five years with a director which cannot be terminated by the company by notice or which can only be terminated in specified circumstances. If a service contract contains such a term and there has been no shareholder approval, the term will be void and the service contract deemed to be terminable on reasonable notice.

6.3.2 The Combined Code

The Combined Code (paragraphs B.1.7–B.1.8) with regard to listed companies, states:

Service Contracts and Remuneration

"There is a strong case for setting notice or contract periods at, or reducing them to, one year or less. Boards should set this as an objective; but they should recognise that it may not be possible to achieve it immediately.

If it is necessary to offer longer notice or contract periods to new directors recruited from outside, such periods should reduce after the initial period."

6.3.3 *The ABI Guidelines on Executive Remuneration*

The Statement by the ABI and the National Association of Pension Funds ("the NAPF") regarding Best Practice on Executive Contracts and Severance ("the ABI/NAPF Statement") now forms part of the ABI's new Guidelines on Executive Remuneration. The ABI and NAPF state that the one-year notice period provided for under the Combined Code should not be seen as a floor, and remuneration committees should be prepared, where appropriate, to consider shorter periods. Equally, change-of-control clauses, giving rise to an entitlement exceeding one year's remuneration, should not normally be included. Only in exceptional circumstances, such as where a new chief executive is being recruited to a troubled company, will a longer notice period (or more generous change-of-control clause) applying during an initial period possibly be appropriate.

The ABI/NAPF Statement also suggests that if a director is dismissed following the use of a disciplinary procedure, the contract could provide for termination on a shorter notice period than otherwise. A further suggestion is that contracts should permit dismissal without notice in cases of serious financial failure, such as a very significant fall of the share price relative to the sector. This would require a specific clause to that effect in the contract.

6.3.4 *Current practice*

Recent practice indicates a trend towards shorter notice periods, well below the legal maximum of five years. An estimate given by the NAPF indicated that, in early 2003, of the top 350 UK listed companies, while 38 per cent had at least one executive director with a notice period of longer than 12 months, 98 per cent had pledged that all new executive director appointments would in future be made on the basis of not more than 12 months' notice.

6.4 Disclosure of service contracts

6.4.1 Statutory requirements – Section 318 CA 1985

Section 318 provides that a company must keep copies of directors' service contracts (or where there is no written contract, a memorandum of the terms) open to inspection by shareholders without charge at an "appropriate place". (In the case of a director employed by a subsidiary of the company, a similar obligation is imposed.) There is an exception for contracts where the unexpired term of the contract is less than 12 months or where the company can terminate the contract within the next 12 months without payment of compensation (Section 318(11)).

An "appropriate place" can be the company's registered office, the place where its register of members is kept (if this is not the registered office) or its principal place of business (provided that this is in the part of Great Britain where the company is registered). These provisions apply equally to variations of a director's service contract and accordingly any documents amending the terms of a service contract must also be open to inspection by shareholders (Section 318(10)). The Company must give notice in the prescribed form to the registrar as to the place of inspection (Section 318(4)). There are heavy financial penalties on a company and a defaulting director for a failure to comply with these requirements (Section 318(8)) and where a shareholder is denied inspection the court can compel inspection (Section 319(9)).

An exception to the disclosure requirement is where the director's contract requires him to work wholly or mainly outside the UK, in which case a note must be available for inspection setting out the director's name and the provisions of the contract relating to its duration (Section 318(5)).

6.4.2 The Listing Rules

Chapter 16 of the Listing Rules imposes various obligations relating to directors of listed companies, including rules as to the disclosures that a company must make about its directors.

Paragraphs 16.9 to 16.11 deal with the disclosure of directors' service contracts. A director's service contract is defined for this purpose as a service contract with a notice period of at least one year, or with provisions for predetermined compensation on termination of at least one year's salary and benefits in kind. Under these provisions, copies of the directors' service contracts must be available for inspection by any person. Note that this is wider than the obligation under Section 319 above, where it is only shareholders who can inspect. Thus, any interested party is entitled to have access to the directors' service contracts including potential investors or journalists. Inspection can take place either at the registered office of the company (or in the case of an overseas company, at the offices of any paying agent in the UK) during normal business hours on each business day (not Saturdays or public holidays), or at the place of the annual general meeting ("the AGM") for at least 15 minutes prior to and during the meeting.

The contracts available for inspection must disclose, or have attached to them, the following information:

(a) the name of the employing company;
(b) the date of the contract, the unexpired term and details of any notice periods;
(c) full particulars of the director's remuneration, including salary and other benefits;
(d) any commission or profit sharing arrangements;
(e) any provision for compensation payable upon early termination of the contract; and
(f) details of any other arrangements which are necessary to enable investors to estimate the possible liability of the company upon early termination of the contract.

Failure by a director to accept and discharge his responsibilities for the company's compliance with the Listing Rules can result in the UKLA censuring the director and publishing such censure. If, following such a censure, the director wilfully or persistently refuses to discharge his responsibilities, the Quotations Committee can issue a public statement to the effect that the retention of office by the director is prejudicial to the interests of investors and, if the director remains in office following such a statement, the Quotations Committee can suspend or cancel the company's listing of all securities or any class of securities (paragraph 1.15).

6.4.3 The Takeover Code

The Takeover Code aims to provide a framework within which takeovers of public companies are conducted and to ensure fair and equal treatment of all shareholders. It does not have the force of law and is not therefore mandatory, but reflects what are considered good business standards.

Rule 26 of the Takeover Code requires various documents to be on display and available for inspection by the other party, or by any competing offeror or potential offeror, from the time that the offer document or offeree board circular is published to the end of the offer period. This includes all service contracts of offeree company directors which have more than 12 months to run.

6.4.4 Persons entitled to inspect

As can be seen from the above, different provisions apply to who is entitled to inspect under the Companies Act 1985, the Listing Rules and the Takeover Code. In summary the position is as shown in Table 6.1.

6.5 Remuneration of directors

6.5.1 Components of directors' remuneration

6.5.1.1 Salary

The most significant part of a director's remuneration is likely to be his salary. Executive salary levels have generated much debate in recent

Table 6.1: Entitlement to inspect

Provision	Who can inspect?	What can be inspected?
Section 318 CA 1985	Shareholders only	Directors' service contracts (except where 12 months or more to run, or where company can terminate in next 12 months without paying compensation)
		Memorandum of terms (where no written directors' service agreement)
		A note of the director's name and contract duration provisions (where the director is required to work wholly/mainly outside the UK)
Listing Rules	Any member of the public	Directors' service contracts (as defined under the Listing Rules) disclosing specified information
Takeover Code	Any member of the public. Copies of relevant copies must, on request, be furnished to the offeror and any competing offeror or potential offeror	Various documents, including all service contracts of offeree company directors more than 12 months to run

years. In relation to listed companies, the level of this should be set by the remuneration committee in accordance with the principles contained in the Combined Code (*see* 6.5.2 below). Further details of the factors influencing the level at which salaries should be set by the remuneration committee are set out below.

6.5.1.2 Bonus

In addition to his salary, a director may be entitled to a bonus under a scheme which is either discretionary or contractual. The nature of the scheme is crucial, particularly in assessing damages on an early termination of the service contract. If discretionary, the director will not be contractually entitled to the bonus even when any targets as to individual/company performance are met, though the company would be under the general duty not to act in breach of the duty of trust and confidence in the way it exercised the scheme – this means that it should not exercise its discretion in bad faith or capriciously. If truly contractual, the director is entitled to the bonus calculated in accordance with the bonus formula and the company cannot refuse to pay it or withhold any part of it. Employers should be wary of pre-contractual statements or representations, for example by headhunters or recruitment consultants, which might be used as evidence of a contractual entitlement where the bonus is intended to be discretionary. Clearly, careful drafting of the scheme is essential where no contractual entitlement is intended.

Entitlement under the scheme will depend on the terms of the scheme, but common factors are the company's performance in the relevant financial year (or the performance of particular subsidiaries for which a director is responsible) by reference to profits and the individual director's performance. The bonus commonly takes the form of a cash payment, but some companies have adopted deferred share bonus plans whereby a part of the bonus is payable in shares which must be held by the director for a significant period. In many cases, the bonus is only payable on production of an auditor's certificate confirming that the amount is due.

6.5.1.3 Long-term incentive schemes

Another component of a director's remuneration can be a long-term incentive scheme which typically offers a director the right to acquire shares in the parent company at nil or nominal cost, dependent on the company's performance, assessed by reference to particular targets. Alternatively they may take the form of a bonus award whereby part of the director's annual cash bonus is taken in the form of shares and, if left with the trustees of the scheme for a certain period, will qualify the director for a matching allocation of additional free shares. Under the Listing Rules, long-term incentive schemes for directors (whether payable in cash, shares or any other security) have to be approved by the shareholders except in specified circumstances (paragraph 13.13).

6.5.1.4 Golden hellos

Offer letters commonly provide for a cash bonus payable when the director commences employment. These are taxable as income in the normal way. They can take the form of an immediate cash payment or a guaranteed bonus for the first year/part year of employment when a discretionary bonus scheme would otherwise operate. An immediate cash payment would normally become repayable if the director left within a specified period of commencing employment. Such payments can be justified where they are needed to attract the best recruits.

6.5.2 Requirements of the Combined Code in relation to the content of directors' remuneration

Paragraphs B1.1 to B1.4 of the Combined Code contain general guidance as to directors' remuneration policy as follows:

(a) the remuneration committee should provide the packages needed to attract, retain and motivate executive directors of the quality required but should avoid paying more than is necessary for this purpose;

(b) remuneration committees should judge where to position their company relative to other companies. They should be aware what comparable companies are paying and should take account of relative performance. However, they should use such comparisons with caution in view of the risk that they can result in an upward ratchet of remuneration levels with no corresponding improvement in performance;

(c) remuneration committees should be sensitive to the wider scene, including pay and employment conditions elsewhere in the group, especially when determining annual salary increases;

(d) the performance related elements of remuneration should form a significant proportion of the total remuneration package of executive directors and should be designed to align their interests with those of shareholders and to give these directors keen incentives to perform to the highest levels.

Service Contracts and Remuneration

Schedule A to the Combined Code sets out various provisions in relation to performance related remuneration. In summary these are:

(a) remuneration committees should consider annual bonuses and if so, performance should be relevant, stretching and designed to enhance the business. Upper limits should be considered;
(b) long-term incentive plans should be considered and any new plans should be approved by shareholders. In normal circumstances, shares granted or deferred remuneration should not vest in under three years. The total rewards under such schemes should not be excessive and payouts should be subject to challenging performance criteria reflecting the company's objectives;
(c) in general, annual bonuses and benefits in kind should not be pensionable and remuneration committees should consider the pension consequences of salary and other increases where a director is close to retirement.

6.5.2.1 The ABI Guidelines on Executive Remuneration
There are 12 principles set out in the ABI guidelines, covering the structuring of remuneration; dialogue with shareholders concerning remuneration; and what should go into the remuneration report.

An important principle is that remuneration committees should maintain a constructive and timely dialogue with their major institutional shareholders and the ABI about remuneration policies, including issues relating to share incentive schemes. Another key principle is that the board should demonstrate that performance based remuneration arrangements are clearly aligned with business strategy and objectives. Remuneration committees should seek to ensure that remuneration reflects market requirements, and should have regard to pay and conditions elsewhere in the company. They should pay particular attention to arrangements for senior executives who are not board directors but have a significant influence over the company's ability to meet its strategic objectives.

Several of the principles relate to relationships with shareholders. Contemplated changes to remuneration policy and practice should be discussed with shareholders in advance, and any proposed departure from the stated remuneration policy should be subject to prior approval by shareholders. Boards should review regularly the potential liabilities associated with all elements of remuneration and make appropriate disclosure to shareholders. There should be transparency on all matters relating to the remuneration of present and past directors and, where appropriate, other senior executives. Shareholders' attention should be drawn to any special arrangements and significant changes since the previous remuneration report.

The ABI Guidelines also contain a more detailed set of principles ("Guidelines for the Structure of Remuneration") aimed at helping remuneration committees to devise remuneration packages that achieve an appropriate balance between fixed and variable pay and between long- and short-term incentives. In summary, these suggest that:

(a) a policy of setting salary levels below the comparator group median can be helpful because it provides more scope for increasing the amount of variable performance based pay and incentive scheme participation. On the other hand, if the company wants to pay salaries at above the median level, it is required to justify this;

(b) annual bonuses are permissible but should be related to performance;

(c) all performance targets should be disclosed in the remuneration report. If there are commercial confidentiality concerns which prevent disclosure of specific short-term targets, that is acceptable provided the basic parameters adopted in the financial year are reported on;

(d) material payments which may be regarded as ex gratia in nature should have prior shareholder approval;

(e) there should be informative disclosure of the value accruing to pension schemes or other superannuation arrangements, which should include the costs to the company, the extent to which liabilities are funded, and aggregate outstanding unfunded liabilities. Remuneration committees should scrutinise all other benefits, including benefits in kind and other financial arrangements.

6.5.3 *Role of the Remuneration Committee*

It will be seen from the provisions of the Combined Code and the ABI Guidelines set out above that the remuneration committee plays a vital role in setting the levels and structure of directors' remuneration. The Combined Code further sets out a procedure for establishing remuneration levels and provides at paragraph B.2 that companies should establish a formal and transparent procedure for developing policy on executive remuneration and for fixing the remuneration packages of individual directors and that no director should be involved in deciding his own remuneration. There should be a Remuneration Committee consisting of independent non-executive directors who:

(a) make recommendations to the board on the remuneration framework and the cost involved; and
(b) determine each director's package (including pension rights and any compensation payments).

Remuneration committees should have access to internal and external professional advice and this could include taking advice from external consultants as to current levels of remuneration within the particular industry at the relevant level.

6.5.4 Disclosure requirements

6.5.4.1 The Companies Act 1985
Section 232 and Schedule 6 CA 1985 require disclosure in the notes to companies' annual accounts of the aggregate amount of directors' emoluments, the aggregate gain made on the exercise of share options and the aggregate amount for pensions and payments for loss of office. Disclosure of directors' emoluments must include details of payments under long-term incentive plans. Companies are also required in certain circumstances to give specific information about the highest-paid director. As set out below, listed companies are also required to comply with the stricter provisions of the Listing Rules, while "quoted companies" (which is a wider definition than listed companies) must, in addition, comply with the requirements of the Directors' Remuneration Report Regulations 2002.

The Directors' Remuneration Report Regulations 2002 ("the Regulations") have now amended CA 1985 so as to require all UK companies which are listed in the UK or in any other EU state, or on the New York Stock Exchange or NASDAQ (with the exception of UK AIM listed companies) to produce a directors' remuneration report for each relevant financial year and to put a resolution to shareholders at each general meeting before which the company's annual accounts are to be laid.[3] There are also specific provisions requiring the board of directors to approve the report and for the report to be signed on behalf of the board by a director or the company secretary. A copy of the report must be sent to all members of the company, debentures holders and those entitled to receive notice of general meetings.

---

[3] Section 241A Companies Act 1985 does not specify the AGM but refers to the "general meeting at which the company's annual accounts are laid".

However, it should be noted that the resolution to gain shareholder approval of the remuneration report has no legal effect. Putting the remuneration report to a vote does not of itself make any director's remuneration conditional on the outcome of that vote. If a company's shareholders do not approve the remuneration report, it does not mean that past or future payments to directors are rendered unlawful. Similarly, even if shareholders refuse to approve the report, the company would not be in breach of CA 1985 if it ignored the outcome of the vote and implemented its defeated remuneration policy anyway. In practice, of course, few listed companies would want to flout shareholder opinion in such a way.

There is also a new personal requirement on directors, or anyone who was a director at any time in the preceding five years, to give notice to the company of anything that the company needs to know in order to comply with the detailed content requirements of the new Schedule 7A. Failure to comply with this requirement will be punishable by a fine. The detail of the information to be included in the remuneration report is set out in Parts 2 and 3 of the new Schedule 7A as follows.

Non-audited information
Part 2 of Schedule 7A sets out key disclosure requirements on policy and performance, many of which are new:

(a) The members of the remuneration committee, the names of any persons who assisted the remuneration committee on matters relating to directors' remuneration and, if any of those who assisted were not themselves directors of the company, information on the nature of any other services they provided during the year. (The Combined Code requires the members of the remuneration committee to be listed in the remuneration report, but the requirements on persons who assisted the committee are new.)
(b) A statement of the company's policy on directors' remuneration for the forthcoming and subsequent financial years. (The Listing Rules require a statement of the company's policy on executive directors' remuneration, but the reference to "forthcoming and subsequent financial years" makes it clearer that the statement should be forward looking.) The statement must include, for each director, a detailed explanation of the performance conditions applicable to his entitlements to share options or under a long-term incentive scheme. In relation to each director's remuneration, the policy statement must explain "the relative importance of those elements which are, and those which are not, related to performance".

(c) The policy statement must also include information on the company's policy on length of contracts with directors, and notice periods and termination payments under those contracts. (This requirement to state the policy is new, although CA 1985 already required disclosure of the aggregate amount of compensation paid to directors for loss of office and, as set out below, the Listing Rules require details of any service contract containing certain notice provisions.)

(d) There is a new requirement for a performance graph, illustrating actual shareholder return on a holding of the company's listed shares over the last five years, compared with the notional shareholder return over the same period on a basket of shares "of the same kinds and number as those by reference to which a broad equity market index is calculated".

(e) Details of directors' service contracts and/or contracts for services. This must include date, unexpired term and notice periods; any provision for compensation on early termination; and details of any other provisions in the contract which shareholders need to know about in order to estimate the liability of the company on early termination. Any "significant award" made to a former director must also be explained.

Audited information
Part 3 of the Schedule requires very detailed information to be set out regarding the actual amounts received in the financial year by way of:

(a) salary and fees, bonuses, expenses and other non-cash benefits, and any compensation for loss of office or other termination payment;
(b) information on each director's share options and interests under long-term incentive schemes; and
(c) information on each director's entitlements under pension schemes.

These are similar to the existing Listing Rules requirements but are more detailed in some respects, such as the disclosure requirements on performance criteria and conditions for share option and long-term incentive schemes. There are also additional requirements on excess retirement benefits, compensation for past directors and sums paid to third parties for directors' services, largely derived from the existing requirements of Schedule 6 CA 1985 (which has also been amended).

The auditors are required to report to shareholders on this part of the remuneration report and state whether in their opinion it has been properly prepared in accordance with CA 1985; so the position is similar to that under the Listing Rules where the auditors' report has to cover the disclosures on individual directors' remuneration packages, share options, long-term incentive schemes and pension schemes.

Some of this reflects the information that has been required under the Listing Rules for some years now, although in some respects the Listing Rules still go further than the new statutory provisions. The UKLA has said that it does not plan to make any immediate changes to the Listing Rules to reflect the Directors' Remuneration Report Regulations. Therefore, listed companies need to have regard not only to the new Schedule 7A CA 1985, but to the Listing Rules and the Combined Code as well.

6.5.4.2 The Listing Rules
Rule 12.43A requires a company to include in its annual report and accounts a report by the board containing, *inter alia*, the following information:

(a) a statement as to how the company has applied the provisions of Section 1 of the Combined Code (including the provisions regarding directors' remuneration) with an explanation enabling shareholders to evaluate how the principles have been applied;
(b) a statement as to whether or not it has complied with Section 1 of the Combined Code (including the provisions regarding directors' remuneration);
(c) a statement of the company's policy on executive directors' remuneration;
(d) the amount of each element of each director's package by reference to each named director;
(e) information on share options and long-term incentive plans for each director by name;
(f) details of directors' service contracts with a notice period of more than one year or with provisions for predetermined compensation exceeding one year's salary and benefits;
(g) a statement of the company's policy on the granting of share options or awards under long-term incentive plans with details of any change in policy from the previous year.

6.5.4.3 The Combined Code
Paragraph B3 of the Combined Code sets out the disclosure requirements for directors' remuneration. The company's annual report should contain

Service Contracts and Remuneration

a statement of remuneration policy and details of the remuneration of each director.

Schedule B sets out in more detail what should be included in the remuneration report as follows:

(a) full details of all elements of each named director's package, such as basic salary, benefits in kind, annual bonuses and long-term incentive schemes including share options;
(b) information on share options, including SAYE options, should be given for each director;
(c) the report should explain why any grants under executive share option or other long-term incentive schemes are awarded in one block rather than phased;
(d) the pension entitlements earned by each individual director during the year;
(e) an explanation as to why any annual bonuses or benefits in kind are pensionable;
(f) service contracts with notice periods in excess of one year (or which have provisions for predetermined compensation on termination which exceed one year's salary and benefits) should be disclosed and the reasons for the longer notice periods explained.

It is clear from the above disclosure obligations that the wider public, and not just shareholders, will have access to information as to the make-up and amount of directors' remuneration by way of the company's published annual accounts.

6.6 Other benefits

6.6.1 *Pension arrangements*

Pension benefits may be a very significant element of a director's remuneration package. Benefits for directors may be provided through an existing company pension scheme set up for all employees (although often special sections may be appropriate offering a higher scale of benefits, a lower retirement age and special terms on early termination of employment), or through a separate tax-approved pension scheme for executives, or via contributions to a director's personal pension arrangement.

The introduction of the "earnings cap" in 1989 (for 2003/04 this is £99,000) set a limit on the amount of earnings in respect of which benefits can be provided under a tax-approved pension scheme. This means that if pension benefits are to be provided in relation to earnings above the cap (as is likely in the case of directors), it must be done by way of an unapproved scheme. The Inland Revenue has proposed introducing a single lifetime limit on retirement savings for tax purposes (the limit put forward in the Inland Revenue Consultation Paper in December 2002 was £1.4 million).

The two most common types of unapproved pension provision for directors to provide a pension in excess of the earnings cap are as follows.

6.6.1.1 Funded unapproved retirement benefit schemes ("FURBS")
FURBS are similar to approved pension schemes in that benefits are paid out of a fund held on trust separately from the assets of the company, made up of contributions from the employer and in some instances the director (although in practice it is rare for the director to pay contributions). The benefits payable from FURBS are commonly calculated on a money purchase basis, although final-salary FURBS are possible, and the employer's liability to contribute may be based upon a target level of benefits.

The Inland Revenue does not impose any limits on benefits payable under FURBS unless they are so excessive that they do not constitute a bona fide retirement benefits scheme. The individual bears tax on any payments made into the scheme except to the extent that they represent scheme establishment and management expenses. The employer's contributions are allowable against corporation tax. The scheme's trustees will pay income tax at the basic rate on income derived from land or trade, and at the lower rate on income (e.g. dividends) if the trustees have discretion over the level of benefits or can accumulate surplus money. The benefits can be paid tax free as a lump sum on retirement.

6.6.1.2 Unfunded unapproved retirement benefits schemes ("UURBS")
An UURBS amounts to a promise by the company to provide a member with retirement or death benefits without any pre-funding by the company. The company makes a provision in its accounts each year and pays the benefits on retirement or death from its revenue. The UURBS can be treated by way of an advance contractual promise in the director's service contract or by means of a separate letter. The director's tax liability will not arise until benefits are payable, and tax relief for the employer's contributions cannot be claimed until the benefit is actually paid under the scheme.

The main disadvantage of such schemes is the uncertainty that the company will in fact remain in business until payment is required when the director retires, although for the company itself this link to performance may not be seen as a disadvantage. It is important that the benefits promises in the initial document are clear, particularly in relation to leaving service and early retirement, in order to avoid dispute later.

6.6.2 Share schemes

Share awards for directors usually involve significant numbers of shares and therefore often involve unapproved schemes in addition to approved schemes. Unapproved schemes are schemes which have not been approved by the Inland Revenue and thus do not have the tax advantages of approved schemes. Under the Listing Rules, any scheme which may involve the issue of new shares requires shareholder approval (paragraph 13.13). Listed companies (and companies considering a listing) will be keen to ensure that their share schemes are supported by institutional shareholders. A scheme which uses existing shares may also require shareholder approval if one or more of the directors is eligible to participate in the scheme and the scheme involves conditions in respect of service and/or performance to be satisfied over more than one financial year. Such companies will also need to take into account the guidelines issued by the ABI when drafting their share schemes. These guidelines provide recommendations on, for example, the maximum amount of new shares which may be used under the schemes and the use of performance targets to link remuneration to performance. The main types of schemes for directors are as follows.

6.6.2.1 Discretionary share option schemes

This type of scheme normally gives the director the right to buy shares in the parent company at an exercise price equal to market value at the date of grant of the option. The option will normally be exercisable from the third anniversary of grant until the tenth anniversary of grant (provided the director is still in employment) although some non-listed technology companies now often allow a proportion of the option to become exercisable on the first anniversary of grant with the balance exercisable in tranches over the following two to three years. The right is to buy shares at a fixed price and so, if the value of the shares increases, the director will want to exercise the option. If the shares decrease in value the director will not have lost money as he will have been granted the option for no consideration, or perhaps nominal consideration. The incentive for the director is thus to improve company performance so that the share price increases as far as possible by the exercise date.

Discretionary share option schemes are usually established in two parts – an approved part (which normally attracts income tax and national insurance reliefs on options over shares with an aggregate value of up to £30,000 per participant at the original grant price provided the options are held for at least three years) and an unapproved part (which provides for unapproved options in excess of this limit and which will usually be subject to PAYE and National Insurance contributions).

6.6.2.2 Enterprise management incentive ("EMI") scheme

EMI is a new type of scheme designed to assist higher-risk trading companies to attract key executives by offering them generous tax relief on share options over shares with a value of up to £100,000 at the date of grant. A company, whether quoted or unquoted, can qualify for EMI provided its gross assets do not exceed £30 million, it is not under the control of another company and it carries on a "qualifying trade" mainly in the UK. Most trades will qualify, but the following activities, amongst others, are deemed insufficiently high risk and therefore will not qualify:

(a) property development;
(b) hotel management;
(c) leasing;
(d) banking;
(e) insurance and other financial services.

There is a £3 million limit on the total value of shares in the company over which unexercised option under an EMI Scheme may exist at any time.

Only 15 employees may hold EMI options at the same time. Unlike an approved discretionary share option scheme (where income tax relief is normally only available where the option is held for at least three years before exercise), there is no requirement under EMI for a minimum period before exercise. Qualifying companies may consequently choose their own exercise periods provided the option can be exercised within 10 years of grant. There will normally be no income tax or National Insurance contributions to pay when an EMI option is exercised provided the option was granted at no less than market value. When the shares are sold, capital gains tax taper relief will normally start from the date of grant of the option, which means that the rate of capital gains tax for a higher-rate taxpayer (who normally pays capital gains tax at 40 per cent) will taper down to 10 per cent provided the shares are sold more than two years after the option was granted.

6.6.2.3 "Phantom" share schemes
Phantom share schemes are cash bonus schemes made to look like a share option scheme, or a long-term incentive plan. They are usually used where a share scheme is not possible, but this part of the director's remuneration is to be linked to the share price as an incentive.

6.7 Compensation for loss of office

6.7.1 Damages for early termination of a service contract

In the absence of a liquidated damages, or payment in lieu, provision in the contract, or any misconduct or other contractual breach on the part of the director entitling the company to dismiss with immediate effect, the director will be entitled to damages for wrongful dismissal if he is dismissed summarily. Damages will be assessed by reference to the net loss he has sustained as a result of the breach of contract for the balance of the term of the service contract or the notice period. The net loss is calculated by assessing the net salary that the director would have received during that period, plus a sum to represent the loss of any other contractual benefits (e.g. a car) for the period. Genuine termination payments have the benefit of a tax-free element. This is currently £30,000 and thus the balance over £30,000 needs to be grossed up to take account of the tax that the director will have to pay on the excess over £30,000. Further, in assessing appropriate damages the board would be entitled to make a deduction for accelerated receipt, that is, a deduction to reflect that the director will receive the sum immediately rather than in monthly instalments had he remained in employment. The percentage deduction should be set by reference to what the director might reasonably be expected to earn by way of interest on the total sum.

Entitlement to damages is subject to the director's duty to attempt to mitigate his loss by seeking suitable alternative employment, thereby reducing the damages payable by the company by the amount that the director might reasonably be expected to earn. The duty to mitigate loss is not onerous. The courts will expect the departing director to do everything he can to find another job. Initially, the director would be entitled to restrict his search to positions at a similar level, offering equivalent salary and other benefits, but after a period he might be expected to look at a lower level. Clearly, if the director already has another job this can be taken into account by the company in assessing what it should pay the departing director – provided that the company knows about it. This is why a director may be required to warrant in any settlement documentation that he has not already obtained another job or been offered one.

In light of this, it will be clear that the unexpired length of the contract is especially significant, as companies cannot assume that mitigation will significantly reduce their liability. In deciding the level of damages payable, the board will have to consider carefully the director's prospects of finding alternative employment and it would not be exercising its powers in the best interests of the company if it failed to do so. To take expert advice from, for example, a recruitment consultant experienced in board-level prospects would assist the board in discharging this responsibility. Board minutes should record the board's consideration of the mitigation issue and how and why it reaches its conclusions.

The duty to act in the company's best interests is illustrated in this context by the case of *Turnbull* v *Glenhazel*.[4] The claimant managing director of the company had been given a service contract two years after the company's incorporation. It was in dispute whether the company, which had been set up to receive the proceeds of sale of an investment trust, was ever intended to have a long-term future. Nonetheless, the board considered the award of a service contract and a £50,000 salary to be in the interests of the company in order to retain the services of its managing director. Shortly after this, the holders of 90 per cent of the company's ordinary shares requisitioned an EGM in order to replace the directors with those who favoured winding up the company immediately. However, on the day prior to the EGM, the board resolved to terminate the managing director's service contract with no notice, subject to a compromise agreement which required his resignation as a director in return for the payment of £65,000. When the company subsequently refused to pay the agreed sum proceedings were issued. On the company's appeal against summary judgment, the court considered that the terms of the service contract and of the compromise agreement were so generous that they raised a prima facie case, which was not rebutted, that the motive behind the board's approval was primarily to benefit the claimant and was not in the best interests of the company.

---

[4] 1998 Chancery Division, 23 November.

Service Contracts and Remuneration

The ABI/NAPF Statement places further emphasis on the board's role in approving termination payments. It makes clear that if the service contract is simply to include a notice period, damages for breach of which would then be subject to the director's duty to mitigate his loss, shareholders will expect reassurance that the board has taken steps to ensure that he has done so to the fullest extent possible – and therefore any termination agreement should reflect this duty fully. In this instance, the institutions suggest that the board should consider providing for claims to go to arbitration rather than litigation.

Indeed, the ABI/NAPF Statement also supports the inclusion of a clause in the service contract providing for phased payments where the company continues to pay the departing executive on the usual basis for the outstanding term of the contract or, if earlier, until the executive finds new employment. The statement suggests that in many cases executives will prefer to seek further employment rather than remain idle. In some cases this may be rather optimistic, but there is nothing to prevent the contract making continued payment conditional on the executive making reasonable efforts to find other employment (and, possibly, providing the company with proof of this).

6.7.2 Section 312 CA 1985

Section 312 CA 1985 states:

> "It is not lawful for a company to make to a director of the company any payment by way of compensation for loss of office, or as consideration for or in connection with his retirement from office, without particulars of the proposed payment (including its amount) being disclosed to members of the company and the proposal being approved by the company."

Section 316(3) contains an exception to this for bona fide payments by way of damages for breach of contract.

6.7.3 Golden parachutes and golden handshakes

A director's service contract may contain a liquidated damages provision setting out the director's entitlement on an early termination of the contract, a golden handshake clause. Frequently, such a sum is also payable when the employing company is taken over or its business is transferred outside the group, in which case it is known as a golden parachute. In order to be enforceable, the liquidated damages provision must be a genuine pre-estimate of the director's loss – if it is not, then it is likely to be unenforceable as a penalty.

The clause will set out a formula as to how the director's entitlement is to be calculated. This is usually a multiplier of the number of years left to run under the service contract/the length of the notice period and the director's gross salary and, usually, a sum representing the other contractual benefits. A similar effect can be achieved by including a payment in lieu of notice or "PILON" clause in the contract.

The advantage of such provisions are that they avoid the uncertainties of quantifying the contractual damages for wrongful dismissal which would otherwise be payable. An advantage for the director is that no account is taken of the director's duty to mitigate his loss by seeking further employment. This, of course, can be a significant disadvantage to the employing company if it sees a former director walk straight into a new job following termination. The real advantage to the company of such a provision is the fact that, by paying out under the liquidated damages clause, the company will be acting in accordance with the service contract and will therefore be able to rely on any enforceable restrictive covenants in the service contract. By contrast, if it breaches the service contract in dismissing the director, it cannot rely on the restrictive covenants.

A liquidated damages payment will be fully taxable and will not attract the tax-free element of a termination payment (currently £30,000). This is because it is construed by the Inland Revenue as a contractual payment and not a payment representing damages for wrongful dismissal.

The cases of *Taupo Totara Timber Co. Ltd v Rowe*[5] and *Lander v Premier Pict Petroleum Ltd*[6] illustrate the way in which the courts have interpreted Section 312 (or in the case of *Taupo Totara*, equivalent New Zealand provisions) as they apply to liquidated damages clauses.

In *Taupo Totara* the Privy Council examined the nature of a provision in a service contract that the director should be entitled to a lump sum payment, on early termination, of five times his annual salary. The company argued that it should not have to make the payment as prior shareholder approval for the payment had not been obtained, in breach

---

[5] [1978] AC 537; [1977] 3 All ER 123; [1977] 3 WLR 466.
[6] [1997] SLT 1361; [1998] BCC 248.

of the provision equivalent to Section 312 in New Zealand. The court took the view that the requirement for shareholder approval did not apply to payments which were made in connection with employment or which the company was contractually bound to make. The true nature of the payment was not "compensation", but a contractual payment payable under the terms of the service contract. The agreement to pay the sum was therefore enforceable. This decision was followed in the Scottish case of *Lander* v *Premier Pict Petroleum Ltd* where a managing director was contractually entitled to a sum representing three times his gross annual salary if the employing company was taken over. Again the court held that Section 312 did not apply to payments which the company was contractually bound to make, and Lord Osborne observed, "I cannot see why the chronological stage at which [the] payment was contracted for has any bearing whatever" on the issue of whether the payment is covered by Section 312.

In another more recent Scottish case of *Mercer* v *Heart of Midlothian plc*[7] the limits of the application of Section 312 were considered again. The case involved a challenge to certain match-day privileges awarded in relation to a director's appointment as life president of a football club, but agreed only a few days prior to his resignation as a director and without disclosure or approval by the company's members. Lord Macfadyen held that the privileges fell outside of Section 312 on those particular facts. However, he also observed that while payments due to a director under an agreement entered into when the director took up office, or subsequently (where followed by a period of continuing office), are outside Section 312, contractual entitlement of itself is not sufficient to take a payment outside of Section 312, in particular where the contract is made immediately before the director resigns office. Furthermore, it was not only a transfer of money that was necessary for a "payment" within Section 312 – in some cases a sufficiently specific payment in a form other than money could suffice.

The ABI/NAPF Statement makes it clear that the liquidated damages approach of agreeing up front how much a director will receive on severance is not generally supported by shareholder institutions. This is on the basis that the amount cannot be varied to reflect under-performance (nor, as set out above, does it allow for mitigating earnings to be offset). Of course, it would be possible to provide expressly in the service contract that the specified amount of damages is reduced if the company

---

[7] [2001] SLT 945.

terminates for poor performance (or misconduct). However, this is not suggested in the ABI/NAPF Statement, which instead recommends that boards adopting liquidated damages clauses should provide that the amount of the damages be determined by arbitration.

6.7.4 The Combined Code

Paragraphs B1.9 and B1.10 of the June 1998 Combined Code set out the remuneration committee's responsibilities in relation to compensation for loss of office. Under these provisions, the remuneration committee should consider what compensation commitments the directors' service contracts would entail in the event of early termination and consider the advantages of expressly providing for compensation commitments, except in the case of a removal for misconduct.

Where the service contract does not make such provision, the remuneration committee should aim for the following approach:

(a) to avoid rewarding poor performance;
(b) to deal fairly with cases where departure is not due to poor performance; and
(c) to take a robust line on reducing compensation to reflect departing directors' obligations to mitigate loss.

6.7.5 Proposals for reform

6.7.5.1 The Higgs Review on the role of non-executive directors

January 2003 saw the publication of Derek Higgs' *Review of the Role and Effectiveness of Non-executive Directors*. The new requirements will have a major impact on all UK listed companies.

The Higgs Review rejects the imposition of change by law or regulation and instead proposes a revised Combined Code and continuing with the "comply or explain" principle. The report also makes a number of best-practice recommendations, which will not form part of the Code. A number of proposals contained in the Higgs Review are of particular relevance to this Chapter, and are considered below (with references to the relevant sections of the July 2003 Combined Code in brackets).

(a) Evaluation of directors: there are new Code provisions on performance evaluation. Boards will be required to evaluate their performance annually (A.6) with evaluation covering the board, the committees and the individual directors. The chairman should act on the results of the evaluation, if necessary by appointing new members or seeking the resignations of existing directors. The annual report should also state whether performance evaluation is taking place and how it is conducted. This will be a significant change for many listed companies, as recent research by KPMG suggests that more than half of non-executive directors do not undergo formal performance evaluation, and of those who are assessed less than a quarter are assessed annually.

(b) Audit and remuneration committees: both committees should comprise at least three, or in the case of smaller companies, two, members (B.2.1, C.3.1). As now, the remuneration committee should consist exclusively of independent directors.

The report echoes the recent ABI/NAPF Statement in recommending that the remuneration and nomination committees work together closely to ensure that incentives are appropriately structured and that severance terms are carefully considered. A new Code provision states that the remuneration committee should consider the advantages of providing explicitly in the initial contract for compensation commitments on severance, except in the case of removal for misconduct, bearing in mind that such provisions should not have the effect of rewarding poor performance (B.1.5).

The Code also provides that the remuneration committee should have responsibility for setting remuneration for all executive directors and the chairman, and should set the level and structure of remuneration for senior executives (B.2.2). It should also make its terms of reference publicly available (B.2.1). A Supporting Principle of the Code also provides that if executive directors or senior managers advise or support the committee, this role should be clearly separated from their role within the business.

A summary of the principal duties of the remuneration committee is set out in Annex E of the Report.

As requested by Derek Higgs, the Institute of Chartered Secretaries & Administrators ("ICSA") issued a Guidance Note in early 2003 entitled "Principles of Executive Service Contracts". This guidance is intended to assist company secretaries to ensure that all issues have been considered prior to the drafting of an executive service contract. The note covers the relevant regulatory requirements and the procedure for negotiation and authorisation of the contract. Also included is a useful checklist of key points for consideration prior to drafting.

The July 2003 Combined Code contains a sample letter for a non-executive director appointment and an Induction Checklist.

6.7.5.2 The Government White Paper "Modernising Company Law"
In July 2002 the Government published its response to the Company Law Review in a White Paper entitled "Modernising Company Law".[8] The consultation was based on draft legislation for simplifying and modernising various aspects of company law, and had a particular focus on smaller companies. In addition to various proposals relating to how companies take decisions, and on corporate reporting, the White Paper also considered directors, their duties, and how their activities are regulated and monitored in the interests of the company. The White Paper concluded that directors' common law duties should be codified, broadly as proposed by the Company Law Review, with the basic objective of directors being the success of the company in the collective best interests of shareholders.

The White Paper also agreed with the current Table A approach towards setting directors' remuneration. Thus, the board may continue to determine the remuneration of the managing and executive directors, provided there is effective disclosure and accountability to shareholders.

6.7.5.3 DTI Consultation on directors' compensation and severance
The issue of "fat cat" pay-outs to departing directors whose companies are performing badly has continued to receive much attention from the press and investors. A private member's bill was introduced early in 2003 in an attempt to require boards to link termination payments to performance, but it was dropped as it did not receive Government support. Instead the DTI has prepared its own consultation document "Rewards for Failure", published in June 2003. This includes proposals to reduce recommended notice periods from the current "industry standard" of one year, to ensure mitigation of earnings by making use of phased compensation payments (subject to the executive still being out of work), and to consider whether the liquidated damages approach could be modified, for example by introducing a recommended cap on the level of damages that may be awarded.

---

[8] Modernising Company Law, Command Paper CM 5553.

Chapter 7

Share Dealing by Directors and Connected Persons

Andrew Peck, Partner
Linklaters

7.1 Introduction

Directors' actions in relation to share dealing are, of course, subject to the general provisions of the law relating to, for example, notification of interests (Part VI of the Companies Act 1985) or insider dealing. It is not the purpose of this Chapter to give a full description of these matters – although section 7.6 does touch on the area. However, by virtue of their position, directors have a special relationship with a company partly because of their duties of good faith in their dealings with the company and partly because of the nature and amount of information they hold about it. This Chapter deals with the obligations which are of particular relevance in relation to dealings in shares by them and by their connected persons.

At common law, the duties of directors in relation to their dealings in shares is limited. The case of *Percival* v *Wright* [1902] 2 Ch 42 made it clear that, in the absence of any misrepresentation on the part of the directors, since the duties of the directors were owed to the company, no action would lie in respect of a purchase of shares in a company by the directors even though the directors had information which, had it been known to the sellers, would have led them to put a higher value on their shares.

However, the obvious inequity of directors dealing in shares with the benefit of price-sensitive information has led to provisions setting out a number of restrictions and disclosures, both statutory and non-statutory, with a view to restricting the freedom which directors would otherwise appear to have at common law. This has meant that English law has not had to become involved in developing theories of liability based on, for example, misuse of company property (confidential information), as has happened in the US. There are also other provisions, such as the market abuse offences introduced by the Financial Services and Markets Act 2000

("FSMA 2000"), which, while not specifically aimed at directors, may well have greater implications for directors than for other shareholders of a company. At the core of these provisions is concern about directors' privileged access to information about the company, its business, its financial position and prospects.

Directors are, by virtue of their position, almost always in a privileged position compared with outsiders when it comes to information about a company of which they are officers. Since it is not considered necessary or desirable to prevent directors from dealing in shares completely (indeed, on the contrary, share incentive plans of one sort or another are thought by many to be a good way of linking, at least in part, the fortunes of the directors to the fortunes of the company), the relevant laws and regulations operate so as to prevent dealings when the information is material or significant. The disclosure obligations provide transparency, to ensure that dealings are subject to scrutiny by the public and by the regulators.

7.2 Restrictions on dealing

7.2.1 Insider dealing

The offence of insider dealing is contained in Part V of the Criminal Justice Act 1993 ("CJA 1993"). The objective of the law is to prevent those with inside information from using this information to their advantage to make a profit when dealing with others. A breach of the law is a criminal offence. The structure of the relevant provisions is complex but depends on there being an individual (and not a body corporate) who is an "insider" and who deals in securities of a company with the benefit of confidential information, or encourages somebody else to deal, or who improperly discloses that information to a third party. As will be seen below, a director who, as a director, has information about the company, will almost always be an insider and the principal problems arise when a determination has to be made as to the materiality or significance of that information or as to the availability of one of the exemptions.

CJA 1993 creates three main offences:

(a) dealing in price-affected securities, that is, dealing in securities on the basis of information which would, if made public, be likely to have a significant effect on the price of the securities;
(b) encouraging another to deal in price-affected securities; and

(c) improperly disclosing information which a person holds as an insider.

To establish liability, a number of elements have to be present. First, there must be inside information. "Inside information" is information which:

(a) relates to particular securities or to a particular issuer, or particular issuers, of securities (including information affecting its business prospects);
(b) is specific or precise;
(c) has not been made public; and
(d) if it were made public would be likely to have a significant effect on the price (or value) of any securities.

No indication is given in CJA 1993 as to the scope of the words "specific or precise" or what is a "significant" effect on the price of securities. This has resulted in a degree of uncertainty, particularly in relation to the meaning of "significant". Although some counsel have expressed the view that significance should be calculated by reference to a (small) percentage of the market value of a share, there is no certainty as to what the percentage might be or even whether it is a percentage at all or an absolute amount. There is no judicial decision on the point and, until there is guidance from the courts, directors who have inside information which might have an effect on a share price should adopt a cautious approach. If there is doubt about whether any particular piece of information might be price sensitive and, if so, to what extent, a director might be well advised to seek professional advice from a stockbroker (probably the company's broker or somebody else who follows the company closely). Although, as will be seen below (*see* section 7.3.2), there is no defence of reasonable belief that information was not price sensitive, a court is likely to look more favourably on a person who at least took reasonable steps to confirm that the information was not price sensitive than one who did not.

In Section 58(2) CJA 1993 some guidance is given as to the meaning of "made public", and four situations are set out in which information *will* be treated as having been made public. These are that:

(a) the information is published in accordance with the rules of a regulated market for the purpose of informing investors and their professional advisers (e.g. by making an announcement via the Regulatory News Service ("RNS") of the UK Listing Authority or through another Regulatory Information Service);

(b) it is contained in records which are required by statute to be open to inspection by the public (e.g. at Companies House);
(c) it can be acquired readily by those likely to deal in any securities (i) to which the information relates, or (ii) in any securities of an issuer to which the information relates; or
(d) it is derived from information which has been made public.

Section 58(3) also states that information *may* still be treated as "made public" even when the information:

(a) can be acquired only by persons exercising diligence or expertise;
(b) is communicated to a section of the public and not to the public at large;
(c) can be acquired only by observation;
(d) is communicated only on payment of a fee; or
(e) is published only outside the UK.

It can be seen that if information is available otherwise than in the four circumstances set out in Section 58(2), it cannot be assumed that it has been made public for the purposes of CJA 1993. This is another area of uncertainty on which there is no judicial guidance.

Secondly, there must be "requisite knowledge". The individual must know that the information is in fact inside information and that he has that information from an inside source. This also applies to secondary insiders who must know that the person from whom they obtain the information is an insider and that the information is inside information.

Thirdly, the information must be from an "inside source". This arises only if the individual:

(a) has the information through:
    (i) being a director, employee or shareholder of an issuer of securities; or
    (ii) having access to the information by virtue of his employment, office or profession; or
(b) the person receives the information directly or indirectly from a person within (i) above.

Generally speaking, an individual, in relation to securities of the company of which he is a director, will fall squarely within (ii) above and will thereby satisfy the test as to requisite knowledge.

Share Dealing by Directors and Connected Persons

Once it has been established that an individual has satisfied the three requirements described above (i.e. that he has inside information, with the requisite knowledge, from an inside source), it must then be established whether he has committed one of the three offences.

Before considering each of the offences, the meaning of the word "securities" in this context should be noted. The term "securities" covers a wide range of investments but the relevant securities for the purpose of CJA 1993 are defined in Section 54(1). By way of a generalisation, it is fair to say that CJA 1993 is primarily concerned with securities dealt in, or under the rules of, a regulated market (such as the London Stock Exchange ("the Exchange") and other European securities and derivatives exchanges) and derivatives of those securities traded off market. The securities may not just be shares but may include debentures and futures, options and contracts for differences.

7.2.1.1 *Dealing in price-affected securities (Section 52(1))*

As noted above (*see* section 7.2.1), price-affected securities are securities in relation to which there is information which would, if made public, be likely to have a significant effect on the price of those securities.

Under Section 52(1) CJA 1993, a person deals in price-affected securities if he:

(a) acquires or disposes of them;
(b) agrees to acquire or dispose of them;
(c) enters into a contract which creates the security;
(d) procures, directly or indirectly, an acquisition or disposal of the securities by any other person (which will often be his agent, nominee or a person acting under his instruction).

The dealing must take place on a regulated market (which includes the Exchange) or the individual must have relied upon (or have been himself) a professional intermediary. A "professional intermediary" is a person who carries on the business of acquiring or disposing of securities (as principal or agent) or of acting as an intermediary between those taking part in any dealing in securities, or indeed any employees of such persons.

7.2.1.2 *Encouraging another to deal (Section 52(2)(a))*

It is also an offence for an individual who has information as an insider to encourage another person to deal in price-affected securities in relation to that information, knowing or having reasonable cause to believe that the dealing would take place on a regulated market or the individual was relying on (or was himself) a professional intermediary.

The person receiving the information does not have to realise that the securities are in fact price-affected securities and the inside information does not actually have to be given to the recipient. It is the act of encouraging that is relevant (and, indeed, there need be no actual dealing).

7.2.1.3 Disclosing information (Section 52(2)(b))

An individual who has information as an insider will commit an offence if he discloses that information to another person otherwise than in the proper performance of his employment, office or profession.

7.2.2 Defences

The defences to the three offences outlined above are contained in Section 53 CJA 1993. The defences vary depending on which of the three offences has prima facie been committed. They are as follows.

7.2.2.1 Defences to dealing and encouraging another to deal

An individual will not be guilty of an offence if he can prove any one of the following three facts:

(a) that he did not at the time of the offence expect the dealing to result in a profit attributable to the fact that the information in question was price-sensitive information in relation to the securities;
(b) that at the time he believed on reasonable grounds that the information had been (or would be in the case of insider dealing by virtue of encouraging) disclosed widely enough to ensure that none of those taking part in the dealing would be prejudiced by not having the information (the "equality of information" defence); or
(c) that he would have done what he did even if he had not had the information.

An individual will also not be guilty of an offence, by virtue of a special defence contained in Schedule 1 CJA 1993, if:

(a) the information that the individual has as an insider is market information and that it was reasonable for a person in his position to have acted as he did despite having that information as an insider at the time; or

(b) he acted in connection with an acquisition or disposal which was under consideration or the subject of negotiation and with a view to facilitating the accomplishment of the relevant transaction, and that the information he had was market information which arose directly out of his involvement in the particular transaction.

For the purpose of this defence, "market information" is information consisting of any of the following facts:

(a) the fact that securities of a particular kind have been or are to be acquired or disposed of, or that the acquisition or disposal is under consideration or the subject of negotiation;
(b) the number or price of those securities;
(c) the identity of those involved or likely to be involved in any capacity in an acquisition or disposal;
(d) the fact that securities of a particular kind have not been or are not to be acquired or disposed of.

In deciding whether it is reasonable for an individual to have acted as he did whilst in possession of market information, three issues have to be taken into account:

(a) the content of the information;
(b) the circumstances in which he first had the information and in what capacity; and
(c) the capacity in which he now acts.

7.2.2.2 Defences to disclosing

An individual will not be guilty of the offence of disclosing if he can show that:

(a) he did not at the time expect any person to deal in the securities on a regulated market or in reliance on a professional intermediary because of the disclosed information; or
(b) although he did expect the above, he did not expect the dealing to result in a profit attributable to the fact that the information was price-sensitive information relating to the securities.

It will be seen that dealings by a director, or encouraged by a director, for the benefit of himself or another person in circumstances in which the securities are price-affected securities, will generally not fall within any of the defences described above. One circumstance in which there may be a defence, however, is when a director is in the exercise period for an option or for the conversion of a convertible security where the final date for the exercise of the option or for conversion falls during a period when the director would otherwise be prevented from dealing by reason of his holding inside information. In this case, it may well be possible to argue that the director would have done what he did even if he had not had the information. In addition, depending on the nature of the information, he may also be able to claim that he had market information and that it was reasonable for an individual in his position to have acted as he did despite having that information as an insider at the time. Nevertheless, these defences must be used with care.

7.2.3 Jurisdiction

There are rules governing the jurisdiction in which the offence is committed, which vary according to the particular offence:

(a) The offence of dealing: in order to commit this offence, the transaction does not have to take place within the UK. However, the following requirements must be satisfied:
 (i) the individual must have been within the UK at the time when he is alleged to have committed any act which constitutes or forms a part of the dealing;
 (ii) the regulated market on which the dealing is alleged to have taken place is a regulated market (see the Insider Dealing (Securities and Regulated Markets) Order 1994 (as amended)); or
 (iii) the professional intermediary was within the UK at the time when he is alleged to have done anything causing the alleged offence to have been committed.
(b) The offences of disclosing and encouraging: these offences can only be committed if:
 (i) the defendant was within the UK at the time when he is alleged to have committed the offence; or
 (ii) the alleged recipient of the information or encouragement was within the UK at the time when he is alleged to have received the information or encouragement.

7.2.4 Penalties

An individual convicted of the offence under CJA 1993 is liable to a fine and/or imprisonment (for a term not exceeding six months on summary conviction, seven years on a conviction on indictment).

However, the transaction will not be void or unenforceable. Further, although there is no provision in CJA 1993 to compensate a "victim" of insider dealing and there are no other civil remedies, there are provisions for compensation or penalties in other statutes. For example, if a person who has suffered loss as a result of insider dealing can be identified, and a prosecutor applies, the Crown Courts have the discretion under Part II of the Proceeds of Crime Act 2002 to order that the proceeds of a crime be confiscated. The court must be satisfied that the defendant has a criminal lifestyle and has benefited from his general criminal conduct or if he does not have a criminal lifestyle that he has benefited from the particular criminal conduct. Cases of insider dealing may fall within either circumstance.

7.2.5 Market abuse

FSMA 2000 has introduced a new offence of market abuse. Unlike insider dealing, which is a criminal offence and therefore requires the more onerous criminal burden of proof ("beyond reasonable doubt"), market abuse is a civil offence with the corresponding lower burden of proof ("balance of probabilities"). The difficulty in proving insider dealing has led to relatively few prosecutions under the insider dealing regime; a factor which is likely to have been part of the rationale behind the introduction of the market abuse regime.

Three types of behaviour can constitute market abuse, namely:

(a) misuse of information;
(b) creating a misleading or false impression to the market; and
(c) market distortion.

The relevant type of behaviour in this context is "misuse of information" which catches behaviour based on information which is not generally available that a reasonable person who regularly deals on that market in investments of the kind in question is likely to consider relevant to trading in the "relevant investment". Generally, "relevant investments" are shares and commodities traded on markets like the Exchange, the London International Financial Futures and Options Exchange ("LIFFE") or the London Metal Exchange ("LME"). Market abuse is not specifically aimed at company directors but directors are more likely to be in a position to misuse information than shareholders and so should be aware of the issues raised by the market abuse regime.

There is an overlap between market abuse and insider dealing because market abuse can cover conduct falling within the existing insider dealing regime. Conduct which amounts to insider dealing will almost invariably also amount to market abuse. However, the market abuse regime has wider territorial scope than the insider dealing regime. This can have significant practical implications; for example, if a director of a UK plc who is in the US discloses inside information about his company (traded on the London Stock Exchange) to a US shareholder with the aim of encouraging that person to buy shares in the company. This would not amount to insider dealing under CJA 1993 because of the Act's limited territorial scope. However, it would be market abuse as it would amount to "requiring or encouraging" another to commit market abuse as the behaviour is in relation to an investment traded on a UK market.

Because of the overlap between the two regimes, there is a risk of multiple jeopardy. The Financial Services Authority ("the FSA") has the power to institute criminal proceedings in respect of insider dealing as well as for market abuse. However, the FSA has stated that it will choose either market abuse charges or criminal (i.e. insider dealing) charges. In practice, because of the high standard of proof and difficulties of proving intention under the criminal regime, it is possible that the FSA will be more inclined to pursue someone for market abuse.

7.2.6 Future developments

The European Commission has published the Market Abuse Directive which may impact on the current insider dealing and market abuse regimes in the UK. This Directive will have to be implemented by the UK within 18 months of publication in the Official Journal (i.e. by October 2004).

The European Commission has indicated that the existing directive dealing with insider dealing is "essentially sound" so that it appears that, insofar as it relates to insider dealing, the Market Abuse Directive will not bring about a significant change in the existing regime. In relation to the UK market abuse regime, the FSA has indicated that it will be consulting on this but has not yet indicated a time frame for the consultation.

7.3 The Model Code

7.3.1 Introduction

The Model Code is to be found in the Appendix to Chapter 16 of the Listing Rules of the Financial Services Authority (acting in its capacity as the UK Listing Authority). The provisions of the Model Code apply in addition to the insider dealing requirements of the CJA 1993. It is principally a code of conduct which, in effect, forms part of the continuing obligations laid down in the Listing Rules.

7.3.2 Restrictions on dealing

In relation to dealings by directors, Chapter 16 of the Listing Rules provides that a listed company must require its directors and appropriate employees to comply with a code of dealing in terms no less exacting than those of the Model Code and must take all proper and reasonable steps to secure such compliance. It is also made clear that companies may impose more rigorous restrictions upon dealings by directors and employees if they so wish.

The Model Code is narrower in its focus than the insider dealing provisions of the CJA 1993; it only regulates dealings by directors (and appropriate employees) and their connected persons in securities listed on the Exchange. However, the restrictions it imposes are in some respects more onerous than the CJA 1993, partly in order to ensure that directors are seen to be above suspicion in relation to their transactions in listed securities of the company of which they are a director. It also covers dealings in certain circumstances not covered by the CJA 1993, specifically:

(a) dealings between directors and/or other relevant employees of the company;
(b) off-market dealings; and
(c) transfers for no consideration by a director (other than transfers where the director retains a beneficial interest under the Companies Act 1985).

The specific restrictions laid down by the Model Code are as follows:

(a) a director may not deal in his company's securities, at any time, on considerations of a short-term nature and must take reasonable steps to prevent any such dealings by a connected person;

(b) a director must not deal in his company's securities at any time when he is in possession of unpublished price-sensitive information (*see* below) in relation to those securities or in circumstances in which he is not given clearance to deal;

(c) a director must not deal in his company's securities in certain prohibited periods, known as "close periods". These close periods are the periods immediately before the announcement of the company's results, that is, the two-month period immediately before the preliminary announcement of the annual results and the announcement of half-yearly results (or if shorter, the period from the end of the relevant financial period up to and including the time of the announcement). It should be noted that companies which announce results on a quarterly basis are subject to a one-month close period prior to publication of interim results (or, if shorter, the period from the end of the relevant financial period to the time of announcement), but the two-month period applies prior to the preliminary announcement of the annual results.

The definition of "unpublished price-sensitive information" is broadly the same as the definition of "inside information" for the purpose of the insider dealing provisions of CJA 1993 and is information which:

(a) relates to particular securities or to a particular issuer(s) of securities;
(b) is specific or precise;
(c) has not been made public within the meaning of Section 58 CJA 1993 (*see* 7.2.1 above); and
(d) if it were made public would be likely to have a significant effect on the price or value of any securities.

The Model Code states that it should be considered whether any unpublished information regarding transactions required to be notified to a Regulatory Information Service (in accordance with the Chapters of the Listing Rules relating to significant transactions or transactions by a company with related parties) should be regarded as price sensitive, as well as information which might fall within the continuing obligations of the company with regard to announcements, such as alterations to capital structure or notification of major interests in shares, as well as purchase of the company's own securities and notification of directors' interests.

A director must always seek clearance from the chairman (or any other director(s) designated for this purpose) before any dealing. The chairman (or designated director(s)) must himself receive the appropriate clearance from the board or another designated director. A director cannot be given clearance for a dealing if "during a prohibited period":

(a) the proposed dealing falls within a close period (*see* above);
(b) the person responsible for the clearance feels that the dealing would contravene the Model Code; or
(c) there is any matter which constitutes unpublished price-sensitive information in relation to the company's securities, and the proposed dealing would occur after the time when it has become reasonably probable that an announcement will be required.

A company must keep a written record of any requests for clearance and of any clearances given. Any director that has requested clearance must also be given written confirmation from the company that there is a written record that his request was made and that he did/did not receive clearance, as appropriate.

The Model Code also provides that "in exceptional circumstances", where it is the only reasonable course of action available to a director, clearance may be given for a director to sell (but not to buy) securities when he would otherwise be prohibited from doing so. The person responsible for deciding whether to give clearance must decide whether such "exceptional circumstances" exist. One example stated in the Model Code of where an exceptional circumstance could exist is where there is "a pressing financial commitment on the part of the director that cannot otherwise be satisfied".

In addition to being prohibited from certain dealings himself, a director is also required to seek to prohibit dealings in his company's securities by connected persons or by an investment manager acting on his behalf or on behalf of a connected person during a close period or at any time when the director would be prohibited from dealing because of the existence of price-sensitive information. In order for the director to comply with this obligation, the Model Code states that the director must advise the connected persons of the following:

(a) the name of the listed company of which he is a director;
(b) the close periods during which they cannot deal;
(c) any other periods when the director knows he is not himself free to deal under the terms of the Model Code unless his duty of confidentiality to company prevents him from disclosing these periods; and

(d) that they must tell him immediately after they have dealt in the company's securities.

For the purpose of the Model Code, references to connected persons are to persons who are connected within the meaning of Section 346 of the Companies Act 1985. The definition contained in this Section is very wide – considerably wider than the class of persons covered by the disclosure obligations of directors (*se/e*, 7.6.1 below). In addition to spouses and infant children, it covers:

(a) "associated" companies (that is companies in which the director and persons connected with him hold at least one-fifth by nominal value of the equity share capital or are entitled to exercise more than one-fifth of the voting power at general meetings);
(b) trustees (acting as such) for the director; or
(c) connected persons and partners (acting as such) of the director or connected persons.

The Model Code provides that details of any such dealings by directors and connected persons must be circulated to the board with the board papers, as well as being notified to a Regulatory Information Service, as provided for in the Listing Rules.

If the director is a sole trustee (but not a bare trustee, i.e. a trustee who has no interest at all in the capital or income of the trust property which is held entirely for one or more other persons who can call for delivery of the trust property), the Model Code will apply as though the director were dealing on his own account. However, if the director is acting as a co-trustee (but not a bare trustee), he must inform his co-trustees of the name of the listed company of which he is a director. It is also worth noting that, if the director is not actually a beneficiary, the Model Code will not regard any dealing in his company's securities undertaken by the trust as a dealing, provided that the other trustees acted independently from the director in deciding whether or not to deal.

An area in which the scope of the Model Code is wider than the scope of the CJA 1993 relates to the grant and the exercise of options, or the award of shares, under employee incentive plans. Directors cannot be granted options or be awarded securities or given other rights or interests to acquire securities during a prohibited period unless:

(a) the award or grant is made under the terms of an employee share scheme; and

(b) the terms of the scheme set out the timing of the award or grant and such terms have either previously been approved by shareholders or summarised to shareholders in a document sent to them or the timing of the award or grant is in accordance with the timing of previous awards or grants under the scheme and the terms of the scheme set out the amount or value of the award or grant or the basis on which the amount or value is calculated; and
(c) the failure to make the award or grant would be likely to indicate that the company is in a prohibited period.

Similarly, the exercise of an option or the exercise of a right under an employee share scheme, or the conversion of a convertible security, is not permitted in a prohibited period unless the final date for the exercise of such option or right or conversion falls during a prohibited period and the director could not reasonably have been expected to exercise it at an earlier time when he was free to deal. It should be noted, however, that where exercise or conversion is permitted, a director shall not be given permission to sell any of the securities he acquires.

The general restrictions applying to employee share schemes do not apply to saving schemes under which the director is contractually bound to pay by way of regular standing order or deduction from his salary or where securities are acquired by way of a standing election to reinvest dividends or other distributions or are acquired as part payment of a director's remuneration without regard to the provisions of the Model Code. However, to benefit from this exemption there are a number of provisions which must be complied with including, generally, his not entering into the scheme during a prohibited period or varying the terms of his participation or selling securities of a listed company within the scheme, during the prohibited period.

The Model Code does not apply to a number of common corporate transactions, including undertakings or elections to take up entitlements under a rights issue or other offer or the actual taking up of those entitlements or allowing entitlements to lapse. It also does not apply to the sale of sufficient entitlements nil-paid to allow take up of the balance of the entitlements under a rights issue. In addition, "dealings" do not include undertakings to accept, or the acceptance of, a takeover offer, or dealings by directors with a person whose interests in securities is to be treated by virtue of Section 328 of the Companies Act 1985 as the director's interest (*see* below) or certain dealings in relation to shares in Inland Revenue approved share option and profit sharing schemes.

A Practitioner's Guide to Directors' Duties and Responsibilities

7.3.3   Interaction with the market abuse regime

It should be noted that a director might fall foul of the market abuse provisions mentioned in 7.2.5 above even though his behaviour is in accordance with the Model Code. However, in relation to the offence of requiring or encouraging another to commit market abuse, the FSA has given guidance that a director of a company will not be regarded as having required or encouraging another person to engage in behaviour amounting to market abuse where the director acts in compliance with provisions of the company's code of dealing implemented in accordance with paragraph 16.18 of the Listing Rules (equivalent to the requirements in paragraphs 11 and 12 (dealings by connected parties and investment managers) of the Model Code).

7.3.4   Future developments

The FSA is currently undertaking a major review of the Listing Rules and has stated that its aim is to publish a new set of rules by the end of 2004. The FSA has not indicated that there will be any significant changes to the Model Code although it is currently consulting on whether the scope of the Model Code should be broadened to include spread bets and other contracts for differences.

7.4   The Takeover Code

The City Code on Takeovers and Mergers ("the Takeover Code") was established to ensure the fair and equal treatment of all shareholders in relation to takeovers and it contains a framework within which takeovers are conducted. The operation of the Takeover Code is overseen by the Panel on Takeovers and Mergers ("the Panel"), which is comprised of people appointed by the Governor of the Bank of England plus representatives from numerous city institutions.

The Takeover Code will apply whenever a person makes an offer to the shareholders of certain types of company to acquire all or some of their shares, where the offeree company is either:

(a)   a public company resident in the UK, the Channel Islands or the Isle of Man, whether listed or unlisted; or
(b)   a private company resident in the UK, the Channel Islands and the Isle of Man but only when there has been some public market in its

shares, or it has filed a prospectus, at any time during the 10 years prior to the relevant date.

Residence for these purposes means the place where the company:

(a) is incorporated; and
(b) has its place of central management.

The introduction to the Takeover Code makes it clear that the "spirit" of the Takeover Code is important and must be observed as well as the precise wording, and the Panel has decided that if the "spirit" of the Takeover Code is not observed this can be viewed as a breach, regardless of whether a particular rule has been broken. Therefore, it can be seen that the Takeover Code is not black and white and is open to interpretation. If in doubt as to the meaning of any provision, it is advisable to seek clarification by consulting the Panel.

Directors, like other persons, are covered by the Takeover Code and will usually be regarded as "acting in concert" with their company. The general consequences of this are not described in this Chapter, but there are a number of rules in the Code which specifically deal with share dealings and their consequences.

(a) Rule 4.1: this Rule prohibits dealings of any kind in securities of an offeree company by any person, other than the offeror, who is privy to confidential, price-sensitive information about an offer or contemplated offer, prior to an announcement of the offer or contemplated offer or of the termination of discussions.
(b) Rule 4.2: this restricts dealings by the offeror and persons acting in concert with it (such as directors) by providing that such persons must not sell any securities in the offeree company during an offer period unless consent from the Panel is obtained and following 24 hours' public notice that such sales might be made. If any such sales are made, neither the offeror nor persons acting in concert with it will generally be permitted to purchase securities in the offeree thereafter.
(c) Rule 5: this Rule, subject to a number of limited exceptions, prevents a person and persons acting in concert with him from acquiring shares carrying 30 per cent or more of the voting rights in a company. If a person (and his concert parties) already holds 30 per cent or more but not more than 50 per cent of the shares carrying voting rights, then the person and his concert parties cannot acquire any further shares.

7.5 Prohibition on dealing in options

It is an offence under Section 323 of the Companies Act 1985 for a director or a shadow director of a company listed on a Stock Exchange, or of a holding company, subsidiary or sister company of a listed company, to buy options in shares or debentures of the listed company. This prohibition is extended (by Section 327) to spouses and infant children. The options covered are options giving the right to call for delivery (call options) or to make delivery (put options) of shares or giving the right to do both. The prohibition does not cover the right to subscribe for new shares (e.g. under an employee share scheme).

A person found guilty of an offence under Section 323 is liable:

(a) on summary conviction, to up to six months' imprisonment or to a fine not exceeding the statutory maximum, or both; and
(b) on conviction on indictment, to up to two years' imprisonment or to a fine of unlimited amount, or both.

7.6 Disclosure of interests

Provided a director complies with the provisions described above and his fiduciary duties to the company, he will be permitted to deal in securities. However, the Companies Act 1985 imposes obligations on a director and, in some cases, on shadow directors to notify the company of their shareholdings and dealings so that the company can maintain a register of those dealings. There are also disclosure requirements imposed by the Takeover Code.

7.6.1 *Disclosure under the Companies Act 1985*

7.6.1.1 Notification of existing and subsequent interests
The Companies Act 1985 imposes an obligation on a director to notify the company of which he is a director of any interests in shares or debentures of that company, its subsidiary, holding company or a subsidiary of the holding company. At the time a person first becomes a director of a company, he is obliged under Section 324(1) to notify the company in writing of his interests at the time of appointment and of the number of shares in each class in, and the amount of debentures of each class of, the company or other such body corporate in which he has an interest at that time.

In addition to the initial duty in Section 324(1), Section 324(2) contains a continuing obligation on a director to notify the company in writing of the occurrence, while he is a director, of any of the following:

(a) any event in consequence of whose occurrence he becomes or ceases to be interested in shares in, or debentures of, the company or any other body corporate, being the company's subsidiary or holding company or a subsidiary of that holding company;
(b) his entering into a contract to sell any such shares or debentures;
(c) the assignment by him of a right granted to him by the company to subscribe for shares in, or debentures of, the company; and
(d) the grant to him by a company's subsidiary or holding company or by another subsidiary of its holding company of a right to subscribe for shares in, or debentures of, that body corporate, the exercise of such a right granted to him and the assignment by him of such a right so granted.

Notification to the company must state the number or amount and class of the shares or debentures involved (Section 324(2)) and the price (Schedule 13, Part III).

A failure to make a notification required by Section 324 or the making of a false statement, made either knowingly or recklessly, is a criminal offence and a person guilty of such an offence is liable to imprisonment or a fine or both (Section 324(7)).

Section 324 includes interests of shadow directors who are therefore under the same duty to notify the company of such information (Section 324(6)).

7.6.1.2 Meaning of "interest"
Schedule 13 CJA 1993 sets out the more detailed provisions governing the obligation on a director to notify his interests to the company. Schedule 13, Part I states that an interest in shares or debentures is to be read as including any interest of any kind whatsoever disregarding any restriction or restraint on the exercise of any right attached to an interest.

The width of this definition is made clear by further details set out in the Schedule, for example:

(a) where any interest in shares or debentures is comprised in trust property, any beneficiary of the trust is taken to have an interest in the shares or debentures;

(b) a person is taken to have an interest in shares or debentures if he enters into a contract for their purchase by him (for cash or for any other consideration) or, not being the registered holder, he is entitled to exercise any right conferred by the holding of shares or debentures or is entitled to control the exercise of any such right (and, for this purpose, a director can be interested in shares or debentures indirectly through a body corporate if the body corporate or its directors are accustomed to act in accordance with his directions or instructions or he is entitled to exercise or control the exercise of one-third or more of the voting power at general meetings of that body corporate);

(c) a person has an interest in shares and debentures if, otherwise under a trust, he has the right to call for the delivery of the shares or debentures to himself or to another or has the right to acquire an interest in shares or debentures or is under an obligation to take an interest in shares or debentures whether in any case the right or obligation is conditional or absolute;

(d) where persons hold joint interests, each of the joint holders is taken to have an interest;

(e) it does not matter that the shares or debentures in which a person has an interest are unidentifiable.

On the other hand, there are a number of interests which do not need to be notified:

(a) where a person has a life interest in income from trust property including shares or debentures, the interest in reversion or remainder in the trust is disregarded;

(b) interests of a bare trustee are disregarded;

(c) a person does not have a notifiable interest by virtue of being appointed a proxy or a corporate representative for a meeting of a company;

(d) a right of pre-emption under the Articles is not notifiable;

(e) a holding of units in a unit trust does not give rise to a notifiable interest.

The Companies (Disclosure of Directors' Interests) (Exceptions) Regulations 1985 also set out a number of other exemptions from the meaning of "interest" including interests in shares or debentures of a person in his capacity as a trustee of, or beneficiary under, a retirement benefit scheme or a superannuation fund. Notification is also not required to a wholly owned subsidiary of a body corporate incorporated outside Great Britain of interests in shares or debentures of that body corporate. Nor is it necessary for a director to notify his interests to a company which is a wholly owned subsidiary of another company, of which the director is also a director, in circumstances in which that other company maintains its own register under Section 325 (*see* 7.6.1.6 below).

7.6.1.3 Spouses and children

Section 328 CJA 1993 extends the scope of the obligation on directors to notify their interests to the company. It requires a director to disclose also the interests of his spouse or infant children (including stepchildren) (if they are not themselves directors) in shares or debentures of the company. The provisions of Schedule 13 governing the meaning of interest apply also to Section 328.

A contract, assignment or right of subscription entered into, exercised or made by, or a grant made to such a spouse or child is to be treated as having been entered into, exercised or made by the director (Section 328(2)).

As with Section 324, the duty under Section 328 includes the grant by the company to the spouse or child of a right to subscribe for shares or debentures and the exercise of such a right (Section 328(3)).

Failure to make a notification required by Section 328 or the making of a false statement, made either knowingly or recklessly, is a criminal offence and a person guilty of such an offence is liable to imprisonment or a fine or both (Section 328(6)).

It will be clear from the above that, in the absence of any provisions which prevent double counting, interests which have to be notified by a director (and, therefore, kept in the register maintained under Section 325 (*see* 7.6.1.6 below) may well exceed the number of shares which are actually subject to the various interests described. For example, if a director and his spouse hold shares jointly, each of them is regarded as having an interest in all of the shares, so that the register will show on its face interests in double the number of shares actually held.

7.6.1.4 Period for making a notification

A notification under Section 324 must generally be made within five days of becoming a director or, where an interest arises once the director is already in office, before the expiration of a period of five days after the event giving rise to the interest which has occurred. In either case, where the director is not aware of the event, the obligation must be fulfilled before the expiration of a period of five days after the occurrence of the event comes to his knowledge (Schedule 13 Part II). Weekends and bank holidays are not included in the calculation.

7.6.1.5 Circumstances in which the obligation is not discharged

By Section 324(5), the obligation to notify under Section 324 is not fulfilled unless the notice is expressed to be given in fulfilment of that obligation. In addition, Part Ill of Schedule 13 describes a number of other circumstances in which notification does not discharge the obligation under Section 324. This is usually where insufficient information has been provided, such as the price paid or received or the consideration given in connection with the acquisition or disposal of the interest.

7.6.1.6 Register of directors' interests

Section 325 CJA 1993 imposes an obligation on a company to maintain a register of the information notified to it under Section 324 (Section 325(1) and (2)). The company must also enter details of the rights granted by it to directors to subscribe for shares, or debentures, in the company (Section 325(3)). Again, this obligation covers the interests of shadow directors (Section 325(6)).

Failure by the company to maintain the register will render the company and every officer of it who is in default to a fine, and for continued contravention, to a daily default fine (Section 326).

Schedule 13 Part IV contains additional guidance for a company on the maintenance of the register. The register must be kept either at the registered office or where the register of members is kept and must be open to inspection by members of the company (for no charge) and other members of the public who may be required to pay a fee.

7.6.1.7 Duty to notify the Exchange

Under Section 329, a company which is listed on a recognised investment exchange and which is notified of an interest of a director or of a spouse or infant child under Sections 324 and 328 is obliged to pass that information to the Exchange. The Exchange may then publish that information (Section 329(1)).

Under Section 329(2), the notification to the Exchange must be made before the end of the day next following that on which the Section 329(1) obligation arises. Failure to comply with Section 329 will render the company and every officer of it who is in default guilty of an offence and liable to a fine and, for continued contravention, to a daily default fine (Section 329(3)).

7.6.2 Disclosure under the Takeover Code

In the case of a takeover offer governed by the Takeover Code there are additional rules for disclosure of a director's dealings in the shares of the offeror and the offeree company.

Rule 8.1 of the Takeover Code requires disclosure of dealings by parties to a takeover offer and by their associates for themselves or for discretionary clients in the relevant securities of the parties to the offer. Relevant securities are, in general, securities of the target which carry, or contingently carry, voting rights and securities of the offeror which carry "substantially the same rights" as any to be issued in consideration for the offer by the offeror. The definition of "associate" includes the directors, their close relatives and related trusts. Close relatives is not defined but would at the least include spouse and infant children (and the definition may, depending on the circumstances, be wider).

Rule 8.1 provides that any dealings in relevant securities by an offeror or offeree company, and by any associates, for their own account during an offer period must be publicly disclosed.

If such dealings are for discretionary clients, they must also be publicly disclosed. However, if the associate is an exempt fund manager connected with the offeror or offeree, the dealings need only be privately disclosed. If such dealings are for non-discretionary clients, Rule 8.2 provides that they must be privately disclosed to the Panel.

Rule 8.3 provides for public disclosure of dealings by any person, whether or not an associate, who owns or controls (directly or indirectly) 1 per cent or more of any class of relevant securities.

Rules 24 and 25 provide for the detailed information which has to be given in offer documents and defence documents respectively. As well as much detailed financial information and general information about the offer, Rule 24.3 (in the case of offer documents) and Rule 25.3 (in the case of defence documents) require that a detailed list of shareholdings and of dealings be disclosed. Thus, in the offer document, there must be disclosed *inter alia*:

(a) shareholdings in the offeror (in the case of a securities exchange offer only) and in the offeree company in which directors of the offeror are interested;

(b) the shareholdings in the offeror (in the case of a securities exchange offer only) and in the offeree company which any persons acting in concert with the offeror own or control (with the names of the persons acting in concert);

(c) the shareholdings in the offeror (in the case of a securities exchange offer only) and in the offeree company owned or controlled by any persons who, prior to the posting of the offer document, have irrevocably committed themselves to accept the offer, together with the names of such persons (in the case of a recommended offer, it is very common for the directors of the offeree company to accept the offer irrevocably);

(d) if any party whose shareholdings are required to be disclosed has dealt for value in the shares in question during the period beginning 12 months prior to the commencement of the offer period (and ending with the latest practicable date before the posting of the offer document), the details, including dates and prices must be stated.

In the case of a defence document, Rule 25.3 requires that the first major circular from the offeree company board advising shareholders on an offer must disclose *inter alia*:

(a) the shareholdings in the offeree company and in the offeror in which directors of the offeree company are interested; and

(b) if any of the directors whose shareholdings are required to be disclosed by this Rule has dealt for value in the shares in question during the period beginning 12 months before the start of the offer period and ending with the latest practicable date before the posting of the circular, the details, including dates and prices.

Chapter 8

Directors' Powers and Proceedings

Caroline Carter, Partner
Ashurst Morris Crisp

8.1 Powers of companies and their directors

8.1.1 Company's constitution – statutory provisions

What is the position where:

(a) a company acts beyond the limits of the objects clause within its memorandum;
(b) a board acts beyond the limits of its collective authority; or
(c) individual directors or other employees act beyond the limits of their own individual authority?

Are resultant transactions enforceable? What is the position of the authorising director(s)? This Section deals with the position in respect of acts which occurred on or after 4 February 1991.[1]

Section 35(1) Companies Act 1985 ("CA 1985") provides that "the validity of an act done by a company shall not be called into question on the ground of lack of capacity by reason of anything in the company's memorandum". This covers the situation where a company enters a transaction which is beyond the scope of its objects, for example starting a pig farm where the company's objects are limited to the financial services sector. Such transactions would previously have been ultra vires at common law and void, but under Section 35 they can now be enforced in many cases by third parties to the transactions.

---

[1] Acts pre-dating 4 February 1991 are dealt with under Section 35 CA 1985, as it was prior to the amendments of the Companies Act 1989. The validity of such acts is dealt with under different principles.

Whilst a failure to comply with an explicit requirement in the memorandum makes a transaction unauthorised, and consequently voidable, it is not of itself void. The third party, if acting in good faith,[2] can invoke Section 35A CA 1985 to prevent the company treating the transaction in question as void. It may enforce against the company the legal obligations that arise from the transaction as if there had been no limit on the company's powers specified in its objects clause. The only time when a transaction entered into by a company is void automatically is where the transaction offends one of the provisions of CA 1985 and is considered illegal.[3]

Can the company's shareholders do anything to stop such transactions? Section 35(2) CA 1985 allows shareholders to seek redress in court to restrain the company from acting in a manner which, but for the impact of Section 35(1), would be beyond its capacity, provided that legal obligations have not yet been created.[4] This right is of limited use. Shareholders will frequently not be aware of the relevant matters before legal obligations have been created and thereby the company will be bound to proceed at the third party's behest.

What if the company itself wants to enforce the legal obligations created with the third party? For the company to enforce the provisions of the transaction against the third party it must first of all ratify the transaction by special resolution of the company's shareholders.[5] Even after this

---

[2] What is good faith? Knowledge of the limitations on the powers of the directors under the company's constitution does not, of itself, equate to bad faith under the new rules. It does not follow that lack of knowledge automatically means that the third party is taken to be acting in good faith. Section 35(A)(2)(b) does not exclude the possibility that, where a vitiating factor is present and the third party dealing with the company deliberately fails to enquire as to the provisions of the company's constitution, he can be found to be acting in bad faith and therefore not entitled to the protection of Section 35A. On this basis, it is advisable for all third parties to check the company's constitution, at least in circumstances where there is a risk of the existence of vitiating factors.

[3] For example, payment of a bribe by a director out of company assets.

[4] Section 35(2) provides that a member may bring proceedings to restrain the doing of an act which, but for Section 35(1), would be beyond the company's capacity. This right is limited almost to the point of disuse because it is extinguished as soon as legal obligations have arisen from the purported act. Legal obligations can now arise by virtue of Section 35(1) together with Section 35A so that an act which is beyond the company's capacity can give rise to legal obligations.

[5] Section 35(3) CA 1985. Commentators are divided as to whether the ratification is required before the company can enforce its rights. For safety, ratification is recommended prior to attempting to enforce.

initial shareholder ratification the director(s) responsible for the transaction in question remain liable for all consequent losses which the company may suffer as a result of such a transaction unless and until a second separate special resolution is passed by the shareholders. For this purpose the directors should be very careful to ensure that the company's objects clause is always wide enough to cover the proposed transaction (*see* 8.1.2 below).

Whose acts bind the company for the purposes of Section 35? The wording of Section 35, "an act done by a company", was originally thought likely to cover an act purported to be done by a company by any of the following:[6]

(a) the company's board;
(b) an individual to whom the board has purported to delegate authority; or
(c) an individual whom the board has held out to third party as having authority to act on the company's behalf.

Since the first edition of this publication, the waters have been muddied by a decision of the Court of Appeal[7] where decisions are taken by improperly constituted boards (e.g. insufficient directors attending to achieve the necessary quorum). It now seems to hinge on the identity of the third party trying to enforce the transaction in question against the company and whether they are an insider or an outsider.

Let us look first at situations where a decision is taken by an inquorate board and where the third party is an outsider. Whether a third party who is an outsider can enforce a transaction against a company in such circumstances depends on whether they obtain the protection of Section 35A CA 1985. This provision works in favour of a person dealing with a company in good faith and has the effect of disapplying fetters found within the company's memorandum and articles on directors' powers to bind the company.

When is a person deemed to be dealing in good faith? Statute[8] helps out to a limited extent stating that: "A person shall not be regarded as acting

---

[6] A narrower interpretation is possible though this would deprive the Section of the protection that the European Communities Act 1972 intended it to give innocent parties dealing with companies.
[7] *Smith v Henniker-Major & Co* [2002] EWCA Civ 762.
[8] Section 35A(2)(b) CA 1985.

in bad faith by reason only of his knowing that an act is beyond the powers of the directors under the company's constitution".

This is less helpful than it appears on first sight because although it does not mean that lack of knowledge automatically means that the person concerned is acting in good faith, there may be some other vitiating factor present which still renders such a person not to be acting in good faith and therefore not able to avail himself of Section 35A(1). The vitiating factors are not clear and there has been insufficient case law to clarify the extent to which the courts are willing to offer protection under this Section to the dealing party. In the meantime it is prudent for those dealing with companies to request copies of their constitutional documents, especially in circumstances where there may be vitiating factors present.

Does the position differ if the company is a charity? By Section 35(4) the provisions of Sections 35 and 35A are modified in relation to companies which are charities. They do not apply to acts of a company which is known to be a charity, except where they are normal commercial transactions entered into for the full market consideration with persons who have no knowledge that the act is beyond the company's memorandum.[9] When considering a change in the company's objects clause to avoid the whole scenario the directors must be sure that they seek prior approval from the charity commissioner.

The second scenario is where a decision is taken by an inquorate board and where the third party is an insider, for example a director of the company. The recent Court of Appeal decision[10] referred to above involved a director of a company attempting, at an inquorate meeting, to assign a legal right which was vested in the company to himself. The Court of Appeal found by a majority that he was unable to benefit from the provisions in Section 35A, but their reasoning was far from clear. They did not go as far as to say that no director could rely on this provision but decided that someone in Mr Smith's specific position could not rely upon it. (Mr Smith was the chairman of the company and as such had a duty to ensure that the constitution was applied properly. He was personally responsible for the error on which he then tried to rely.) The decision seems to have been taken, at least in part, to get away from a clear, logical but otherwise unpalatable High Court

---

[9] These provisions for charities were inserted by Section 65 Charities Act 1993.
[10] *Smith* v *Henniker-Major & Co* [2002] EWCA Civ 762.

decision that a decision of an inquorate board was not a decision of the board at all and therefore that no third party, whether an insider or an outsider, could rely on its protection. In the meantime, directors should be aware that they will have difficulties enforcing a transaction where they contract with their own companies and purport to hold a board meeting, either alone or with other board members, which is inquorate or otherwise improperly convened, to approve the transaction in question.

Even if a director can rely on Section 35A, this is not their last hurdle. Section 322A CA 1985[11] qualifies Section 35A by providing that a transaction with a director (or other connected person) is "voidable" at the company's instance where the board's constitutional limits have been exceeded. (This Section covers transactions both where the directors carry out acts beyond the company's powers under its objects clause or where they exceed their own powers to act under the company's constitution.) It is a provision designed to deprive "insiders" of the benefits otherwise afforded by Sections 35 and 35A (as described above) to persons who deal with a company. It takes effect where directors have exceeded any limitation on their powers within the company's constitution (whether in the memorandum, articles, a shareholder resolution[12] or an agreement between members)[13] in connection with a transaction where one of the other parties is an insider. Who are "insiders" for the purposes of Section 322? Insiders for this purpose are directors of either the company or of its holding company and persons connected[14] with those directors or companies associated with those directors.

This Section applies to any director (or other insider) who deals with his company, whether or not he plays an active part in the company's decision to conclude that transaction. Such transactions are voidable at

---

[11] Section 322A was inserted in Part X CA 1985 by Section 109 Companies Act 1989.
[12] The shareholder resolution can be in a general meeting or a resolution by a particular class of shareholders.
[13] The agreement can be between all members or the shareholders of a particular class of shares.
[14] "Connected persons" are defined in Section 346 CA 1985 as a person who is not a director of the company who falls into one of five categories specified therein, including spouses, children, stepchildren and partners.

the instance of the company until the circumstances specified in Section 322A(5) arise.[15]

If ratified by the shareholders in general meeting, the transaction ceases to be void, but this ratification does not of itself relieve the director(s) concerned of liability. The resolutions required to ratify must be either ordinary or special, whichever is appropriate. If the transaction was beyond the scope of the company's capacity, for example beyond the scope of the company's objects clause, then a special resolution will be required, otherwise an ordinary resolution will suffice. Recent case law[16] indicates that where a company seeks to ratify a commitment entered into by a company, it is safer not to seek simultaneously to amend the terms of the original commitment.

The directors who authorised the transaction in question, whether or not the transaction is avoided by the company, must:

(a) account to the company for any gain (whether direct or indirect) under the transaction; and
(b) indemnify the company against any resultant loss or damage.

Insiders other than directors can avoid this liability in certain circumstances.[17]

8.1.2 Drafting and interpretation of objects clauses

As discussed above, the drafting of a company's objects clause may no longer affect whether or not a transaction is enforceable by a third party against a company, but the scope of this clause is still crucial for

---

[15] A transaction cannot be avoided by the company where the legal rights of a third party, who has acted:

(a) in good faith;
(b) for value; and
(c) without actual notice that the directors had exceeded their powers in entering the transaction on behalf of the company,
(d) would be affected.

[16] *Smith v Henniker-Major & Co* [2002] EWCA Civ 762.

[17] To avoid liability under Section 322(6) CA 1985 the insider must prove that at the time of the transaction he did not know that the directors were exceeding their powers.

determining whether director(s) authorising the transaction acted outside the company's scope and are thus subject to personal liability for any resultant loss that may be suffered by the company in relation to the transaction concerned.

Many companies have taken to including very broad wording within their objects clause to try to increase its scope to cover any business in which the company may want to be involved. To give the intended interpretation to such general wording in the objects clause it is advisable for the memorandum to state that each paragraph is to be read separately and without limitation by reference to other clauses.[18] This prevents the courts from limiting the ambit provided by the extra wording to matters related and auxiliary to those laid out expressly in the clause.

But if the memorandum authorises an act expressly to a limited extent, this by implication forbids any act outside of that limit. For example, a power to borrow up to £1,000 will be read so that borrowing in excess of £1,000 will be unlawful under the company's constitution.

Where the memorandum is unclear or the articles of association ("the articles") contradict provisions in the former then the following rules of construction must be observed. The memorandum takes precedence over the articles; the articles cannot vary the memorandum by purportedly giving the memorandum powers inconsistent with it. However, if the memorandum is ambiguous or silent then contemporaneous articles may explain the meaning.

In view of the ever-lengthening objects clauses being drafted, Section 110 Companies Act 1989 ("CA 1989") made provision for a general commercial company to have a standard statement of objects which takes the form of a new Section 3A inserted into CA 1985. Many companies have taken to using this short statement of objects in addition to, rather than in place of, the earlier multi-part clauses. For the time being commentators recommend that this course be adopted until the courts have had a chance to rule on the effect of the current statutory clause.

---

[18] This interpretation can be seen in the case *Cotman v Brougham* [1918] AC 514 where it was held that providing the registrar of companies had accepted the clause this was conclusive that the company had all of the powers set forth in the memorandum, however dissimilar they may be from what appeared to be the main object of the company.

If the objects of the company do not cover adequately and clearly the matter proposed, then the board should seek to have them changed. Section 110 CA 1989 inserted a new Section 4 into CA 1985 enabling the objects clause to be changed for any reason[19] by means of a shareholder special resolution. If the company concerned is a charity then any proposed change to the objects clause should have the prior approval of the charity commissioner.

8.1.3 Directors' personal liability

A director is liable under a Section 35 transaction even if the company ratifies the transaction by shareholder special resolution itself, unless the company also separately ratifies by shareholder special resolution the director's breach of authority as required by Section 35(3). Unless and until such ratification is given, the director is liable for any damages suffered by the company as a result of the transaction. There is no financial cap on potential liability.

A director will also be liable under Section 322A[20] CA 1985 where he deals with the company in respect of which he holds a directorship or that company's subsidiary. Liability under this Section is strict. It does not matter that the director may not have played an active part in the company's decision to conclude that transaction.

It is not just the directors against whom the company can have legal recourse. If the matter in question has involved a breach of trust by a director[21] and company property has been misappropriated, then the court may find that there is a constructive trust and that the third party holds the property in question on trust for the company. Other remedies that may also be open to the company such as common law tracing and seeking tortuous remedies from the director for having induced a breach of contract or for breach of his fiduciary duty.

The position is different if the "transaction" occurred before 4 February 1991.

---

[19] Previously the change of objects clause had to fall within certain specified grounds.
[20] Directors' liability under Section 322A is more strict than that under Section 322 CA 1985, that is relating to substantial property transactions.
[21] Not all breaches of directorial duty are a breach of trust, though all breaches of trust are by necessity a breach of duty. Breach of trust requires misappropriation of company assets.

Directors' Powers and Proceedings

8.1.4 Limiting directors' personal liability

As described above, current statute allows third parties to enforce agreements against companies which are a party to them even if the directors of the company in question exceeded their authority or the nature of the transaction exceeds the company's objects under its memorandum. The company in question can ratify all such agreements by shareholder resolution but a second separate resolution is required to absolve the director(s) concerned from personal liability.

Prospective directors will often seek to limit the effects of this potential personal liability before accepting their appointments to a board, whether by way of an insurance policy or an indemnity agreement.

8.1.4.1 Indemnity agreements

Commonly indemnity agreements are entered into between a director and one or more shareholders of the company, or by other persons in respect of personal liability that may be incurred by the director during and as a result of his office. Care must be taken that such agreements do not infringe Section 310 CA 1985, which makes void any exception or indemnity given by a company to a director for negligence, default, breach of duty or breach of trust in relation to the company. This is not a problem if the indemnity is given by one or more shareholders or other third parties, but even these parties are unlikely to indemnify against fraud.

A company can indemnify one of its directors in respect of his negligence, default, breach of duty or breach of trust to it:

(a) to the extent of costs he incurs in a successful claim for relief from personal liability under Section 727 CA 1985 (*see* 8.1.4.3 below); and/or

(b) to the extent of buying and keeping in force insurance (*see* 8.1.4.2 below) for the director against any such liability.

Section 310 CA 1985 prohibits the company giving an advance indemnity to one of its directors in respect of liabilities to third parties under any provision of CA 1985 and related legislation by which personal liability is imposed on directors.

8.1.4.2 Insurance policies against directors' personal liability

Since the end of the 1980s it has been clear that insurance policies may be taken out by companies in favour of their own directors. A typical directors' and officers' liability insurance policy (frequently referred to as "D&O insurance") typically comprises:

(a) directors' and officers' liability insurance; and
(b) companies' reimbursement insurance.

Frequently companies will buy D&O insurance policies covering both of these elements, but policies covering just the first element above (directors' and officers' liability insurance) can be purchased by directors in an individual capacity.

What matters are covered by these policies? Typical policies on the market cover liability arising from actual or alleged:

(a) negligent acts;
(b) errors;
(c) omissions;
(d) misstatements;
(e) misleading statements;
(f) neglect; and
(g) breach of duty,

and are likely to extend to:

(a) damages;
(b) settlements;
(c) legal fees; and
(d) expenses.

Matters unlikely to be protected include:

(a) the consequences of defamation;
(b) injury or death;
(c) pollution;
(d) dishonest, fraudulent or criminal acts or omissions;
(e) payments for punitive or exemplary damages;
(f) criminal or civil fines;
(g) penalties imposed by law; and
(h) taxes.

It is important to note that policies sometimes do not protect directors where they are being sued by their own company. Since it is precisely the risk that the company may be seeking to recover loss suffered as a

Directors' Powers and Proceedings

result as a result of a director's unauthorised or *ultra vires* act, such a policy will not serve the director well.

Companies considering taking out such an insurance policy to protect the directors should make sure that:

(a) the company's memorandum and articles permit such policies to be effected. If they do not, or the ambit of the objects clause is unclear, the objects clause should be altered (*see* 8.1.2 above);
(b) the company's articles do not limit the company to only giving certain types of indemnity or taking out certain types of insurance, in which case the articles may need to be amended;
(c) the company's articles require an independent quorum of directors when such matters are discussed, in which case the articles may need to be amended;[22] and
(d) the insurance policy proposed covers all liabilities which may lawfully be insured against where the premium is paid by the company; and
(e) subject to this, the policy provides cover effectively in the areas allowed.

Clearly the director must also make sure that a policy is renewed when required in order to prevent the cover lapsing. Where a company effects such a policy in respect of one of its directors it must state this fact in the next directors' report.

Recently there has been press coverage of a considerable hike in premiums for D&O insurance, presumably in part due to the publicity surrounding Equitable Life's decision to sue its former directors. As well as premiums for cover increasing, insurance providers have started to add more onerous provisions into policies, for example adding in geographical exclusions (e.g. aimed at carving out payment of directors' defence costs in respect of US litigation) and onerous cancellation clauses.

---

[22] If all of the directors are intended to be covered by a single policy, it may not be possible to convene a board meeting with an independent quorum if the articles do not permit interested directors to either count in quorum or to vote on matters in which they have an interest. Most public companies and some private companies would need to alter their articles inserting a new provision relaxing the quorum requirement in these circumstances if the policies are to be approved by resolution of the directors and not by the shareholders.

Directors should scrutinise the terms of their company's D&O insurance policies in order to assess whether there are significant gaps and if so whether they should take out personal cover. (The argument that not having cover makes directors less likely to be sued is cold comfort to those faced with lawsuits.)

The Higgs Review (January 2003) into the role and effectiveness of non-executive directors (as discussed in more detail in Chapter 9 below) made some recommendations in respect of D&O insurance including that companies should:

(a) provide appropriate D&O insurance to directors; and
(b) supply details of their insurance cover to potential non-executive directors before they are appointed.

The former recommendation is proposed as a new provision (A.1.5) in the Combined Code annexed to the UK Listing Authority ("UKLA") Listing Rules (the "Listing Rules").

Various bodies[23] have agreed, subsequent to the publication of the Higgs review, to draw up guidance for companies to use when obtaining D&O insurance. At the time of this edition going to print no guidance had been produced. Matters which the Higgs Review indicated could be covered by such guidance included:

(a) details of risks that should be covered and those that cannot be;
(b) advice on aggregate limits for cover; and
(c) advice on exposure to claims outside the UK.

8.1.4.3 Court order
The court may relieve a director of his personal liability under the powers granted to it in Section 727 CA 1985 where it finds that:

(a) the director has acted honestly and reasonably; and
(b) having regard to all the circumstances of the case he ought fairly to be excused.

In such circumstances the court may relieve the director, either wholly or in part, from his personal liability on such terms as the court thinks

---

[23] The City of London Law Society, the Institute of Chartered Secretaries and Administrators, the Association of British Insurers and the British Insurance Brokers' Association.

fit. As mentioned above, a company may indemnify a director for the costs of bringing a successful claim under this Section.

8.2 Delegation

8.2.1 General

Certain powers are reserved to the members by statute,[24] otherwise the starting point is that the company, unless otherwise expressly provided for in its constitution or by board resolution, can only act after proposals have been agreed by the passing of a board resolution at a board meeting by the majority of the directors attending, provided quorum requirements for the meeting are satisfied. Without express delegation of authority having been given to a group of directors, it is inappropriate for such directors to act without meeting or at a meeting of which notice has not been given to the whole body of directors. Decisions of a majority of the directors made at board meetings which were not duly convened will be invalid. (An exception to the requirement to hold meetings may be permitted where all directors are agreed or acquiesce and a decision is taken informally,[25] though this should not be relied upon unless absolutely necessary.)

For each board meeting reasonable notice must be given to all directors unless they are out of the country. The articles will provide for the business of the company to be managed by the directors. If the company has Table A articles, then Regulation 70 permits the directors to manage the company's business by exercising the powers provided by CA 1985 and the memorandum and articles. Directors do not have any power to act beyond that capacity.

Company affairs would grind to a halt if this were the only legal method of making company decisions. Often, therefore, express provision will be made for committees of directors or even solely executive directors to manage limited matters on behalf of the company. There are some matters which in the interests of good corporate governance should not be delegated down from a board level. For listed companies the

---

[24] Powers reserved to a company's shareholders include the power to change the objects of the company, the power to change the articles, the power to change the company name and the power to ratify actions by directors otherwise beyond the capacity of the company, to name but a few.
[25] *Charterhouse Investment Trust Limited* v *Tempest Diesels Limited* (1986) BCLC 1 at p. 9.

A Practitioner's Guide to Directors' Duties and Responsibilities

Combined Code of the Rules requires boards of directors to produce a schedule of matters which are reserved for the approval of the main board.[26] Paragraph 424 of the Cadbury Report (from which the Code originated) states that such a schedule would include at least:

(a) acquisitions and disposals of assets of the company or its subsidiaries that are material to the company; and
(b) management of investments, capital projects, authority levels, treasury policies and risk management policies.

The rules to determine the materiality of any transaction are expected to be produced and used by boards. Once the materiality of a transaction has been established using these rules the number of board signatures required for the transaction in question will be evident. These rules necessitate that more directors are directly involved the more substantial a transaction is, thus minimising the scope for misjudgement and possible illegality.

The Cadbury Committee also stated that boards should agree the procedures to be followed when, exceptionally, decisions are required between board meetings. Care should be taken before agreement is reached on delegating approval of any of the following:

(a) interim and final dividend recommendation;
(b) significant changes in accounting policies or practices;
(c) material circulars to shareholders and listings particulars;
(d) press releases concerning matters decided by the board;
(e) board appointments and removals; and
(f) terms of reference for executive directors.

8.2.2 Delegation to committees

A company must have express provision within its constitutional documents before it may delegate any functions to a committee of directors. There will usually be a provision in the company's articles. Regulation 72 of Table A provides that the directors of the company may (clearly by board resolution) delegate any of their powers[27] to any committee consisting of one or more directors, such delegation may be

---

[26] Code provision A.1.1.
[27] Whilst "any" powers can be delegated, the comments on good corporate governance above, particularly for listed companies, should be borne in mind.

subject to any conditions that the directors may impose. The board, when resolving to make such delegation, must not only clearly define the ambit of the committee's authority, but also specify whether the powers granted to the committee are granted in exclusion or in addition to the board of directors' own powers.

Even if powers are granted exclusively to a committee, the board in all cases retains the ability to alter or revoke any authority given.[28] Such revocation occurs automatically if the board passes a resolution expressly revoking the authority of the committee, but can also occur implicitly where the board exercises a power that has been delegated to the committee where the original delegation gave authority solely to the committee. The membership of a committee must be set out by the board, specifying if membership is to be for a fixed period or for such period until they resign their position or are replaced. However, even if the appointment of a particular person to a committee was for a fixed period it may be revoked immediately by the board.[29]

The ability to delegate some of the board's decision-making powers to committees is an invaluable way of facilitating company management, by allowing directors to attend overall fewer management meetings each and thereby freeing up more time to develop the commercial aspects of a company. Abuse of the committee structure as a means of excluding a particular director or minority of directors who are properly entitled and obliged to participate in the management, not just by voting but also by having general corporate financial and commercial information available to them, is not allowed by the courts.[30]

The aim of releasing some directors from the need to attend some meetings (as allowed by the committee structure) does not mean that it entitles a company to take matters discussed at committee meetings any less seriously. Minutes should be kept of all committee proceedings in the same way as is required by Regulation 10(b) of Table A for board meetings.

Good corporate governance recognises that some matters are better dealt with by committees rather than by the whole board, particularly where

---

[28] Any agreement that purports irrevocably to delegate the directors' powers would be viewed by the courts to be contrary to public policy and unenforceable.
[29] *Manton v Brighton Corporation* [1951] 2 KB 393.
[30] *Bray v Smith* [1908] 124 LT Jo 293.

factions of directors are bound to be interested in the outcome, for example producing general company policy on directors' pay. The Cadbury Report recommends that companies should maintain three committees:

(a) an audit committee;
(b) a nominations committee; and
(c) a remuneration committee.

It was a recommendation of the Higgs Review (*see* Chapter 9 for more details) that the Combined Code be amended to add the requirement for these three committees to have written terms of reference and that those of the remuneration and audit committees should be made public (adopted as Provisions A.4.1, B.2.1 and C.3.2). In January 2003, the Financial Reporting Council ("FRC") published a revised version of the Combined Code incorporating the changes recommended by the Higgs and Smith Reviews. A 12-week consultation period followed. The FRC initially said that it would not re-open the substance of the recommendations and that the new Code would come into effect on 1 July 2003. It subsequently announced on 14 May 2003 that it was setting up a working group to produce a revised version of the Combined Code in the light of comments received. The working group produced a revised text in July 2003 with a view to the new Combined Code coming into effect "as soon as possible consistent with a high quality output". It seemed that the strong criticism of the revised Code forced the FRC to do a more fundamental review of the changes than they initially intended.

If a board delegates power to a committee without any provision relating to the committee's quorum, all acts of the committee must be carried out in the presence of all members of the committee. The committee apparently has no power to add to their number or to fill a vacancy.

Whatever matters are delegated to committees for listed companies, the Code requires that the board should still meet regularly.[31]

8.2.3 Delegation to individual executives

Delegation may be to individuals, particularly to executive directors of a company who have various areas of specialised business flair. The usual executive posts that a reasonable sized company will fill include

---

[31] Code provision A.1.1.

that of managing director or chief executive officer, chairman, sales director and finance director. Regulation 91 of Table A permits directors to appoint a chairman of the board who may be provided with a casting vote where votes are otherwise evenly distributed in a directors' board meeting.[32] The chairman by his title does not have any particular areas of responsibility other than those set out expressly. The authority to delegate matters down to other individual directors comes from Regulation 72 of Table A which, in addition to allowing delegation by the board to a managing director, also allow the appointment by the directors of the board of "any one or more of their number ... to any other executive office". If the company does not have Table A then there must be an article expressly on this point. The board are unable to delegate to a managing director unless the articles or a resolution enable them to do so.[33] Any such delegation to an executive, as to a committee, may be:

(a) made subject to any conditions that the directors may impose;
(b) either alongside or to the exclusion of their own powers; and
(c) may be revoked or altered.

Executives other than the managing director are usually appointed with a restricted area of responsibility such as finance, marketing etc. Any such executive appointee will not be required to retire by rotation.[34] In the *Hely-Hutchinson* case[35] Justice Roskill disagreed that "mere status, derived from the holding of a particular office ... [of itself] implies an authority which would not otherwise exist".[36] The case itself concerned a chairman acting as managing director.

The level of power that ought to be delegated to a particular individual is reflected partly by the executive status given in his service contract and partly by his area of expertise and past experience. Some executive posts have connotations of holding more power than others, though the exact remit in each case is a matter to be set by the board. The most important director of a company is often described as the "managing director" or as the "chief executive". In relation to listed companies the Combined Code, the product of the Cadbury, Greenbury and Hampel Reports,

---

[32] *See* Regulation 88 of Table A. Incidentally the chairman is usually also given the power to chair general meetings and to have a casting vote at such meetings under Regulations 42 and 50 of Table A.
[33] *Nelson v James Nelson & Sons* [1914] 2 KB 770.
[34] *See* Regulation 84 of Table A.
[35] *Hely-Hutchinson v Brayhead Limited* [1968] 1 QB 549.
[36] Though he conceded such an implication might be made in some cases.

recognises the power that is frequently delegated to the managing director and recommends that a single person should not hold both the roles of managing director and chairman. The 1998 Code[37] required that a decision to combine the posts of chairman and chief executive officer in one person should be publicly justified and that, whether the posts are held by different people or the same person, there should be a strong and independent non-executive element, with a recognised senior member, on the board. The Higgs Review recommended that the division of duties between the chairman and the chief executive officer should be set out in writing and that a chief executive officer should not become a chairman of his company even once he has stepped down from the former role (A.2.1, A.2.2).

There can in certain circumstances be cases of implied delegation, though these generally arise when something has gone wrong and the company has sought to limit its liability by claiming that a particular director had not had the requisite power delegated to him and that consequently the company was still bound. Where an individual has matters of authority implicitly delegated down to him, the company can be held to any transactions completed with third parties in good faith as discussed in 8.1.1 above. In the *Charterhouse* case above, Justice Hoffmann found that there had been acquiescence by two of the three directors of a company that the third agreed to surrender tax losses for the company. Such a finding was on the basis that the other two directors were content to acquiesce in whatever lawful terms were agreed between the third and the other party. It did not matter that there had not been a formal board meeting delegating such power. This is not to say that there can be an implied delegation of all matters by acquiescence.[38]

8.2.4 Delegation by directors to non-officer employees and other parties

It was Justice Romer's view in *Re City Equitable Fire Insurance Company*[39] that the larger the business the more numerous, and the more important, the matters that must of necessity be left to the managers, the accountants and the rest of the staff.

---

[37] 1998 Code provision A.2.1.
[38] The case *Mitchell & Hobbs (UK) Limited* v *Mill* [1996] 2BCLC 102 is the authority that there is no unilateral right on the part of a managing director to take proceedings on a company's behalf in absence of express delegation by the board.
[39] *Re City Equitable Fire Insurance Company* [1925] Ch 407.

Directors' Powers and Proceedings

Directors will almost invariably pass down a certain level of responsibility and day-to-day running of aspects of the areas which they oversee whilst retaining ultimate responsibility for internal management of more junior members.

Directors are permitted to rely upon non-employee advisers in particular circumstances. In *Stephens* v *Hoare* (1904) 20 TLR 407 it was ruled that in the context of the preparation of a prospectus the directors are entitled to rely upon the assistance and advice of the company's legal advisers. Indeed for listed companies the Code[40] provides that there should be a procedure agreed by the board of directors in the furtherance of their duties to take independent professional advice if necessary, at the company's expense.

8.2.5 Continuing duties of a director towards matters delegated

A director is entitled, in the absence of any matters that should put him on notice, to trust his fellow directors and all other officers of the company to perform those matters which may be properly delegated to them. But whilst the board may make these delegations, they cannot abdicate responsibility for these powers and they cannot relieve themselves of the duty to continue to supervise the management of these matters. This principle was most publicly borne out in the trial of the various directors of the Barings group after the collapse of Barings Bank with total losses of £927 million caused largely by a single trader, Nick Leeson.

In the *Barings*[41] case, it was accepted by the Companies Court that boards may delegate specific tasks and functions within the company or group to managers and/or employees. The judge emphasised, however, that this does not mean that directors (either individually or collectively) cease to bear any responsibility for the discharge of the delegated function. Directors have, collectively and individually, an ongoing duty to acquire and maintain sufficient knowledge and understanding of the company's business, including supervision of the discharge of delegated functions, to enable them properly to discharge their duties as directors. The judge did not attempt to formulate a rule of universal application as to directors' residual duties of monitoring and supervision referred to above. The extent of these duties, and the question of whether they have

---

[40] Code provision A.5.2.
[41] *Re Barings plc (No. 6)* [1999] 1BCLC 433.

been discharged, depend upon the particular facts of each case, including the director's role in the management of the company.

As a result of *Barings* all directors, whatever their status, have a basic duty to keep themselves regularly informed of company affairs (especially finance matters) and to participate at least to some degree in the supervision and monitoring of their co-directors and other delegates. This duty continues to exist even if directors are kept very busy by other particular aspects of their work. The management structure is not obliged to accommodate the amount of time that a director may be spending dealing with particular aspects of the company's business, for example winning deals.[42] Less time to spend on supervision does not lead to a lessening of the duty to supervise. Merely sitting in on meetings without making inquiries and without having acquired the background knowledge to understand at least a proportion of the content does not aid fulfilment of the duty.

Though previous law[43] had led to the conclusion that non-executive directors had an equivalent level of directorial responsibility, one implication of *Barings* is that more will be expected of executive directors than of non-executive directors, although it would be wrong to assume that non-executive directors have no responsibility.

The level of the individual director's remuneration is now a relevant factor in determining the extent of his duty;[44] more is expected of a highly paid director. Similarly, the standard of the basic duty may be scaled upwards to reflect the level of each director's skill and experience,[45]

---

[42] The court rejected such a submission by one of the Barings directors, Mr Turkey.
[43] After the case of *Dorchester Finance Co. Limited* v *Stebbing* [1989] BCLC 498 a strong message was received that non-executive directors have the same legal responsibilities as any other director and will be subject to all the statutory restrictions affecting directors.
[44] Sir Richard Scott VC in his judgment commented:

> "Status in an organisation carries with it commensurate rewards. These rewards are matched by the weight of the responsibility that the office carries with it, and those responsibilities require diligent attention from time to time to the question of whether the system that has been put in place over which the individual is presiding is operating efficiently, and whether individuals to whom duties in accordance with the system have been delegated are discharging those duties efficiently."

[45] *Re Continental Assurance of London plc* [1997] 1 BCLC 48.

though generally one expects strong attributes in this area to be rewarded by higher remuneration, so perhaps this is less of an issue than might at first appear to those whose hard work has taken them to such a fortuitous position.

The directors in the *Barings* case were disqualified under the Company Directors Disqualification Act 1986 following the failures of the internal management controls which allowed Mr Leeson to operate in the manner that he had which were found to be crass and absolute. There was no challenge to the honesty or integrity of the three respondents, but as a result of such disqualification they were nevertheless prevented from taking up directorships for considerable periods.[46]

What has been the impact of *Barings*? The Combined Code now expressly requires listed companies' boards to maintain a sound system of internal control to safeguard shareholders' investment and the company's assets. In September 1999 the Institute of Chartered Accountants in England and Wales published its final guidance on the implementation of the internal control requirements of the Combined Code on Corporate Governance. The practical guidance *Internal Control: Guidance for Directors on the Combined Code*, which has the support and endorsement of the Stock Exchange (competence has now been transferred to the FSA as the new UKLA), states: "a company's system of internal control has a key role in the management of risks that are significant to the fulfilment of its business objectives".

The guidance indicates that the company's internal control system should:

(a) be embedded within its operations and not be treated as a separate exercise;
(b) be able to respond to changing risks within and outside the company; and
(c) enable each company to apply it in an appropriate manner related to its key risks.

The guidance requires companies to identify, evaluate and manage their significant risks and to assess the effectiveness of the related internal control system. Boards of directors are called on to review regularly reports on the effectiveness of the system of internal control in managing

---

[46] The court can fix an appropriate period between two and 15 years.

key risks, and to undertake an annual assessment for the purpose of making their statements on internal control in the annual report.[47]

Executive management is responsible for managing risks through maintaining an effective system of internal control, and the board as a whole is responsible for reporting on it. An appendix to the guidance suggests questions the board may want to consider and discuss with management when carrying out its annual assessment of internal control. The guidance, including the appendix, can be found on the Institute's website.[48]

8.2.6 Where there has been no official delegation of authority

Whilst Section 35A (as discussed in 8.1.1 above) does not operate to extend directly the powers of anyone else other than the board of directors, such as a committee or any individual director, it is possible that under the law of agency the acts of an individual may still bind the company where there has been no official delegation of authority.

When can the third party rely on agreements it has made with this unauthorised person who acts beyond the bounds of his authority? The individual may bind the company to the agreement if he acts as the company's agent. The law of agency is complex but essentially the individual agent must have either actual authority (which clearly is not applicable here) or ostensible authority to do the thing which he does on behalf of the company (his principal).

When will an individual have ostensible authority? What amounts to ostensible authority will vary with circumstances. If a company (or a person with actual authority for a particular matter) represents that an individual has authority delegated down for that matter then the company will, if the third party relies on this representation, be bound by the acts of the individual and prevented from claiming that the individual did not have such authority. There is no such thing as a self-authorising agent. In some cases ostensible authority arises not from a positive act, but sometimes by acquiescence by the company of an individual's assumed role such as permitting a director or ex-director to continue to act as if he still was authorised even though his authority has been terminated.

---

[47] As required by Principle C.2.1 of the Combined Code.
[48] www.icaew.co.uk/internal control/.

Directors' Powers and Proceedings

To determine what is usually or customarily within the scope of the authority of a particular agent, the relevant factors include the principal's kind of business, the role of the office holder in that business, current business practices and all other material circumstances. The main executive posts and the ostensible authority that a third party can generally attribute to them are set out below.

(a) Managing director: a company's managing director may generally be presumed to have wide authority to manage the company's ordinary business. An individual permitted to manage the company's day-to-day business may be treated as if he were a managing director.

(b) Chairman: the chairman, by virtue of that office alone, enjoys no special authority to act on behalf of the company in dealings with third parties.[49] He should be treated, in the absence of holding any particular executive posts (e.g. managing director, marketing director or sales director), as any other director.

(c) Company secretary: whilst in the past company secretaries had limited roles, some of which are now encapsulated within their duties under CA 1985, nowadays the company secretary enjoys a wider range of responsibilities for the company's administrative and legal activities.[50]

(d) Finance director: finance directors generally have ostensible authority for accounting and treasury matters.

(e) Other executive directors: in addition to their authority as ordinary directors, other executive directors generally have such authority as is usual for somebody occupying the position they hold as a result of their service contract with the company. This will therefore vary largely from domain to domain.

(f) Ordinary directors: unless the articles provide otherwise, a director does not have authority to bind the company unless he acts as part of the board passing resolutions. Subsequently, an individual director's ostensible authority to act for the company is so limited as to be almost negligible.

---

[49] *Hely-Hutchinson* v *Brayhead Limited* [1968] 1 QB 549 – although in this case the chairman was held to have actual implied authority on the basis that he was also the *de facto* managing director.

[50] The earlier case law as regards the ostensible authority of a company secretary must be regarded with caution since the role of the secretary has blossomed. It is reasonable now to expect a wider scope of ostensible authority.

8.3 Access to company books

8.3.1 Directors' access to company books

Directors have long had an acknowledged right to inspect the company's books either at a board meeting or elsewhere. This right extends to the minutes of directors' meetings and to the company's accounting records. In *Conway* v *Petronius Clothing Co.*[51] Justice Slade clarified that this right of inspection derived not from Section 147[52] Companies Act 1948 but from common law.[53] (Section 147 CA 1985 was altered and the current applicable provision is Section 221 CA 1985.) This right was conferred on a director not for his own advantage but to enable him to carry out his duties as a director.

As a corollary to this right the courts will intervene where a director is improperly excluded from board meetings by his fellow directors by granting an injunction restraining the exclusion,[54] although in *Petronius* it should be noted that the director seeking the injunction was also a shareholder.

As the right to inspect is for the benefit of the company, it terminates on a director's removal from office. Almost invariably in cases where directors are refused access to the company books the majority of directors will be seeking to get those denied access removed expediently as directors. Where an application by those refused access comes before the court and a general meeting of the company has already been convened for the purpose of removing the applicant(s) as director(s), the

---

[51] [1978] 1 WLR 72.
[52] Section 147 Companies Act 1948 was intended merely to impose sanctions if the books were not kept properly.
[53] Justice Slade in *Petronius*, however, slightly muddies the water when he:

"[leaves] open the question whether this right conferred on (the director) at common law is to be regarded on the one hand as a right incident to his office and independent of contract or on the other hand, as a right dependent on the express or implied terms of his contract of employment with the company, so that it may be excluded by express provision to the contrary."

If the latter is found to be the case then express terms in directors' service contracts might limit or exclude this right in the event of a board resolution. So far there have been no further cases exploring this *obiter dictum*.

[54] *Pulbrook* v *Richmond Consolidated Mining Co.* [1878] 9 ChD 610.

Directors' Powers and Proceedings

court will normally intervene only if it considers such intervention necessary for the protection of the company.

It will often be argued in such cases that the applicant plans to abuse the inspection, if granted by the court, to damage the interests of the company. Though a court will not allow a director to abuse his right by disregarding the confidence that his office imposes, in absence of clear proof from the respondent it will be assumed that the applicant will inspect in the company's best interests and for its benefit. The court has a discretion as to whether or not to order an inspection. Such were the allegations in the *Petronius* case, where misconduct was alleged against the applicant director, that the court ruled that the balance of convenience was against making the order before a meeting had been held to consider the director's removal.

Where the court uses its discretion to enforce the right to inspect, particularly where the applicant is not a finance director, he is entitled to the assistance of an expert, for example an accountant (subject to the court's discretion to order otherwise or impose conditions). But the company in its turn is entitled to a reasonable time to consider whether to object to the proposed expert.

8.3.2 Third-party rights to view the company books

Section 8.4.1 above dealt with the rights of directors to view the company books. Directors must be aware of the circumstances in which third parties can insist on inspecting the company books so that they do not breach the relevant Sections in CA 1985 and render themselves liable for a personal fine.

8.3.2.1 General viewing
This Section gives a non-exhaustive list of various company books and related matters and their required circulation or "inspectability".

Register of charges
The register of charges must be open for inspection by members and creditors[55] for at least two hours on each business day at the company's registered office. Any refusal by an officer of the company to such inspection is liable to a penalty. On a winding up, however, no one may inspect this register without a court order.

---

[55] This right of inspection does not extend to prospective creditors.

Company accounts
A limited company is required to keep accounts sufficient to show and explain the company's transactions. These records[56] must be kept at the company's registered office, or such other place as the directors think fit, and must be open to inspection by the company's officers at all times.[57] The accounting records must be kept for at least six years (or a reduced minimum of three years for a private company) from the date on which they were made. The accounts must be laid each year before the members of the company in general meeting. This requirement can, however, be avoided where a private company has passed an elective resolution.[58]

The register of directors and secretaries
The company is obliged to keep a register of all directors and secretaries of the company, including shadow directors, and send a copy of this to the registrar of companies.[59] The register must be open to members. If there is a refusal to allow an inspection, the company and every officer in default is liable to be fined.

The register of directors' interests in shares and debentures
Companies are required to keep a register to record the information about those interests in shares and debentures regarding which their directors are required[60] to notify the company. This register should usually be kept in the same place as the register of members and must be open to inspection by members free of charge and by other members of the public for £2.50 an hour. The register must also be produced at the company's general meetings and must remain open and accessible throughout such meetings so that it can be viewed by those attending.

Liquidation/receivership
When a company goes into liquidation the appointed liquidator clearly has a right to view the company books as he will deal with the liquidation

---

[56] The right to inspect applies to the records whether or not they are in a legible format or are on a computer system as permitted by Section 723 CA 1985.
[57] The directors are required to refer to the company accounts. Failure can amount to serious incompetence as in *Re Continental Assurance Co of London PLC* (1996) 93(28) LSG 29 where an interest-free loan amounted to financial assistance prohibited under Section 151 CA 1985. The director's failure to appreciate what would have been obvious if he had viewed the accounts amounted to allowing the loans and this gross incompetence resulted in his disqualification.
[58] Section 252 CA 1985.
[59] Sections 288 and 289 CA 1985.
[60] Under Section 324 CA 1985.

Directors' Powers and Proceedings

matters on the company's behalf, with the sanction of the court or the liquidation committee if required. The court may also enforce delivery to the appointed liquidator of any of the books, property, paper and records to which the company appears to be entitled,[61] though this power is exercisable by the liquidator himself. The liquidator's requirements must be complied with without any avoidable delay.

An administrative receiver has similar rights. Amongst those who have a duty to cooperate with him are persons who have at any point been officers of the company concerned. The administrative receiver can apply to the court for a private examination of any officer of the company.[62]

---

[61] Section 234 Insolvency Act 1986.
[62] Section 236 Insolvency Act 1986.

Chapter 9
Corporate Governance

David Johnson, Partner
Slaughter and May

9.1 Introduction

Following the collapse of Enron and other high-profile corporate failures, there has been a good deal of public comment and speculation regarding the future of corporate governance in the UK. It seems to be accepted that the UK enjoys a relatively well-developed system of corporate governance and this has led to a tendency to view corporate governance as the device that should prevent corporate failures. Realistically, no system of corporate governance could ever achieve this lofty ambition.

When looking at recent corporate failures to assess what went wrong, there seem to be two apparent causes:

(a) a disregard of normal standards of conduct by a powerful individual or individuals (the so-called "Maxwell syndrome"); and
(b) an ill-judged strategic decision or a simple business failing due to an external development (or a failure to respond appropriately to such development).

A more worrying recent trend seems to be for initial problems to be compounded by management action after the problem is identified, whether it be action to obscure the problem or to improve financial performance elsewhere in a business to compensate for the problem.

Corporate governance cannot guard against the "determined rogues". Moreover, it is clear that corporate governance cannot influence external developments. The market may move against a company and no system of corporate governance will prevent that. However, corporate governance can assist businesses to be mindful of potential causes of failure, and plan and act accordingly. In addition, corporate governance can, and should, ensure that the management response to problems is not to compound them by subsequent action.

In 1992 the Cadbury Report[1] defined corporate governance as the system by which companies are directed and controlled for the benefit of shareholders and identified as an objective of good corporate governance the need to give management the freedom to create prosperity without undue bureaucracy or over-regulation, but within a framework of effective accountability. The position occupied by the board of directors is central as it is at the helm of the company, setting the company's strategic aims and supervising the management of the business. However, the shareholders also have a role to play since they appoint the directors and, as a body, they have the power through their votes at general meetings to influence the stewardship of the company.

In theory, through their power to appoint and remove directors, the shareholders of a public company have substantial control over how the company is managed. In practice, it is rare for shareholders to operate collectively, except in response to a corporate initiative such as a takeover or merger. Shareholders usually spread their risk over many investments rather than concentrating their resources in a few companies, and may not have the time or motivation to take a very active interest in the management of the individual companies in which they invest. In recent years, one of the primary concerns of good corporate governance has, therefore, been to address the question of how to strengthen the accountability of boards of directors to their shareholders and promote the relationship between the two.

9.2 Background

The separate roles of the board and the shareholders are long established. By the middle of the nineteenth century it had become established practice for the shareholders to elect the directors and for the directors to run the company. If the members were unhappy with the running of the company they could, in theory, change the board but not intervene in the management. Until their removal, the existing board continued to have control over the management of the company.

This has been an enduring theme in company law, reinforced by the Cadbury Report:

> "The formal relationship between the shareholders and the board of directors is that ... the directors report on their stewardship to the

---

[1] "The Financial Aspects of Corporate Governance", 1 December 1992.

shareholders and ... the shareholders as owners of the company elect the directors to run the business on their behalf and hold them accountable for its progress."[2]

In the post-war years, some institutional investors took the view that it was cheaper to invest in successful companies and to avoid or divest from the unsuccessful ones. Where institutional intervention did take place, it was often on an informal basis rather than through representations or other action at formal shareholder meetings. If the company under-performed, shareholders just sold their shares. As the share price fell, it was at least possible that the acquisitive and more successful companies might move in with takeover proposals. This environment provoked debate about the appropriate standards of corporate governance which it was desirable to promote.

The law currently provides a basic framework of corporate governance by specifying the minimum number of directors that companies may have, by regulating the conduct of directors in a limited way and by providing for certain decisions to be taken by the shareholders. Apart from these requirements, however, companies are generally free to establish their own systems of governance by means of provisions in their memorandum and articles of association ("the articles") or by less formal internal rules. As a result, governance structures are largely not prescribed by law but have developed out of business and commercial practice. The governance of listed companies is also influenced by the additional rules promulgated and administered by the Financial Services Authority ("the FSA"), which are mainly directed towards the protection of investors.

In March 1998 the then Trade & Industry Secretary, Margaret Beckett, launched the three-year review of UK company law, one of the purposes of which is to address whether the law has any greater role to play in the establishment of high standards of corporate governance. During the 1990s the codes of practice developed by three committees which were set up to examine corporate governance issues introduced a new dimension. The approach adopted in those codes was to use self-regulation as a means of promoting and maintaining practices of good governance. The intention in each case was to establish a voluntary code, but with an emphasis on disclosure. The idea was to encourage

---

[2] "The Financial Aspects of Corporate Governance", 1 December 1992; paragraph 6.1.

transparency in corporate governance through disclosure obligations which would promote shareholder pressure to comply with best practice in appropriate cases.

The Cadbury Committee was set up in May 1990 as a result of public concern over high-profile corporate failures such as Polly Peck, BCCI and Maxwell. The objective of the Cadbury Committee was to help to raise the standards of corporate governance and the level of confidence in financial reporting and auditing by setting out clearly the responsibilities of the directors and their relationship with the auditors. The committee published its report, accompanied by its Code of Best Practice, in December 1992.[3]

Concern over what were considered to be excessive remuneration and compensation packages awarded to some directors resulted in the establishment of the Greenbury Committee in January 1995 to identify good practice in determining directors' remuneration. The committee published its report and Code of Best Practice in July 1995.[4]

Unlike the Cadbury and Greenbury Committees, the establishment of the Hampel Committee in November 1995 was not a reaction to public concern about the way in which companies regulated themselves, but rather to the two reports which had preceded it. The Hampel Committee was born out of the recommendation of Cadbury and Greenbury that a committee should follow up on the implementation of their findings. The aim was to draw up a set of principles and a code, based on Cadbury, Greenbury and its own conclusions.

Following the publication of the final report of the Hampel Committee,[5] the London Stock Exchange ("the Exchange") issued the Principles of Good Governance and the Code of Best Practice ("the Combined Code") in June 1998, which was derived from the reports of the three committees on corporate governance. At the same time, the Exchange published a new listing rule,[6] requiring listed companies to include in their annual reports and accounts specified details as to how they had complied

---

[3] "The Financial Aspects of Corporate Governance", 1 December 1992; The Code of Best Practice, 1 December 1992.
[4] "Directors' Remuneration – Report of a Study Group chaired by Sir Richard Greenbury", 17 July 1995.
[5] Committee on Corporate Governance, Final Report, January 1998.
[6] Listing Rule 12.43A.

with the Combined Code during the year under review, but it did not require listed companies to comply with the Combined Code. This is the "comply or explain" philosophy that still underpins corporate governance.

The Turnbull Committee was set up by the Institute of Chartered Accountants in England and Wales to provide guidance for listed companies on how to implement the requirements in the Combined Code relating to internal control. Its report set guidelines for ensuring that companies have in place effective risk management and internal control systems.[7]

Following the collapse of Enron in 2001, the Government appointed Derek Higgs in April 2002 to head a review of "the role and effectiveness of non-executive directors in the UK". This followed the Myners review of institutional investment, "Institutional Investment in the United Kingdom, a Review", March 2001. In addition, the Financial Reporting Council ("FRC") commissioned a report by Sir Robert Smith to clarify the responsibilities of audit committees and to develop the existing Combined Code guidance in this area.[8] The final reports from these exercises were published in January 2003 and included a revised version of the Combined Code which was due to take effect from 1 July 2003. However, following criticism of both the substance of certain findings of the Higgs Review and the speed at which its findings were to be implemented through the revised Combined Code, the FRC did not publish the final version of the revised Combined Code until 23 July 2003. The revised version will now take effect from 1 November 2003.

The three-year review of company law is also reaching its conclusion. The Government White Paper, "Modernising Company Law", together with a draft Companies Bill, was published in July 2002. Among other things, it is proposed that the duties of directors be codified, although the proposed statutory provisions seem to add little to the current common law position. In addition, the Directors' Remuneration Report Regulations came into force in August 2002 and these oblige companies to publish a report on directors' remuneration as part of the company's annual reporting cycle and to submit this report to a shareholder vote at the annual general meeting. Although this vote is advisory in nature (i.e. there are no legal consequences if the report is voted down), it provides

---

[7] "Internal Control: Guidance for Directors on the Combined Code", September 1999.
[8] The Smith Report "Audit committees: Combined Code guidance", January 2003.

shareholders with an opportunity to register any objection to remuneration policy.

Notwithstanding recent and proposed statutory provisions, the structure for corporate governance in the UK is not based on firm legal rules but rather on codes of best practice. This Chapter focuses on the present corporate governance regime in the UK, of which the Combined Code forms a cornerstone.

9.3 The Combined Code

> "Good corporate governance is not just a matter of prescribing particular corporate structures and complying with a number of hard and fast rules. There is a need for broad principles. All concerned should then apply these flexibly and with common sense to the varying circumstances of individual companies."[9]

This statement highlights the approach taken by the Hampel Committee to corporate governance in the UK. The Hampel Committee adopted the same philosophy as its two predecessors, namely that successful corporate governance could not be delivered by rules and regulations designed to be rigidly applied and complied with by all listed companies. The principles set out by the Hampel Committee were incorporated into the Combined Code, most of them having provisions appended to them to indicate how the principles might be applied in practice.

The Higgs Review has precipitated further changes to the Combined Code and has set out a summary of the principal duties of remuneration and nomination committees, a pre-appointment due diligence checklist for new board members[10] and a guide for evaluating the performance of the board.[11] However, the Higgs Review remained rooted in the existing approach to corporate governance in the UK, that is the "comply or explain" philosophy. It also endorsed the UK's unitary board system and included thinly veiled criticism of the typical US board model where a limited number of executive directors are supplemented by a large number of non-executive directors.

---

[9] Hampel Report, paragraph 1.11.
[10] The Higgs Report, Annex G.
[11] Ibid, Annex J.

9.3.1 Board structure

"Every listed company should be headed by an effective board, which is collectively responsible for the success of the company."[12]

One of the ways in which the Hampel Committee recommended that the board of a company can achieve its role effectively was to ensure that the board was not dominated by one individual or a group of individuals. To promote this end, the Combined Code stated that the board should include non-executive directors of sufficient calibre and number for their views to carry significant weight in the board's decisions. It recommended that non-executive directors should comprise not less than one-third of the board.

The Higgs Review went further, putting particular emphasis on greater independent non-executive presence and refining the definition of "independence". The revised version of the Combined Code states that at least half of the board, excluding the Chairman, should be non-executive directors who satisfy the new definition, and that the board should identify in its annual report the non-executive directors that it determines to be independent. Following concern about the ability of smaller companies to recruit sufficient independent non-executive directors to meet this requirement, the FRC amended the revised version of the Combined Code so that it requires companies below FTSE-350 level to have at least two independent non-executive directors rather than a majority.[13]

The role of non-executive directors in making the work of the board effective to promote the best interests of the company is seen as crucial. This view has been promoted by institutional investors for many years. One of the important functions of non-executive directors is viewed as being to prevent the self interest of directors from hampering the effective running of the company. The independence of non-executives has traditionally been seen as important in achieving this. The determination of independence in this context has been a concern of institutional investors. Much has been written as to the criteria for establishing "independence", and institutional shareholder guidelines offer definitions. The Association of British Insurers ("the ABI") and the National

---

[12] The Higgs Review, Annex A: suggested revised (Combined) Code, Part I, Section 1, A.1.
[13] Combined Code, Section 1, A.3.2.

A Practitioner's Guide to Directors' Duties and Responsibilities

Association of Pension Funds ("the NAPF") dealt with this issue in a joint statement.[14]

The Higgs Review made additions to the Combined Code on the role of the board and, in particular, it strengthened and clarified the position of non-executive directors and the role they should play in corporate governance. Whilst the revised version of the Combined Code leaves the final judgement as to whether a director can be considered independent in the hands of the board, it lists a number of circumstances that may lead the board to conclude that a director should not be considered independent. In essence, a director is considered independent when the board determines that the director is independent in character and judgement and there are no relationships or circumstances which could affect, or appear to affect, the director's judgement. Relationships or circumstances which may affect judgement include where the director:

(a) has been an employee of the company or group within the last five years;
(b) has, or has had within the last three years, a material business relationship with the company either directly or as a partner, shareholder, director or senior employee of a body that has such a relationship with the company;
(c) has received or receives additional remuneration from the company apart from a director's fee, participates in the company's share option or a performance related pay scheme, or is a member of the company's pension scheme;
(d) has close family ties with any of the company's advisers, directors or senior employees;
(e) holds cross-directorships or has significant links with other directors through involvement in other companies or bodies;
(f) represents a significant shareholder; or
(g) has served on the board for more than nine years from the date of his or her first election.

Whilst the board is free to disregard the presence of any of these relationships or circumstances, it must explain in the annual report why it considers a director to be independent notwithstanding their existence. As a practical matter, the extent to which companies will be able to ignore these relationships or circumstances in the face of investor discontent remains to be seen. Indeed, the Pensions Investment Research

---

[14] A Joint ABI/NAPF Statement "Responsible Voting", July 1999, Appendix 1,19.

Consultants Limited ("PIRC") applies a more stringent test for independence for directors in their PIRC Shareholder Voting Guidelines 2003.

The revised version of the Combined Code also seeks to ensure an appropriate balance within the board of directors by recommending that the posts of chairman and chief executive be the responsibility of different individuals. The Hampel Report cited with approval Cadbury's description of the role of the chairman. The chairman is primarily responsible for the working of the board, for the balance of its membership (subject to board and shareholders approval), and for ensuring that all directors, executive and non-executive alike, are able to play their full part in its activities. In contrast, the role of the chief executive is to run the business and to implement the policies and strategies adopted by the board. The aim of separating the two roles is to "ensure a balance of power and authority, such that no one individual has unfettered powers of decision".[15] The Combined Code also recommends that, even where the roles of chairman and chief executive are held by different people, there should be a recognised senior independent non-executive director, who must meet the test of independence, other than the chairman, to whom concerns can be conveyed.[16] The Higgs Review concluded that the senior independent non-executive director should be available to shareholders if they have reason for concern that contact through the normal channels (i.e. the chairman or chief executive) has failed, although this conclusion was criticised as undermining the role of the chairman.[17] The revised version of the Combined Code also requires the senior independent non-executive director to attend sufficient meetings with shareholders to obtain a balanced understanding of their concerns.[18]

The various corporate governance reports suggest that one way of promoting an effective and balanced board is for there to be a transparent system and policy for recruiting new directors to the board. This is advocated in the Combined Code,[19] which provides that the board should make new appointments on the recommendation of a nomination committee. The members of the nomination committee and the process by which nominations are made should be identified in the annual report, and a majority of them should be independent non-executives.

---

[15] The Cadbury Report, Paragraph 4.9.
[16] Combined Code, Section 1, A.3.3.
[17] The Higgs Report, paragraphs 7.4 and 7.5.
[18] Combined Code, Section 1, D.1.1.
[19] Combined Code, Section 1, A.4.

The aim of the nomination committee is to promote objectivity in the appointment of directors, which is crucial in guaranteeing a balanced board not dominated by a particular individual or group of individuals. Whilst the Higgs Review suggested that the chairman should not chair the nomination committee, this was not incorporated into the revised Combined Code. The chairman should, however, stand down when the recruitment of a new chairman is under discussion.[20]

The reports also suggest that accountability following appointment can be fostered through the requirement for regular re-appointment by the shareholders in general meeting. The Listing Rules require directors to submit themselves for election at the first Annual General Meeting ("AGM") after their appointment. The Combined Code[21] recommends that directors should be required to submit themselves for re-election at least every three years. The Code also suggests that the names of directors submitted for election or re-election should be accompanied by sufficient biographical details to enable shareholders to take an informed decision on their election. The revised version of the Combined Code requires the performance of the board (including its committees and members) to be evaluated and the annual report to state whether such performance reviews are taking place and how they are conducted.

9.3.2 Accountability and audit

> "The board should present a balanced and understandable assessment of the company's position and prospects."[22]

The Combined Code emphasises the need to report that the business is a going concern, with supporting assumptions or qualifications as necessary.[23] This recommendation was adopted from the same recommendation made by the Cadbury Committee. Following publication of the Cadbury Report, a working group comprising members of the "100 Group" of finance directors and representatives of the chartered accountants' institutes published guidance for directors on how to comply with this requirement.[24]

---

[20] Financial Reporting Council Press Notice, 14 May 2003; Combined Code, Section 1, A.4.1.
[21] Combined Code, Section 1, A.7.1.
[22] Combined Code, Section 1, C.1.
[23] Combined Code, Section 1, C.1.2.
[24] "Going Concern and Financial Reporting", November 1994.

The presumption that a company is a going concern – namely that the company will continue in operational existence for the foreseeable future – is one of the fundamental accounting concepts[25] upon which the preparation of a company's accounts is based. It is presumed that a company is a going concern unless the published accounts contain a clear statement to the contrary. In any case, the directors are under a duty to ensure that the accounts present a true and fair view of the financial affairs of the company, and so the application of this basic principle would require a disclosure in a note to the accounts if there are factors which cast doubt on the going concern presumption.

9.3.3 Internal control

> "The board should maintain a sound system of internal control to safeguard shareholders' investment and the company's assets."[26]

The Combined Code requires the directors to conduct a review, at least annually, of the effectiveness of the systems of internal controls, and the directors should report to shareholders that they have done so. Companies that do not have an internal audit function should review the need for one from time to time. The Combined Code contains no guidance as to what would constitute a sound system of internal control, nor how a company might go about establishing one.

The Turnbull Committee produced guidance for directors on how to comply with this aspect of the Combined Code. The guidance is based on the adoption by a company's board of a risk-based approach to establishing a sound system of internal control and to reviewing its effectiveness. Both the Combined Code and the Turnbull Report make it clear that the internal controls to be reviewed by the board apply not only to internal financial controls, but to all types of controls, including those of an operational and compliance nature.

The Turnbull Committee considered that the board should take several factors into account when determining what would constitute a sound system of internal control for their particular company:

(a) the nature and extent of the risks facing the company;

---

[25] SSAP 2 Disclosure of Accounting Policies (November 1971).
[26] Combined Code, Section 1, C.2.

(b) the extent and categories of risk which the board regard as acceptable for the company to bear;
(c) the likelihood of the risks concerned materialising;
(d) the company's ability to reduce the incidence and impact on the business of risks that do materialise; and
(e) the costs of operating particular controls relative to the benefit thereby obtained in managing the related risks.[27]

Turnbull also identified characteristics which an effective system of internal control should have. The system should:

(a) be embedded in the operations of the company and form part of its culture;
(b) be capable of responding quickly to evolving risks to the business arising from factors within the company and to changes in the business environment; and
(c) include procedures for reporting immediately to appropriate levels of management any significant control failings or weaknesses that are identified together with details of corrective action being undertaken.[28]

The board should design a process for reviewing the effectiveness of the system, an essential part of which should be the receipt of regular reports from management. These reports should provide a balanced assessment of the significant risks facing the company and the effectiveness of the system of internal control in managing those risks. A process should be established for an annual assessment of the company's system of internal control in support of the board's annual public statement on internal control.

Although the board formulates the company's policies on internal control, it is the role of management to implement the policies by identifying and evaluating risks for consideration by the board and designing, operating and monitoring a suitable system of internal control. All employees have some responsibility for internal control, and they should collectively have the necessary skill, authority and understanding of the company, its business and its markets to carry out this responsibility effectively.

---

[27] The Turnbull Report, paragraph 17.
[28] Ibid, paragraph 22.

Corporate Governance

The Exchange wrote to all listed companies in 1999[29] stating that compliance with the internal control aspects covered by the Combined Code would be required for accounting periods ending on or after 23 December 2000.

9.3.4 Audit committee and auditors

> "The board should establish formal and transparent arrangements for considering how they should apply the financial reporting and internal control principles and for maintaining an appropriate relationship with the company's auditors."[30]

The Combined Code recommends that this objective should be achieved by establishing an audit committee of at least three members (or, in the case of companies below FTSE-350 level, at least two members), who should all be independent non-executive directors. At least one member should have significant, recent and relevant financial experience. The role of the audit committee was clarified by the Smith Report to include monitoring of financial statements, reviewing financial reporting judgments and reviewing the company's internal audit function and financial controls.

The audit committee is responsible for making recommendations to the board concerning the appointment of the external auditor and for monitoring the external auditor's independence, objectivity and effectiveness. The audit committee should also develop and implement policy on the engagement of the external auditor to supply non-audit services.

9.3.5 Disclosure requirements and the relationship with shareholders

> "Institutional shareholders have a responsibility to make considered use of their votes."[31]

In recent years, there has been no shortage of authoritative and informed commentary upon the role of shareholder meetings in the governance of companies. In 1995, with the encouragement of the Department of Trade and Industry ("the DTI"), a joint city/industry working group was

---

[29] London Stock Exchange letter to all listed companies, 27 September 1999.
[30] Combined Code, Section 1, C.3.
[31] Combined Code, Section 2, E.3.

established[32] "to suggest practical ways in which the relationship between UK industry and institutional shareholders can be improved as a stimulus for long-term investment and development".

Virtually all participants in the working group's consultation exercise viewed the AGM as then constituted as an "expensive waste of time and money". Criticisms referred to poor attendance by institutional shareholders and to the hijacking of proceedings by special-interest groups or by individuals with questions irrelevant to most people attending the meeting.

The solution recommended by the working party was to change the format of the AGM to make it a more interesting and rewarding event so that major investors saw value in attending. Thus:

(a) an updated trading statement would be provided at the meeting and operational managers would make presentations;
(b) shareholders would be encouraged to submit their questions in advance;
(c) questions which were not of general interest would be referred to the relevant director or manager after the meeting; and
(d) institutions should accept their responsibilities to take an active and involved interest in constitutional governance.

In 1996 the DTI issued a consultative document[33] raising a number of specific questions in this context:

(a) Should the Companies Act be amended to render it easier for shareholders to requisition resolutions?
(b) Should there be additional provisions to allow and regulate questions asked by members, both private and corporate, at AGMs?
(c) Should the law make it easier for the beneficial owners of shares (particularly with the introduction of CREST) to attend shareholder meetings when their shares were held by nominees?

The Institute of Chartered Secretaries and Administrators, with support from the DTI, established a working party to deal with the issues raised by the responses to the DTI's consultative document. The working party issued a Guide to what was considered best practice in the conduct of

---

[32] Developing a Winning Partnership – How Companies and Institutional Investors are Working Together (The Myners Report), February 1995.
[33] Shareholder Communications at the General Meeting, April 1996.

Corporate Governance

AGMs.[34] The Guide sets out 24 principles as to best practice at AGMs. None is particularly startling or radical and the Guide contained no dramatic departures from established practice.

The Guide emphasises the importance of good communication with shareholders, including in relation to questions at the AGM (which should be encouraged) about past performance, results and intended future performance. The Guide also advocates the provision of an updated trading statement at the AGM, together with a report from at least one executive director. Given the length of time which can elapse between the release of the preliminary announcement and the holding of the annual meeting, this may be a useful way in which to encourage attendance.

The Hampel Committee had two main recommendations in this area:

(a) the practice of some companies in mounting a full business presentation with a question and answer session should be examined and perhaps followed by other companies;
(b) without a poll being demanded, companies should announce the total proxy votes for and against each resolution once it has been dealt with by the meeting on a show of hands. This, the Committee said, would be likely to encourage an increase in shareholder voting.

The Government's White Paper "Modernising Company Law"[35] sets out that:

(a) the rights of proxies at company meetings should be improved so that they have a right to speak, vote on a show of hands and join others in demanding a poll;[36]
(b) there should be no change to the threshold for circulation of members' resolutions, but if received in time, resolutions circulated with the meeting notice should be free of charge;[37] and
(c) that Section 360 Companies Act 1985 should be amended to make it clear that companies are enabled to recognise the rights of persons other than the registered holder (i.e. beneficial owners), including

---

[34] A Guide to Best Practice for AGMs, September 1996.
[35] HM Government White Paper CM 5553-I; Modernising Company Law, July 2002.
[36] Ibid; Section 2.18.
[37] Ibid; Section 2.24.

the rights of such a person to appoint a proxy. This is to reflect CREST developments.[38]

The Combined Code contains various provisions relating to AGMs. Boards should use the AGM to communicate with private investors and encourage their participation. Institutional shareholders have a responsibility to make a considered use of their votes. Specifically in relation to the companies themselves:

(a) they should indicate the level of proxies lodged on each resolution, and the balance for and against the resolution, after it has been dealt with on a show of hands;

(b) separate resolutions should be proposed on each substantially separate issue, and there should be a resolution on the report and accounts;

(c) chairmen of the audit, remuneration and nomination committees should be available to answer questions at the AGM; and

(d) at least 20 working days' notice of the AGM should be given. The revised Combined Code makes it clear that institutional investors should be expected to attend AGMs where practicable.

The March 2001 Myners review of shareholder activism recommended that those responsible for pension scheme investments should have a duty actively to monitor and communicate with the management of investee companies and to exercise shareholder votes where those would enhance the value of the investment. The Department of Work and Pensions jointly with the Treasury then issued a consultation paper in February 2002, "Encouraging Shareholder Activism".[39] In response to this, the Institutional Shareholders' Committee ("the ISC") issued a Statement of Principles on 21 October 2002, entitled "The Responsibilities of Institutional Shareholders and Agents in the UK". This is a voluntary code of practice, which sets out the responsibilities of institutional investors in relation the companies in which they invest. Under the principles institutional shareholders should:

(a) maintain and publish statements of their policies in respect of active engagement with the companies in which they invest;

(b) monitor the performance of and maintain an appropriate dialogue with those companies;

---

[38] Ibid; Section 2.40.
[39] "Encouraging Shareholder Activism – A Consultation Document", 4 February 2002.

(c) intervene where necessary – including voting all shares held wherever practicable;
(d) evaluate the impact of their policies; and
(e) in the case of investment managers, report back to the clients on whose behalf they invest.

The Government has approved the ISC proposal to maintain a best practice approach to shareholder activism. The Higgs Review recommended that institutional investors apply the ISC code of activism and this is reflected in the revised Combined Code. This non-legislative approach will be reviewed by the Government in 2004 to see whether the best practice approach is working or whether there is a need to legislate in this areas.

The Combined Code, and the related modifications to the Listing Rules, seeks to encourage shareholder interest and action in corporate governance by requiring the directors to address certain identified key areas of corporate governance in their reports to the shareholders. Thus, the Listing Rules require the following items to be included in the annual report and accounts of a listed company incorporated in the UK:

(a) a narrative statement of how the company has applied the relevant principles set out in the Combined Code, providing an explanation which enables its shareholders to evaluate how the principles have been applied;
(b) a statement as to whether or not the company has complied throughout the accounting period with the relevant provisions set out in the Combined Code. A company which has not complied with the Code provisions, or has complied with only some of them or complied for only part of an accounting period, must specify those with which it has not complied, and (where relevant) for what part of the period such non-compliance continued, and give reasons for any non-compliance;
(c) a report to the shareholders by the board on directors' remuneration which must include certain specified information.[40]

These disclosures are intended to enable shareholders to assess how effectively the board is following the recommendations of the Combined Code. Shareholders are then able to decide whether it is necessary to put pressure on the board to make changes to the way that the company is

---

[40] The Listing Rules, paragraph 12.43A.

governed. Flexibility in the application of principles of good corporate governance is seen as being achievable by fostering an informed dialogue between the company and its shareholders. Companies are to review and explain their governance policies, including any special circumstances which in their view justify departure from generally accepted best practice, and shareholders and others should show flexibility in the interpretation of the Code, taking into account the explanations they receive and judging them on their merits.

9.4 Is the present system of corporate governance adequate?

9.4.1 The stakeholder debate

"From a practical point of view, to redefine directors' responsibilities in terms of the stakeholders would mean identifying all the various stakeholder groups; and deciding the nature and extent of the directors' responsibility to each. The result would be that the directors were not effectively accountable to anyone, since there would be no clear yardstick for judging their performance. This is a recipe neither for good governance nor for corporate success."[41]

The Hampel Committee reaffirmed the position under English law that directors owe their duties to the shareholders collectively, both present and future, through the company itself and do not owe duties to differing groups of stakeholders. Section 309 of the Companies Act 1985 requires directors to consider the interests of employees. Nevertheless, the section provides that "the duty imposed by this section ... is owed by [the directors] to the company (and the company alone)".

There has been much debate as to whether or not directors' responsibilities should be extended to take into account other stakeholder groups, in addition to the interests of shareholders. Hampel adopted the traditional view that the directors' overall objectives in fulfilling their duties are to promote the welfare of shareholders' interests.[42] It is estimated that companies account for 50 of the world's 100 largest economies, and the 500 largest corporations control 25 per cent of the

---

[41] Hampel Report, paragraph 1.17.
[42] Hampel Report, paragraph 1.16.

world's economic output.[43] As a result of the considerable power and influence which they exercise, the proposition is advanced that it is now time to extend the responsibilities of directors to include the interests of employees, customers, suppliers and the wider community generally. In Germany, for example, although directors' duties are owed to the company itself, the interests of the company are not, as a matter of practice, seen as being synonymous with the interests of the shareholders alone. Directors are obliged not only to promote the interests of the shareholders, but also to take into account the welfare of the employees, creditors and the wider community.

There has been some interest in political circles in reshaping corporate governance in the UK more along the lines of the German model. In February 1999 the Company Law Review Steering Group issued a Consultation Document[44] canvassing opinion on the proposition that companies should have an inclusive relationship with stakeholders, who could include employees, customers, suppliers and local residents as well as shareholders. This would mean that directors would have to consider "the need to ensure productive relationships with a range of interested parties" and not simply favour the interests of shareholders where these conflict with the interests of stakeholders.[45]

The paper offered two possible models to achieve this. The enlightened shareholder value approach would involve the pursuit of shareholder interests in an "enlightened and inclusive way" under existing principles. Alternatively, the pluralist approach envisages that directors would be "permitted (or required)" to "balance shareholders' interests with those of others committed to the company".

In its response to this paper, the Law Society's Company Law Committee strongly opposed the introduction of the pluralist approach.[46] The committee suggested that there is scope, within the flexibility of the existing law, for companies to apply pluralist principles, and that most boards of directors already take account of relevant stakeholder interests in deciding the best course of action in the interests of the company. This is essentially the conclusion reached by Hampel:

---

[43] IALS Company Law Lecture "Shareholders v Stakeholders: the bogus argument", *The Company Lawyer*, Vol. 19 No. 2 (February 1999).
[44] Modern Company Law for a Competitive Economy: The Strategic Framework (February 1999), paragraph 3.7.
[45] Ibid; Executive Summary, paragraph 5.
[46] Law Society Memorandum No. 377, May 1999, pages 1 and 2.

"As regards stakeholders, different types of company will have different relationships, and directors can meet their legal duties to shareholders, and can pursue the objective of long-term shareholder value successfully, only by developing and sustaining these stakeholder relationships."

In commenting on the interests of stakeholders in April 1999, the corporate governance section of the Institute of Directors ("IoD") expressed their opposition to any attempt to impose a duty upon directors which could be enforced by stakeholders. Such a step would, it contended, lead to a plethora of claims against directors and prove deleterious to the smooth running of business. However, it did accept that the law should be worded as to *entitle* directors to consider the interests of non-equity stakeholders in their decision-making process.[47]

Making companies more responsive to the interests of non-equity stakeholders continues to remain a topic of interest at a political level. In 2000 the Prime Minister issued a challenge to the top 350 companies to publish annual environment reports. A survey carried out by consultants Environmental Context and Salter Baxter for 2000/2001 initially found that many companies had failed to heed the Prime Minister's call for greater disclosure of environmental information.[48] However, the most recent survey carried out by the same consultants for 2001/2002 found that a significant increase had occurred in reporting on environmental and employee affairs.[49]

This high-level political concern about the interests of stakeholders has manifested itself in proposed changes to the law, which will replace the duties owed by directors to the company in Section 309 of the Companies Act 1985. In the proposed codification of directors' duties in the new Company Law White Paper put forward by the Government in July 2002, the concerns and interests of non-equity stakeholders are now one of the "material factors" which directors can consider when carrying out their duty of promoting the company's objectives. However, as some commentators have noted, these material factors are subordinate to the directors'

---

[47] M Watson, 'Companies in a Global Society: Issues for Stakeholders in the Company Law Review', 13 April 1999.
[48] Cited in L Miles, "Company Stakeholders: Their position under the new framework", *Company Lawyer*, Volume 24, No. 2 (February 2003) page 57.
[49] Ibid, page 57.

primary duty of promoting the success of the company for the benefit of the members.[50]

9.4.2 Board structure and the monitoring of directors

"The benefit of the unitary board, strongly supported in consultation responses, is the value of executive knowledge within the board, alongside non-executive directors who can bring wider experience."[51]

The Combined Code places considerable emphasis on the role played by non-executive directors on the boards of companies. They not only supervise and monitor the management of the company but also contribute to the management of the company by bringing added skills and experience to the board. The non-executives are expected to help resolve conflicts between the chairman or chief executive and other directors and differences over corporate strategy among the executive directors. They work on board committees, especially the remuneration, nomination and audit committees.

Some commentators on corporate governance, as it is practised in the UK, have criticised a system based on the role of non-executive directors who, together with the senior executive management they are charged with monitoring, are responsible and accountable collectively to the shareholders. This system, so it is said, can confuse the management and supervisory roles, and the corresponding responsibilities and account-abilities. Such commentators have looked to other systems to find alternatives which, they argue, would serve British industry better.

In German public companies and larger private companies (with more than 500 employees), it is a requirement that the board consist of two tiers: the management board and the supervisory board. The management board manages the day-to-day affairs of the company, while the supervisory board is made up of outside directors who control and supervise the activities of the management board.[52]

The constitution of the supervisory board of a German company is a direct result of the recognition given to a wider range of stakeholders

---

[50] L Miles, "Company Stakeholders: Their position under the new framework" *Company Lawyer*, Volume 24, No. 2 (February 2003) pages 56–59.
[51] The Higgs Review, Chapter 4, paragraph 4.2.
[52] Giles Proctor and Lilian Miles, "Cutting the Mustard: Stakeholders in the Boardroom?" *Business Law Review*, July 1998.

and company employee representatives. By law, half of the members of the supervisory board of companies with more than 2,000 employees must be appointed by the employees, while the other half are appointed by the shareholders. In smaller companies the ratio is different, with one-third of the members of the supervisory board being appointed by the employees.[53] Furthermore, it is common in Germany for customers and creditors of the company to be shareholders of the company, and so they too tend to be represented on the supervisory board.[54] The management board therefore plays no role in the selection of the supervisory board, and the selection process is designed to enable the different interest groups within the company to appoint representatives to monitor the activities of the management board.

As Proctor and Miles explain in their article,[55] although the supervisory board has no direct management responsibilities, it nevertheless has considerable influence over the management board. They explain that:

> "it can request the management board to report to it at regular intervals in relation to matters of policy, profitability and other transactions of significant importance. It determines the appointment, removal and remuneration of members of the management board. It can inspect the books and accounts of the company ... it represents the company in any disputes between the latter and the management board."

The article also makes the important point that the supervisory board can be held negligent if it does not carry out its duties adequately.

In the past, the selection of non-executive directors was largely in the hands of the chairman or chief executive, who might, in some cases, be more concerned with candidates who would support them than candidates who might prove effective. This concern should diminish with the use of nomination committees which provide more formal and transparent selection methods. There is also increasingly less reliance on

---

[53] Giles Proctor and Lilian Miles, "Cutting the Mustard: Stakeholders in the Boardroom?" *Business Law Review*, July 1998.
[54] Giles Proctor and Lilian Miles, "Cutting the Mustard: Stakeholders in the Boardroom?" *Business Law Review*, July 1998.
[55] Giles Proctor and Lilian Miles, "Cutting the Mustard: Stakeholders in the Boardroom?" *Business Law Review*, July 1998.

personal contacts and more use of outside consultants to find new board members.

The principle of separating the roles of directors between supervision and management, as in the German system, has some intellectual merits. It results in a system in which power is not concentrated in a single body of people. Because of their legal responsibilities and the manner of their appointment, the supervisory directors are not under the same level of influence from the chief executive as the directors of a UK board. And the fact that shareholders are represented on the supervisory board encourages greater direct accountability of the management to the body of shareholders when contrasted with the more indirect accountability between the unitary board of a UK company and its shareholders.[56]

Nevertheless, there are also disadvantages to the two-tier board system. It does not necessarily guarantee an adequate system of checks and balances on management. By virtue of having less contact with senior executive management, the members of the supervisory board may be less well informed than UK non-executive directors. In the UK, non-executive directors are likely to attend more board meetings alongside their executive colleagues. And increasingly, in accordance with the Combined Code, non-executive directors are playing active roles on board committees. The supervisory board in a two-tier structure, on the other hand, may become proactive only when problems have already emerged within the company. As a result of its being more divorced from the management of the company, there may be less scope for intervention by the supervisory board to avoid a problem arising in the first place. For example, there has been concern in Germany that many supervisory boards are not sufficiently involved in the affairs of their companies. A new law has recently been passed requiring supervisory boards of listed companies to meet at least twice every six months. Previously, the legal minimum had been once every six months.

In France a company has the right to choose whether or not to have a two-tier board or a unitary board. It is therefore interesting to note that the vast majority of French companies do not have two-tier boards. It is also possible to conceive of structures within the framework of the unitary board which clarify the separation of management and monitoring functions without introducing the disadvantages sometimes

---

[56] Modern Company Law for a Competitive Economy: The Strategic Framework, Executive Summary, paragraph 5.1.32.

inherent in adopting a formal two-tier board structure. The boards of many US companies, for example, comprise a clear majority of independent directors. Typically, the board of a US company retains responsibility for major strategic and other decisions as well as for monitoring management's performance, but day-to-day management is delegated to an executive committee. Whilst it is arguable that such a structure may still compromise the ability of non-executives to perform their monitoring role, the advantages of a strong independent platform for strategic decisions and supervision by individuals who are well informed as to the company's affairs and goals are clear.

The UK Government's consultation paper on the review of company law states that the replacement of a unitary board by a two-tier board structure would "represent a very radical change to British corporate culture and would be unlikely to command wide support".[57] However, the paper did acknowledge that there may be a case for enabling companies to adopt such board structures if they wished to do so.[58]

In his review of corporate governance in the UK, Derek Higgs endorsed the view of the Hampel Report of 1998 and the opinions put forward by the Government's consultation document relating to the replacement of the unitary board with a two-tier board. His lack of enthusiasm for change was clear from his statement, "evidence collected during the Review has not convinced me of the merits of moving away from the unitary board structure in the UK".[59]

This is not to say that the supervisory board in Germany is not an effective institution, but rather that the structure does not of itself guarantee effective monitoring of the executive directors. Indeed, what is crucial to effective monitoring is not necessarily the structure of the arrangements themselves so much as the calibre and motivation of the outside directors who are charged with this duty and the direct access they enjoy to material information and to management (whether or not appointed to the board). It may not be necessary to introduce changes to the structure of the board to enhance the effectiveness of the outside directors. It may be more productive to devise ways of ensuring that their various roles are more effectively discharged.

---

[57] Modern Company Law for a Competitive Economy: The Strategic Framework, Executive Summary, paragraph 5.1.33.
[58] The Higgs Review, Chapter 4, paragraph 4.3.
[59] HM Government White Paper CM 5553-I, Modernising Company Law, July 2002, Section 7.3.

9.4.3 The draft Companies Bill and the White Paper "Modernising Company Law"

9.4.3.1 Introduction

> "The law needs to balance various interests, including those of shareholders, directors, employees, creditors and customers, but it should avoid imposing unnecessary or inappropriate burdens."[60]

In response to the Company Law Review, which was completed in July 2001, the Government published its White Paper, Modernising Company Law, along with a draft Companies Bill in July 2002.

The Company Law Review Steering Group had considered and proposed recommendations on the following topics in its examination of the state of company law:

(a) the duties of directors, with particular reference to the interests of non-equity stakeholders;
(b) strengthening the position of non-executive directors;
(c) the recognition of the separation of legal and beneficial ownership of shares;
(d) communications with shareholders and the retention of Annual General Meetings ("AGMs");
(e) the current reporting and accounting systems.

The White Paper and draft Bill approved many of the Steering Group's recommendations. Its aims are to simplify the law, reduce burdens on small businesses, improve transparency and governance, and take account of modern technology.

9.4.3.2 The position of directors

Whilst the Steering Group of the Company Law Review did not wish to turn directors into "moral, political or economic arbiters", it identified the need for the scope of director's duties to be codified and broadened to include non-equity stakeholder interests.

In its recently published White Paper, the Government has expressed its general approval of the recommendations of the Steering Group and

---

[60] HM Government White Paper CM 5553-I, Modernising Company Law: The Government's Policy, July 2002, Section 3.3.

endorsed their proposal that a director's duties should be widened to now include the interests of customers, suppliers, the community and the environment.[61] The draft clauses in the Companies Bill state that a director must:

(a) act in a way which promotes the success of the company for the benefit of the shareholders; and
(b) consider in good faith all material factors which it is practicable in the circumstances for him to identify.[62]

The aforementioned material factors which directors should take into account in their decision-making process are:

(a) the company's need to foster business relationships, including those with its employees, suppliers and customers;
(b) concern about the impact of its operations on communities and the environment;
(c) the company's need to maintain a reputation for high standards of business conduct;
(d) the company's need to achieve outcomes which are fair as between its shareholders.[63]

The draft clauses also seek to define the care, skill and diligence which are expected from a director when carrying out his duties. Under the Companies Bill, a director is to exercise the care, skill and diligence which would be exercised by a reasonably diligent person with both:

(a) the knowledge, skill and diligence which may be reasonably expected of a director in his position; and
(b) any additional knowledge, skill and experience which he has.[64]

The Steering Group had suggested that directors should be required to sign a statement acknowledging that they had read and understood the statutory duties expected of them. The Government perceived some inherent problems with this approach. In its view, the proposal of the

---

[61] HM Government White Paper CM 5553-II Modernising Company Law (Draft Companies Bill), Schedule 2, Section 2(a) and (b).
[62] Draft Companies Bill, Schedule 2, Section 2, Note 2(a)(b)(c) and (d).
[63] Draft Companies Bill, Schedule 2, Section 4.
[64] HM Government White Paper CM 5553-I, Modernising Company Law: The Government's Policy, July 2002, Sections 3.16–3.17.

Steering Group might create the impression that the contents of the statute constituted a comprehensive statement of directors' duties, which would not be the case. Equally importantly, the director's signature would be of no legal effect as the statutory duties would be automatically binding on all directors. Accordingly, the Government will seek to further expand on its current policy of sending directors leaflets setting out their obligations under the Companies Act 1985. In future, directors will receive leaflets which will provide guidance as to their responsibilities and new statutory duties.[65]

At the time of writing, these proposals are subject to revision as the Department of Trade and Industry is seeking comments and responses to the draft Companies Bill from directors and practitioners.

The Steering Group also examined the corporate governance regime in the UK and considered the effectiveness of the Combined Code, with particular emphasis on the role of non-executive directors. It found that the existing system was in need of some reform and advocated bolstering the position of non-executive directors, either through increased non-executive membership, a more rigorous appointment method or strengthening the independence of the chairman.

This matter was not considered extensively by the Government in its White Paper. Instead, it decided to explore further the issue of the role of non-executive directors under the auspices of the Higgs Review.

9.4.3.3 The position of shareholders

> "We believe that it is very important for effective company governance that there should be no unnecessary inhibitions on the means by which shareholders exercise their control rights. In particular, the law should not inhibit arrangements to enable beneficial owners of shares, or their representatives, to exercise control rights through the most efficient means possible."[66]

In an attempt to ensure that beneficial owners of shares were able to exercise their voting rights more efficiently, the Steering Group proposed

---

[65] "Modern Company Law for a Competitive Economy: Developing the Framework", a consultative document from the Company Law Review Steering Group (March 2000), paragraph 4.27.

[66] HM Government White Paper CM 5553-I, Modernising Company Law. The Government's Policy, July 2002, Section 2.41.

the introduction of a voluntary system in which the company could recognise the rights of beneficial owners of shares even though the shares were in the name of the registered member. The alternative course of action advanced by the Steering Group was to introduce a mandatory system in which the registered owner could compel the company to recognise the rights of another person (the beneficial owner).

The Government found much to commend in the voluntary regime as outlined by the Steering Group and agreed that companies should be able to recognise the rights of the beneficial owners of shares at the request of the registered owner. It noted that under the current system, these beneficial owners are reliant on arrangements with the registered member to secure access to information and to provide any instructions. Moreover, it is easier for larger investors to secure such contractual arrangements than for smaller ones. However, the Government expressed less enthusiasm for the mandatory regime, stating that it would examine the practicality of the proposal.[67]

Another major topic for scrutiny in the Steering Group's review was the AGM. The Steering Group expressed its hostility to any plans to permit public companies to dispense with AGMs. The retention of the AGM was deemed to be essential in ensuring that directors could not act untrammelled and that the voice of shareholders would be heard in the highest echelons of the company. However, these objectives would be also be furthered through reform of the existing AGM system. In particular, it called for greater shareholder involvement in setting the agenda of an AGM and more openness in the dialogue between the board and the shareholders. However, it doubted the utility of a codification of a set of principles for the conduct of AGMs.

Whilst the Government appeared to share the views of the Steering Group in relation to the use of AGMs by public companies, it has, in the draft Companies Bill, made provisions for private companies to dispense with AGMs with the unanimous consent of its shareholders.[68]

Under the draft clauses, a private company will not be required to hold an AGM unless it is subject to the mandatory scheme.

---

[67] HM Government White Paper CM 5553-I, Modernising Company Law: The Government's Policy, July 2002, Section 2.11.
[68] Draft Companies Bill, Section 127(2)(a) and Section 5(1)(g).

A private company will only be subject to the mandatory scheme if:

(a) it has given notification to the registrar at Companies House upon formation stating that it wishes to opt in to the mandatory scheme;[69] or
(b) it has passed an ordinary resolution stating that it will opt into the mandatory scheme.[70]

If the private company is part of the mandatory scheme, it must hold an AGM for the financial year.[71] This provision was included out of a recognition that an AGM would be likely to be a useful procedure for larger private companies with a wider shareholder base.[72]

Public companies are to be deemed to be part of the mandatory scheme unless they have passed a resolution which enables them to opt out of the mandatory scheme.[73] However, the resolution must have been approved by all of the members who are entitled to vote at the AGM.[74] Moreover, the decision to opt out may also be reversed by a shareholder who gives notice to the company of his wish that the company be subject to the mandatory scheme.[75]

As part of the approach to strengthen the position of shareholders, the Steering Group recommended empowering proxies with the ability to speak and vote at AGMs. The Government gave its approval to this proposal based on the principle that shareholders should be able to exercise their rights at meetings even though they might not be able to attend. Accordingly, proxies are to be given the right to speak, vote on a show of hands and join with others in demanding a poll. Shareholders will also be able to demand a poll in advance of a meeting and vote on the poll without needing to attend or appoint a proxy.[76]

---

[69] Draft Companies Bill, Section 127(2)(a) and Section 128(1).
[70] Draft Companies Bill, Section 135(1) and (2).
[71] HM Government White Paper CM 5553-I, Modernising Company Law, July 2002, Section 2.12.
[72] Draft Companies Bill, Section 127(3)(a) and Section 130(1).
[73] Draft Companies Bill, Section 130(2).
[74] Draft Companies Bill, Section 131(1)(a).
[75] HM Government White Paper CM 5553-I, Modernising Company Law, July 2002, Section 2.18.
[76] HM Government White Paper CM 5553-I, Modernising Company Law, July 2002, Sections 2.42–2.44.

The Steering Group also perceived the need to increase the active participation of shareholders in the decision-making process, in particular that of institutional investors. The Review had highlighted the need for some of these institutional investors to intervene to protect the value of their investment in companies which are mismanaged. The Government appeared to realise the significance of these investors in the decision-making process of companies, noting that the majority of shares in listed companies in the UK are held by these investors. However, it declined to advance any proposals on this matter in its White Paper as it is currently being considered in response to the report on institutional investment submitted by Paul Myners to the Chancellor.[77]

9.4.3.4 *Reporting and accounting*
The Steering Group launched a number of criticisms direct at the reporting and accounting systems which apply to companies. It found that these documents were often inaccessible to shareholders because of their complexity and technicality. Equally, significant documents such as preliminary and interim announcements were not sent to shareholders. The Steering Group also found that the annual reports and accounts did not consider future strategy and prospects in sufficient depth because of an absence of statutory requirements relating to these subjects. The director's report was also the target of some criticism by the Steering Group as it was an ill-assorted mix of public interest matters and functional matters.

To address these failings, the Steering Group advocated the introduction of a new regime for accounting and reporting. Under its proposals, shareholders would receive a statutory version of the preliminary announcement. The annual report would include a cash flow statement and a new Operating and Financial Review ("OFR"), but would only be sent to investors. The Steering Group expressed some scepticism about the retention of the summary financial statement used by listed companies and suggested that these companies might be given the option of either publishing a preliminary announcement or a summary financial statement.

The Government concurred with many of the views of the Steering Group and put forward the following major proposals:

---

[77] HM Government White Paper CM 5553-I, Modernising Company Law, July 2002, Section 4.10.

(a) the narrative directors' report should be replaced with a short supplementary statement to the financial statement;
(b) "economically significant companies" will be required to produce OFRs;
(c) listed companies will be required to provide a director's remuneration report;[78]
(d) rules on the content of the financial statements will be drawn up by a new Standards Board;[79]
(e) the time in which private companies are to deliver their accounts is to be reduced from 10 months to seven months. Public companies are to deliver their accounting documents within six months.[80] This change reflects the fact that information often becomes out of date rapidly.[81]

Under the draft Companies Bill, the economically significant companies who are required to produce an OFR are "major companies". The criteria for determining the status of a company, be it public or private, are the size of the company's turnover, the size of the company's balance sheet and the number of employees in a financial year. A public company must have turnover of at least £50 million, a balance sheet of at least £25 million and a minimum of 500 employees. A private company must have turnover of at least £500 million, a balance sheet of at least £250 million and a minimum of 5,000 employees in order to be a major company.[82]

The OFR is to contain:

(a) a statement of the company's business, a review of the company's performance;
(b) a fair review of the company's performance and its position at the end of the financial year; and
(c) a projection of the prospects of the company's business and any events which might or will substantially affect that business.[83]

---

[78] HM Government White Paper CM 5553-I, Modernising Company Law, July 2002, Sections 4.11–4.12.
[79] Draft Companies Bill, Section 84(1)(a) and (b).
[80] HM Government White Paper CM 5553-I, Modernising Company Law, July 2002, Section 4.24.
[81] Draft Companies Bill, Section 77(3)(4) and (5) and Section 78(3)(4) and (5).
[82] HM Government White Paper CM 5553-I, Modernising Company Law, July 2002, Section 4.36.
[83] HM Government White Paper CM 5553-I, Modernising Company Law, Section 4.30.

This last requirement is designed to give effect to the objective of the Steering Group that reporting should be more prospective.[84] The Government has also used the OFR as a means of promoting the interests of stakeholders; directors will now also be required to consider whether matters relating to the company's employment policies and its policies on social and community issues should be included in the OFR.

9.5 Conclusion

It is unlikely that the eventual publication of the revised version of the Combined Code and the enactment of legislation reflecting the conclusions of the Company Law Review will bring the corporate governance debate in the UK to an end. As with the work of the committees on corporate governance preceding it, this latest round of changes is likely to be seen as constituting another important milestone in progress rather than the end of a journey. This is undoubtedly a good thing. Corporate activity is itself taking place in a rapidly changing environment and standards of corporate governance need to reflect these changes.

Although a definitive conclusion may not have been reached, the corporate governance debate in the UK has nevertheless underlined two relatively constant themes:

(a) the absence of any necessary correlation between the structure of governance and its quality; and
(b) the importance of allowing companies some flexibility to adapt the model governance structure to their own individual circumstances, subject to the discipline of public justification of departures from the model.

The immediate reaction of companies, investors and commentators to the revised Combined Code and new legislation provided an interesting test of whether these constants held good in light of recent events. The Higgs Review was much criticised for expanding the list of recommendations in a manner that might encourage institutions to require absolute compliance which would in turn undermine the "comply or explain" philosophy. Indeed, until the FRC announced amendments to the revised

---

[84] Draft Companies Bill, Section 75(2)(c) and (e).

Combined Code and a delay in its implementation, there were concerns that the lack of further consultation on the revised form of the Combined Code would be used by companies as justification for explanation rather than compliance. This, of course, cannot have been the aim of the Higgs Review as the revised Combined Code would lack credibility if little or no account is paid to companies' legitimate concerns.

At the same time, others have raised concerns that the increased compliance culture of corporate governance in the UK, coupled with a continued absence of strict delineation between the legal duties of executive and non-executive directors and the growing spectre of litigation, will serve to reduce the pool of talented individuals prepared to serve as non-executive directors. Whilst the Higgs Review concluded from the submissions that it received that this was not yet proving to be the case, it is clearly a matter for concern. In the final analysis, any system of corporate governance is reliant upon diligent and able individuals overseeing the management of companies. It is possible that the next chapter in the development of corporate governance in the UK will reflect a need for companies to be able to attract and retain high-calibre individuals to safeguard accepted principles of corporate governance.

Chapter 10
Directors Facing Disputes

Michael Hatchard, Partner
Skadden, Arps, Slate, Meagher & Flom (UK) LLP

This Chapter is divided into two parts. Part 10.1 covers disputes within the board of a company. Parts 10.2 to 10.5 cover disputes between the board and members of the company.

All Section references in this Chapter refer to the Companies Act 1985 unless otherwise stated.

10.1 Disputes within the board

The actions and attitude of a board of directors reflect the sum of its parts. Individuals differ in their backgrounds, opinions and objectives. While diversity is a strength, it is not surprising that one or more members of a board can sometimes find themselves at odds with the others.

In practice, a board may continue running a company for years without rigid formality. There is nothing inherently wrong in this. Differences are resolved by a measure of compromise on all sides, or by persuasion.

However, situations can arise where compromise goes out of the window and irreconcilable positions are taken. It is these situations that this part of this Chapter addresses, first from the standpoint of the majority and then from that of the minority. It also addresses the position where the board is deadlocked.

10.1.1 Majority standpoint

The basic instinct of the majority of the board when faced with an objectionable director may be to exclude the director from board discussions or, ultimately, to remove the director from the board.

10.1.1.1 Exclusion from proceedings
Each director has the right:

(a) to be notified of a proposed board meeting in sufficient time to attend (or the meeting may be invalid); and
(b) to attend board meetings.

This right of attendance is fundamental, given the responsibilities associated with the office of director, and has proved to be enforceable by injunction.[1]

The procedures for notification of board meetings may be qualified by the articles of association, which for example customarily provide that notice of a board meeting does not have to be given to a director who is for the time being out of the UK (*see* Regulation 88 of the 1985 Table A). Nonetheless, it may be unwise to attempt to convene a meeting without giving notice to a particular director in slavish reliance on a provision in the articles even though apparently permitted so to do. The failure to notify may conflict with some working practice previously observed by the company or improperly ignore readily available means of communication;[2] the failure may come under attack where there has been no reasonable effort to give notice and the consequences for the excluded director are material. To a great extent the effect of exclusion may be achieved more safely by controlling the circulation of information and by delegating management to committees or officers. An article or procedural determination of the board may be a safe and effective way of denying the relevant director the right to participate in debate or to vote (*see* for example Regulation 94 of the 1985 Table A), subject to the Section 459 implications of exclusion from management (*see* 10.4.1.7 below).

10.1.1.2 Removal of directors
The articles can include procedures to remove a director, for example by conferring on a specified majority of the directors the power to remove a director. In the absence of such a power the board has no inherent right

---

[1] *Hayes* v *Bristol Plant Hire Ltd* [1957] 1 WLR 499. Case holds that a director has a sufficient proprietary interest to maintain an action for the injunction. The underlying conclusion is founded on a Sir George Jessel, M.R. judgment that may itself have relied on an assumption that the relevant articles gave a right to attend meetings that must be upheld.

[2] *Mitropoulos* v *The Greek Orthodox Church and Community of Marrickville & District Ltd* (1993) 10 ACSR 134.

to remove one of its number from office as director (as distinct from termination of employment or curtailment of delegated authority). Absent special provision in the articles, the directors are removable only by some action on the part of the members. This can be achieved either:

(a) by a power conferred by or introduced into the articles; or
(b) through use of the statutory procedure in Section 303.

Before starting the process of removal of a director, it is worth checking to see whether he is already disqualified from acting as such or whether there was any procedural defect in his appointment. The various bases of disqualification are reviewed in Chapter 2, Section 4.4.

Also consider whether there were any special terms of office conferred at the time of appointment and any implications of removal that need to be managed. Assess whether the board can function effectively without the relevant director, for example as a result of quorum requirements or contractual commitments dictating board procedure. Review whether the relevant director exercises any delegated authority that must be cancelled. Determine whether removal of the director will trigger any breach of commitment and if so, whether the rights of appointment are contractual or class rights.[3] The financial implications, especially in the case of executive directors, will also need to be anticipated.

The statutory procedure for removal of a director under Section 303 is inalienable and by its terms operates notwithstanding any inconsistency in the articles[4] or agreement between the company and the director.[5] However, it does rely upon shareholders voting by the necessary

---

[3] *Cumbrian Newspapers* v *Cumberland Co* [1987] Ch 1. *See* Peter Gibson LJ at 39 in *Union Music Limited and Arias Limited* v *Russell John Watson and another* [2003] EWCA Cir 180 (CA) in which the decision in Cumbrian Newspapers was questioned.

[4] Section 303(1). *See* also *Link Agricultural Pty Ltd* v *Shanahan* (1998) 28 ACSR 498, CA (Vic).

[5] Section 303(1). *See Bushell* v *Faith* [1970] AC 1099, in which articles conferring weighted voting rights on shares held by a director in the event of a resolution being proposed to remove him as a director were held not to contradict and therefore not infringe Section 303. In *Criterion Properties plc* v *Stratford UK Properties LLC and Others* [2003] BCC 50 where provisions in an agreement with the company would give rise to significant, negative commercial consequences for the company in the event of removal of identified directors from office and thereby act as a fetter on the freedom of shareholders to remove directors under Section 303, the possibility that approval of such an agreement might demonstrate an improper exercise of board power was acknowledged.

majority and the shareholders are free to fetter contractually their voting rights as they choose.[6]

Special notice is required of a resolution to remove a director under Section 303.[7] Section 379 contains the relevant provisions governing the giving of special notice, which appear incongruous in this context because Section 379 contains in effect a warning procedure that serves a more helpful purpose where the resolution is being sponsored by a member rather than by the board. The board can of course give the requisite special notice to the company and otherwise ensure that the requirements in Section 379 are observed. While the Section 379 procedure would apparently require a meeting convened by the board to remove a director under Section 303 to be held on a minimum of 28 days notice, the effect of the relief in Section 379(3) is to allow the meeting to be convened within a shorter period, provided notice of the intention to move the resolution has first been given to the company.

Section 304 imposes certain procedures for notification to be given to the relevant director and confers rights on the director to publish a response of a reasonable length, at the expense of the company, save where his representations are defamatory. The board will be concerned to manage the surrounding publicity and will have the resources of the company at its disposal for that purpose. It will also have the initiative and in particular will control the timing and procedure of the meeting.

There is no particular form that the removal resolution must take although often expressed to the following effect:

> "THAT, special notice having been received by the Company, Mr X be removed as a director of the Company pursuant to Section 303 of the Companies Act 1985."

The director concerned, even if not a member of the company, is entitled to speak at the meeting, in addition to requiring his written representations to be read out (if not previously sent to members).[8]

The Section 303 procedure is reviewed and summarised in Chapter 2.

---

[6] *Holmes* v *Life Funds of Australia Ltd* [1971] 1 NSWLR 860.
[7] Section 303(2).
[8] Section 304(1) and (3).

Directors Facing Disputes

Articles sometimes provide for the removal of a director by shareholder resolution. Unless by its terms it effectively replicates the statutory procedure, such an article may be useful in bypassing the detailed statutory procedures under Section 303. An article permitting shareholders by extraordinary resolution to remove a director was at one time required by the London Stock Exchange for listed companies. While Section 303(5) provides that the statutory power does not derogate from any power to remove a director that may exist apart from Section 303, a power in the articles to remove a director by ordinary resolution might be open to question as subverting the statutory procedure. Removal by special resolution is amply supported by precedent as an effective alternative to the power and procedures in Section 303.

If a company's articles do not contain a provision enabling removal of a director, in the absence of any class rights to appoint and remove directors,[9] there is no reason why a general meeting should not pass two resolutions, the first a special resolution altering the articles so as to insert such a power, and the second implementing the removal.

Unless the vacancy created by the removal is filled at the meeting, the board can fill it if so permitted by the articles (*see* for example Regulation 79 of the 1985 Table A) but if appointed at the meeting the appointee will assume the rotation features of the director he replaces whereas if appointed by the board under a power to fill casual vacancies, the appointee will typically be subject to renewal at the next succeeding annual general meeting.[10]

Removal of a director under Section 303 or under a power in the articles does not, unless otherwise agreed, deprive him of any compensation or damages (*see* the discussion at Chapter 6.7) payable on termination either as a director or in respect of any appointment that terminates with his directorship.[11] It may also, in certain circumstances, be the foundation of a claim by the director under Section 459 (*see* 10.4.1.7(a) below).

---

[9] *Cumbrian Newspapers* v *Cumberland Co* [1987] Ch 1.
[10] Section 303(3) and (4).
[11] Section 303(5). While the entitlement to directors' fees may be qualified under the articles in the event of termination, entitlements under a contract of employment are unaffected save by their terms, certainly for early termination of a fixed-term contract. *Southern Foundries (1926) Ltd* v *Shirlaw* [1940] AC 701 (note the dissenting judgments in relation to the particular operation of the principle in circumstances where a controlling shareholder exercised rights conferred post contract to remove a director rather than the company acting itself and the pragmatic if

In the case of a private company, the current statutory written resolution procedure laid down in Sections 381A to 382B is not available[12] to pass a resolution to remove a director under Section 303. In relation to articles permitting members' resolutions to be in writing, it is clearly not possible to rely on an article such as Regulation 5 of Part II of the 1948 Table A, which is expressly "Subject to the provisions of the Act", and it is questionable whether reliance can be placed on an article such as Regulation 53 of the 1985 Table A, even though not so qualified, because it is inconsistent with the statutory special notice provisions and the provisions of the Act conferring on the director concerned the right to speak in his own defence at the meeting.

10.1.2 Minority standpoint

The position of the director who is in dispute with the other members of the board is to some extent the corollary of the above. The director has the right:

(a) to be informed about the company's affairs;
(b) to inspect the company's accounting records in accordance with Section 222 and a residual common law right.[13] The director is entitled to have the assistance of an expert when making such an inspection.[14] The ability to enforce such rights where removal from office is pending is, however, questionable;
(c) to call, or require the company secretary to call, a meeting of the board in compliance with the applicable notice provisions (*see above*);

---

[11] *(continued)* somewhat strained analysis supporting the majority conclusion that the actions of the shareholder and the company were either merged or interdependent); *Shindler v Northern Raincoat Company* [1960] 1 WLR 1038. See *Read v Astoria Garage (Streatham) Ltd* [1952] Ch 637 which may support the theory that where there is no specified contractual duration, termination by removal from office may not found a claim in damages for contractual breach if the terms of the contract provide for automatic termination of appointment on loss of directorship. Much depends on the form of the articles in any particular case.

[12] Section 381(A)(7) and Schedule 15A paragraph 1(a).

[13] *Conway v Petronius Clothing Co.* [1978] 1 All ER 185. There is no clear basis to argue that the right to inspect extends beyond the scope of the statutory right under Section 122 to inspect accounting records. However, *see Burn v London and South Wales* (1890) 7 TLR 118, 9 Digest (Reissue) 197, 1190 which suggests a more general right of access to any document belonging to the company.

[14] *Wes-Transvaalse Boeresake (Edms) Bpk v Pieterse* 1955 (2) SA 464, PD (Tvaal); cf. *Conway v Petronius Clothing Co.* [1978] 1 All ER 185.

Directors Facing Disputes

(d) not to be excluded from board meetings.[15] Any director under threat of ejection should take care to give instructions for notification of board meetings that are both efficient and consistent with any notification provisions in the articles; and

(e) in the case of a company which is governed by, or voluntarily adopts the Combined Code, to take independent professional advice, if necessary, at the company's expense.

As described above, the director also has the right to make representations to the members in the event that a resolution for his removal from office is proposed under Section 303,[16] and to speak at the meeting at which the resolution is proposed.[17]

10.1.3 Boardroom deadlock

The board of a company may be deadlocked because one or more directors refuses to attend board meetings (so as to prevent there being a quorum) or because the directors are equally divided on a question and the chairman either does not have or is not prepared to use a casting vote.

In these circumstances, as an alternative or perhaps an adjunct to removal of a director, the members in general meeting have an inherent default power to fill vacancies in the board[18] subject to any limit on the total number of directors imposed by the articles that cannot by its terms be adjusted by ordinary resolution. In addition, an article in the form of Regulation 78 of the 1985 Table A empowers the general meeting to appoint additional directors.

The members can pass a special resolution to take the conduct of the business of the company away from the directors, but an ordinary

---

[15] *Hayes* v *Bristol Plant Hire Ltd* (supra).
[16] Section 304(2) to (4).
[17] Section 304(1).
[18] *Munster* v *Cammell Co.* (1882) 21 Ch D 183; *Barron* v *Potter* [1914] 1 Ch 895 which distinguished *Blair Open Hearth Furnace Co.* v *Reigart* (1913) 108 LT 665 in which held that if the directors have delegated power to fill vacancies that excludes any implied concurrent right of members; see also *Integrated Medical Technologies Ltd* v *Macel Nominees Pty Ltd* (1988) 13 ACLR 110, SC (NSW) which held that any attempt in the articles to confer an exclusive power of appointment on the board must be clearly expressed. The principle in *Blair* was doubted by Lord Hanworth MR in *Worcester Corsetry Ltd* v *Witting* [1936] 1 Ch 640 although the ratio of the decision turned on construction of the particular articles.

resolution is insufficient except and to the extent that the articles require the directors to comply with directions given by the members in general meeting.[19]

Under articles which follow Regulation 70 of the 1985 Table A, the general meeting can give directions to the board by special resolution; the regulation provides that no such direction is to invalidate any prior act of the directors which would have been valid if that direction had not been given.

However, if the directors are unable by reason of disfunction (e.g. because they cannot secure a quorum whether by reason of overall lack of numbers or dispute) to exercise the powers given to them under the articles, the company in general meeting can perform the functions delegated to the board, certainly to appoint additional directors and perhaps to exercise other powers.[20]

The procedure by which to convene a general meeting in the absence of an effective board is addressed at Chapter 8.

As a last resort, a member may apply to the court either under its inherent power or under Section 37(1) of the Supreme Court Act 1981 for the appointment of a receiver to manage the affairs of the company. Alternatively, if the deadlock reflects a stalemate at the shareholder level, the remedy discussed in 10.4 below or a winding up on the just and equitable ground may provide the solution.

10.2 Disputes between the board and the members

The board of a company can find itself under attack from one or more of the members of the company for a variety of reasons, including claims that some action of the company has been taken in breach of a shareholder's personal rights; that the directors, or some of them, have committed some wrong against the company; or that the actions of the board have been unfairly prejudicial to one or more of the members.

---

[19] *Automatic Self-Cleansing Filter Co.* v *Cunninghame* [1906] 2 Ch 34, CA; *The Gramophone and Typewriter Ltd* v *Stanley* [1908] 2 KB 89 at 105, CA, dicta of Fletcher Moulton and Buckley LJJ; *Salmon* v *Quin & Axtens* [1909] AC 442, HL.

[20] *Barron* v *Potter* [1914] 1 Ch 895.

The remaining parts of this Chapter examine this complex area of company law, and set out some practical guidelines in relation to the claims procedure for derivative and unfair prejudice complaints. Section 10.2 below considers first the rights which a shareholder has under the company's constitution, and the extent to which those rights can be enforced by the shareholder; then the rights which are conferred on the shareholder by particular statutory provisions. Section 10.3 below considers the circumstances in which a shareholder can bring an action in the name of the company to obtain redress for a wrong done to the company (a "derivative" action). Section 10.4 below addresses the right of a shareholder to bring an action under Section 459 to obtain a remedy for unfairly prejudicial conduct. Section 10.5 below then summarises the Law Commission's recommendations for reform of the law in these areas.

As an alternative to reliance upon the remedies considered in this Chapter, an aggrieved minority might instead draw the matters complained of to the attention of the Department for Trade and Industry ("the DTI") or another body with powers of investigation. The alternatives are considered in Chapter 12.

10.2.1 Personal actions

This Section identifies a range of contractual and statutory rights and protections that form a key element of the broader minority shareholder protections. In exercising their powers, the directors need to be sensitive to the inherent limits on their authority or ability to take action reflected in the expectations of all shareholders at least in so far as any one of these remedies might come into play.

There is a complex interaction between a member's right to bring proceedings in an individual capacity and the derivative action discussed in 10.3 below where the acts complained of cause damage to the company. However, if the claimant can establish that the conduct has constituted a breach of some legal duty owed to him personally and the court is satisfied that such breach has caused him personal loss, separate and distinct from any loss occasioned to the company, a personal action can be mounted.[21]

---

[21] *Jason Walker and Others* v *James Nicholas Stones and Others* (2000) WTLR 79.

10.2.1.1 Shareholders' personal rights

Section 14 of the Companies Act 1985 creates a contract which is generally recognised as the basis of the legal relationship between the company and its members in addition to its operation as between the members themselves. It provides that:

> "Subject to the provisions of this Act, the memorandum and articles, when registered, bind the company and its members to the same extent as if they respectively had been signed and sealed by each member, and contained covenants on the part of each member to observe all the provisions of the memorandum and of the articles."

However, this does not mean that every shareholder necessarily has the right to enforce all of the rights which the contract appears on its face to confer on him. The decided cases are not entirely consistent and to some extent turn on their facts. Nonetheless, the general view is that Section 14 confers contractual effect on a provision in the memorandum and articles only insofar as it gives rights to or imposes obligations on a member in his capacity as a member,[22] most certainly when in common with other members or a class of members ("insider rights") and not, for example, as a director[23] or as a professional adviser to the company[24] whether or not also a shareholder ("outsider rights"). It is certainly the case that a member seeking to enforce a provision vested in him as a member should expect to succeed under established principle more readily than in an action to uphold a provision that does not touch on the member qua member. The difficulty faced by any attempt to uphold outsider rights by enforcing provisions in a company's articles has not been affected by the Contracts (Rights of Third Parties) Act 1999, which expressly excludes Section 14 from its scope.[25]

---

[22] *Hickman* v *Kent or Romney Marsh Sheep Breeders' Association* [1915] 1 Ch 881. For further analysis, *see* Section A Part 2 Law Commission Consultation Paper 142. See cases referred to in footnote 56 for discussion of the distinction between rights enjoyed by the company and those of individual shareholders.

[23] *Browne* v *La Trinidad* (1888) 37 Ch D 1; but *see John* v *Price Waterhouse* [2002] 1 WLR 953 – an appointment made "on the footing of the Articles" may have the effect of incorporating provisions of the articles into a director's terms of appointment.

[24] *Eley* v *Positive Government Security Life Assurance Co. Ltd* (1876) 1 Ex D 88.

[25] Section 6(2) Contracts (Rights of Third Parties) Act 1999.

Even if the provision of the company's constitution which has been breached is one which creates "insider rights", the member may not be able to bring a personal action to enforce it. This will be so if the breach involves only an internal corporate irregularity, such as an irregularity in the conduct of a meeting which is trivial or can readily be remedied by reconvening a meeting at which it is expected that a majority will prevail in a manner that renders the breach nugatory.

10.2.1.2 Impact of the rule in Foss v Harbottle[26]

The refusal by the courts to uphold personal actions by shareholders in respect of breaches of internal corporate irregularities stems from the "majority rule"[27] and "proper claimant"[28] principles generally attributed to the decision in *Foss* v *Harbottle*, set out in the case of *Edwards* v *Halliwell*[29] and restated in *Prudential Assurance Co. Ltd* v *Newman Industries Ltd (No. 2)*.[30] The "rule in *Foss* v *Harbottle*" is discussed in more detail in 10.3.1 below.

The courts have not always been consistent in relation to the ability of a shareholder to challenge internal corporate irregularities; in certain instances the line adopted has been to restrain individual action in reliance on an extension of the *Foss* v *Harbottle* principle while in other cases the courts have permitted a shareholder to enforce his contractual right under the articles. Shareholders have for example been allowed to bring personal actions involving defective or inadequate notices of meeting,[31] improper adjournment of meetings[32] or the right to have their votes counted[33] but have been refused any remedy when a valid demand for a poll was wrongfully rejected by the chairman of the meeting even though, so it appears, the outcome of the particular poll would have reversed the result on a show of hands.[34]

---

[26] [1843] 2 Hare 461; 67 ER 189.
[27] The will of the majority of members of the company should in general prevail.
[28] A breach of duty owed to the company is a wrong for which the company and not its investors should seek a remedy. In determining whether to seek redress, the company may legitimately take into account balancing factors such as the relative return on investment of time and other resources in litigation.
[29] [1950] 2 All ER 1064.
[30] [1982] Ch 204.
[31] *Musselwhite* v *C H Musselwhite & Son* [1962] Ch 964.
[32] *Byng* v *London Life Association Ltd* [1989] 2 WLR 738.
[33] *Pender* v *Lushington; Oliver* v *Dalgleish* [1963] 1 WLR 1274.
[34] *MacDougall* v *Gardiner* (1875) LR 1 Ch D 13.

If a general principle can be extracted from the authorities,[35] it may be that where a breach of internal procedure damages the company first and foremost and incidentally affects all members, it should be resolved by corporate action, save where an exception to the rule in *Foss* v *Harbottle* applies (*see* 10.3.1 below). Contrastingly, where the principal wrong is done to an individual member, that individual may seek redress unless the matter complained of is open to ratification by ordinary resolution. In cases of substantial wrongdoing, it is in any event likely to be appropriate to seek a remedy under Section 459.

10.2.1.3 Transactions outside the company's powers
The rule in *Foss* v *Harbottle* does not prevent a shareholder from bringing a personal action to restrain the company from committing an ultra vires act. This right is not undermined by the third party protection conferred by Section 35. The rule in *Foss* v *Harbottle* does not prevent a shareholder from bringing a personal action to restrain the company from committing an ultra vires act including, for example, a planned misapplication of funds.[36] This right is not undermined by the third party protection conferred by Section 35. However, in *Smith* v *Croft (No. 2)*,[37] while the principle was acknowledged that a shareholder can have locus standi to bring an action to recover on behalf of a company property or money transferred or paid in an ultra vires transaction, and that an ultra vires act cannot be ratified by any majority of the members, it was held that if a majority of independent shareholders, acting in good faith, do not wish such an action to be continued, the will of that majority should prevail. This assumes that the shareholder promoting the action is not able to demonstrate a loss beyond that which is merely reflective of the loss suffered by the company as a result of the ultra vires transaction.

10.2.1.4 Amendments to the company's articles
A shareholder may be able to challenge a special resolution altering the company's articles on the grounds that the resolution was not passed bona fide (that is, without fraud or malice) for the benefit of the company as a whole (i.e. the shareholders as a general body) or breached a class or special right or discriminated between majority and minority

---

[35] *MacDougall* v *Gardiner* (supra); *see* also *Burland* v *Earle* [1902] AC 83 at 93: "It is an elementary principle of the law relating to joint stock companies that the court will not interfere with the internal management of companies acting within their powers and in fact has no jurisdiction to do so". This rule is attributed by Lord Davey at page 93 to the decision in *Foss* v *Harbottle*.
[36] *Smith* v *Croft (No. 2)* [1988] Ch 114, at 129.
[37] [1988] Ch 114.

shareholders[38] or (as discussed below) that the alteration was unfairly prejudicial to his interests for the purposes of Section 459.

The High Court of Australia has taken a novel but attractive approach in relation to the assessment of validity of amendments made to the constitution of a company in *Gambotto WCP Limited*.[39] The High Court stressed the proprietary nature of a share and rejected a test based simply on the amendments being bona fide in the interests of the company as a whole. Instead, the Court distinguished between amendments allowing expropriation by the majority of the shares of the minority or of valuable proprietary rights attaching to the shares and other amendments to the constitution giving rise to a conflict of interest. The Court determined that the test applicable to the first category would be whether the power to alter the constitution had been exercised for a proper purpose and if so, whether the exercise of that power would not operate oppressively in relation to minority shareholders. For amendments falling into the second category, the Court decided that, if regularly approved, such amendments would prima facie be fair unless shown to be beyond a purpose contemplated by the constitution or oppressive.

10.2.1.5 Shareholders' agreements

Accepting that the law relating to enforcement of rights and obligations provided for in the articles is complex and, depending on what is intended, may not provide complete protection for an individual shareholder, those wishing to regulate their participation should consider the relative attractions of a shareholders' agreement. A shareholder may enforce his contractual rights under a shareholders' agreement to which he and other members of the company are parties.[40]

If the company is a party to the agreement, then any restriction on its statutory powers contained in the agreement (such as a restriction

---

[38] *Allen v Gold Reefs of West Africa Ltd* [1900] 1 Ch 656; *Greenhalgh v Arderne Cinemas Ltd* [1951] Ch 286; cf. *Sidebottom v Kershaw, Leese & Co* [1920] 1 Ch 154, CA and *Shuttleworth v Cox Bros & Co* [1927] 2 KB 9, CA. In determining whether an amendment of the articles was bona fide for the benefit of the company, the test is by reference to the opinion of the shareholders; their bona fides will only be called into question if the circumstances are so oppressive or extravagant as to cast suspicion on their honesty. Benefit of the company will be assumed unless no reasonable man could consider it so (p. 11, 17d et seq.).

[39] [1995] 16 ASCR 1.

[40] Provisions in a shareholders' agreement may also attach as class rights to shares; see *Harman v BML Group Ltd* [1994] 1 WLR 893.

preventing it from increasing its authorised share capital except by special resolution) will be void as far as the company is concerned, but assuming the severability of the provision in as far as it binds the company, parallel restrictions assumed by shareholders who are parties to the agreement will be enforceable amongst them since they do not fetter the inalienable statutory powers of the company.[41]

10.2.1.6 Statutory rights

The Companies Act 1985 and the Insolvency Act 1986 provide shareholders with a somewhat disparate collection of other direct or indirect rights. The principal rights in the Companies Act 1985,[42] which may in relevant circumstances be considered in parallel with the minority protection regime, are:

(a) if representing not less than 15 per cent of the relevant class or shares, to challenge an amendment to the company's memorandum of association (Section 5);

(b) if representing not less than 5 per cent of the relevant class or shares,[43] to challenge a special resolution of a public company to re-register as a private company (Section 54);

(c) if representing not less than 15 per cent of the relevant class, to challenge a resolution varying the rights attaching to a class of shares passed in accordance with Section 125 (Section 127);

(d) if representing not less than 10 per cent of the relevant class or shares, to challenge a special resolution passed by a private company "whitewashing" financial assistance for the purchase of the company's shares (Section 157(2));

(e) to challenge a special resolution passed by a private company approving a payment out of capital for the redemption or purchase of its shares (Section 176);

(f) if the company is a private company and has passed an elective resolution to dispense with annual general meetings, to require the holding of an annual general meeting (Section 366A(3));

(g) if representing not less than 10 per cent of the total voting rights, to requisition an extraordinary general meeting (Section 368(1)) or, in the event that it proves impracticable to call or conduct a meeting by conventional means, to apply to the court under Section 371;

---

[41] *Russell v Northern Bank Development Corp. Ltd* [1992] 1 WLR 588; applying the principle established in *Southern Foundries (1926) Ltd v Shirlaw* [1940] AC 701 at 739 and *Allen v Gold Reefs of West Africa Ltd* [1900] 1 Ch 656 at 671.

[42] Others can be found in Sections 92, 214, 228, 253, 303, 318, 359, 386, 393 and 430.

[43] Or being not less than 50 members.

(h) if representing not less than 5 per cent of the total voting rights,[44] to require distribution of notice of a resolution to be proposed at the next annual general meeting (Section 376);
(i) if representing not less than 10 per cent of the shares[45]; to apply for the appointment of inspectors under Section 431, which may lead to the Secretary of State bringing a petition under Section 460 for an unfair prejudice remedy similar to that provided by Section 459 (*see* 10.4 below); and
(j) to call upon the Secretary of State to appoint inspectors (Section 432).

Principal rights available under the Insolvency Act 1986 are:

(a) to object to a business or property transaction approved under Section 110 of the Insolvency Act 1986 (Section 111 Insolvency Act 1986);
(b) to petition the court for the company to be wound up on the ground that it is just and equitable to do so (Section 122(1) of the Insolvency Act 1986) and a related restraining remedy under Section 126 Insolvency Act 1986.[46]

10.3 Derivative actions

The expression "derivative action" is used to mean proceedings which a shareholder brings to enforce a cause of action vested in the company. It has to be distinguished from a personal action of the type described in 10.2.1 above, which a shareholder may bring in his own right to enforce a right vested in him personally.

Since the introduction in 1948[47] of the prejudice remedy (now in Section 459 Companies Act 1989) the significance of the derivative action has diminished. The Law Commission has, in its "Shareholder Remedies" Report 246,[48] nonetheless identified in the derivative action a remedy that

---

[44] Or being not less than 100 members holding shares in the company on which there has been paid up an average sum, per member, of not less than £100.
[45] Or being not less than 200 members.
[46] Other rights that may be available to a contributory during a winding up can be found in Sections 133, 147, 155, 167, 168, 188 and 212 and operate in addition to powers exercisable by the liquidator.
[47] Section 210 Companies Act 1948.
[48] Part 6, the Law Commission Report 246.

still serves a useful purpose. However, it is complicated and unwieldy in its current guise. As a result, the Law Commission has recommended a new derivative procedure that would replace the common law derivative action entirely and operate subject to tight judicial control at all stages with the objective of mitigating the substantial costs typically associated with derivative actions and guarding against nuisance litigation.

Although there are a number of problems associated with the current procedure, a claimant in a derivative action has the advantage (when compared with a Section 459 prejudice action) of not needing to prove unfairly prejudicial conduct by the defendants.[49] Furthermore, whereas Section 459 has to a substantial extent evolved as an exit remedy, the derivative action is designed to provide a solution for shareholders that wish to retain their investment.[50] This part of this Chapter contains a summary of the current law on the subject.

10.3.1 *The rule in* Foss *v* Harbottle

The derivative action has its origins in the rule in the case of *Foss* v *Harbottle*,[51] referred to briefly in 10.2.1.2 above. This rule, substantially restated in *Prudential Assurance Co. Ltd* v *Newman Industries Ltd (No. 2)*,[52] is understood to provide that:

(a) the proper claimant in an action in respect of a wrong alleged to be done to a corporation is prima facie the corporation;
(b) where the alleged wrong is a transaction which might be made binding on the corporation by a simple majority of the members, no individual member of the corporation is allowed to maintain an action in respect of that matter because, if the majority confirms the transaction, *cadit quaestio* (the question is at an end); or, if the majority challenges the transaction, there is no valid reason why the company should not sue;
(c) there is no room for the operation of the rule if the alleged wrong is ultra vires the corporation, because the majority of members cannot confirm the transaction;

---

[49] Note also that the remedy under Section 460 is only available where the court is satisfied that an unfair prejudice has occurred.
[50] Paragraph 6.11, the Law Commission Report 246.
[51] [1843] 2 Hare 461; 67 ER 189.
[52] [1982] Ch 204.

Directors Facing Disputes

(d) there is no room for the operation of the rule if the transaction complained of could be validly done or sanctioned only by a special resolution or the like, because a simple majority cannot confirm a transaction which requires the concurrence of a greater majority; and
(e) there is an exception to the rule where what has been done amounts to fraud or possibly oppression or unfairness[53] and the wrongdoers are themselves in control of the company.

At first instance in *Prudential Assurance Co. Ltd v Newman Industries Ltd (No. 2)*,[54] Vinelott J promulgated a broader exception to the rule in *Foss v Harbottle*, so as to allow individual shareholder action whenever the justice of the case so requires. This broad exception was disapproved of on appeal.[55] The decision at first instance that, as a result of a finding of fraud, individual shareholders were entitled to damages for the loss of value in their shares as a personal claim was also held to be misconceived in that the damage complained of was damage suffered by the company. To recover under a personal claim would require a case to be made of loss to personal assets caused by the fraudulent act, separate and distinct from the loss suffered by the company. No claim can be founded for personal loss that is merely a reflection of the loss suffered by the company unless the company has no cause of action to sue and recover the loss.[56]

---

[53] *MacDougall v Gardiner* (supra); *Edwards v Halliwell* (supra).
[54] [1982] Ch 257.
[55] [1982] Ch 204 at 221. This does not appear to be the case in Australia's *Biala Pty. Ltd v Mallina Holdings Ltd (No. 2)* (1993) 11 ACSR 785.
[56] [1982] Ch 204 at 223; see also *Johnson v Gore Wood* [2001 1 AER 481] in which the House of Lords identified two circumstances in which an individual shareholder may sue, namely (i) where the company had no cause for action, the shareholder claim then being for reflective loss of value in the shares and (ii) where the shareholder has a separate cause of action in respect of a breach of duty owed to him; also *Giles v Rhind* [2003] 1 BCLC 1, *Day v Cook* [2003] BCC 256, *Ellison Property Leeds (UK) Ltd* [2002] 2 BCLC 175 and *Shaker v Al-Bedrawi* [2003] 2 WLR 922.

In the US, where courts have held that directors and controlling shareholders of closely held corporations owe other investors a higher level of fiduciary duty that needs to be observed in the case of publicly held corporations, there is also precedent permitting a personal action as a means of providing direct compensation to a shareholder for loss sustained by a close corporation where all shareholders are joined in the action. However this tendency to permit personal actions is more evident in states that do not make statutory provision for oppression actions. US courts have also been prepared to provide an individual remedy where the corporation is no longer a going concern or where there has been a change of control of the corporation and derivative action would not provide an adequate remedy.

This emphasises the scope and essential character of derivative action; it seeks relief to the extent and no larger than that which the company itself would have if it were the claimant. For this reason, a shareholder is able to assert a cause of action which arose before he became a shareholder because it is the company's and not his substantive right that is being enforced.[57]

10.3.2 Fraud on the minority

The exception in 10.3.1 (e) above exists because, if it did not, the minority's grievance could never reach the court since the wrongdoers themselves, being in control, would not allow the company to sue.[58] To come within the exception, the claimant must show:

(a) that what has been done amounts to fraud; and
(b) that the wrongdoers are in control. However, an individual shareholder may be prevented from pursuing his action if an "independent organ" of the company does not wish the action to proceed.

In this context, "fraud" means "fraud in the wider equitable sense of that term, as in the equitable concept of a fraud on a power" and does not require proof of deceit.[59] Examples are:

(a) attempts by the majority to sell worthless assets to the company, while concealing a commission paid to a director who procured the arrangement;[60]
(b) the majority diverting business from the company to themselves in breach of their fiduciary duties;[61] and
(c) the majority compromising, on terms which are disadvantageous to the company, litigation against bodies in which the majority are interested.[62]

---

[57] *Season v Grant* (1867) LR 2 Ch App 459.
[58] *Prudential Assurance Co. Ltd v Newman Industries Ltd (No. 2)* [1982] Ch 204 at 211.
[59] *Eastmanco (Kilner House) Ltd v Greater London Council* [1982] 1 WLR 2 at 12. Further held on the facts that the sum total of the facts represented such an abuse of power as to have the same effect as a fraud on the minority.
[60] *Atwool v Merryweather* (1867) LR 5 Eq 464.
[61] *Cook v Deeks* [1916] 1 AC 554 (PC).
[62] *Menier v Hooper's Telegraph Works* (1874) 9 Ch App 350.

The fraud exception probably has no application where the wrongdoers do not themselves benefit, it certainly does not extend to mere negligence on the part of the directors,[63] unless the negligence is in failing (for their own benefit) to procure that the company takes action against them and even in such a case, if an independent majority can vote that proceedings not be taken in respect of the negligence, the action would fail.

It is also necessary for the claimant to show that the wrongdoers control the company. This may amount to a direct or indirect holding of a majority of the shares in the company, but could extend to a situation where control lies with the wrongdoers together with those likely to vote with them as a result of influence or apathy.[64]

A major problem for the claimant is the need to show that there is a prima facie case of fraud and the element of control by the wrongdoers at a preliminary hearing, as the court will make no assumptions on these issues.[65] This may have the effect of turning the preliminary application into a mini trial, but it serves to uphold the purpose of the rule, to avoid multiple claims where the company itself is competent to bring proceedings but may for its own reasons determine not to do so. It was even suggested in the Prudential appeal proceedings[66] that it might be right for a judge trying the preliminary issue to grant a sufficient adjournment to enable a meeting of shareholders to be convened, so that a conclusion can be reached in the light of the conduct of the members.

In *Smith v Croft (No. 2)*,[67] a case in which the purported wrongdoers had voting control, it was held that a minority shareholder's derivative action should not be allowed to continue if an "independent organ" of the company did not wish it to be pursued. The nature of an independent organ will vary from one company to another, but it could consist of a majority of the independent shareholders or directors (i.e. those not associated with the wrongdoers). The test of independence is whether the relevant parties are capable of reaching a determination as to a course

---

[63] *Pavlides v Jensen* [1956] Ch 565. However, in *Daniels v Daniels* [1978] Ch 406, the court suggests that if directors benefit personally from the negligence at the company's expense, this may constitute fraud on the minority.
[64] *Prudential Assurance* (supra) at 219.
[65] *Ibid*; at pages 221–222. This was described in *Smith v Croft* (supra) at 139 as giving rise to a half-way house in this very special type of case.
[66] *Prudential v Newman* (supra) at 222.
[67] [1988] Ch 114.

of action that in their view is bona fide for the benefit of the company as a whole.[68]

10.3.3 Ultra vires transactions

If the alleged wrong is ultra vires the company or illegal (such as the unlawful reduction of its capital or unlawful financial assistance for the purpose of acquiring its own shares) or criminal, there is a prima facie basis for the shareholder's derivative action and it is not necessary for him to show fraud on the minority.[69] Again, that action will not be allowed to proceed if an independent organ of the company does not wish it to be pursued.[70]

If the alleged wrong is not unlawful but is ultra vires the company based on the powers contained in its memorandum of association, Section 35 allows the company to ratify, by special resolution, a director's act which is ultra vires the company, and to absolve the directors from liability. However, a minority shareholder could challenge the resolution on the grounds that it was not passed for the purposes of securing a benefit for the company, and so was a fraud on the minority (i.e. the resolution was passed for an improper purpose).[71]

10.3.4 Where a special or extraordinary resolution is required

A further limb of the rule in *Foss* v *Harbottle* (as set out in 10.3.1 (d) above) provides, in effect, that a shareholder can bring an action to prevent the company from relying on an ordinary resolution to sanction a transaction if a special or extraordinary resolution is required by the Act or the articles.[72] Although packaged with the general concept of derivative action, this limb is probably more accurately viewed as a personal action in response to irregularities in voting procedure, in breach of the contract to which the relevant shareholder is a party.

10.3.5 Further obstacles

Assuming that the minority shareholder is able to bring his complaint within one of the exceptions to the rule in *Foss* v *Harbottle*, there are a

---

[68] *Smith* v *Croft* (supra) at 186.
[69] *Smith* v *Croft* (supra).
[70] *Smith* v *Croft* (supra) page 185.
[71] *Smith* v *Croft* (supra) page 186.
[72] *Pavlides* v *Jensen* (supra).

Directors Facing Disputes

number of further tests which need to be satisfied if he is to persuade the court to allow his action to proceed. These are:

(a) as referred to above, no independent organ of the company must disapprove of his continuing with the action;
(b) whether the wrong complained of can, as a matter of law, properly be ratified;
(c) whether the minority shareholder comes "with clean hands";
(d) whether some other adequate remedy is available to the minority shareholder; and
(e) whether the company is in liquidation.

In relation to ratification, the position varies according to the nature of the defect. If the act complained of is lawful but ultra vires the company, then it cannot be authorised in advance but may, as discussed in 10.3.3 above, be ratified (and the breach of authority by the directors absolved) under Section 35(3). If the act is within the powers of the company but outside the authority of the directors, then it cannot be authorised in advance but may be ratified by subsequent ordinary resolution. However, if the act complained of amounts to a breach of fiduciary duty by the directors, whether or not the majority may seek to ratify the actions of the directors, should the effect be to transfer benefit from the minority to the majority or otherwise discriminate between the minority and the majority, the purported ratification will be no bar to the minority shareholder's action.[73]

The next test is whether the claimant comes with "clean hands". A derivative action is an equitable remedy and so the minority shareholder will be barred from bringing it if he has knowingly benefited from the relevant ultra vires act or misappropriation of assets.[74]

---

[73] *Cook v Deeks* [1916] 1 AC 554 (PC). Had a relevant majority previously determined to dissolve the company or that it should close business, there would have been no breach of duty in subsequently taking the benefit of a contract personally; cf. *Regal (Hastings) Ltd v Gulliver* [1967] 2 AC 134 if a breach of fiduciary duty in the guise of a director making a profit from his position is not waived or ratified by a majority, the director will be liable to account; see also *Hogg v Cramphorn* [1967] Ch 254 and *Bamford v Bamford* [1970] Ch 212.

[74] *Nurcombe v Nurcombe* [1985] 1 WLR 370 at page 378; *Barrett v Duckett* [1995] 1 BCLC 243.

The minority shareholder will also be prevented from bringing a derivative action if there is another adequate remedy (e.g. the winding up of the company) available.[75]

If the company is in liquidation, there is normally no need for a minority shareholder to bring a derivative action to obtain redress against the wrongdoers, as the liquidator can bring an action in the name of the company if there is a reasonable cause of action; and if he refuses, the shareholder may be able to obtain an order requiring the liquidator to bring the action[76] or an order permitting the shareholder to bring an action in the name of the company.[77]

10.3.6 Costs

A further, and potentially substantial, obstacle is the burden of the costs of the action. It was held by the Court of Appeal in *Wallersteiner v Moir (No. 2)*[78] that legal aid was not available to a shareholder bringing a derivative action, and legal aid is now largely unavailable anyway for money claims.[79] However, following *Wallersteiner v Moir (No. 2)*, the claimant may apply for an indemnity out of the assets of the company (commonly called a Wallersteiner order).

The procedure is now set out in CPR Part 19, rule 19.9(7).[80] Under this rule, at the same time as giving permission for the claimant to continue the claim, the court may order the company "to indemnify the claimant against any liability in respect of costs incurred in the claim".[81]

The court will consider whether the claimant has acted reasonably and in good faith in bringing the action, it may have regard to the ability of

---

[75] *Barrett v Duckett* supra at page 250.
[76] Sections 112(1) and 168(5) of the Insolvency Act 1986.
[77] *Barrett v Duckett* supra at page 255.
[78] [1975] QB 373.
[79] The Access to Justice Act 1999 set up alternative systems of funding for civil cases in England & Wales, including funding under the Community Legal Service, conditional fee agreements and litigation funding agreements.
[80] The former provision was RSC, O.15, r.12A(13). The new procedure is contained in the Civil Procedure (Amendment) Rules 2000, SI 2000/221, Schedule 2, paragraph 1.
[81] The same procedure for a "derivative claim" is available where a claim is made by members of a trade union or by members of an incorporated body other than a company (CPR rule 19.9(1)).

the claimant to finance the claim himself[82] and may order that part of the costs be borne by the claimant regardless of his means.[83]

The majority of the Court of Appeal in *Wallersteiner* v *Moir (No. 2)*[84] considered that contingency fees (where the advisers to the petitioner are entitled to a share in the proceeds if the action is successful) could not be used as a mechanism to fund derivative actions. However, the introduction of new rules permitting conditional fee arrangements[85] (allowing recovery from losing opponents of uplifted success fees, in addition to normal fees, and premiums for after-the-event legal expenses insurance) has heralded a new way by which a claimant may be able to protect himself from full exposure to costs unless and until he obtains an indemnity out of the assets of the company.

10.3.7 Procedure

The title to the proceedings in a derivative action must state that the claimant makes the claim on behalf of himself and all other shareholders in the company, other than the defendants. The company must, perhaps somewhat illogically, also be named as a defendant,[86] the reason being so that it can be bound by any order made by the court.

The claim in a derivative action is started by issuing a claim form under Part 7 of the Civil Procedure Rules in the usual way. However, after the claim form has been issued, the claimant must apply to the court for permission to continue the claim, and he may not take any other step, other than arranging for service of the claim form and of his application upon the defendant,[87] without the court's permission.[88] The application must be supported by written evidence[89] (typically a witness statement) verifying the facts on which the claim and the entitlement to sue on behalf of the company are based.

---

[82] *Smith* v *Croft* [1986] 1 WLR 580. In this case, Walton J suggested that it was for the claimant to show that he did not have sufficient resources to finance the action and that he genuinely needed an indemnity from the company. However, this more restrictive approach was not followed in *Jaybird Group Ltd* v *Greenwood* [1986] BCLC 319 at 327.
[83] *Smith* v *Croft* [1986] 1 WLR 580 at pages 597–598.
[84] [1975] QB 373 at page 403.
[85] Under the Access to Justice Act 1999.
[86] CPR rule 19.9(2).
[87] CPR rule 19.9(5).
[88] CPR rule 19.9(3).
[89] CPR rule 19.9(4).

It was held in *Prudential Assurance Co. Ltd v Newman Industries Ltd*[90] that a minority shareholder must establish a prima facie case that:

(a) the company is entitled to the relief claimed; and
(b) that the action falls within the proper boundaries of the exception to the rule in *Foss v Harbottle*.

Despite protestations of appellate judges to the contrary,[91] these requirements can easily convert the preliminary hearing into a "mini-trial". The main practical consideration which emerges from this is that the preliminary hearing required under the court rules can be lengthy and expensive. In the case of *Smith v Croft (No. 2)*,[92] the preliminary hearing lasted 18 days.

Following the preliminary hearing, the court has discretion to decide the extent to which permission to continue will be granted: "until close of pleadings, or until discovery or until trial".[93]

10.4 Statutory unfair prejudice remedy (Section 459)

10.4.1 *The requirements of Section 459*

Section 459(1) provides:

> "A member of a company may apply to the court by petition for an order under [Companies Act 1985 Part XVII] on the ground that the company's affairs are being or have been conducted in a manner which is *unfairly prejudicial to the interests of its members generally or of some part of its members*[94] (including at least himself) or that any actual or proposed act or omission of the company (including an act or omission on its behalf) is or would be so prejudicial."

---

[90] Supra at page 222.
[91] For instance, Lord Denning MR in *Wallersteiner v Moir (No. 2)* [1975] QB 373 at 392.
[92] [1988] Ch 114; *see Law Commission, Shareholder Remedies* (Law Commission Report No. 142, HMSO, London, 1996) page 50.
[93] *Wallersteiner v Moir (No. 2)* [1975] QB 373 at 392 per Denning MR.
[94] Wording in italics substituted by Companies Act 1989, Section 145, Sch 19, paragraph 11, effective 4 February 1991.

This Section contains a number of elements, which are considered separately below. This remedy was first introduced as Section 210 of the Companies Act 1948 but originally related only to conduct that was oppressive to some part of the members. The narrower concept of oppression has been replaced by the requirement in Section 459[95] that the relevant conduct be unfairly prejudicial. The opportunity was also taken to address other defects in Section 2.

Under Section 210 it was necessary to demonstrate that the facts would have justified a winding up on the just and equitable ground. Section 459 imposes no such requirement. It also makes clear that a single act or omission, and threatened conduct of a kind that would otherwise support a petition, can justify relief. Further, to supplement the fraud on the minority exception to the rule in *Foss* v *Harbottle*, the power of the court was extended to authorise proceedings to be brought against a third party in the name of the company and on such terms as the court should direct. Finally the right of persons entitled to shares by transmission to petition was specifically confirmed.[96] It was anticipated that the amendments reflected in Section 459 should enable a petitioner to obtain relief where he could demonstrate a sufficient prejudice to his interests as a result of conduct that damaged the value of the company but where the conduct complained of might fall short of fraud on the minority, as a result, for example, of negligence or abuse of corporate assets. Nonetheless there was a concern to achieve an appropriate balance such that the court should not interfere with bona fide commercial decisions taken on behalf of the company.

An amendment introduced in the Companies Act 1989 removed a defect in Section 459 that impeded reliance upon the remedy where the interests of some but not all of the members were unfairly prejudiced.

While successful petitions under Section 210 were rare, Section 459 has spawned a very high level of activity and has generally proved far more successful although a strong case for further reform has been made as reflected in the Law Commission "Shareholder Remedies" Report 246 to which reference is made in 10.5 below.

The remedy was introduced as an alternative to a winding up on the just and equitable ground and is substantially relied upon as an exit

---

[95] Originally Section 75 Companies Act 1980.
[96] These changes were all recommended by the Jenkins Committee command 1749 of 1962, *see* paragraphs 199–212.

mechanism for the damaged shareholder while not destroying the company.

While the remedy applies to all Companies Act companies,[97] it has proved particularly relevant in the case of private companies, in circumstances where shareholders may also be directors and, in the mind of the protagonists, the distinction between the interests of an individual as an investor and his responsibilities as a director is unclear. Proposed reforms of the remedy focus on streamlining procedure and reducing the significant cost hurdle. Regardless, shareholders in private companies where disputes of the kind to which Section 459 applies are more likely to arise will generally be better served by anticipating dispute and making appropriate provision in shareholders' agreements or the articles. Such provisions should cater for controls over the conduct of the company's affairs, management of disputes and an exit solution in the event that issues in dispute cannot otherwise be resolved satisfactorily.

10.4.1.1 *The complainant must be a member*

In general, the petitioner must be a member at the time of bringing the petition, but it is unclear whether he must also have been a member at the time of the conduct to which the complaint relates. Any person to whom shares have been transferred or transmitted by operation of law is, although not a registered member, permitted to petition.[98] A former member is unable to petition under Section 459, even if he discovers that unfairly prejudicial conduct occurred while he was a member.

A separate, but similar, right is given by Section 460(1) to the Secretary of State to petition if he has received an inspector's report or obtained information by exercising his powers to do so, and it appears to him that the affairs of the company are being, or have been, conducted in a manner which is unfairly prejudicial to the interests of its members generally or of some part of the members or that any actual or proposed act or omission of the company (including an act or omission on its behalf) is or would be so prejudicial.

10.4.1.2 *The complaint must be made in the petitioner's capacity as a member*

The Section refers to members' interests including at least the petitioner. It has been held that, while the expression "interests" is wider than "strict

---

[97] Section 459(3).
[98] Section 459(2).

legal rights",[99] those interests must be those of the petitioner qua member, and not in some other capacity; that is, the conduct complained of must adversely affect or jeopardise the value or quality of the shareholder's interest.[100] There may be circumstances where conduct affecting a member in some other capacity may nonetheless also affect the member as a member because it breaches a term on which he agreed to participate as a member. For example, where the value of membership is inextricably connected with a management role, removal from management may prejudice the member's interests as a member.[101]

10.4.1.3 Effect on other members

The matter complained of need not affect the petitioner alone: it can affect all members (e.g. a fall in share value), even though the others do not complain.

10.4.1.4 Conduct of the company's affairs

It is not necessary for the conduct to be continuing at the time of the presentation of the petition.[102] While the act complained of need not be continuing and a failure to act may prove sufficient,[103] if the offending conduct has been put right and cannot recur or can be remedied by the petitioner, no court-imposed remedy will be required or made available.[104] In effect, it is difficult to envisage circumstances in which persons in control of a company as directors and shareholders could bring a petition, even where relations with a minority shareholder have totally broken down, in an effort to squeeze out the minority in reliance on Section 459, notwithstanding some prior or even current improper conduct of the minority shareholder in any management role.[105]

---

[99] See Re a Company [1986] BCLC 376 page 378; Re JE Cade & Son Ltd [1992] BCLC 213.

[100] Re a Company (No. 004475 of 1982) [1983] Ch 178 page 189; Re JE Cade & Son Ltd (supra); but see the remarks of Vinelott J in Re a Company [1983] 1 WLR 927. See also O'Neill and Another v Phillips and Others [1999] 2 BCLC 1, HL which, while confirming that the prejudice must be suffered as a member, noted that the requirement should not be too narrowly or technically construed. See also commentary of Ralph Gibson LJ in Nicholas v Soundcraft Electronics Ltd and Another [1993] BCLC 360.

[101] O'Neill and Another v Phillips and Others (supra).

[102] Re a Company (No. 001761 of 1986) [1987] BCLC 141 page 143.

[103] Re a Company (No. 001761 of 1986) [1987] BCLC 141.

[104] Re Legal Costs Negotiators Ltd [1999] BCC 547 or 1999 2 BCLC 171, aka: Morris and Others v Hateley and Another (1999) The Times March 10 (CA).

[105] Re Legal Costs Negotiators Ltd (supra).

There is no limitation period applicable to a petition under Section 459, and so historic conduct can be relied upon, but inexcusable delay may bar relief.[106]

Although Section 459 makes reference to a proposed act or omission of the company, a petition brought when proposed conduct of the company is merely speculative may be insufficient.

10.4.1.5 Meaning of "the company's affairs"
The conduct complained of must be conduct by the defendant of the company's affairs, rather than conduct by shareholders of their own affairs or the exercise of their individual rights. The offending conduct must be concerned with acts done by the company or those authorised to act as its organs.[107] Conduct merely in another capacity (even if that conduct affects the company) will not support a complaint.[108]

A refusal by a minority shareholder to sell shares, or disagreements between shareholders relating to their disposal of or dealings with their shares, will not constitute conduct of the company's affairs. Similarly, disagreements as to the operation of a shareholders' agreement typically will not relate to the conduct of the company's affairs.[109]

Should controlling shareholders procure that a company take no action to preserve its interests in the face of competing objectives of the controlling shareholders, maintaining that policy of passive neglect of the company's interests will qualify as conduct of the company's affairs in a manner that is unfairly prejudicial for these purposes. Particularly in a group context, where a subsidiary has an independent minority, the parent company must accept that, insofar as it competes, there will be an obligation to conduct affairs so as to deal fairly with the subsidiary. Representative directors of the majority shareholder may find themselves in a delicate position where competing demands arise, but in those circumstances the burden on the controlling shareholder to behave with scrupulous fairness towards the minority shareholders becomes the benchmark for the remedy. Exploiting control to guide the company to

---

[106] *Re a company (No. 005134 of 1986), ex parte Harries* [1989] BCLC 383, pages 397–398.
[107] *Re Legal Costs Negotiators Ltd* (supra); *Arrow Nominees Inc and Another* v *Blackledge and Others* [2000] 2 BCLC 167.
[108] *Re a Company (No. 001761 of 1986)* [1987] BCLC 141; *O'Neill and Another* v *Phillips and Others* (supra).
[109] *Re Unisoft Group Ltd (No. 3)* [1994] 1 BCLC 609; *Re Leeds United Holdings plc* [1996] 2 BCLC 545, but see *Scottish Cooperative Wholesale Society* v *Meyer* [1959] AC 324.

a policy of inaction is sufficient connection between the conduct of the controlling shareholders and the company's affairs for these purposes.

Where the affairs of members of a group of companies are to any relevant extent treated as if a single enterprise, actions taken by the parent company in its own interests may be regarded as acts done in the conduct of the affairs of the subsidiary, even if the two companies are engaged in different types of business.[110]

10.4.1.6 Meaning of "interests"

Although the expression "interests of the members" in Section 459 limits the interests in question to those of the members qua members, it is not limited to strict legal rights under the company's constitution, and the court may have regard to wider equitable considerations.[111] However, the petitioner must usually show some breach of the terms on which the members have agreed or have an understanding that the affairs of the company should be conducted.[112]

This agreement will not necessarily be a formal agreement, but in appropriate circumstances can be a "legitimate expectation"[113] of the petitioner,

---

[110] *Nicholas* v *Soundcraft Electronics Ltd* [1993] BCLC 360, CA.

[111] *see Re Macro (Ipswich) Ltd* [1994] 2 BCLC 354 page 404 – examples of interests included damage to the value of the company and the absence of independent directors; *Re Rotadata Ltd* [2000] 1 BCLC 122.

[112] *O'Neill and Another* v *Phillips and Others* (supra).

[113] *Re Saul D Harrison* [1995] 1 BCLC 14, although this expression was qualified in *O'Neill and Another* v *Phillips and Others* (supra) such that only to the extent equitable principles dictate should a remedy be available. Most US states provide a remedy in response to misconduct by those that control a corporation. A common theme in the development of such remedies is to relate them closely to breach of good faith and fair-dealing obligations by majority shareholders or, at its broadest, the frustration of "reasonable expectations" of shareholders. The reasonable expectations standard has enabled US courts to adapt the remedy to address the greater intimacy of business relationships that tend to exist in close corporations, permitting the court to assess the understanding of the parties and then determine whether the conduct of controlling shareholders is contrary to that understanding.

In determining the particular characteristics that bind participants in a close corporation, US courts have tended to distinguish subjective aspirations, frustration of which would not justify relief, and expectations that were known to and concurred with by other shareholders. In assessing expectations, the US courts have been prepared to look beyond rights and benefits anticipated by a shareholder in that capacity, to take account of an individual's collateral expectations as an officer or employee.

breach of which might have formed the basis of a petition to wind up the company on the "just and equitable" ground set out in Section 122(1)(g) of the Insolvency Act 1986. In the case of *Ebrahimi v Westbourne Galleries Ltd*[114] (where the majority had exercised their legal right to remove the petitioner from his directorship) the House of Lords said that it was both impossible and undesirable to give an exhaustive statement of the circumstances in which equitable considerations should be taken into account in determining whether a person's rights had been interfered with, but indicated that the circumstances might include one or probably more of the following elements:

(a) an association formed or continued on the basis of a personal relationship, involving mutual confidence – this element will often be found where a pre-existing partnership has been converted into a limited company;
(b) an agreement, or understanding, that all or (if there are sleeping shareholders) some of the shareholders shall participate in the conduct of the business;
(c) restriction upon the transfer of the members' interest in the company – so that, if confidence is lost or one member is removed from management, he cannot take out his stake and go elsewhere.

This parallel between circumstances in which an exercise of strict legal rights will nonetheless justify a remedy under Section 459 akin to the "just and equitable" ground for winding up is not intended to mean that the conduct complained of will not be unfair unless it would justify a winding up order on that ground. It is quite clear that whereas there was such a requirement in the former Section 210 Companies Act 1948, that standard was not replicated in Section 459. The parallel is not in the conduct which the court will treat as justifying the remedy but in the principles upon which it determines that the conduct is unjust, inequitable or unfair.[115]

The expression "quasi-partnership" has been used to describe companies in which some or all of the elements in (a) to (c) above exist, and the distinction between companies which are quasi-partnerships and those which are not is important in understanding what attitude a court will take on a petition under Section 459. Where it is established that the company has the characteristics of a quasi-partnership, minority

---

[114] [1973] AC 360 (HL).
[115] *O'Neill and Another v Phillips and Others* (supra).

participants will in effect have a second string upon which to rely, namely the breach of legitimate expectations which may go beyond the articles or agreements between shareholders, statutory obligations or directors duties. However, it is not sufficient for the petitioner merely to establish that the company is a quasi-partnership in order to obtain a remedy under Section 459. He must also show either a breach of the legal terms on which the business of the company is to be conducted or, in the context of a quasi-partnership, use by the majority of their strict legal entitlements in a way which equity would regard as contrary to good faith.[116]

In identifying these hurdles, the House of Lords decision in *O'Neill v Phillips* represents a landmark limitation on excessive reliance upon Section 459 by shareholders petitioning on the strength of broad based disappointments. Section 459 does not provide a right to exit at will, even if it is possible to establish that the company is a quasi-partnership, simply because there has been a loss of trust, confidence or good relations.

Nonetheless, where an event occurs that puts an end to the basis upon which parties have entered into a quasi-partnership making it unfair that some shareholders should insist upon the continuance of the association, the conduct of the majority in insisting upon that continuation in changed circumstances may be sufficient to support a petition.[117]

It is clear that only small, possibly very small, companies can be quasi-partnerships. It is highly unlikely that a petitioner would be able to demonstrate that all members of a public company with a substantial number of shareholders were parties to some informal arrangement such as to qualify the contractual obligations and rights conferred by the constitution.[118]

---

[116] *O'Neill and Another v Phillips and Others* (supra). The *Law Commission, Shareholder Remedies* Report 246 at paragraph 4.11 references its suggestion that conduct could be unfairly prejudicial merely based on breaches of legitimate expectations, a concept adopted in *Re Saul D. Harrison & Sons plc* (supra). In *O'Neill*, Lord Hoffmann qualified this broad interpretation on the basis that a balance must be struck between the breadth of discretion given to the court and the principle of legal certainty.

[117] *Re Guidezone Ltd* [2000] 2 BCLC 321.

[118] *Re Blue Arrow plc* [1987] BCLC 585; *Re Tottenham Hotspur plc* [1994] 1 BCLC 655; *Re Astec (BSR) plc* [1998] 2 BCLC 556 at 590.

10.4.1.7 Meaning of "unfairly prejudicial"

This leads to a consideration of the meaning of the expression "unfairly prejudicial". There is a vast body of case law under Section 459, which is not surprising as the courts have acknowledged that the protection afforded by the Section has had to be worked out on a case-by-case basis.[119] In its 1996 Consultation Paper,[120] the Law Commission analysed the petitions under Section 459 presented to the Companies Court at the Royal Courts of Justice between January 1994 and December 1995, and disclosed the following principal allegations pleaded (listed in order of frequency):

(a) Exclusion from management: by far the most common allegation was that the petitioner had been excluded from the management of the company,[121] and this exclusion will be likely to entitle the petitioner to relief if the court finds that he had a legitimate expectation to participate and that exclusion was unfairly prejudicial to his interests qua member.[122] The conduct of the petitioner, and the way in which he was excluded, will be relevant.[123] The Law Commission has recommended that in the case of a private company limited by shares, in which substantially all the members are directors, there should be a statutory presumption that the removal of a shareholder as a director or from substantially all his functions as a director is unfairly prejudicial conduct. As noted in *O'Neill v Phillips*, this will not seem very different in practice from current law. The key point, however, is that the unfairness is not so much in the exclusion alone as in the exclusion without a reasonable offer to buy out the relevant shareholder (*see* 10.4.2 below).

(b) Failure to provide information: although the failure to comply with the various requirements of the Companies Act 1985 to provide members with information may be grounds for a petition under Section 459 (unless the failure is trivial), it is more commonly linked to an allegation of exclusion from management. However, a deliberate policy not to consult the petitioner on major issues on which he had a legitimate expectation to be consulted could amount to unfair prejudice.[124]

---

[119] Per Neill LJ in *Re Saul D Harrison & Sons plc* (supra) at page 30.
[120] The Law Commission Consultation Paper No. 142, Appendix E, Table 1.
[121] *Richards v Lundy and Others* [1999] BCC 786 or [2000] 1 BCLC 376.
[122] *Quinlan v Essex Hinge Co. Ltd* [1996] 2 BCLC 417.
[123] *Re R A Noble & Sons (Clothing) Ltd* [1983] BCLC 273.
[124] Per Nourse J in *Re R A Noble & Sons (Clothing) Ltd* (supra) at page 289.

Directors Facing Disputes

(c) Misappropriation of assets: there have been a number of successful petitions under Section 459 where the majority have been shown to have misappropriated the company's assets (often by selling them at an undervalue to a company controlled by them) or diverted business, which should have gone to the company, to another business owned by them or otherwise acted to run down the value of the company while transferring value to themselves.[125] These cases show that a petition under Section 459 is not barred even though the facts would have warranted the bringing of a derivative action or a personal action based on the directors' breach of fiduciary duties.

(d) Failure to remunerate/pay a dividend: the fact that a company's failure to pay a dividend affects all shareholders equally is no longer relevant following the amendments made by the Companies Act 1989. The petitioner will, however, have to show a legitimate expectation that dividends would be paid in order to overcome the objection that it is for the directors to decide what the company's policy should be on the retention or distribution of the company's profits. Failure to pay dividends is often linked to a complaint about excessive remuneration of the directors (*see* (f) below).[126]

(e) Mismanagement: the courts have been reluctant to interfere in the management of the company's business by the directors. Mere disagreement over the manner in which the business of a company is being operated or the policies of the board will not support action under Section 459. Section 459 will not provide an exit mechanism for a shareholder who is simply disappointed with the company's performance or disagrees with decisions of the board over the direction the company should take or who has fallen out with the majority. However, it has been acknowledged[127] that serious or persistent mismanagement which the majority did nothing to correct could amount to unfair prejudice.

(f) Excessive remuneration: if the remuneration paid to the defendant has clearly been in excess of what he deserved by comparison to his contribution to the company's business, this has been held to be unfairly prejudicial to the interests of the petitioner.[128]

---

[125] For example *Re London School of Electronics Ltd* [1986] Ch 211; *Re a Company* [1986] 1 WLR 281; *Re Antoniades v Wong and Others* [1997] 2 BCLC 419.
[126] *Shamsallah Holdings Pty. Ltd v CBD Refrigeration and Airconditioning Services Pty. Ltd* (2001) 19 ACLC 517.
[127] *Re Elgindata Ltd* [1991] BCLC 959; *Re Macro (Ipswich) Ltd* [1994] 2 BCLC 354.
[128] *Re Cumana Ltd* [1986] BCLC 430, *see* also *Re Dalkeith Investments Pty. Ltd* (1984) 1 ACLR 247.

Other commonplace allegations include oppressive conduct of board meetings,[129] breach of agreement, breach of statute,[130] improper allotment of shares,[131] breach of articles, decisions made for the benefit of related companies rather than shareholders in the company,[132] use of company funds to defend oppressive proceedings[133] and other breach of fiduciary duty.

The test of unfair prejudice is an objective one to be applied flexibly according to the circumstances in the context of the commercial relationship. It is not necessary for the petitioner to show bad faith or a conscious intention to prejudice the petitioner. Rather, the test is one of unfairness, not unlawful or even underhand conduct.[134] Indeed, as noted above, in the context of quasi-partnerships, the unfairness may consist of reliance on legal rights in circumstances where ethical considerations make it unfair to do so because the proposed exercise is outside either what can fairly be regarded as having been in the contemplation of the parties when they became members or some later established understanding.[135] Thus, what may be fair between competing business people may not be fair in a family company context.

10.4.2 Obstacles

Even if the petitioner is able to demonstrate unfairly prejudicial conduct within the ambit of Section 459, there are further obstacles which he must overcome in order to obtain relief under Section 459. These are:

(a) Conduct of the petitioner: in contrast to the situation where the shareholder wishes to bring a derivative action (*see* 10.3 above), in the case of a petition under Section 459 it is not necessary for him to come "with clean hands". However, his conduct will be taken into account by the court in deciding whether conduct which was clearly prejudicial was also unfair.[136]

---

[129] Young J in *John J Star (Real Estate) Pty. Ltd v Robert R Andrew (Australasia) Pty. Ltd* (1991) 6 ASCR 63 at 66.
[130] *DR Chemicals Ltd* (supra).
[131] *DR Chemicals Ltd* (supra) but *see* for contrast *CAS (Nominees) Ltd v Nottingham Forest FC plc and Others* [2001] 1 AER 954.
[132] See *Brenfield Squash Racquets Club Ltd* [1999] 2 BCLC 184.
[133] *Re DG Brims & Sons Pty. Ltd* (1965) 16 ACSR 559.
[134] *DR Chemicals Ltd* (supra).
[135] *O'Neill and Another v Phillips and Others* (supra).
[136] *Re London School of Electronics Ltd* (supra); and *see Re DR Chemicals Ltd* (supra).

(b) Availability of an alternative remedy: this divides itself into two, namely: (i) the existence of pre-emption rights in the company's articles of association; and (ii) in the absence of pre-emption rights, the existence of a fair offer by the other shareholder(s) to buy the petitioner's shares.

    (i) Pre-emption rights: if the company's articles contain (as the articles of many private companies do) provisions requiring (or entitling) a shareholder to offer his shares for purchase by the other shareholders (or, in some cases, by the company itself) before he can transfer them elsewhere, and he does not take advantage of those provisions, it might be argued that he has failed to exploit a remedy that is available in the alternative to an order under Section 459. However, such provisions often require the shares to be valued on an "open market value" basis, and the value of a minority shareholding will normally be valued on a discounted basis (i.e. at less than the pro rata value of the shares), and so to the detriment of the shareholder. There may be other factors (such as the valuation procedures or the commercial impact of the conduct complained of) that render the provisions inappropriate as a fair alternative to a remedy under Section 459. It is now accepted that the existence of such provisions does not represent a bar to proceedings under Section 459, but an open offer to purchase the minority shareholder's shares at a fair price, which is calculated on a pro rata basis and otherwise fairly will make it an abuse of process for the petitioner to continue.[137]

    (ii) Offer to buy the petitioner's shares: a reasonable offer to buy the petitioner's shares at a fair price (to be determined by competent expert valuation if not agreed), with equality of access to relevant company information and a fair mechanism to deal with the petitioner's shares may be enough to prevent the petition under Section 459 from being successful. If the company is a quasi-partnership, the basis of valuation may need to be on a pro rata, rather than discounted, basis to be sure of success, although the court has a discretion in all cases.[138] There may be difficulties in deciding the date as at

---

[137] *Virdi* v *Abbey Leisure Ltd and others* [1990] BCLC 342 (CA); *Re a Company* [1996] 2 BCLC 192; but *see Re Rotadata Ltd* (supra) at page 132.

[138] *Re Bird Precision Bellows Ltd* [1986] Ch 658 page 669; and *see O'Neill and Another* v *Phillips and Others* (supra) also *North Holdings Ltd* v *Southern Tropics Ltd* [1999] 2 BCLC 625 at 639.

which the valuation is to be made, as this will need to be fair in context[139] and so will vary with the circumstances of the case. An offer that fails to make provision for costs reasonably incurred by the petitioner may not prove to be an obstacle. In framing an offer, the majority shareholder should have a reasonable time to do so before he should be obliged also to pay costs.[140]

(c) Costs: as with derivative actions (*see* 10.3.6 above) the issue of costs is pervasive. The old legal aid regime has been replaced by a new system of public funding that expressly excludes funding for matters relating to company law.[141] Moreover, as the petition is by the shareholder in his own right, the court has no discretion to grant the petitioner an indemnity out of the company's assets for his costs. The Law Commission, in its 1996 Consultation Paper,[142] cites examples of the cost and length of proceedings under Section 459, including the case of *Re Elgindata Ltd*,[143] in which the hearing of the petition lasted 43 days, costs totalled £320,000 and the shares, originally purchased for £40,000, were finally valued at only £24,600. In the case of *O'Neill* v *Phillips*,[144] the original petition was issued in January 1992 and the House of Lords decision was handed down in May 1999. The new rules permitting conditional fee and litigation funding arrangements have now provided an alternative method of funding these petitions.[145]

10.4.3 Remedies available

Section 461 provides:

> "(1) If the court is satisfied that a petition under [Companies Act 1985 Part XVII] is well founded, it may make such order as it thinks fit for giving relief in respect of the matters complained of.

---

[139] *see Re London School of Electronics Ltd* (supra).
[140] *O'Neill and Another* v *Phillips and Others* (supra).
[141] The new system has been brought in under the Access to Justice Act 1999 (*see* note 79 above). Schedule 2 to the Access to Justice Act 1999 sets out services that are excluded from funding under the Community Legal Service regime.
[142] The Law Commission Consultation Paper No. 142, page 104 ff.
[143] [1991] BCLC 959.
[144] [1999] 2 BCLC 1.
[145] These alternative means of funding are referred to in Part II to the Access to Justice Act 1999.

(2) Without prejudice to the generality of subsection (1), the court's order may –

(a) regulate the conduct of the company's affairs in the future;

(b) require the company to refrain from doing or continuing an act complained of by the petitioner or to do an act which the petitioner has complained it has omitted to do;

(c) authorise civil proceedings to be brought in the name and on behalf of the company by such person or persons and on such terms as the court may direct;

(d) provide for the purchase of the shares of any members of the company by other members or by the company itself and, in the case of a purchase by the company itself, the reduction of the company's capital accordingly."

By far the most common form of relief sought is the purchase of the petitioner's shares.[146] In its 1996 Consultation Paper,[147] the Law Commission noted that, in petitions presented to the Companies Court at the Royal Courts of Justice between January 1994 and December 1995 seeking relief under Section 459, 69.9 per cent[148] sought this form of relief. As noted in Section 4.2 (b) (ii) above, difficulties can arise in such cases in relation to the basis of valuation of the shares (whether on a discounted – more likely where the shareholding is an investment[149] or pro rata basis, if they are a minority's shares) and the date as at which the valuation is to be made.[150] The courts will apply equitable considerations so as to arrive at a result which is, in all the circumstances, fair as between the parties.[151]

---

[146] But see Re Brenfield Squash Racquets Club Ltd [1996] 2 BCLC 184; also Re Planet Organic Ltd [2000] 1 BCLC 366.

[147] The Law Commission Consultation Paper No. 142 Appendix E.

[148] Taking into account that any given petition may include reference to more than one form of relief.

[149] See Re Elgindata Ltd (supra).

[150] See Profinance Trust SA v Gladstone [2002] 1 WLR 1024 for a review of relevant considerations in selecting a valuation date; also Re Cumana Ltd [1986] BCLC 430.

[151] See Re Bird Precision Bellows Ltd [1986] Ch 658 page 672; Scottish Cooperative Wholesale Society v Meyer [1959] AC 324 page 369; Re Jermyn Street Baths Ltd [1970] 1 WLR 1194 page 1208; Guinness Peat Group plc v British Land Co. plc & Others [1999] BCC 536, CA or [1999] 2 BCLC 243; O'Neill and Another v Phillips and Others (supra); Re Elgindata Ltd (supra).

A Practitioner's Guide to Directors' Duties and Responsibilities

10.4.4 Procedure

In *Re a Company (No. 004837 of 1998), North Holdings Ltd* v *Southern Tropics Ltd & Others*,[152] the first appeal concerning Section 459 proceedings since the introduction of the new Civil Procedure Rules, the judges emphasised the need for active case management at an early stage in order to reduce the time and expense involved in ascertaining a fair price for the petitioner's shares, and for use of the power to require the use of a joint expert or the appointment of an assessor, which would lead to a reduction in the number of striking out applications.

Applications under Section 459 are governed by the Companies (Unfair Prejudice Applications) Proceedings Rules 1986[153] and (as far as not inconsistent with those Rules) the CPR, in particular Part 49 of the CPR (Specialist Proceedings) and the Practice Directions made under it.[154]

---

[152] [1999] BCC 746; and *see* also *Re Rotadata Ltd* (supra). In terms of fashioning remedies, the US courts have provided a rich seam of alternatives for consideration. In addition to dissolution or buy-out, in many US states a court can appoint a provisional director to resolve deadlock and to enable the corporation to function. The appointment of a custodian represents an alternative that is more intrusive in the sense that a custodian need not operate with the approval or acquiescence of board members. Other remedies recognised in many US states include:

(a) alteration of the corporation's constitution;
(b) aintervention in actions of the corporation;
(c) prohibition of planned actions;
(d) sale of assets;
(e) alterations to the board of directors;
(f) ordering an account of corporate assets or an investigation;
(g) requiring declaration of a dividend;
(h) identifying constructive dividends paid through controlling shareholder remuneration and directing a corresponding dividend to non-participating shareholders;
(i) ordering a rebalancing in the shareholding structure;
(j) treating related corporations as grouped for the purposes of determining appropriate relief;
(k) imposing damages payments;
(l) installation of effective accounting systems or management controls; and
(m) directing dissolution at a future date if differences have not in the meantime been resolved.

[153] SI 1986/2000, made under Section 411 of the Insolvency Act 1986 and not altered on the introduction of the CPR.
[154] *See* the Chancery Guide issued by the Chancery Division, paragraphs 20.2 and 20.3.

Every application under Section 459 has to be made by petition rather than by use of a claim form,[155] is to be allocated to the multi-track, and the provisions of the CPR relating to allocation questionnaires and track allocation do not apply.[156] The 1986 Rules lay down a timetable for the filing and service of the petition, and the Schedule to those Rules sets out the form which the petition must take ("with such variations, if any, as the circumstances may require"[157]).

In line with the active case management role of judges now encouraged under the CPR, the petitioner is required, after presenting his petition, to apply for directions from the court by filing an application notice. A directions hearing will subsequently be held at which the court will give such directions for the hearing of the petition as it thinks appropriate including whether the petition is to be advertised and, if so, by what means, the manner in which evidence relating to the petition is to be put before the court (for example, orally or in writing) and directions on any other matter relevant to the hearing and disposal of the petition.[158]

The petition itself needs to set out the grounds on which it is presented and include all allegations on which the claim of unfairly prejudicial conduct is based in order to avoid these allegations subsequently being ruled inadmissible. It should also state the grounds on which any claim of the existence of a quasi-partnership is founded.

The petition may additionally ask for a winding-up order on "just and equitable" grounds under Section 122(1)(g) of the Insolvency Act 1986 in the alternative, relief which is not available under Section 459.[159] However, Section 125(2) of the Insolvency Act 1986 provides that the court is not to make a winding-up order on these grounds "if the court is . . . of the opinion both that some other remedy is available to the petitioners and that they are acting unreasonably in seeking to have the company wound up instead of pursuing that other remedy". The remedy of winding up is outside the scope of this Chapter, but it will be seen that

---

[155] CPR Part 49, Practice Direction 49B paragraph 4.
[156] CPR Part 49, Practice Direction 49B paragraph.
[157] Rule 3(1) of the 1986 Rules.
[158] Rule 5 of the 1986 Rules; CPR Part 49, Practice Direction 49B paragraph 5.
[159] Although the Law Commission has proposed that the law should be altered to make it so available in its "Shareholder Remedies" Report 246, paragraph 4.35. It also established that, in the period between January 1994 and December 1995, 39.1 per cent of petitions under Section 459 pleaded Section 122(1)(g) in the alternative.

there may be circumstances in which relief under Section 459 could be such an "alternative remedy". Since Section 124 of the Insolvency Act 1986 requires a winding-up petition to be brought by (among others) a "contributory", a member can only petition as such if he holds shares on which there is some liability, or if the company is solvent and there is some reasonable possibility of a surplus being available to the members.

A Practice Direction introduced in 1990, and now re-enacted in the CPR,[160] states:

> "(1) Attention is drawn to the undesirability of asking as a matter of course for a winding up order as an alternative to an order under Section 459 Companies Act 1985. The petition should not ask for a winding up order unless that is the relief which the petitioner prefers or it is thought that it may be the only relief to which the petitioner is entitled."

A petition to wind up a company can lead to devastating consequences for the company, not least under its contractual commitments. Further, under Section 127 of the Insolvency Act 1986, any disposition of the company's property made after the commencement of the winding up is void unless the court otherwise orders; under Section 129 of the Insolvency Act 1986, the winding up is deemed to have commenced at the time of the presentation of the petition. The Practice Direction referred to above therefore provides:

> "(2) Whenever a winding up order is asked for in a contributory's petition, the petition must state whether the petitioner consents or objects to an order under Section 127 of the [Insolvency Act 1986] in the standard form. If he objects, the written evidence in support must contain a short statement of his reasons.
> (3) If the petitioner objects to a Section 127 order in the standard form but consents to such an order in a modified form, the petition must set out the form of order to which he consents, and the written evidence in support must contain a short statement of his reasons for seeking the modification.
> (4) . . .
> (5) If the petition contains a statement that the petitioner consents to a Section 127 order, whether in the standard or modified form, the

---

[160] Paragraph 9 of Practice Direction 49B to CPR Part 49, misleadingly under the title: Schemes and Reductions in the Long Vacatio.

Registrar shall without further inquiry make an order in such form at the first hearing unless an order to the contrary has been made by the Judge in the meantime.

(6) If the petition contains a statement that the petitioner objects to a Section 127 order in the standard form, the company may apply (in the case of urgency, without notice) to the Judge for an order."

Paragraph 7 of the Practice Direction sets out the terms of the standard order as follows:

"(Title etc.)
ORDER that notwithstanding the presentation of the said Petition

(1) payments made into or out of the bank accounts of the Company in the ordinary course of the business of the Company and
(2) dispositions of the property of the Company made in the ordinary course of its business for proper value between the date of presentation of the Petition and the date of judgment on the Petition or further order in the meantime shall not be void by virtue of the provisions of Section 127 of the Insolvency Act 1986 in the event of an Order for the winding up of the Company being made on the said Petition Provided that (the relevant bank) shall be under no obligation to verify for itself whether any transaction through the company's bank accounts is in the ordinary course of business, or that it represents full market value for the relevant transaction.

This form of Order may be departed from where the circumstances of the case require."

10.5 Proposals for reform

Improvement in the statutory support for shareholders in the context of disputes with a company and its management is expected to form a significant part of the current review of company law.[161] A clear route for individual members to enforce obligations imposed in the constitution of a company is being promoted subject only to exclusion of trivial or fruitless objections. It is recognised that this may result attempts to

---

[161] *See* the Company Law Review Steering Group Final Report 2001, Chapter 7.

develop constitutional constraints on the freedom of individual shareholders to mount challenges. However, there is the prospect of improved transparency of rights and related attempts to introduce constitutional constraints will be open to challenge under Section 459.

There appears to be significant support for the introduction of a statutory derivative action along the lines recommended by the Law Commission as described below. Consideration is also being given to a requirement that to ratify a wrong on the company, or decision by the board not to pursue the wrong, it will be necessary to reach the required majority without support of the wrongdoers or those operating under their influence.

As regards the scope of the unfair prejudice remedy, there appears to be less interest in promoting the detailed initiatives proposed by the Law Commission and described below, in so far as they would require statutory provision.

Generally, in the context of codification of directors duties, it is likely that some attention will be paid both to the circumstances in which individual shareholders are entitled to see that those duties are observed and to the obligations as between shareholders in relation to corporate constitutional issues.

10.5.1 Derivative actions

The Law Commission has proposed a new derivative action,[162] to apply in the event of negligence, default, breach of duty or breach of trust by a director of the company or where a director had put himself in a position where his personal interests compete with his duties to the company. The proposal defines the remedy strictly by reference to circumstances in which the company's rights are being infringed. By comparison, the current common law derivative action remedy has been applied in circumstances where the relevant abuse reflected conduct of a third party such as a majority shareholder. However, the Law Commission did recommend that the new remedy should encompass claims against shadow directors. The proposal extends the derivative action insofar as it would be applicable in cases of negligence or breach of duties of skill and care where directors have not benefited personally. The new action would be available only to members of the company and

---

[162] The Law Commission Report 246.

would replace entirely the common law fraud on minority derivative action. A statutory derivative action was introduced into the Australian Corporations Law in 1999. Sections 236–242 of the Corporations Law provide the structure for members and others bringing derivative actions in Australia. Actions may be brought by a member, former member, persons entitled to be registered as a member, a related body corporate, or an officer or former officer of the company on behalf of the company in all cases with leave of the court. The statutory derivative action replaces the common law derivative action.

Sections 239 and 240 of the Canada Business Corporations Act 1985 incorporate a statutory derivative action. Standing is granted to "complainants" which is defined to include present and former security holders, directors, officers, security holders and other persons whom the court believes to be a proper person to make an application. A similar statutory derivative action is found in New Zealand under the Company's Act 1993 (Section 165).

However, it would not impair the right to bring personal actions, thereby preserving the fourth limb of the Prudential restatement of the *Foss* v *Harbottle* rule that deals with the invalidity of a transaction for which a special majority is required but has not been obtained. The proposal envisages a number of procedural requirements such as prior notification to the company specifying the grounds of a proposed derivative action[163] and requirements for leave of court to be obtained to continue a derivative claim beyond its preliminary stages. The court would be bound to take account of relevant circumstances including the interest of the company, the extent of any independent ratification and the availability of alternative remedies. As a generality, the procedure would confer discretion on the court to develop a principled approach in determining whether or not an action should proceed.

10.5.2 Unfair prejudice claims

The Law Commission has also made a number of proposals with the aim of simplifying the unfair prejudice remedy and, in particular,

---

[163] There are significant parallels between the derivative remedy available in many US states and the English remedy. Certain US states impose an obligation that the shareholder plaintiff first make demand either of the corporation or its shareholders to remedy an alleged wrong before instituting proceedings.

recommended that active case management by the court is the key to reducing what the Law Commission perceived to be "the excessive length and costs"[164] involved in pursuing the remedy.

Many of the Law Commission's proposals on procedure have been addressed by the CPR.[165] For example, the court now has the power to strike out a claim or a defence which, in the court's view, discloses no reasonable grounds for bringing or defending the claim.[166] Another important innovation is that the CPR have given the court greater flexibility to make costs orders which take account of the way a party has conducted the proceedings and, in making an order for costs, the court will now consider whether it is reasonable for a party to raise, pursue or contest a particular allegation or issue.[167] Such increased powers should act as a deterrent to a party who is contemplating pressing ahead with weak or insubstantial allegations in a Section 459 case.

Moreover, the Law Commission's recommendation that Alternative Dispute Resolution (ADR) should be encouraged in shareholder disputes wherever appropriate is also reflected in the CPR.[168] However, the recommendation of the Law Commission that an amendment be made to the 1986 Rules so as to include an express reference to the use of ADR, has not so far led to any amendment of the 1986 Rules. However, such amendment may prove to be unnecessary in light of the provisions of the CPR on ADR.[169]

---

[164] The Law Commission Report 246, paragraph 1.23(i). The main proposals for procedural reform are contained in Part 2 of the Law Commission Report 246.

[165] CPR, Part 3 sets out the Court's Case Management Powers.

[166] CPR, Part 3, rule 3.4. This rule refers to the ability of the court to strikeout a "statement of case". Though this term is defined to cover formal pleadings such as a particulars of claim and a defence, a similar application of the rule can likely be achieved by the court in the case of petitions under Section 459, using its inherent power to make any order of its own initiative as part of the exercise of its case management powers (CPR Part 3, rule 3.3).

[167] CPR, Part 44, rule 44.3.

[168] CPR, Part 1, rule 1.4(e) (*see* also Chancery Guide, Chapter 17).

[169] It is also worth noting that despite its support of ADR, the Law Commission eventually recommended against the inclusion of an arbitration and ADR provision in Table A in light of the less than enthusiastic response it received from consultees who feared, amongst other things, that there was scope for abuse in cases where a shareholder, dissatisfied with a proposed resolution, might commence arbitration proceedings which may not be disposed of as easily as court proceedings.

Directors Facing Disputes

Other proposals for reform made by the Commission include:

(a) the addition of winding up to the list of Section 461 remedies available in proceedings under Section 459;

(b) the amendment of Sections 459–461 to raise the following presumptions:

    (i) that in certain circumstances,[170] exclusion from participation in the management of a company will be presumed to be unfairly prejudicial (unless the respondent shows otherwise); and

    (ii) where the first presumption is not rebutted, and the court is satisfied that it ought to order a buy-out of the petitioner's shares, a presumption that the shares will be valued on a pro rata (rather than a discounted) basis;

(c) the introduction of a time limit for bringing a Section 459 claim, although it is recommended that the time limit would apply only to the conduct which forms the basis of the unfair prejudice claim and there should be no time limit imposed on other "background" matters to which the parties may refer in order to support or refute the claim;[171]

(d) the amendment of the 1985 Table A by the insertion of a new regulation providing a "no-fault" exit route for disgruntled shareholders so that they do not have to resort to bringing costly proceedings under Section 459 in order to have their shares bought out.[172] The inclusion of this new regulation would be optional and would allow the company to decide on the circumstances giving rise to the exit rights and the method of valuation of the shares in question. Such regulation or equivalent provisions in a shareholders' agreement should ideally be developed at the inception of a relationship rather than thrashed out once disagreement has begun to emerge.

---

[170] The circumstances in which a presumption of unfair prejudice on exclusion from management will arise are set out in the draft Bill in Appendix A of the 1997 Report. The type of companies envisaged are private companies limited by shares where substantially all the members of the company are directors and where prior to his removal as a director or his exclusion from management, the petitioner held, in his own name, at least 10 per cent of the voting rights in the company (Law Commission Report 246, paragraphs 3.26–3.70).

[171] The Law Commission Report 246, paragraphs 4.22 and 4.23.

[172] The exit article is set out in draft regulation 119 in Appendix C of the Law Commission Report 246.

A Practitioner's Guide to Directors' Duties and Responsibilities

As a generality, sensible anticipation and a structure to address a disagreement between shareholders and their representatives should ideally be developed at the outset of a relationship, whether in the constitution or the broader commercial framework regulating affairs between the members.

Chapter 11

Duties of Directors Facing Insolvency

Hamish Anderson, Partner
Norton Rose

11.1 Introduction

Company directors who are facing the actual or prospective insolvency of their companies retain, of course, all of the duties they would have even if the company was fully solvent. However, the onset of insolvency imposes a further set of duties, mostly under the Insolvency Act 1986 ("IA 1986"), and adds a new dimension to fiduciary duties of directors given the significant position of the company's creditors as opposed to its shareholders when insolvency is in prospect. In addition there are certain duties to the company's shareholders which apply in all cases but, by their nature, are most likely to be a problem on insolvency. Consequently, this Chapter deals with a number of statutory duties under the Insolvency Act 1986 which were enacted specifically to protect the creditors of insolvent companies, the cases surrounding the issue of directors' fiduciary duties when the company is insolvent or prospectively insolvent, and certain duties under the Companies Act 1985 ("CA 1985") and the UK Listing Authority's ("the UKLA") Listing Rules which frequently become an issue on the prospective insolvency of the company. This Chapter does not cover those sections of the Company Directors' Disqualification Act 1986 ("CDDA 1986") which deal with insolvency, as this is dealt with in Chapter 13.

11.2 Statutory duties under the Insolvency Act 1986

All of the provisions relate to a situation where a company enters into a formal insolvency procedure such as liquidation or administration. The liquidator or administrator has the power to look back to the period shortly before a formal insolvency and bring proceedings, either for compensation against the directors personally or to undo certain transactions entered into by the directors during that period.

11.2.1 Wrongful trading (Section 214 IA 1986)

This provision applies where a company goes into liquidation. The liquidator is entitled to apply to the court for an order making a person liable to contribute to the company's assets if the following conditions apply (Section 214(2) IA 1986):

(a) the company has gone into insolvent liquidation;
(b) at some time before the commencement of the winding up of the company, that person knew or ought to have concluded that there was no reasonable prospect that the company would avoid going into insolvent liquidation; and
(c) that person was a director of the company at the time.

IA 1986 provides for a defence to proceedings for wrongful trading in the following terms (Section 214(3) IA 1986):

"The court shall not make a declaration under this section with respect to any person if it is satisfied that after the condition specified in subsection (2(b) [i.e. that that person knew or ought to have concluded that there was no reasonable prospect that the company would avoid going into insolvent liquidation] was first satisfied in relation to him that person took every step with a view to minimising the potential loss to the company's creditors as (assuming him to have known that there was no reasonable prospect that the company would avoid going into insolvent liquidation) he ought to have taken."

The Section also provides guidance on the knowledge, skill and experience which is expected of directors in the following terms (Section 214(4) and (5) IA 1986):

"(4) For the purposes of subsections (2) and (3), the facts which a director of a company ought to know or ascertain, the conclusions which he ought to reach and the steps which he ought to take are those which would be known or ascertained, or reached or taken, by a reasonably diligent person having both –
(a) the general knowledge, skill and experience that may reasonably be expected of a person carrying out the same functions as are carried out by that director in relation to the company, and
(b) the general knowledge, skill and experience that that director has.

"(5) The reference in subsection (4) to the functions carried out in relation to the company by a director of the company includes any functions which he does not carry out but which have been entrusted to him."

The Section defines "insolvent liquidation" as a "liquidation where the assets of the company are insufficient for the payment of its debts and other liabilities and the expenses of the winding up" (Section 214(6)).

11.2.1.1 Comments

There are relatively few reported cases in which this Section has been considered. However, in the leading case on wrongful trading (*Re Produce Marketing Consortium Ltd (No. 2)*[1] Knox J characterised the method of establishing the quantum of the relevant director's liability as follows (at 553):

> "In my judgment the jurisdiction under s 214 is primarily compensatory rather than penal. Prima facie the appropriate amount that a director is declared to be liable to contribute is the amount by which the company's assets can be discerned to have been depleted by the director's conduct which caused the discretion under sub-s (I) to arise. But Parliament has indeed chosen very wide words of discretion ... the fact that there was no fraudulent intent is not of itself a reason for fixing the amount at a nominal or low figure, for that would amount to frustrating what I discern as Parliament's intention in adding s 214 to s 213 in the 1986 Act, but I am not persuaded that it is right to ignore that fact totally."

In the subsequent case of *Re DKG Contractors Ltd*[2] the court simply ascertained the date on which the directors ought to have concluded that there was no reasonable prospect of avoiding insolvent liquidation and made an order rendering the directors liable to pay a contribution equal to the amount of trade debts incurred by the company after that date. Although a precise method of calculating the liability has not been established, the principle that it is compensatory and not penal is not in doubt. In the recent case of *In re Continental Assurance Company of London plc*,[3] it was held that it was not enough merely to say that, if the company had not

---

[1] [1989] BCLC 520.
[2] [1990] BCC 903.
[3] [2001] BPIR 733.

still been trading, a particular loss would not have been suffered by the company. In order to impose liability on directors there must be sufficient connection between the wrongfulness of the directors' conduct and the company's losses.

In practice, if the directors of a company cease trading as soon as they reach the conclusion that there is no reasonable prospect of avoiding insolvent liquidation, then, assuming that their opinion was a reasonable one and they were not dilatory in reaching it, there should be little risk of a successful claim for wrongful trading being brought. This is because there will be no time for losses to accumulate between the directors reaching the relevant decision and the commencement of the liquidation of the company. In *In re Continental Assurance Company of London plc* (above), Park J considered the difficult position of directors balancing their wish to avoid liability for wrongful trading with making proper efforts to avoid liquidation if possible. He said (at page 817):

> "An overall point which needs to be kept in mind throughout is that, whenever a company is in financial trouble and the directors have a difficult decision to make whether to close down and go into liquidation, or whether instead to trade on and hope to turn the corner, they can be in a real and unenviable dilemma. On the one hand, if they decide to trade on but things do not work out and the company, later rather than sooner, goes into liquidation, they may find themselves in the situation of the respondents in this case – being sued for wrongful trading. On the other hand, if the directors decide to close down immediately and cause the company to go into an early liquidation, although they are not at risk of being sued for wrongful trading, they are at risk of being criticised on other grounds. A decision to close down will almost certainly mean that the ensuing liquidation will be an insolvent one. Apart from anything else liquidations are expensive operations, and in addition debtors are commonly obstructive about paying their debts to a company which is in liquidation. Many creditors of the company from a time before the liquidation are likely to find that their debts do not get paid in full. They will complain bitterly that the directors shut down too soon; they will say that the directors ought to have had more courage and kept going. If they had done so, the complaining creditors will say, the company probably would have survived and all of its debts would have been paid. Ceasing to trade and liquidating too soon can be stigmatised as the cowards' way out."

Directors whose companies are facing financial difficulties should always have regular board meetings and at each meeting consider the prospects for the company and minute their reasons for the view they take and their reasons for any decision to continue trading. Up-to-date financial information must be available. In the context of disqualification proceedings, it has been held that a director must keep himself informed about the financial affairs of the company and play an appropriate role in its management (*Re Galeforce Pleating Co Ltd*[4]). This is directly relevant to the "functions" of the directors when applying the wrongful trading test. Ignorance of the financial position will not be a valid defence to any claim for wrongful trading. Directors are expected to apply the general knowledge, skill and experience that may reasonably be expected of a person carrying out the same functions as are carried out (or entrusted to) the relevant director in relation to the company. This point was also emphasised in *Re Produce Marketing Consortium Ltd (No. 2)* (above).

Once the directors of a company have reached the conclusion that there is no reasonable prospect of avoiding an insolvent liquidation, they have a choice. Either the company must cease trading immediately and go into liquidation or another suitable insolvency procedure, or they may attempt to rely on the defence set out in subsection (3), that the director took every step with a view to minimising the potential loss to the company's creditors as he ought to have taken.

This second option is a high-risk option for the following reasons:

(a) it is a defence to wrongful trading for the director to prove that he has taken these steps. In other words, the burden of proof shifts from the liquidator to the director himself;

(b) in the absence of detailed case law on this subsection, it is unclear in practical terms what is meant by "every step he ought to have taken". One point which has been noted by many commentators is that there is no qualification to state that such steps should be reasonable. Consequently, the courts may insist on a very high standard for any director who wishes to rely on this Section. Any director who considers that he will have to rely on this defence should take detailed legal advice at the time.

Practical problems often arise in relation to wrongful trading in circumstances where a period of continued trading may enhance the value of

---

[4] [1999] 2 BCLC 704.

an asset which the company wishes to sell. It is sometimes argued that in such circumstances the directors of a company have a positive duty to continue trading after reaching the point where they consider there is no reasonable prospect of avoiding insolvent liquidation. Such continued trade will have the effect of minimising the potential loss to creditors by a better value being achieved for the asset in question than would be achieved on a liquidation or other insolvency procedure. The author's view is that this interpretation is incorrect. As has been shown above, Section 214 IA 1986 does not impose an obligation upon directors to minimise the potential loss to creditors. The Section which refers to the concept of minimising potential loss to creditors is a defence to proceedings for wrongful trading. A director who manages to avoid any proceedings for wrongful trading being brought against him in the first place will not be relying on this Section. The usual way to avoid the possibility of proceedings for wrongful trading being brought would be to cease trading as soon as it became clear that the insolvent liquidation of the company was inevitable.

Continuing to trade in order to enhance the sale proceeds of an asset may increase the actual proceeds of sale of the company's assets, but may not necessarily benefit the creditors of the company as a whole. It is often the case that secured creditors put pressure on company directors to maximise the proceeds of a particular asset by continued trading. However, if that continued trading involves incurring further credit from unsecured creditors, those unsecured creditors will in fact have suffered increased losses as a result of the continued trading. The directors will, effectively, have benefited one set of creditors at the expense of another set. Under such circumstances, the author sees no reason why the directors of the company should not be made liable for wrongful trading in respect of the losses caused to their unsecured trade creditors. This point was, in fact, touched upon by Knox J in the *Produce Marketing* case in his comment (at page 554):

> "The affairs of PMC were conducted during the last seven months of trading in a way which reduced the indebtedness to the bank, to which Mr David had given a guarantee, at the expense of trade creditors . . . the bank is, if not fully, at least substantially secured. If this jurisdiction is to be exercised, as in my judgement it should be in this case, it needs to be exercised in a way which will benefit unsecured creditors."

An issue which has been discussed in the case law surrounding wrongful trading is whether a director can plead Section 727 CA 1985 in his defence to wrongful trading proceedings. Section 727(1) CA 1985 provides as follows:

> "If in any proceedings for negligence, default, breach of duty or breach of trust against an officer of a company or a person employed by a company as auditor (whether he is or is not an officer of the company) it appears to the court hearing the case that that officer or person is or may be liable in respect of the negligence, default, breach of duty or breach of trust, but that he has acted honestly and reasonably, and that having regard to all the circumstances of the case (including those connected with his appointment) he ought fairly to be excused for the negligence, default, breach of duty or breach of trust, that court may relieve him, either wholly or partly, from his liability on such terms as it thinks fit."

In an earlier judgment in the *Produce Marketing* case, Knox J held that in Section 727 CA 1985 a subjective test applied whereas in Section 214 IA 1986, particularly in subsections (3) and (4) an objective test applied. It was difficult to see how the two Sections could be used in conjunction. Knox J therefore held that Section 727 CA 1985 was not available to the directors in wrongful trading proceedings (*Re Produce Marketing Consortium (No. 1) Ltd*[5]). However, in the later case of *Re DKG Contracts Limited* (above), Section 727 CA 1985 was pleaded. The judge held that the directors had acted honestly but not reasonably and declined to grant the relief sought. It is notable in this case that there were other breaches of duty in addition to wrongful trading and that the earlier decision of Knox J appears not to have been drawn to the attention of the court. In *Re Brian D Pierson (Contractors) Ltd*,[6] the court followed *Produce Marketing* in holding that Section 727 does not apply to wrongful trading claims. In the author's view, the point should now be regarded as settled.

11.2.2 Fraudulent trading

Fraudulent trading is set out in Section 213 IA 1986. It is as follows:

> "(1) If in the course of the winding up of a company it appears that any business of the company has been carried on with intent to defraud creditors of the company or creditors of any other person, or for any fraudulent purpose, the following has effect.

---

[5] [1989] 1 WLR 745.
[6] [2001] 1 BCLC 275.

(2) The court, on the application of the liquidator may declare that any persons who were knowingly parties to the carrying on of the business in the manner above-mentioned are to be liable to make such contributions (if any) to the company's assets as the court thinks proper."

The essential difference between fraudulent trading and wrongful trading is that fraudulent trading involves dishonest intent, described in this Section as "intent to defraud". Fraudulent trading is also a criminal offence under Section 458 CA 1985.

Given the criminal connotations of fraudulent trading, a criminal standard of proof is required, and this Section is consequently rarely used. The Court of Appeal held that a business can be carried on with intent to defraud creditors even though only one creditor is actually defrauded by a single transaction.[7] However, the section does not apply in every case where an individual creditor is defrauded but only where the business has been carried on with intent to defraud.[8]

One further point must be borne in mind in the light of *Re Sarflax Ltd*.[9] Even where the company is insolvent, preferring one creditor over another is conduct which a company is entitled to engage in, subject only to subsequent challenge as a voidable preference under section 239. The bare fact of a preferential payment does not, per se, constitute fraud within the meaning of section 213.

It might be thought, in the light of the offence of wrongful trading, that the fraudulent trading jurisdiction has become redundant. This, however, may be wrong. Fraudulent trading is available as a civil claim against any person who is "knowingly a party to" the carrying on of the company business with intent to defraud. Thus on this aspect, liability under section 213 is wider than liability for wrongful trading, because mere participants are potentially liable, while the only people being made liable under section 214 are directors, albeit including shadow directors (*Re BCCI, Banque Arabe Internationale d'Investissement SA v Morris*[10]), in which the alleged participant was a bank.

---

[7] *Re Gerald Cooper Chemical Ltd* (1978) Ch 262.
[8] *Morphitis v Bernasconi and others* [2003] EWCA Civ 289.
[9] [1979] Ch 592.
[10] [2001] BCLC 263.

Duties of Directors Facing Insolvency

The second circumstance in which fraudulent trading liability is more widely available than wrongful trading arises because the fraud does not have to be directed at the company itself or even the company's own creditors. If the business of the company is being conducted (a) with intent to defraud the creditors of another person or (b) for any fraudulent purpose the knowing participant is exposed to potential liability. This means that unlike section 214 the focus of the liability is not necessarily on the imminence of the company's liquidation and the putative defendant's awareness of that fact.

Doubtlessly it will normally be proper to infer intent to defraud where a company continues to carry on incurring credit when the directors know that there is no reasonable prospect of the creditors receiving payment (*Re William Leitch Bros*[11]) but that is not the only circumstance in which fraud may be established. Thus it may be fraudulent to promise creditors that a parent company will stand behind its subsidiaries when the promisor knows that this is not true, even though he might genuinely, properly and reasonably consider that the subsidiary is sound (*Augustus Barnett & Sons*[12]). In that kind of case, wrongful trading would not be established, but fraudulent trading may be.

11.2.3 Transactions which can be overturned by liquidators or administrators

11.2.3.1 Transactions at an undervalue

Section 238 IA 1986 deals with transactions at an undervalue. The Section applies where a company goes into administration or into liquidation. For the purposes of this Section and for Section 239 (*see* 2.3.3 below) the administrator or liquidator is referred to as the "office holder".

A company enters into a transaction with a person at an undervalue if (Section 238(4) IA 1986):

"(a) the company makes a gift to that person or otherwise enters into a transaction with that person on terms that provide for the company to receive no consideration, or
(b) the company enters into a transaction with that person for a consideration the value of which, in money or money's worth,

---

[11] [1932] 2 Ch 71, 77.
[12] [1986] BCLC 170.

is significantly less than the value, in money or money's worth, of the consideration provided by the company."

The Act further provides, in subsection (5), as follows (Section 238(5) IA 1986):

> "The court shall not make an order under this section in respect of a transaction at an undervalue if it is satisfied –
> (a) that the company which entered into the transaction did so in good faith and for the purpose of carrying on its business, and
> (b) that at the time it did so there were reasonable grounds for believing that the transaction would benefit the company."

The question sometimes arises as to whether security given by a borrower for indebtedness which has been outstanding for a period before the giving of security could be characterised as a transaction at an undervalue. This point was considered in *Re MC Bacon Ltd*,[13] which is the leading case on transactions at an undervalue and preferences. This case concerned a company which was in financial difficulties and had given security in respect of its existing overdraft at the time when it was insolvent. When the company subsequently went into liquidation, the liquidator commenced proceedings under Sections 238 and 239 to have the security set aside. Millett J held that a transaction of this type could not be a transaction at an undervalue, and stated:

> "In my judgment, the applicant's claim to characterise the granting of the bank's debenture as a transaction at an undervalue is misconceived. The mere creation of a security over a company's assets does not deplete them and does not come within the paragraph. By charging its assets the company appropriates them to meet the liabilities due to the secured creditor and adversely affects the rights of other creditors in the event of insolvency. But it does not deplete its assets or diminish their value. It retains the right to redeem and the right to sell or remortgage the charged assets. All it loses is the ability to apply the proceeds otherwise than in satisfaction of the secured debt. That is not something capable of valuation in monetary terms and is not customarily disposed of for value . . . in my judgment, the transaction does not fall within sub-s (4), and it is unnecessary to consider the application of sub-s (5) which provides a defence to the claim in certain circumstances."

---

[13] [1990] BCLC 324.

In *Barnes* v *Premium Credit Ltd*[14] it was held that a re-grant of security where the previously granted security was void for want of registration did not amount to a transaction at an undervalue, but was a preference (*see* 2.3.3 below).

11.2.3.2   *Relevant time*
The Act contains specific provisions as to the relevant time that the company entered into a transaction at an undervalue in Section 240. The court will not make an order in respect of a transaction at an undervalue unless the following conditions apply:

(a)   the transaction must take place at a time in the period of two years ending with the "onset of insolvency" (*see* 2.3.4 below) (or while an administration is pending); and
(b)   at the time of the transaction the company must be unable to pay its debts within the meaning of Section 123 IA 1986 or become unable to pay its debts within the meaning of that Section in consequence of the transaction.

This last requirement is presumed where a person who benefits from the transaction is connected with the company.

11.2.3.3   *Preferences: Section 239 IA 1986*
This provision applies in similar circumstances to those relating to Section 238 IA 1986: that is, if a company goes into administration or liquidation. Section 239(4) describes the nature of a preference:

> "For the purposes of this Section ... a company gives a preference to a person if –
> (a) that person is one of the company's creditors or a surety or guarantor for any of the company's debts or other liabilities, and
> (b) the company does anything or suffers anything to be done which (in either case) has the effect of putting that person into a position which, in the event of the company going into insolvent liquidation, will be better than the position he would have been in if that thing had not been done."

Under subsection 5, the court shall not make an order unless the company which gave the preference was "influenced in deciding to give

---

[14] Unreported, 20 January 2000.

it by a desire to produce in relation to that person the effect mentioned in subsection (4)(b)".

The concept of the "desire to prefer" was introduced in the Insolvency Act 1986 when the previous law of "fraudulent preference" was radically recast. The leading case on both transactions at an undervalue and preferences, *Re MC Bacon Ltd* (above), gives some guidance as to the interpretation of this subsection. As mentioned in 2.3.1 above, the case concerned a company which had encountered financial difficulties. It gave security to its bank to secure its overdraft facilities, which were advanced to it before the security was given. This situation is clearly extremely common in the negotiations that companies have with their bankers when the company is in financial difficulties and facing insolvency. Millett J held that the giving of security in these circumstances was not a preference because the company was not "influenced by a desire to prefer" the bank. Millett J interpreted the concept of being "influenced by a desire to prefer" as follows (at 335–336):

> "It is no longer necessary to establish a *dominant* intention to prefer. It is sufficient that the decision was *influenced* by the requisite desire. That is the first change. . . . The second change is made necessary by the first, for without it it would be virtually impossible to uphold the validity of a security taken in exchange for the injection of fresh funds into a company in financial difficulties. A man is taken to intend the necessary consequences of his actions, so that an intention to grant a security to a creditor necessarily involves an intention to prefer that creditor in the event of insolvency. The need to establish that such intention was dominant was essential under the old law to prevent perfectly proper transactions from being struck down. With the abolition of that requirement intention could not remain the relevant test. Desire has been substituted. That is a very different matter. Intention is objective, desire is subjective. A man can choose the lesser of two evils without desiring either. It is not, however, sufficient to establish a desire to make the payment or grant the security which it is sought to avoid. There must have been a desire to produce the effect mentioned in the subsection, that is to say, to improve the creditor's position in the event of an insolvent liquidation. A man is not to be taken as *desiring* all the necessary consequences of his actions. Some consequences may be of advantage to him and be desired by him; others may not affect him and be matters of indifference to him; while still others may be positively disadvantageous to him and not be desired by him, but be regarded by him as the unavoidable price of obtaining the desired advantages.

It will still be possible to provide assistance to a company in financial difficulties provided that the company is actuated only by proper commercial considerations. Under the new regime a transaction will not be set aside as a voidable preference unless the company positively wished to improve the creditor's position in the event of its own insolvent liquidation. There is, of course, no need for there to be direct evidence of the requisite desire. Its existence may be inferred from the circumstances of the case, just as the dominant intention could be inferred under the old law. But the mere presence of the requisite desire will not be sufficient by itself. It must have influenced the decision to enter into the transaction. It was submitted on behalf of the bank that it must have been the factor which 'tipped the scales'. I disagree. That is not what sub-s (5) says; it requires only that the desire should have influenced the decision. That requirement is satisfied if it was one of the factors which operated on the minds of those who made the decision. It need not have been the only factor or even the decisive one. In my judgment, it is not necessary to prove that, if the requisite desire had not been present, the company would not have entered into the transaction. That would be too high a test."

This approach was supported in *Re Fairway Magazines Ltd*[15] where a company issued security for advances utilised to reduce an overdraft liability guaranteed by a director. It was held that the debenture was not a preference because the company was solely influenced by commercial considerations, namely the need to raise money from another source in order to continue trading. However, Mummery J made the point, however, that the desire to influence the creditor does not have to be the sole or decisive influence in making the decision.

Where the beneficiary of the preference is connected with the company otherwise than by reason only of being its employee at the time the preference was given, the desire to prefer is presumed (Section 239(6)).

This Section also provides that the fact that something was done in pursuance of the order of a court is not enough to prevent the doing or suffering of that thing from constituting the giving of a preference (Section 239(7)).

---

[15] [1992] BCC 924.

As in the case of a transaction at an undervalue, IA 1986 provides that a transaction of this type will only be a preference if the company enters into it at a "relevant time". The "relevant time" is described as follows in Section 240 of IA 1986:

(a) where the beneficiary of the preference is a person who is connected with the company (otherwise than by reason only of being its employee) at a time in the period of two years ending with the onset of insolvency;

(b) where the preference is not given in favour of a connected person, a time in the period of six months ending with the onset of insolvency (Section 240(1)); and

(c) in either case, when an administration is pending.

As for transactions at an undervalue, the company must be unable to pay its debts within the meaning of Section 123 IA 1986 at the time of, or as a consequence of, the preference.

11.2.3.4 The onset of insolvency
The "onset of insolvency" is relevant to both transactions at an undervalue and preferences, and is defined as follows (Section 240(3)):

"(a) in a case where section 238 or 239 applies by reason of the making of an administration order or of a company going into liquidation immediately upon the discharge of an administration order, the date of the presentation of the petition on which the administration order was made; and

(b) in a case where the section applies by reason of a company going into liquidation at any other time, the date of commencement of the winding up."

11.2.3.5 Effect of an order
The court has a wide discretion in the order it makes under Section 238 or Section 239, but the essential principle is that these are "clawback" provisions. The relevant office holder will be seeking to undo a transaction which has either depleted the assets of the insolvent estate (in the case of a transaction at an undervalue) or given one creditor a privileged position in relation to the general body of creditors (in the case of a preference). As such, the beneficiary of the transaction is the prime target of the proceedings (subject to the provisions of Section 241(2) to (3C) IA 1986 which provides protection for beneficiaries who did not have full knowledge of the circumstances of the transactions from which they benefited) rather than the director of the company responsible for

entering into the transaction. However, the sanctions against directors who are responsible for procuring companies to carry out such transactions are equally significant and are set out in CDDA 1986, which is described in 11.4 below. It is therefore quite clear that these provisions have the practical effect of imposing on directors a duty not to enter into transactions of those types.

11.2.3.6 Transactions defrauding creditors

Directors should also be aware of the provisions of Section 423 IA 1986 which concerns transactions defrauding creditors. This provision applies to all companies, whether or not insolvent, and applies to individuals as well as companies. The essential ingredients of a transaction defrauding creditors are as follows:

(a) a person must enter into a transaction at an undervalue. The definition of "transaction at an undervalue" is exactly the same as in relation to Section 238 IA 1986 except that it contains a further provision which is relevant to individuals and not to companies (Section 423(1) IA 1986);
(b) the court may make an order under Section 423 if it is satisfied that the person entered into such a transaction for the purpose of:
  (i) "putting assets beyond the reach of a person who is making, or may at some time make, a claim against him"; or
  (ii) "otherwise prejudicing the interests of such a person in relation to the claim which he is making or may make" (Section 423(3) IA 1986).

The court may in such circumstances make such order as it thinks fit for (Section 423(2) IA 1986) for:

"(a) restoring the position to what it would have been if the transaction had not been entered into, and
(b) protecting the interests of persons who are victims of the transaction."

Proceedings may be brought by the liquidator or administrator of the company, or by the person who had a claim which was affected by the transaction.

As will be seen from the above Sections, there is no requirement for a Section 423 application that the company be insolvent or go into liquidation or administration within a time limit from the date that the company entered into the transaction. In order to obtain an order under

Section 423 it is necessary to show that the purpose was either to put assets beyond the reach of the creditor or of otherwise prejudicing his interests. Given the need to establish purpose, this section is relatively rarely used. However, the Court of Appeal held in *Commissioners of Inland Revenue* v *Hashmi & Anor*[16] that prejudice to the creditor does not need to be the sole or even dominant purpose – it is enough if it is a real and substantial purpose of the transaction and not merely a consequence or by-product. Establishing purpose requires the court to have regard to the subjective state of mind of the transferor (see *Pagemanor Ltd* v *Ryan (No. 2)*[17]). In addition, any transaction which could be attacked under Section 423 is likely, in the case of a company, to be actionable by virtue of a breach of fiduciary duties by the directors, as is set out in more detail below. Most of the cases on this Section in fact relate to individuals. However, company directors should be aware of this Section since the types of transaction it refers to, those which involve taking assets "out of the reach" of creditors, of course will almost inevitably end in the insolvency of the relevant company. Clearly, directors should be aware of the fact that any deliberate attempt to try to make a company "judgment proof" can be attacked under the Insolvency Act and lead to sanctions being taken against the directors under the CDDA 1986, which is described below in 11.4 below.

11.3 Fiduciary duties of directors

The fiduciary duties of directors are of crucial importance for all company directors, not just those whose companies are facing insolvency. However, where a company is insolvent, or prospectively insolvent, recent cases have emphasised the role of directors' fiduciary duties in protecting creditors as a class, not just shareholders, where it is the creditors as well as the shareholders of the company who stand to lose if the directors breach their duties.

11.3.1 Nature of fiduciary duties

The fiduciary duties of directors consist of duties to act bona fide in the interests of the company (*Re Smith and Fawcett*[18]). If they do so, the courts will not interfere in their actions unless there are no reasonable grounds

---

[16] [2002] 2 BCLC 489.
[17] [2002] BPIR 593.
[18] [1942] Ch 304.

for that belief. This duty is owed to the company, not to individual shareholders or creditors. Where the company is solvent, the company means shareholders as a class (*Regal (Hastings) v Gulliver*[19]). The shareholders as a class can therefore choose to approve the directors' acts. Shareholder approval of the transaction will be sufficient in the case of a solvent company to absolve the directors from liability for the breach (*Parke v Daily News (No. 2)*[20]). However, if the company is insolvent its shareholders are not the only people concerned. Creditors also stand to lose if, for example, the directors procure that the company makes a gift to a third party.

11.3.2 Insolvent companies

This situation had to be considered in the decision of the High Court of Australia in *Walker v Wimborne*.[21] The company went into liquidation and the liquidator challenged certain transactions which had taken place while the company was insolvent. These transactions included the payment of salaries to employees of other group companies and the making of an unsecured loan to another insolvent group member. It was held by the court that these acts amounted to misfeasance by the directors. Mason J made the following comments:

> "In this respect it should be emphasized that the directors of a company in discharging their duty to the company must take account of the interests of its shareholders and its creditors. Any failure by the directors to take into account the interests of creditors will have adverse consequences for the company as well as for them....
>
> The transaction offered no prospect of advantage to [the company], it exposed [the company] to the probable prospect of substantial loss, and thereby seriously prejudiced the unsecured creditors of [the company]."

One mistake sometimes made by the directors of companies facing insolvency is that they attempt to protect their position by obtaining a resolution of shareholders approving the transaction made in breach of their duties. Logically, if the breach of fiduciary duties have implications

---

[19] [1967] 2 AC 134.
[20] [1962] 1 Ch 927.
[21] (1976) 137 CLR 1.

for creditors as well as shareholders, the shareholders' consent will be insufficient to absolve the directors of liability for breach of fiduciary duty. This point was considered in the Australian case of *Kinsela* v *Russell Kinsela Pty.*[22] In that case, the company leased its premises to its shareholders, at a time when it was insolvent, for a very low rent. The court held that the transaction was effected in breach of duty to the company and Street CJ made the following observation in relation to the ineffectiveness of authorisation by the shareholders:

> "It is, to my mind, legally and logically acceptable to recognise that, where directors are involved in a breach of their duty to the company affecting the interests of shareholders, then shareholders can either authorize that breach in prospect or ratify it in retrospect. Where, however, the interests at risk are those of creditors I see no reason in law or in logic to recognize that the shareholders can authorize the breach. Once it is accepted, as in my view it must be, that the directors' duty to the company as a whole extends in an insolvency context to not prejudicing the interests of creditors . . . the shareholders do not have the power or authority to absolve the directors from that breach."

A similar point was considered in *West Mercia Safetywear Ltd* v *Dodd.*[23] In this case the company, West Mercia, was a wholly-owned subsidiary of A.J. Dodd & Co. Ltd. Both companies were insolvent. Mr Dodd, a director of both companies, caused sums to be transferred by West Mercia to Dodd. This had the effect of reducing Mr Dodd's liability under a personal guarantee he had given in support of Dodd's overdraft. Clearly, the payment was made for the benefit of its shareholder. The Court of Appeal held that once a company was insolvent the interests of the creditors overrode those of the shareholders. Since West Mercia was known by Mr Dodd to be insolvent when the transfer took place and the transfer was a preference made to relieve Mr Dodd of his personal liability, Mr Dodd had breached his duty. The approval of the shareholders was in this case ineffective because creditors become prospectively entitled, through the mechanism of liquidation, to displace the power of the shareholders and directors to deal with the company's assets.

---

[22] (1986) 4 NSWLR 722.
[23] [1988] BCLC 250.

In *Gwyer & Associates Ltd* v *London Wharf (Limehouse) Ltd*[24] this point was reinforced. Where a company is solvent the court has to ask itself "could an honest and intelligent man, in the position of the directors, in all the circumstances, reasonably have believed that the decision in question was for the benefit of the company". Where the company is insolvent, the question is asked with the substitution of "creditors" for "company". However, this does not restrict directors from acting inconsistently with the interests of a particular creditor where it is in the interests of the general body of creditors (*see Re Pantone 485 Ltd*[25]).

11.3.3 Prospectively insolvent companies

A practical problem for directors emerges when considering at what point the creditors begin to become significant for the directors in considering their fiduciary duties? In a case such as *West Mercia Safetywear Ltd* v *Dodd*, where both companies were very clearly insolvent, there is no doubt that the creditors' interests must be taken into account. However, it is not always easy for directors to assess whether the company's financial difficulties are sufficiently serious for the creditors' interests to become a legal issue. An interesting case on this point is *Aveling Barford Ltd* v *Perion Ltd*.[26]

In this case, a motion to set aside a judgment in default of defence was taken to the High Court. Aveling Barford Ltd was in liquidation. Perion Limited was controlled by the same person as Aveling Barford (a Dr Lee). A property owned by Aveling Barford had been sold to Perion at an undervalue; and this fact was known to the directors of both Aveling Barford and Perion. The shareholders of Aveling Barford had consented to the transaction. Aveling Barford was solvent at the time but did not have any distributable reserves: it had an accumulated deficit on the profit and loss account. It would not have been able to make distributions to its shareholders.

Hoffmann J took the view that the directors of Aveling Barford had acted in breach of their fiduciary duty to the company by selling the property at an undervalue and that Perion had the necessary notice of the breach of fiduciary duty to be held a constructive trustee of the benefit. Hoffman J also held that the consent of the shareholders was ineffective to waive

---

[24] [2002] EWHC 2748.
[25] [2002] 1 BCLC 266.
[26] [1989] BCLC 626.

the breach even though Aveling Barford was solvent at the time. His reasoning was based on the fact that the company did not have distributable reserves and was effectively a dressed up distribution to shareholders because of the close connection between Perion and Dr Lee, the company's ultimate shareholder.

This authority is interesting in that it appears to be saying that, where a company enters into a transaction for the benefit of a person connected with its shareholder, the directors must consider not just whether the company is solvent but also whether the company had distributable reserves, and that the approval of the controlling shareholder to a transaction benefiting an associate of the shareholder will not be sufficient to absolve the directors from liability if an equivalent dividend could not have been paid.

In the light of this decision, company directors should always consider the position of creditors if there is any prospect of entering into a transaction which benefits a party associated with a shareholder, even though the company may be technically solvent at the time.

This point was also discussed in the judgment of Cooke J in the New Zealand Court of Appeal in *Nicholson v Permakraft (NW) Ltd*.[27] This case considered a dividend which had been paid to shareholders where the company which had paid the dividend subsequently went into insolvent liquidation. The court considered the point as to whether the directors breached their fiduciary duties when they recommended the distribution, in which case they would have been liable to refund the payment. In this case the New Zealand Court of Appeal held that the directors had not, on the facts, acted in breach of fiduciary duty. However, in the speech of Cooke J, some interesting dicta were made on the issue of the circumstances in which the shareholders could waive a breach of fiduciary duty by the directors. Cooke J made the following remarks at page 249:

> "The duties of directors are owed to the company. On the facts of particular cases this may require the directors to consider *inter alia* the interests of creditors. For instance creditors are entitled to consideration, in my opinion, if the company is insolvent, or near-insolvent, or of doubtful solvency, or if a contemplated payment or other course of action would jeopardise its solvency.

---

[27] [1985] 1 NZLR 242.

The criterion should not be simply whether the step will leave a state of ultimate solvency according to the balance sheet, in that total assets will exceed total liabilities. Nor should it be decisive that on the balance sheet the subscribed capital will remain intact, so that a capital dividend can be paid without returning capital to shareholders. Balance sheet solvency and the ability to pay a capital dividend are certainly important factors tending to justify proposed action. But as a matter of business ethics it is appropriate for directors to consider also whether what they will do will prejudice their company's practical ability to discharge promptly debts owed to current and likely continuing trade creditors.

To translate this into a legal obligation accords with the now pervasive concepts of duty to a neighbour and the linking of power with obligation ... in a situation of marginal commercial solvency such creditors may fairly be seen as beneficially interested in the company or contingently so."

Clearly there are difficult issues to consider here. It may be that the English courts will develop a form of doctrine surrounding circumstances where a company may be solvent and have sufficient distributable reserves but that it may not be prudent for a distribution to be made. In these circumstances, the creditors of the company will be the class who are most affected by such decisions, and shareholder approval of distributions or other transfers of value out of the company should not be effective to absolve the directors of their breach of fiduciary duty. Whilst the law in this area is still developing, directors would always be well advised to consider carefully the interests of creditors if there is any possibility that the company may be prospectively insolvent.

11.4 Public companies and listed companies: duties to shareholders

The duties of the directors of public companies and listed companies to their shareholders are complex and are covered elsewhere in this Guide. However, there are one or two legal provisions which, although relevant to all directors of such companies, tend to pose particular problems on insolvency and are therefore areas which the directors of such companies should always consider if there is any danger that an insolvency may be approaching. These provisions include the maintenance of capital provisions under the Companies Act 1985 and (in relation to listed companies) the disclosure of information requirements under the Listing Rules.

11.4.1 Serious loss of capital: Section 142 CA 1985

Section 142 CA 1985 provides as follows:

> "(1) Where the net assets of a public company are half or less of its called up share capital, the directors shall, not later than 28 days from the earliest day on which that fact is known to a director of the company, duly convene an extraordinary general meeting of the company for a date not later than 56 days from that day for the purpose of considering whether any, and if so what, steps should be taken to deal with the situation.
> (2) If there is a failure to convene an extraordinary general meeting as required by sub-section (1), each of the directors of the company who –
> (a) knowingly and wilfully authorises or permits the failure, or
> (b) after the expiry of the period during which that meeting should have been convened, knowingly and wilfully authorises or permits the failure to continue,
> is liable to a fine."

This provision is an important one for directors of public companies. A company which is coming close to insolvency is likely to be affected by this Section. It is, of course, a problematic Section for directors who are in emergency negotiations for some scheme to save the company, since the publicity involved in convening at an extraordinary general meeting ("EGM") at this time may be inconvenient for the company. However, it is essential that directors are aware of this Section and convene the necessary EGM to avoid incurring penalties under the CA 1985. The directors should also be aware that the Section does not impose upon them a duty to remedy the situation in any way, but simply to call an EGM to consider what steps, if any, should be taken to deal with the situation.

11.4.2 The Listing Rules

Where a company is listed on the London Stock Exchange, the directors will, of course, have to ensure that it continues to comply with the obligations under the Listing Rules. A crucial obligation, set out in Chapter 9 of the Listing Rules, requires disclosure of information where, to the knowledge of the company's directors, there is a change in the:

(a) company's financial condition; or
(b) performance of its business or the company's expectations of its performance,

if knowledge of the change would be likely to lead to a substantial movement in the price of its listed securities.

Clearly, this principle can become an issue for the directors of listed companies where insolvency is a prospect. It is highly likely that the impending insolvency is a sufficient change in the company's financial condition to warrant disclosure under the Listing Rules. Equally, the directors may well be unwilling to disclose information about the company's financial condition if they are involved in such negotiations for a rescue of the company, since the announcement may clearly prejudice such negotiations. This issue, together with all of the other duties which company directors must consider when their company enters into financial difficulties must be kept under consideration at all times if the directors are to comply with their duty under the Listing Rules.

11.5 Practical matters

The combined effect of the statutory provisions set out in this Chapter, together with the cases in the areas of fiduciary duties and the powers of the court to make disqualification orders against directors (*see* Chapter 1), require the directors of companies facing insolvency to take into account a wide range of duties when carrying out their functions. Clearly, no two companies are the same and detailed legal advice should be take in relation to the circumstances of the company. However, directors of a company facing insolvency should always consider the following practical guidelines:

(a) the board should convene regular meetings to consider the company's financial position and keep under constant review the issue of whether the company has a reasonable prospect of avoiding insolvent liquidation;
(b) every member of the board should ensure that he is adequately informed of the position of the company and should perform (and be seen to perform) his functions actively. Directors who leave other directors to cover for them can be penalised;
(c) ensure that all information about the company, in particular its financial details, is adequate and up to date and available to all directors;

(d) careful consideration should be given to deciding whether all actions taken by the board are in the commercial interests of the company;

(e) the effect of any proposed transaction on the interests of creditors should be considered. Even where the company is of doubtful solvency rather than clearly insolvent, the interests of creditors may become the determining factor in any allegations of breach of fiduciary duty. The board must never attempt to rely on shareholder approval to absolve it from a breach of fiduciary duty where its solvency is in doubt;

(f) the board should consider the interests of all its creditors and not just a particular class (e.g. its bankers). It is not infrequent that boards of directors are pressurised by certain powerful creditors to take action which is detrimental to other creditors. Directors can be penalised for acting in this way;

(g) where the company is a listed company, the board should consider carefully its duties in relation to disclosure of information which could cause movements in the price of its shares;

(h) each member of the board should consider his conduct carefully in relation to all relevant duties, not just those relating to insolvency. The insolvency of a company may be the trigger for scrutiny of the conduct of a director in relation to any aspect of his conduct;

(i) where there is conflict amongst members of the board, each member must be seen to act positively to comply with his duties, since the sanctions relate to members individually not collectively. Where a member of the board disagrees with his co-directors, he should take active steps to make his views known and to obtain the information he needs to make the necessary decisions;

(j) all proceedings of the board should be carefully minuted and checked by each member of the board. In particular, the reasons for entering into any transaction and the reasons for the board's belief that the company can continue to trade should be recorded fully. Clearly the members of the board will need evidence that they behaved properly.

Chapter 12

Regulatory Investigations

Angela Hayes, Partner
Lawrence Graham

12.1 Introduction

Investigations are conducted in many different ways. The processes by which they operate impose a variety of obligations and duties which are enforceable in different ways. The focus of this Chapter is statutory investigations. The term "statutory investigation" includes any investigation conducted by a person whose authority to conduct such an investigation derives from statute and whose powers to demand information, whether by production of documents or by means of interview, are backed by sanctions imposed either by civil or criminal penalties, whether financial or custodial.

The common law right to remain silent has been contested since compulsive powers to demand information were introduced into the bankruptcy legislation in the nineteenth century to enable creditors to identify and recover assets from a bankrupt's estate. Since then, there have been many examples of Parliament voting similar powers in support of other regulatory functions, for example to the Secretary of State for Trade and Industry in support of his responsibilities to regulate companies; to the Inland Revenue and Customs and Excise in support of their responsibilities to maximise revenue collection; to the Financial Services Authority ("the FSA") in support of its duty to regulate the conduct of banking, investment and insurance business in the UK; and to the Director of the Serious Fraud Office ("the SFO") in support of his duty to investigate and prosecute serious and complex fraud. Other important examples include the powers given to the Health and Safety Executive, the environmental agencies, marine and air accident investigators, office-holders appointed under the insolvency regime and the competition agencies.

The introduction of these various powers at different times for various purposes and in different political circumstances means that the substance and form of these powers vary considerably and it is not possible within the scope of this Chapter to give a comprehensive guide to all the various provisions to which a director of a company may possibly be exposed. Instead, this Chapter seeks to identify the principal features which are common to most instances of statutory investigation by reference to the more likely examples in the general commercial sector, namely the Companies Act 1985 ("CA 1985"), the Financial Services and Markets Act 2000 ("FSMA 2000"), and the Criminal Justice Act 1987 ("CJA 1987"), The main provisions in each of these statutes relating to investigations are summarised in the Tables at the end of this Chapter. The Chapter also looks at what remains of the individual's common law rights and how they may be invoked in any given situation. This has become a particular issue with the incorporation into English law of the European Convention on Human Rights ("ECHR") by the Human Rights Act 1998. This Chapter concludes with some practical advice on how to respond to a statutory investigation.

The Chapter is structured so that the relevant issues are addressed in the order in which they are likely to occur in the course of the investigation. It examines:

(a) the potential scope of the investigation and the issues relating to the appointment of investigators, namely the notice of appointment and the effect of the appointment;
(b) the confidentiality or otherwise of the investigation, the autonomy and the powers of the investigators and the sanctions for failure to cooperate and obstruction;
(c) the limits on the powers and the rules of natural justice which apply; and
(d) the product of the investigation and what use can be made of its findings and the information which has been collected.

12.2 Scope of the investigation

The relevant statute will prescribe the circumstances in which and/or the purposes for which an investigator[1] can be appointed and the powers that the investigator can exercise during the conduct of an investigation. Statutes and specific provisions within them vary in the breadth of circumstances and purposes for which an investigator can

---

[1] The term "investigator" is intended to refer to all statutory investigators however described in the statute, for example persons appointed under CA 1985 are often described as "inspectors".

Regulatory Investigations

be appointed, for example: the director of the SFO may exercise his power to require information and documents under Section 2 CJA 1987 in order to "investigate any suspected offence which appears to him on reasonable grounds to involve serious and complex fraud" in any case in which "it appears to him that there is good reason to do so for the purposes of investigating the affairs of any person".[2] The DTI can launch an investigation under CA 1985 into the affairs of a company on the application of a company or its members (Section 431 CA 1985) or if there are circumstances suggesting that there is "fraud, misfeasance or other misconduct towards the company or towards its members" (Section 432(2) CA 1985), the FSA may appoint investigators to investigate "the nature, conduct or state of the business of an authorised person" where it appears to them that there is "good reason" for doing so (Section 167 FSMA 2000).

In contrast to these provisions there some which more precisely prescribe the scope of the investigation. For example: under CA 1985, the DTI can launch investigations into the membership of a company (Section 442 CA 1985) or its investigation may confine itself to the books and records of a company (Section 447 CA 1985); under Section 168 FSMA 2000 investigators can be appointed for various specified purposes, such as investigating whether an authorised firm is carrying on a particular type of regulated business without FSA permission.

In theory, therefore, the legitimate scope of the investigation will be limited and there should be grounds for challenge if the circumstances of the appointment of an investigator and the scope of the investigation extend beyond what is permitted by the relevant statute. In practice, as the grounds for appointment are often widely prescribed, it can be difficult to challenge investigations. In particular, there is very

---

[2] The SFO's criteria for accepting a case for investigation are where:

(a) there is a very significant public interest;
(b) the sums at risk exceed £1 million;
(c) the offences involve the public sector;
(d) the evidence or the issues have an international dimension;
(e) there is a highly complex and esoteric market where specialist market knowledge is needed;
(f) the transactions themselves are particularly complex;
(g) where accountancy help is essential; and
(h) overall where it is felt that the conduct of the investigation should be in the hands of those responsible for the ultimate prosecution of the case.

limited scope to challenge the decision to appoint investigators because the courts have held that there is no requirement on the appointing authority to disclose the material facts before it or the reasons for the appointment, provided it acts in good faith and does not use its discretion improperly. In *Norwest Holst Ltd v Secretary of State for Trade*[3] it was held, on appeal, that the wide discretion which had been conferred on the DTI to appoint inspectors to investigate a company's affairs and report to it, was exercised at a preliminary stage for the purposes of good administration, and carried with it no implication that there was any case against the company; accordingly, the rules of natural justice were, at that stage, inapplicable so that the appointment of inspectors could not be challenged where the DTI had acted in good faith and within the powers conferred by the relevant statute. It was further held that the court could not, and would not, review the exercise of that discretion where the company had not discharged the onus on it of showing that there was any lack of good faith on the part of the DTI.

Even though it is difficult successfully to challenge the appointment of investigators or the scope of an investigation, nevertheless it is crucial that a company's directors understand fully at an early stage the statutory basis of the investigation and its intended scope. In acting in the best interests of the company that he serves, a director needs to ensure that the assistance given to investigators by the company and its directors is focused appropriately. That may well entail an exchange of views with an over-zealous investigator. Success in cutting back the scope of specific requests for information or documents is often achieved by a timely challenge on whether particular materials are really relevant to the matters under investigation. Statutory investigations can be expensive and time consuming for target companies and their management. Investigators not infrequently request broad categories of documents and records without appreciating when they do so the volume of material they are asking for or the time it may take to compile. Initial requests for documents and information sometimes go well beyond what is reasonable in the context of the investigation being conducted. Directors need to be vigilant, therefore, to ensure that investigators' requests are made reasonably and properly.

---

[3] [1978] Ch 201. Also *see* the discussion of this decision in *R v Secretary of State for Trade ex parte Perestrello and another* [1980] 3 All ER 28.

12.3 The notice of appointment

For the reasons stated above, this is an important document. Powers vest in investigators as a consequence of their appointment by the designated authority, for example the DTI or the FSA. Investigators ought to produce a notice of their appointment to any person in respect of whom they seek to exercise their powers. In some cases this is obligatory.[4] The notice should contain: evidence of the identity of the appointing authority; the statutory provisions under which the appointment was made; the reasons for the appointment; the names of the individuals appointed and thereby authorised to exercise the powers prescribed; and the date of the appointment (which may, of course, substantially precede the date on which it is produced).[5]

The statement of reasons for the appointment is usually very brief, often little more than a recital of the grounds prescribed by statute, but there should be as much clarity as possible about which entities and/or individuals may be the target of the investigation. It is important to be clear whether the information being requested is to assist an investigation into others, or whether the company supplying the details (and/or individuals within it) are or could become a target of the investigation. If the notice is not clear about this then further written confirmation should be sought.

Special powers exercisable by investigators in certain restricted circumstances to enter and search premises without notice will invariably only be granted by a justice of the peace and will be contained in a warrant.

12.4 Effect of the notice

The notice of investigation is important not just because of the insight it may give into the scope and purpose of an investigation, but also because receipt of it will impose on the recipient certain duties and obligations which need to be recognised at an early stage. It will impose

---

[4] Under Section 170 FSMA 2000 it is obligatory, save in exceptional circumstances, for the investigating authority to give written notice of the appointment of an investigator to the person who is the subject of the investigation and to give written notice to that person of any change in the scope of the investigation.
[5] Under Section 170(4) FSMA 2000 the notice of appointment must specify the provisions under which, and as a result of which, the investigator was appointed and state the reasons for his appointment.

duties and obligations to ensure that all relevant information is preserved. An obligation to keep the investigation confidential may also be imposed. Often it will also be accompanied by a specific request for information and/or documents that must be responded to by a specific date. Sometimes, however, the notice of appointment is served first, with a formal request for information following later.

All statutes providing for the appointment of an inspector will have provisions reinforcing the inspector's powers by imposing criminal sanctions on those who falsify, conceal or destroy documents relating to the subject of the inquiry.[6] Each of the relevant enabling statutes will also impose obligations to retain relevant material on those who are the subject of an investigation, but some statutes are more prescriptive than others.

Under Section 434 CA 1985, "When inspectors are appointed" it is the duty of all officers and agents of the company "to produce to the inspectors all documents of or relating to the company . . . in their custody or power". A strict interpretation would impose an obligation on the directors, once they have received notice that an appointment has been made, to disclose relevant material in their custody or power despite the lack of a specific request . However, where it would be unreasonable to expect a director to be able to identify what is relevant to the investigation, in practical terms this can only be read as creating a duty to preserve all existing company material. In circumstances where the relevance of an important document is apparent, then under Section 434 a positive duty to produce it, without any specific request, would also arise. Under FSMA 2000, persons under investigation are only under a duty to produce documents or other information in response to a specific request by the investigator. But persons authorised under FSMA 2000 are also bound to comply with FSA principles, under which they are bound to deal with the FSA in an open and cooperative manner and "to disclose to the FSA appropriately anything relating to the firm of which the FSA would reasonably expect notice". Breach of a principle by an authorised person is a disciplinary matter so that a failure by an authorised person to volunteer disclosure of relevant material would be a disciplinary offence under FSMA 2000.

---

[6] Section 450 CA 1985; Section 177(3) FSMA 2000.

12.5 Confidentiality of the investigation

The existence of a statutory investigation is rarely made public. The DTI's practice, for example, is to commence its fact-finding enquiry with a confidential investigation using its powers under Section 447 CA 1985 to inspect the books and records of the company.[7] The DTI will neither announce nor acknowledge the commencement of such an investigation nor will it give any notification of when it has been concluded. Any report produced will be confidential. Only on rare occasions will the DTI launch a full-scale investigation with the announcement of the appointment of inspectors under Section 432 CA 1985, the usual outcome of which is a published report.[8] Part XIV CA 1985 does give a discretionary power to the Secretary of State to direct the publication of reports following investigations conducted under the provisions of this part of the Act.

The FSA's policy is that it will not normally make public the fact that it is conducting an investigation or the findings of an investigation. It is bound by statutory restrictions under FSMA 2000 on the disclosure of confidential information (Section 348) and on the publication of its decisions (Section 391). Under the latter, both the FSA and recipients are prohibited from publishing details about an FSA warning notice or decision notice. The FSA is only entitled to publish information about its decision when that decision takes effect (when a final notice or effective supervisory notice is issued). However, in exceptional circumstances the FSA will publish the fact that an investigation is under way, for example if this is desirable to maintain public confidence, such as where the matters under investigation have become the subject of public concern, speculation or rumour. In doing so it must still have regard to the statutory restrictions.[9]

---

[7] This is the most widely used power of the DTI and will almost always be used as a quick fact-finding exercise. In a typical year, the DTI's Companies Investigation Bureau receives over 3,000 complaints (although in its year end 2001 and 2002 figures this had increased to over 4,000) and, of these, approximately 800 are considered for the use of statutory investigative powers. Approximately 200 are accepted for investigation and the vast majority of these are investigated under Section 447 CA 1985.

[8] This is a rarely used power. The most recent example of the appointment of inspectors under this Section remains the Transtec investigation. Before that, the last such appointments were in relation to Queens Moat Houses PLC and Chancery PLC.

[9] Examples of recent investigations that the FSA has acknowledged include South African Breweries/Interbrew, Cyprotex and Winchester.

Where the existence of a statutory investigation has not been announced by the appointing authority, that information itself will be considered confidential within the meaning ascribed to it by the statute.

SFO investigations, if not formally announced, are publicly acknowledged following an initial period in which investigations are made for the purposes of assessing whether or not it is a suitable case for the SFO to take on.

12.6 The autonomy of the investigators

One feature of an investigation which may affect the way in which it is likely to be conducted is the degree of autonomy given to the investigator by the authority appointing him.

Statutory investigations fall broadly into two categories:

(a) those which are essentially conducted by or on behalf of the authority itself, such as investigations under Section 447 CA 1985 or Section 165 FSMA 2000; and
(b) those which are conducted by investigators appointed by the authority (usually in these circumstances referred to as "inspectors") to investigate and report back (e.g. Sections 167 and 168 FSMA 2000 and Section 432 CA 1985).

As far as the latter are concerned, the earlier statutes provided for limited formal means of control exercisable by the appointing authority over the direction of the investigation. No doubt the intention was to ensure that the inquiry would be seen as being independent and objective. More recently, however, the regulators are being increasingly empowered to limit the period of the investigation or confine it to a particular matter. Significantly in FSMA 2000, specific provisions enable the FSA to give directions to the investigators to control the scope of the investigation, the period during which it is to be conducted, the conduct of the investigation and the reporting of the investigation.[10]

One type of investigation carried forward from the Banking Act 1987 to FSMA 2000 is the power of the FSA to require an authorised person under the Act to provide the FSA with a written report by a suitably

---

[10] Section 170 FSMA 2000.

skilled person nominated or approved by the FSA about any aspect of the business including that relating to other members of the group or partnership of which that person is a member.[11] The advantages of this to the regulator are that the costs of the exercise are borne by the institution and the regulator retains control over the "form" of the report. The Bank of England's practice was to use this power on a routine basis as a way of auditing discrete areas of a bank's business such as accounting and internal control systems or the bank's financial returns. It is likely that the FSA will continue to use it in the same way, but it is now available across the full spectrum of the financial services industry rather than confined just to banks.

12.7 Powers of the investigators

The powers themselves, sometimes described as draconian, are broadly consistent across the spectrum of legislation. There are basically two:

(a) the power to require the production of documents; and
(b) the power to require persons to answer questions.

In addition, some statutes make provision for the power to take evidence on oath, the power to require the production of information "without delay" (that is, then and there),[12] and the power to require the production of original documents as opposed to copies.

These powers will usually be reinforced by the invasive powers of entry, search and seizure pursuant to warrants issued by justices of the peace.[13] Warrants will only be issued if the justice of the peace can be satisfied that certain preconditions are met. These will typically comprise reasonable grounds for believing either:

(a) that documents which a person has failed to provide pursuant to a previous request are to be found on the premises; or
(b) that documents on the premises of an authorised person (for the purposes of FSMA 2000) or any person's premises (if a relevant indictable offence has been or is being committed) are likely to be removed, tampered with or destroyed if a request for them was made.

---

[11] Section 166 FSMA 2000.
[12] Section 165(3) FSMA 2000; under Section 447(3) CA 1985 the DTI may authorise an officer to require the production "forthwith" of any specified documents.
[13] Section 448 CA 1985; Section 176 FSMA 2000.

12.8 Sanctions

12.8.1 Sanctions for failure

Failure to cooperate with a statutory investigation may result in any number of possible sanctions (unless a defence of reasonable excuse can be made out, *see* 12.9 below).

Usually a failure to cooperate will itself be a criminal offence punishable with imprisonment or a fine. Under Section 2(13) CJA 1987 a person may be liable on summary conviction to imprisonment for a term not exceeding six months and/or a fine not exceeding level 5 on the standard scale. A recurring theme throughout this regulatory legislation, which applies not only to the conduct of investigations but to all substantive matters dealt with in this legislation, is the statutory liability of directors for offences committed by the company if it can be shown that the offence had been committed with the director's consent or connivance, or it was attributable to any neglect on his part.[14]

However, some statutes provide for the investigators to refer any failure to cooperate to the court which will then be required to decide whether such failure amounts to a contempt of court punishable by imprisonment or a fine.[15] This is the approach adopted under FSMA 2000. Such referrals are rare and, when they occur, the court's usual initial response, where it judges the failure to be unreasonable, is to give the defendant a second chance.

Authorised persons under FSMA 2000 have obligations to cooperate with their regulator pursuant to the FSA's Principles and rules which govern their business, breach of which will render them liable to disciplinary action by the regulator. They can be fined or, in the worst cases, removed temporarily or permanently from the register of authorised persons.

With regard to investigations concerning share ownership under CA 1985,[16] where there is difficulty in finding out the relevant facts about shares, the DTI or the court may impose restrictions on dealings in those shares under Part XV CA 1985.

---

[14] Section 733(2) CA 1985; Section 400 FSMA 2000.
[15] Section 436 CA 1985; Section 177(1) and (2) FSMA 2000.
[16] Sections 442 and 444 CA 1985.

12.8.2 Sanctions for obstruction

The provision of false or misleading information is a criminal offence. It is not necessary to prove that it was intentional. It will be enough to prove that it was done recklessly. FSMA 2000 does not contain an equivalent provision to the offence under the Banking Act 1987 (now repealed) of withholding of information. However, as explained above, to do so could lead to disciplinary sanctions.

The falsification, concealment, destruction or disposal of documents will similarly attract criminal sanctions and it will be enough to prove that a person caused or permitted this to happen.

12.9 Limits on the powers of investigators

An investigator's statutory powers will be subject to certain limitations. Any offence of failing to provide information pursuant to requirements imposed by any legislation will typically permit a defence of reasonable excuse. What amounts to a reasonable excuse will always be judged by reference to the facts of the particular case, but by implication it imposes on investigators a duty to respect the rules of natural justice, to act fairly and to act in accordance with their terms of reference.

12.9.1 The duty to act fairly

Investigators are obliged to act fairly.

Kevin Maxwell succeeded in persuading the Vice-Chancellor, Sir Richard Scott, that, in the exceptional circumstances applying to his case, the potential burden that the questioning proposed by the inspectors imposed on him risked going beyond that which an unrepresented individual could be required to accept. The court therefore held that, until steps were taken by the inspectors to reduce that burden, his refusal to answer questions did not constitute a breach of his statutory obligations.[17] Inspectors may not, therefore, place on persons demands that are unreasonable whether as to the time they have to expend, or the expense they have to incur in preparation, but it is likely that these

---

[17] *Re an Inquiry into Mirror Group Newspapers* [1999] 1 BCLC 690. Kevin Maxwell's circumstances were highly unusual given the interrogations over 61 days that he had already undergone and his criminal trial and acquittal.

demands will have to be exceptional before a court will respond sympathetically.

A witness should be given reasonable notice that he is required to attend before the investigators for examination. Advance notice in general terms of the matters on which the witness is to be examined is also appropriate. Witnesses will be allowed to attend with a legal adviser, but legal advisers will not be permitted to answer on behalf of the witness. As the process of a statutory investigation is inquisitorial, a witness will not have the right to cross-examine other witnesses or to see the transcripts of evidence of other witnesses. Witnesses should not be led to believe that the evidence they give will be confidential; investigators may wish to put their evidence to other witnesses or include it in a report. Witnesses will normally be supplied with a transcript of their evidence which they will be invited to review for transcription errors. They should be invited to correct any errors in the information provided and add any extra information or comments. SFO and FSA interviews will also usually be taped or recorded by a stenographer and a transcript of the tape provided following the interview.

12.9.2 The duty to act within the terms of reference

The investigators will be bound by the terms of reference of their appointment. They will not be permitted to ask for information which extends beyond that which could conceivably be relevant. Often, it will be difficult for the recipient of a request for information to form a view as to relevance and thereby legitimately challenge any such request, especially in the more wide-ranging, large-scale DTI investigations. But where, for example, inspectors have been appointed to look into share dealings in one particular company, they would not be allowed to extend the scope of their inquiry to look at share dealings in other companies unless specifically authorised to do so.

12.9.3 Legal professional privilege

Information (whether in documentary form or otherwise) which falls within the scope of a person's legal professional privilege is usually (but not always) exempt from production, but not all communications between a lawyer and his client are necessarily privileged. In broad terms, there are two types of legal professional privilege:

(a) legal advice privilege: these are confidential communications between a lawyer and his client which come into existence for the purpose of giving or getting legal advice; and
(b) litigation privilege: when litigation is contemplated or pending, any communications between the client, his lawyer or agent and a third party will be privileged if they come into existence for the sole or dominant purpose of giving or getting advice in relation to the litigation or collecting evidence for use in the litigation.

"Litigation" privilege may apply to any proceedings that are adversarial in nature. Communications falling into either of these two categories will not be covered if they occurred for the purpose of committing a fraud or a crime. However, lawyers will usually be required to furnish details of their client's name and address. Regulatory statutes have tended expressly to confirm the availability of legal professional privilege at the investigation stage (see Table 12).

The application of legal professional privilege to particular documents needs to be considered carefully in the context of a regulatory investigation. The precise boundaries of legal professional privilege and its application to particular documents or classes of documents is frequently the subject of debate. A recent example in the civil courts is the decision of the Court of Appeal in the Three Rivers case, which gave legal advice privilege a narrow scope.[18] However, regulatory statutes may themselves modify the concept of legal professional privilege. In particular the FSMA has a specific definition of "protected items" that a person is not obliged to produce to investigators. This is FSMA's own specific definition of legal professional privilege that, although it appears broadly to mirror the common law definition, in some respects is unclear and will need careful interpretation.

12.9.4 Other obligations of confidentiality

Documents and other information in respect of which a person owes an obligation of confidentiality by virtue of carrying on the business of banking also usually attract a degree of privilege. No one can be required to disclose such information unless:

(a) he is the person under investigation or a member of that person's group;

---

[18] Three Rivers DC v Bank of England (Disclosure) (No. 3) (2003) EWCA Civ 474.

(b) the person to whom the obligation is owed is the person under investigation or a member of that person's group;
(c) the person under investigation consents; or
(d) the making of the requirement has been specifically authorised.[19]

12.10 Privilege against self-incrimination

The privilege against self-incrimination is the common law right of any individual not to be required to give evidence against himself. The right has been eroded significantly by regulatory statutes enabling investigators to compel a person to answer questions or produce information. However, the position has changed as a result of the decision of the European Court of Human Rights in the *Saunders*[20] case and the incorporation of the ECHR into domestic law in October 2000. Since then amendments to regulatory statutes have been introduced by the Youth Justice and Criminal Evidence Act 1999 to bring them more expressly into line with ECHR principles. Prior to these developments the English courts had held that the privilege was overridden by statutes providing that questions must be answered under compulsion, so that evidence provided under compulsion could be used in any proceedings, including criminal proceedings, against the person who had given it.

The current position is that a distinction needs to be drawn between the right to remain silent in response to questions and the restrictions on the use that can be made of answers given under compulsion in subsequent proceedings. An "inviolable" common law right not to incriminate oneself still exists only in respect of criminal proceedings, where a qualified right of silence remains.[21] In regulatory investigations the right of silence has generally been abrogated completely by the statutory compulsory powers, but answers to questions so obtained cannot be used (with two exceptions discussed below) as evidence in criminal proceedings against the person giving them. In fact, even before

---

[19] Section 452 CA 1985; Section 175(5) FSMA 2000.
[20] [1997] BCC 872.
[21] The Detention Code prescribes the following caution:

"You do not have to say anything. But it may harm your defence if you do not mention when questioned something which you later rely on in court. Anything you do say may be given in evidence."

See Section 34 Criminal Justice and Public Order Act 1994.

Saunders this was the position in relation to evidence obtained by the SFO pursuant to their Section 2 Criminal Justice Act 1987 powers as a result of express protections in that Act.

In civil proceedings generally (as distinct from statutory investigations using compulsory powers) a privilege against self-incrimination can be claimed to enable a person to refuse to answer a question or to refuse to allow inspection of a document if answering the question or producing the document would expose that person or their spouse to criminal proceedings or to proceedings for the purpose of recovering a penalty. However, the privilege can only be claimed if the criminal offence or penalty concerned is under UK law; it cannot be claimed as against foreign criminal proceedings.[22] In fact it is very hard to persuade a court that the privilege can rightly be claimed. The court will be looking for evidence that the person's likelihood of being involved in criminal proceedings will be significantly greater if the information is provided. The claim of privilege will not succeed if the person is already in real danger of criminal proceedings bring brought.

Article 6 of the ECHR,[23] which addresses the issue of procedural fairness in the determination of both "criminal charges" and "civil rights and obligations", guarantees the right to a fair hearing by an independent and impartial tribunal. Article 6 has been interpreted as not permitting the use in evidence in criminal proceedings of answers given in response to compulsory questioning. In *Saunders* the European Court of Human Rights confirmed that the use by the prosecution at his criminal trial of transcripts of statements made by Saunders to DTI inspectors appointed under Sections 432 and 442 CA 1985 was in breach of Article 6 such that Saunders had been denied a fair hearing. Following this decision the Government's policy changed, with an acceptance that even in cases where there were express statutory provisions to the contrary (such as Section 434(5) CA 1985) answers obtained in response to compulsory questions could not be used as evidence in criminal proceedings (apart from the two exceptions). Since

---

[22] *Arab Monetary Fund* v *Hashim and Others* [1989] 3 All ER 466. *AT&T Istel Ltd* v *Tully* (1992) 3 All ER 522.

[23] Article 6 states:

> "In the determination of his civil rights and obligations or of any criminal charges against him, everyone is entitled to a fair and public hearing within a reasonable time by an independent and impartial tribunal".

then, as mentioned above, specific statutory amendments have been made by the Youth Justice and Criminal Evidence Act 1999 (including the addition of a new subsection 5A to Section 434 CA 1985). The two exceptions are:

(a) where evidence relating to answers given by a person under compulsion is adduced or questions relating to them are asked in the criminal proceedings by or on behalf of that person; and
(b) they can be used in proceedings the purpose of which is to prove the falsity of those answers.

The Article 6 protection does not extend to the conduct of DTI investigations themselves as distinct from any criminal proceedings that might follow. The court ruled in *Fayed v UK*[24] that DTI inspectors did not make legal determinations as to civil or criminal liability and the findings of DTI inspectors were not dispositive in any way. The court went on to hold that if the protections available under Article 6 were to be applied to DTI investigations it would "unduly hamper the effective regulation in the public interest of complex financial and commercial activities". The same principles would apply to all statutory investigations.

12.11 The product of the investigation

Statutory investigators fall into two broad categories:

(a) those who have been appointed to investigate and report; and
(b) those whose powers to investigate are ancillary to statutory functions whether these be to prosecute serious fraud (the SFO), to regulate financial services business (the FSA), or to collect revenue (the Inland Revenue or Customs and Excise).

As regards (a) above, the report may itself be only a prelude to prosecution or other enforcement action, in which case the opportunity to respond to the content of that report or challenge the veracity of the evidence on which its conclusions are based will arise in the context of the legal or disciplinary process which ensues.

However, where the report is to be published, the investigators' duty to act fairly requires that those who are the subject of criticism in the

---

[24] [1994] 18 EHRR 393.

report be given an opportunity to respond to that criticism. This principle was established through the late Robert Maxwell's challenges to DTI inspectors' powers before the Court of Appeal in 1970 and 1974 arising from investigations into Pergamon Press. In the first case, he argued that he should not be compelled to give evidence to DTI inspectors unless he also had the right to read the transcripts of the evidence of other witnesses and, if necessary, meet any allegations by evidence or by written or oral submissions. On the second occasion, following completion of the report, he argued that the inspectors had acted in breach of the rules of natural justice in failing to give him an opportunity to answer any tentative criticisms they were minded to make of him in the final report or put to him any relevant statements made by other witnesses or in documents which were prejudicial to him.

In the first case it was held that Mr Maxwell's refusal to give evidence was unjustified. Although the proceedings before the inspectors were only administrative and not judicial or quasi-judicial, the characteristics of the proceedings required the inspectors to act fairly, in that if they were disposed to condemn or criticise anyone in a report they must first give him a fair opportunity to correct or contradict the allegation. However, for this purpose an outline of the charge would usually suffice and, save for the requirement to act fairly, the inspectors should not be subject to any set rules of procedure but should be free to act at their own discretion. As a matter of fact, the court found that the inspectors had shown that they intended to act fairly and had given every assurance that could reasonably be required.

In the second case, it was held that a clear distinction was to be drawn between an inquiry based on a charge or accusation and one such as that on which the inspectors had been engaged in which they were asked to establish what had happened and, in the course of so doing, to form certain views or conclusions. Having heard the evidence and reached their conclusions, the inspectors were under no obligation to put to a witness such of those conclusions as might be critical of him. All that was necessary was that the inspectors should put to the witness the points that they proposed to consider when he first came to give evidence. Once the inspectors had heard the evidence they were entitled to come to the final conclusions which would be embodied in their report. The inspectors had conducted the enquiry fairly; the fact that certain matters of detail had not been put to Robert Maxwell when he was giving evidence was not a ground for impugning the report. Nevertheless, the DTI's policy and practice did change following this decision, to offer more than these minimum safeguards. The DTI's "Notes for the

Guidance of Inspectors" (published in 1990 in its *Investigations Handbook*, now out of print) suggested that, even where a witness has had the substance of the evidence against him put to him at interview, it might be appropriate when the inspectors have prepared a first draft of their report to write to a witness setting out any intended criticisms and inviting him to respond within a fixed period. Subsequently it may be appropriate in fairness to the witness to include the response in the report either in whole or in part.

12.12 How may the information be used?

12.12.1 Criminal proceedings

As we have seen, Article 6 of the ECHR has had an impact on the admissibility of compulsorily acquired testimony against self-interest in the context of criminal proceedings. It is now established that answers obtained in response to compulsory questioning cannot (apart from the two exceptions mentioned in Section 10 above) be used in evidence in criminal proceedings against the person giving them.

The issue that remains, which determines the extent of the protections under Article 6, is whether a matter will be characterised as "civil" or "criminal". These concepts are autonomous ECHR terms and, if a matter is categorised under the ECHR as criminal, then additional protections will apply. So even if a matter is characterised as "civil" in the UK, it could still be "criminal" under the ECHR. Where there is a power to imprison someone for the offence involved, this is generally determinative of it being a "criminal" matter. Proceedings which include a power to impose large financial penalties (e.g. tax evasion proceedings)[25] could also be classed as criminal proceedings. How are regulatory investigations generally to be classified?

This issue was widely debated during the Bill phase of the FSMA 2000 and a distinction has been drawn in the FSMA 2000 between enforcement action taken for breach of the market abuse provisions, which can be taken against any person, and enforcement action taken for breach of the FSA rules or principles, which could only be taken against an authorised person. The FSA's policy is to treat the former as criminal proceedings for the purposes of Article 6 and the defendants are

---

[25] *Bendenoun v France* (1994) 18 ECHR 54.

therefore entitled to all the procedural safeguards provided under Article 6 for criminal proceedings. The latter are viewed by the FSA as regulatory civil proceedings and the full protections provided by Article 6 will not apply. The rationale for this is that, although in both cases unlimited financial penalties may be imposed and in respect of an authorised person his authorisation and potentially, therefore, his livelihood can be removed, the authorised person has volunteered to be subject to the enforcement regime. The subsequent decision of the Court of Appeal in the *Fleurose*[26] case tends to confirm that the FSA's policy as regards disciplinary proceedings is correct. The Court of Appeal had to consider the correct classification for the purposes of the ECHR of disciplinary proceedings under the rules of the former financial services regulator, the Securities and Futures Authority. It held, applying the principles set out in *Han & Yau*,[27] that the FSA's disciplinary proceedings had been civil in nature so that the full Article 6 protections did not apply. The English court has also expressed a view on this point in the context of proceedings under the Company Directors Disqualification Act 1986 ("CDDA 1986").[28] The court was asked to consider whether, in the circumstances of disqualification proceedings, the use in evidence of information provided by the respondents under Section 235 Insolvency Act 1986 ("IA 1986") was permissible under Article 6. The court held that directors' disqualification proceedings were regulatory civil proceedings not "criminal" proceedings in ECHR terms; and that, although evidence obtained under Section 235 IA 86 was obtained under compulsion, its use in evidence in regulatory civil proceedings would not, except perhaps in rare cases, make the hearing unfair for the purposes of Article 6 of the ECHR.

12.12.2 Civil proceedings

Although Article 6 of the ECHR has restricted the use that can be made of compulsorily acquired evidence in criminal proceedings, such evidence could still be used in civil proceedings. In *British and Commonwealth Holdings plc (in administration)* v *Barclays de Zoete Wedd Ltd and others*[29] one of the parties applied for inspection of the transcripts of

---

[26] *Fleurose* v *Disciplinary Appeal Tribunal of the Securities and Futures Authority Limited* [2002] IRLR 297.
[27] *Han & Yau and others* v *Customs & Excise Commissioners* [2001] EWCA Civ 1048.
[28] *Re Westminster Property Limited, The Times*, 19 January 2000. In the matter of Westminster Property Management Ltd (No. 1) (2001) 1 All ER 633.
[29] [1999] 1 BCLC 86.

evidence given to DTI inspectors appointed under Section 432 CA 1985. The court held that the fact that the evidence had been given in circumstances which were confidential and that the transcripts contained evidence which had been given under compulsion were not reasons why they should not be produced for inspection in the civil proceedings. The civil court has discretion as to whether to admit such evidence.

Directors should therefore be aware that evidence given to DTI inspectors may be used in civil proceedings. However, before the transcripts are produced, they may be edited (or "redacted") in two important respects:

(a) witnesses who are not parties to the civil proceedings and whose evidence is quoted in the transcripts should be notified and given the opportunity to object to the disclosure of their evidence (*Soden v Burns*);[30] and

(b) the transcripts may contain provisional criticism material and such material may validly be the subject of a public interest immunity certificate (*Re Atlantic Computers plc*).[31]

Under Section 441 CA 1985, a copy of any report of inspectors appointed under Part XIV CA 1985 which is certified as a true copy is admissible in any proceedings as evidence of the inspectors' opinion on any matter in their report and in any proceedings on an application under Section 8 of the Directors Disqualification Act 1986 as evidence of any fact stated therein.

12.13 To whom may the information be disclosed?

Confidential information received during a statutory investigation, whether by the authority conducting the investigation or by those to whom information has been imparted for the purposes of conducting the investigation, will generally be subject to restrictions on its further disclosure, breach of which can attract criminal sanctions. FSMA 2000 contains a general prohibition on the disclosure of confidential information. The provisions in CA 1985 are less comprehensive.

---

[30] [1996] 2 BCLC 636.
[31] [1998] BCC 200.

Regulatory Investigations

Confidential information is defined under FSMA 2000 as information which relates to the business or other affairs of any person and which is received under or for the purposes of the Act. Under CA 1985 the restrictions on disclosure attach to information received pursuant to specified investigatory powers. Each statute then provides for circumstances in which confidential information may lawfully be disclosed. These include:

(a) where the person from whom the confidential information was received or, if different, the person to whom it relates has given his consent; or
(b) where at the time of disclosure the information is already available to the public from other sources; or
(c) where the information is in the form of an anonymous summary or collection of information such that information relating to any particular person cannot be ascertained from it.

Each statute provides for a large number of exceptions to the disclosure restrictions which typically include disclosure to other bodies exercising similar regulatory functions. These exceptions are colloquially known as "gateways". There is no obligation to disclose confidential information where a gateway applies; the gateways are permissive rather than mandatory. It is an offence to disclose such information other than in accordance with the gateways.

It is stated DTI policy to treat the transcripts of evidence before inspectors appointed under CA 1985 as confidential but available for release in certain circumstances (at the discretion of the DTI). These circumstances include:

(a) release to the Director of Public Prosecutions, the SFO and other prosecuting authorities and the police where to do so will assist the investigation and prosecution of crime;
(b) on application for a disqualification order under CDDA 1986;
(c) to the liquidators of companies being investigated (although there is no gateway in the CA 1985 for transcripts or other information to be so disclosed) for the purposes of civil proceedings as a result of an application by the liquidator to the court under Section 236 IA 1986;
(d) in accordance with Section 451A CA 1985 which states that information may be disclosed to a competent authority listed in Section 449(3) CA 1985; or

(e) in any circumstance in which, or for any purpose for which, disclosure is permitted under Section 449 CA 1985.

Any such disclosure is discretionary and the DTI may impose preconditions for its release and/or redact passages which the DTI considers that it would not be in the public interest to disclose. As such, witnesses who give evidence to inspectors appointed under CA 1985 can have no assurance that their evidence will remain confidential.

The permissive gateways available to the FSA under FSMA 2000 are set out in a statutory instrument[32] (the "Gateways Regulations"). The pattern of permitted disclosures and purposes for which that disclosure can be made under the Gateways Regulations is complex. This is because EU directives applicable to various of the FSA's activities impose their own specific restrictions on the UK implementing legislation in relation to the disclosure of information. The Gateways Regulations consequently draw a distinction between directive information and non-directive information and the FSA can disclose the latter for a wider range of purposes. The gateways include:

(a) disclosure for the purposes of any criminal investigation or proceedings whether in the UK or elsewhere;
(b) disclosure for the purposes of certain specified civil proceedings, including under the Company Directors Disqualification Act 1986;
(c) disclosure broadly of the information covered by the single-market directives or the UCITS Directive to a long list of designated persons and bodies set out in Schedule 1 to the Gateways Regulations for the purposes of their particular functions specified there. These include central banks, monetary authorities, recognised investment exchanges, the Panel on Takeovers and Mergers, the Director General of Fair Trading, the Competition Commission, designated professional bodies and investigators, auditors and actuaries appointed under FSMA 2000;
(d) disclosure of other information, not covered by directive restrictions, can also be disclosed to the bodies and persons listed in Schedule 2 for the purposes of their wider functions specified there and to a prescribed disciplinary proceedings authority.

---

[32] Financial Services and Market Act 2000 (Disclosure of Confidential Information) Regulations 2001, SI 2001/2188.

12.14 Practical considerations

Having examined the principal features of statutory investigations, this Chapter concludes by considering some of the practical issues which arise for directors when a statutory investigation is commenced. However, the approach to the investigation will depend on the particular circumstances of the case. This list of practical issues will therefore have to be tailored to suit the particular facts of each case.

Throughout the course of the investigation, it is important to bear in mind that as much reputational damage may result from the way in which a person responds to an investigation as can arise from the underlying complaint itself.

12.14.1 *Conflicts of interest*

Following the appointment of investigators, the director's first duty should be to consider whether there is any risk of a conflict between his personal interests and those of the company. If there is such a risk it will need to be managed properly. This can be achieved either by excluding himself from the responsibility of managing the company's response to the investigation or, if alternative appropriate representation is not available, by relying on independent external advice. A director who is not himself in a conflict situation should, together with the other directors, take steps to ensure that no other director who has any such conflicts remains involved. In some circumstances, it may be necessary to rely on the non-executive directors to perform the role of ensuring that the investigation is properly dealt with from the company's perspective.

12.14.2 *Centralise management*

Consideration will need to be given to how the investigation is to be dealt with by the company. It is usually sensible for one person at board level to be charged with overall responsibility for dealing with the investigation and coordinating responses to the investigators' requests for documents and information.

It may also be necessary and appropriate to establish a team to deal with the investigation. Typically, as the investigation proceeds, the range and mix of skills required will change. In addition to the obvious need to involve senior management, lawyers, accountants and the compliance function, it may also be appropriate to involve a non-executive director, who may provide someone with sufficient independence and authority but may also be perceived by the investigators to be impartial in relation to the matters under investigation.

The number of company staff assisting with the investigation should be kept to a minimum to ensure that confidentiality can be maintained and that tight control can be kept of evidence and material gathered and created during the investigation, in particular internal communications generated (*see* 12.14.9 below).

If the investigation has been announced publicly, it is likely that it will attract press comment. It may be appropriate to appoint public relations consultants to deal with press enquiries and to monitor the press for adverse publicity.

Prompt consideration may need to be given to whether it is appropriate to suspend or dismiss any employees.

12.14.3   External advisers

In appropriate cases some regulators (for example, the FSA) may be prepared to hold off from commencing their own formal investigation in order to allow a company time to conduct internal investigations and produce a report. This can happen in cases where there is no ongoing misconduct or no immediate danger to interested parties and the regulator can see that the company is taking its responsibilities seriously and has engaged appropriate external professional expertise. This can be a sound reason for directors to bring in professional advisers early.

In any event there can be difficult questions of judgement and interpretation involved in ensuring, in the best interests of the company, that a regulator's requests are reasonable and that the company does not go further than it needs in responding to them. This means it will usually be in the best interests of the company to take legal advice. Commonly where the investigation relates to matters of a financial nature the directors' first reaction will be to call on the company's usual accountants to assist. However, this could create material disclosable to the regulator as their work may not be covered by legal professional privilege unless a company's in-house legal team or external legal advisers are involved at the outset. A firm's usual accountants may also have a conflict of interest with the company in relation to the matters under investigation. Directors will also need to consider whether it is appropriate to engage the company's usual external legal advisers or whether a new team is needed. That may be the case if the company's usual lawyers have in the past advised on the matters under investigation or have been aware of them in giving other advice, which means that a conflict of interest between the company and its lawyers could arise.

Any directors or other company staff who may be called upon to assist in an investigation but may have a conflict of interest with the company should be advised to obtain independent legal advice. The company may wish to fund the costs of that independent legal advice but directors will need to consider carefully whether that is in the best interests of the company and whether it is permissible within the limitations of CA 1985.[33] The extent to which legal and professional costs of the investigation are covered under Directors and Officers ("D&O") liability insurance is also relevant (*see* below).

12.14.4 *Insurance*

If there is D&O insurance cover in place, consideration will need to be given to the terms of the policy and whether the insurers should be notified. Underwriters may wish to be involved and it is sensible to obtain their consent to the steps being taken and to inform them regularly of developments.

Similarly, in cases where there has been a substantial loss to the company as a result of, for example, a fraud, consideration will need to be given to notifying the company's insurers. It is usually prudent to do so at an early stage.

D&O policies in the past have tended to be unclear as to how far costs of legal advice in relation to regulatory investigations are covered and there is considerable variation between insurers in the policy wording that has been used. Where the potential legal costs are significant, insurers not infrequently seek to rely on policy interpretation to avoid covering those costs. Such arguments are open to challenge but this

---

[33] Section 310 CA 1985 allows a company to indemnify a director against third-party claims provided the director is not in breach of any duty or obligation to the company. Unless it is contingent on a successful defence, a commitment in advance to indemnify against legal costs is invalid. The Company Law Review and the Higgs Review of the role and effectiveness of non-executive directors (January 2003) have both recommended that companies should be able to indemnify in advance against the cost to directors of defending proceedings.

often means that costs must start being incurred with these issues unresolved, which can put directors and officers in a difficult position if they must be self-funding.[34]

12.14.5 Notification

The Listing Rules require companies to notify a Regulatory Information Service without delay of any "major new developments within the company's sphere of activity" which are not public knowledge but which may lead to substantial movement in the price of its listed securities. Listed companies will need to consider whether the matters that an inspector has been appointed to investigate are something that should be disclosed to the market or even whether the fact of the appointment itself should be announced. The latter will not be appropriate if the investigation itself is confidential, but a listed company may need to seek guidance from the Listing Authority, particularly if there are rumours or press speculation.

The appointment of investigators may trigger an obligation to notify the company's regulator. For example, under Rule 15.3.15 of the FSA's Supervision Manual, a firm must notify the FSA immediately if it becomes aware that any statutory or regulatory authority, professional organisation or trade body has started an investigation into its affairs.

12.14.6 Preservation of evidence

At the outset, every possible step needs to be taken to secure and preserve all the evidence which could be relevant to the investigation. This will entail identifying the key players and the documentation which they may have and where it might be. It will also be necessary to establish how far-reaching the problem is within the company.

---

[34] Also *see* footnote 33. Section 310 CA 1985 allows a company to insure its directors against action by the company or third parties. The Higgs Review recommended that a revised Combined Code should refer to the need for companies to provide appropriate D&O insurance and that companies should supply details of their insurance cover to potential non-executive directors before they are appointed. Higgs felt that guidance for companies would be useful on what insurance should be provided for directors. The City of London Law Society, ICSA, the ABI and BIBA have agreed to work together to draw up guidance, which would include the risks that should be covered and specimen policy terms.

Regulatory Investigations

All possible sources of evidence will need to be identified. Immediate steps may need to be taken to avoid evidence being inadvertently lost through a routine destruction policy or being recorded over or even deliberately tampered with.

12.14.6.1 Documents
Consideration will need to be given to what classes of documents (such as correspondence, notes, minutes, diaries, internal memoranda, audit documentation and emails) may have been created and which need to be preserved.

12.14 6.2 Telephones
Often telephone calls will have been taped, particularly in cases involving the securities industry. Tapes will need to be retrieved and transcribed. Telephone logs of calls made and received and voicemail messages sometimes provide useful evidence.

12.14.6.3 Computer records
Specialist IT assistance will be required to ensure that computer records (including emails) are not lost and that computers are quarantined effectively and the forensic integrity of the evidence is preserved. The overriding factor in the securing of computer evidence is time. The faster the relevant computers are taken out of use or their hard disks copied (imaged), the greater the chance of recovering usable evidence from them.

All these types of documentation will need to be collated and held in a single, secure place. Records will need to be kept of the source of each file or document and procedures may need to be introduced to ensure that accurate records are kept if files are removed from the central collation point. Ideally, if a document is required for use, a photocopy should be used.

12.14.7 Production of evidence

As stated above, investigators have wide powers to require the production of documents and to require witnesses to attend interviews. Information (whether documentary or oral) which falls within the scope of legal professional privilege is usually – but not always – privileged from production so it is necessary to consider carefully each request for information from the investigators to ensure that privileged information is not disclosed.

The law in this area is complex and, in places, uncertain. As a result, it is a very real reason why legal advice should be sought at the outset of the investigation.

A practice used by some authorities when exercising search warrants is for independent counsel to be appointed to review documents for which a claim is asserted. The practice was considered and approved by Moses J in R v *Commissioners of Inland Revenue ex parte Tamosius*.[35]

12.14.8 Witnesses

The investigators will usually also require witnesses to attend interviews. It will be necessary to consider whether an individual should obtain separate legal representation. If it appears that the interests of the individual may be at variance with those of the company, the individual should be advised to obtain separate legal representation.

12.14.9 *Material gathered during the investigation*

It is very important to monitor and control communications generated during the course of the investigation about the subject matter of the investigation. As much as possible of the work that a company does in its own internal investigations and in gathering information to be provided to the inspectors should be prepared in such a way that it is covered by legal professional privilege. Again, legal advice will be appropriate at an early stage to ensure that communications are structured in such a way that an effective claim to privilege can be made. Such privileged materials should be segregated. Materials not covered by privilege will potentially be disclosable to the inspectors and "idle gossip" could be very damaging.

It is also important to monitor the information which is passed to the investigators so that a full record is retained of the documents and information which has been handed to them. Consideration should also be given to seeking to agree with the investigators, to the extent possible, restrictions on the use which may be made of the material disclosed to them.

---

[35] The *Independent*, 12 November 1999.

Regulatory Investigations

Table 12.1: *Criminal Justice Act 1987*

Appointment and scope of investigation	Production of documents and evidence	Privileged documents/ restrictions on production etc.	Entry and search of premises	Sanctions for obstruction
Serious or complex fraud Section 2(1): Where it appears to the Director of the SFO ("the Director") on reasonable grounds to involve serious or complex fraud. Upon notification in writing to any person where it appears to the Director that there is good reason to investigate the affairs, or any aspect of the affairs, of such person.	Section 2(2): The person under investigation or any other person whom the Director has reason to believe has relevant information may be required by notice to answer questions or otherwise furnish information with respect to any matter relevant to the investigation at a specified place and either at a specified time or forthwith. Section 2(3): The person under investigation or any other person may be required by notice in writing to produce at a specified place and time (which may be forthwith) any specified documents which appear to the Director to be relevant to the investigation. There is power to take copies or extracts and to require a person to provide an explanation of any documents. If documents are not produced, the person required to produce them may be required to state, to the best of his knowledge or belief, where they are.	Section 2(9): No requirement to disclose any information/ document protected by legal professional privilege except that a lawyer may be required to furnish the name and address of his client. Section 2(10): No requirement to produce information covered by banking confidentiality unless the customer consents or the Director requires.	Section 2(4): If there are reasonable grounds for believing that: (a) a person has failed to comply with an obligation to produce documents; (b) it is not practicable to serve a notice; or (c) the service of such notice may seriously prejudice the investigation; and (d) they are on premises specified in the information a warrant may be obtained. Section 2(5): A warrant authorises a constable to enter using such force as is reasonably necessary and search premises and to take possession of any documents. Section 2(6): Unless it is not practicable in the circumstances, the constable should be accompanied by an "appropriate person" (SFO member or person authorised by the Director).	Section 2(13): it is an offence for a person without reasonable excuse to fail to comply with a requirement imposed on him. Section 2(14): It is an offence for a person to make or recklessly make a false or misleading statement in purported compliance with a notice. Section 2(16): It is an offence for a person to falsify, conceal, destroy or otherwise dispose of (or permit any of these) documents which he knows or suspects are relevant to the investigation.

385

A Practitioner's Guide to Directors' Duties and Responsibilities

Table 12.2: *Companies Act 1985*

Appointment and scope of investigation	Production of documents and evidence	Privileged documents/ restrictions on production etc.	Entry and search of premises	Sanctions for obstruction
The affairs of the company Section 431: Inspectors may be appointed either on the application of the company's own members or on the application of the company. Section 432: Inspectors may be appointed where the court orders or where it appears to the DTI that circumstances exist suggesting: (a) that the company's affairs are being or have been conducted with intent to defraud its creditors or the creditors of any other persons or otherwise for a fraudulent or unlawful purpose, or in a manner which is unfairly prejudicial to some part of its members; or (b) that any actual or proposed act or omission of the company (including an act or omission on its behalf) is or would be so prejudicial or that the company was formed for any fraudulent or unlawful purpose; or (c) that persons concerned with the company's formation or management of the company's affairs have "in connection therewith been guilty of fraud,	Section 434(1): The officers and agents of the company under investigation have a duty: (a) to produce all documents of or relating to the company which are in their custody or power; (b) to attend before the inspectors when required to do so; and (c) otherwise to give the inspectors all assistance in connection with the investigation which they are reasonably able to give. Section 434(2): The same applies to any other person who has or may have in his possession information relating to a matter which may be relevant to the investigation.	Section 452: No requirement to disclose any information which a person would be entitled to refuse to disclose on grounds of legal professional privilege in the High Court except if he is a lawyer, the name and address of his client. Section 452(1A): No requirement to produce documents covered by banking confidentiality unless: (a) the person to whom the obligation is owed is the company under investigation; (b) the person to whom the obligation of confidence is owed consents; or (c) the making of the requirement is authorised by the Secretary of State.	Section 448: If there are reasonable grounds for believing that there are on the premises documents whose production has been required and which have not been produced, a warrant may be obtained. A warrant authorises a constable, together with any other person named in it: (a) to enter the premises specified (using such force as is reasonably necessary); (b) to search the premises and take possession of documents or any other steps necessary for preserving them or preventing interference with them; (c) to take copies of such documents; (d) to require any person named in the warrant to provide an explanation of documents or state where they may be found.	Section 436: If a person fails to comply with the requirements to produce documents or give assistance or refuses to attend interviews or to answer any questions, the Inspectors may certify that fact to the court and the court may then treat any such obstruction as contempt of court. Section 448(7): It is an offence to obstruct intentionally or fail without reasonable excuse to comply with any requirement under a warrant. Section 450: It is an offence for an officer of a company to destroy, mutilate or falsify a document or make a false entry or to be a party to the same unless he had no intention to conceal the company's state of affairs or to defeat the law.

386

Regulatory Investigations

Table 12.2: *Companies Act 1985* (continued)

Appointment and scope of investigation	Production of documents and evidence	Privileged documents/ restrictions on production etc.	Entry and search of premises	Sanctions for obstruction
misfeasance or other misconduct towards it or its members"; or (d) that the company's members have not been given all the information with respect to its affairs which they might reasonably expect. *The Membership of a Company* Section 442: Inspectors may be appointed either where it appears to the DTI that there is good reason to do so or on the application of the company's own members for the purpose of determining the true persons who are or have been financially interested in the success or failure of the company or able to control or materially to influence its policy. *Share Dealings* Section 446: Inspectors may be appointed where it appears to the DTI that there are circumstances suggesting contraventions of a director's obligations concerning dealings in shares or obligations to disclose interests.				

387

Table 12.2: *Companies Act 1985* (continued)

Appointment and scope of investigation	Production of documents and evidence	Privileged documents/ restrictions on production etc.	Entry and search of premises	Sanctions for obstruction
Company's Books and Records Section .447: If the DTI thinks there is good reason, it may require a company to produce specified documents at a specified time and place.	Section 447(5): There is power to take extracts or copies and to require a person to provide an explanation of any documents. If documents are not produced, the person required to produce them may be required to state to the best of his knowledge or belief, where they are.			Section 447(6): It is offence for the company or other person on whom the requirement was imposed to fail to produce documents or to provide an explanation (unless it can be shown that it was not reasonably practicable for him to produce them). Section 451: It is an offence intentionally or recklessly to provide false information.

Regulatory Investigations

Table 12.3: *Financial Services and Markets Act 2000*

Appointment and scope of investigation	Production of documents and evidence	Privileged documents/restrictions on production etc.	Entry and search of premises	Sanctions for obstruction
General investigations Section 167: In any case where it appears to the FSA or the Secretary of State there is good reason for doing so, investigators may be appointed to investigate: (a) the nature, conduct or state of an authorised person or of an appointed representative; (b) a particular aspect of that business; or (c) the ownership or control of an authorised person. *Particular cases* Section 168(3): Investigators may be appointed where there are circumstances suggesting that contraventions of specified provisions may have occurred including: (1) provision of false or misleading information to an auditor or actuary; (2) failure to comply with various requirements relating to notifications to the FSA and the provision of false or misleading information to the FSA; (3) the criminal offences of insider dealing, misleading statements or practices or falsely claiming to be exempt	Section 165: The FSA can by notice in writing to an authorised person require him to provide or produce information or documents before the end of such reasonable period as may be specified; or through an officer or member of staff or agent of the FSA with written authorisation require the person to provide or produce information or documents without delay. Section 171: A person under investigation pursuant to Section 167 or any connected person may be required to attend an interview or provide such information as the investigator may require. There is power to require the production of documents. Section 172: An investigator appointed under Section 168 in addition to the powers of Section 171 may also require a person who is neither the person being investigated nor a connected person to attend an interview or provide such information as the investigator may require where necessary	Section 175(5): No requirement for any person to disclose information or produce documents in respect of which he owes banking confidentiality, unless: (a) he is the person being investigated or a member of the person's group; (b) the person owed the obligation is being investigated or is a member of their group; (c) the person owed the obligation of confidence consents; or (d) it has been specifically authorised by the investigating authority. Section 175(4): A lawyer may be required to give the name and address of his client. Section 413: No requirement to disclose "protected items", namely legally privileged items.	Section 176(1)–(4): If there are reasonable grounds for believing that: (1) a person has failed to comply (in whole or in part) with a requirement to produce information and that on the premises there are documents or information which have been required; (2) the premises are the premises of an authorised person or appointed representative, that there are on the premises documents or information in relation to which a requirement could be imposed and that if such a requirement was imposed, it would not be complied with or the documents or information would be removed, tampered with or destroyed; (3) a specified offence under Section 168 has been committed and that there are on the premises relevant documents and that a requirement to produce them could be imposed and that if such a requirement was imposed it would not be complied with or the documents or information	Section 177(1) and (2): If a person (the "defaulter") fails to comply with a requirement imposed on him, the person imposing the requirement may certify the matter to the court. If the court is satisfied that the defaulter failed to comply without reasonable excuse, the court may treat the matter as a contempt of court. Section 177(3): It is an offence for any person to falsify, conceal, destroy or otherwise dispose of (or permit any of these) documents which he knows or suspects are relevant to the investigation. Section 177(4): It is an offence for a person to provide false or misleading information in purported compliance with a requirement imposed on him or to recklessly provide such confirmation. Section 177(5): A person guilty of an offence under subsections (3) or (4) is liable on summary conviction to imprisonment for a term not exceeding six months or a fine not exceeding the statutory maximum and on

389

Table 12.3: Financial Services and Markets Act 2000 (continued)

Appointment and scope of investigation	Production of documents and evidence	Privileged documents/ restrictions on production etc.	Entry and search of premises	Sanctions for obstruction
or authorised may have been committed; (4) there may have been a breach of the general prohibition; (5) there may have been a contravention of the financial promotion restrictions; or (6) market abuse may have taken place. Section 168(5): Investigators may also be appointed where there are circumstances suggesting that: (1) an authorised person is carrying on a regulated activity without permission; (2) a person may be guilty of an offence under the money laundering regulations; (3) an authorised person may have contravened an FSA rule; (4) an individual may not be fit and proper to perform functions relating to a regulated activity or a firm has allowed an individual to perform such functions without obtaining FSA approval; (5) an individual may have performed or agreed to perform a function in breach of a prohibition order or a firm has engaged someone to do so; (6) there may have been regulatory misconduct by an approved person.	or expedient for the purposes of the investigation. Section 173: An investigation appointed under Section 168(2) may require *any* person to attend an interview or provide such information as may be required for the purposes of the investigation. Section 175: If documents are not produced, the person required to produce them may be required to state to the best of his knowledge and belief where they are.		would be removed, tampered with or destroyed. A warrant may be obtained. Section 176(5): A warrant authorises a constable: (a) to enter premises specified in the warrant; (b) to search the premises and take possession of documents or information; (c) to take copies of documents; (d) to require any person on the premises to provide an explanation of the documents or state where they may be found; (e) to use such force as is reasonably necessary.	conviction on indictment to imprisonment for a term not exceeding two years or a fine or both. Section 177(6): It is an offence to obstruct intentionally the exercise of any rights conferred by a warrant and a person guilty of this offence is liable on summary conviction to imprisonment for a term not exceeding three months or a fine not exceeding level 5 on the standard scale or both.

Chapter 13
Disqualification of Directors

David Allison and Stephen Robins
3/4 South Square Chambers, Gray's Inn

13.1 Introduction

It should come as no surprise that a book addressing the subject of directors' duties contains an analysis of the area of disqualification of directors. The ever-increasing number of decisions made in disqualification proceedings are of paramount importance when seeking to define the duties to which the directors of today are subject. Although the majority of disqualification orders are made against directors of insolvent companies, the fact that a company is trading at a considerable profit and is clearly solvent will not necessarily save a director from being disqualified. It is the conduct of the director which determines whether a disqualification order is appropriate, and not the success or otherwise of the company.

The last National Audit Office report on the issue of disqualification was published in May 1999. The report revealed that disqualification orders made on the grounds of unfitness under Section 6 of the Company Directors Disqualification Act 1986 ("the CDDA 1986") had trebled in less than a decade.

The report estimated that the disqualification of directors of insolvent companies under Section 6 of the CDDA 1986 saves creditors around £11 million per year, this figure being based upon the likely proportion of disqualified directors who would otherwise set up new companies which would become insolvent. This figure demonstrates the protection which can be afforded to the public by virtue of the disqualification of errant directors.

Although the report concluded that disqualification orders are financially beneficial to those who trade with companies, the statistics included within the report reflected the vast amount of time which is consumed in both the preparation and the trial of disqualification cases. An average one year and eight months are spent to prepare a case, and an average of a further one year and two months are needed from the issue of the claim form through to the determination of the proceedings.

13.2 Grounds for disqualification

The CDDA 1986 provides the statutory basis for the commencement of disqualification proceedings. Section 1 CDDA 1986 prescribes the scope of the disqualification order which can be made by the court. The CDDA 1986 separates into three broad categories those Sections which make provision for the basis for a disqualification order:

(a) general misconduct in connection with companies;[1]
(b) unfitness to act as a director of a company;[2] and
(c) other cases.[3]

Section 2 CDDA 1986 provides for disqualification where a person is convicted of an indictable offence "in connection with the promotion, formation, management, liquidation or striking off of a company, or with the receivership or management of a company's property". The court which convicts the person is able to make the disqualification order of its own motion. An example is the decision in *R v Georgiou*.[4] In the event that the criminal court does not impose a period of disqualification, Section 16(2) CDDA 1986 provides that an application for a disqualification order may be made to a court having jurisdiction to wind up the company. The period of disqualification that the court may impose is dependent upon which court makes the order. Where the disqualification order is made by a court of summary jurisdiction, a period of up to five years may be imposed, and in any other case a period of up to 15 years may be imposed.[5] The principles that the criminal courts apply when determining whether to make a disqualification order and the period of such order should be consistent with those applied by the civil courts.[6]

Section 3 CDDA 1986 provides for disqualification of up to five years where a person has been:

---

[1] Sections 2–5 CDDA 1986.
[2] Sections 6–9 CDDA 1986.
[3] Sections 10–12 CDDA 1986. Section 9A will fall somewhere between the last two categories when it comes into force.
[4] [1988] 4 BCC 322 CA.
[5] Section 2(3) CDDA 1986.
[6] *SOS v Tjolle* [1998] 1 BCLC 333, at 336e–g.

"persistently in default in relation to provisions of the companies legislation requiring any return, account or other document to be filed with, delivered or sent, or notice of any matter to be given, to the registrar of companies."

Section 3(2) CDDA 1986 provides that the required persistent default can be proved conclusively if the director is found guilty of three or more defaults in any five-year period.

Section 4 CDDA 1986 provides that a disqualification order of up to 15 years may be made where, in the course of the winding up of a company, it appears that the director has been guilty of fraudulent trading under Section 458 of the Companies Act 1985[7] or any other fraud in relation to the company.[8]

Disqualification orders may be made in respect of conduct in relation to a solvent company under this Section. Where the company is insolvent, the proceedings will tend to be brought under Section 6 CDDA 1986.

Section 5 CDDA 1986 enables the court to make a disqualification order of up to five years where a person has been convicted of an offence due to:

"a contravention of, or failure to comply with, any provision of the companies legislation requiring a return, account or other document to be filed with, delivered or sent, or notice to be given, to the registrar of companies"[9]

and during the five years preceding the conviction the person has had three or more default orders and offences within Section 5.[10]

Section 6 CDDA 1986 enables the court to make a disqualification order against a person who has been a director of a company which has become insolvent, and the conduct of the director makes him unfit to be concerned in the management of a company.[11] Section 8 CDDA 1986 provides for the Secretary of State to make an application for a disqualification order if he believes it to be in the public interest to do so based on

---

[7] Section 4(1) CDDA 1986.
[8] Section 4(2) CDDA 1986.
[9] Section 5(1) CDDA 1986.
[10] Section 5(3) CDDA 1986.
[11] Section 6(1) CDDA 1986.

reports following, or documents obtained during, an investigation into the affairs of a company.[12] The maximum period of disqualification which the court can impose under Section 8 is 15 years. There is no need for the company to have become insolvent for a disqualification order to be made under Section 8.

Section 9A was added to CDDA 1986 by Section 204(2) of the Enterprise Act 2002. At the time of writing, it has not come into force. When it comes into force, the court will be obliged to make a disqualification order against a person provided that two conditions are satisfied in relation to him. The first condition is that a company of which he is a director commits a breach of competition law. Section 9A(4) defines the phrase "breach of competition law" by reference to the Competition Act 1998 and Articles 81 and 82 of the EC Treaty establishing the European Community. The second condition is that the court considers that his conduct as a director makes him unfit to be concerned in the management of a company. For the purpose of deciding whether a person is unfit to be concerned in the management of a company within the meaning of Section 9A, the court will not be permitted to have regard to the usual considerations set out in Schedule 1. Instead, the court will be obliged to consider:

(a) whether the director's conduct contributed to the breach of competition law;
(b) whether the director had reasonable grounds to suspect that the conduct of the undertaking constituted the breach and he took no steps to prevent it;
(c) whether the director did not know but ought to have known that the conduct of the undertaking constituted the breach.

The court will also be permitted to have regard to the director's conduct as a director of a company in connection with any other breach of competition law. The maximum period of disqualification under Section 9A is 15 years. The Office of Fair Trading will be permitted to apply for a disqualification order under Section 9A.

Section 10 CDDA 1986 provides that where a court has made an order under either Section 213 or Section 214 of the Insolvency Act 1986 ("IA

---

[12] The reports include those by inspectors under Section 437 of the Companies Act 1985, or under Section 94 or 177 of the Financial Services Act 1986, or from information and documents obtained under Section 447 or 448 of the Companies Act 1985.

1986")[13] a person is liable to contribute to the assets of a company, the court may, of its own motion, make a disqualification order of up to 15 years.

Section 11 CDDA 1986 makes it an offence for an undischarged bankrupt to act as a "director of, or directly or indirectly to take part in or be concerned in the promotion, formation or management of, a company" without the permission of the court which adjudged him bankrupt.[14] The offence of acting as a company director while being an undisclosed bankrupt is an offence of strict liability. Whether a defendant has been concerned in the promotion, formation or management of a company will be a question of fact for the jury and will not depend on the defendant's own view of his actions.[15]

For the purposes of the limited examination of law on directors' disqualification which will be afforded by this Chapter, it is only appropriate to examine the procedure applicable to applications for disqualification orders under Sections 6 and 8 CDDA 1986, namely disqualification on the grounds of unfitness.

13.3 The purpose of disqualification

The prime question in this regard is whether the act of disqualification is to be characterised as a means of punishing the errant director for the conduct which justifies the making of the disqualification order against him, or whether it is to protect the public from such conduct. An analysis of the case law conveys the fact that the purpose of imposing a disqualification is to protect the public.[16] Disqualification proceedings do not amount to a criminal charge.[17]

The protection conferred upon the public by the making of a disqualification order has two constituent elements, namely:

(a) prohibiting a disqualified director from forming, promoting or managing a company without the permission of the court;[18] and

---

[13] For fraudulent trading and wrongful trading respectively.
[14] Section 11(1) CDDA 1986.
[15] *R v Doring* (2002) Crim LR 817.
[16] *See*, for example, *Shuttleworth v Secretary of State* [2000] BCC 204.
[17] *R v Secretary for State, ex parte McCormick* [1998] BCC 379.
[18] *Secretary of State for Trade and Industry v Bannister* [1996] 1 All ER 993.

(b) the deterrent effect of a disqualification upon both the person disqualified and others in order to raise the standard of conduct of company directors.[19]

13.4 Territorial limits of CDDA 1986

CDDA 1986 undoubtedly has extraterritorial effect. Section 22(2)(b) CDDA 1986 provides that the word "company" includes any company which may be wound up under Part V IA 1986. By virtue of Sections 220 and 221 IA 1986, companies incorporated in foreign jurisdictions may be wound up by the English courts. To wind up a foreign company under Sections 220 and 221 IA1986, the court must be satisfied that there is a sufficient connection with the jurisdiction, that there is a potential benefit to creditors and that the creditors are subject to the jurisdiction. These criteria were recently reiterated in the case of *Re Latreefers Ltd*.[20]

Pursuant to Section 6 CDDA 1986, the court can make a disqualification order in respect of any person who is or has been a director of a foreign company that may be wound up under Part V IA 1986. Similarly, the prohibition in a disqualification order against acting as a director of a company extends to prohibit the disqualified person from undertaking directorships of any company that may be wound up under Part V IA 1986.

It should be noted that there are two possible interpretations of the words "any company which may be wound up under Part V of the IA 1986". On the one hand, all foreign companies can be wound up under Part V provided that the court is satisfied that there is a sufficient connection with the jurisdiction, that there is a potential benefit to creditors and that the creditors are subject to the jurisdiction. Therefore the words may be wide enough to include all foreign companies. If this interpretation is preferred, the court will have jurisdiction over directors of all companies throughout the world, and the court may prohibit individuals from acting as directors of all companies throughout the world.

On the other hand, no foreign company can be wound up under Part V unless the court is satisfied that there is a sufficient connection with the

---

[19] *Re Swift 736 Ltd* [1993] BCLC 896, at 899; *Re Grayan Building Services Ltd* [1995] Ch 241, at 253G; *Re Westmid Packaging Services Ltd* [1998] 2 BCLC 646, at 654; *Re Landhurst Leasing plc* [1999] 1 BCLC 286, at 344d.
[20] [2001] BCC 174.

jurisdiction, that there is a potential benefit to creditors and that the creditors are subject to the jurisdiction. Therefore, the words may denote only those foreign companies that are in fact susceptible to winding up under Part V. If this interpretation is preferred, the court will have a limited jurisdiction over directors of only those companies that currently pass the *Re Latreefers* test. The disqualification order will prohibit individuals from acting as directors of only those foreign companies that currently pass the *Re Latreefers* test.

In *Re Westminster Property Management Ltd*,[21] the Court of Appeal acted on an underlying assumption that the second interpretation was correct. The Court of Appeal did not discuss the first interpretation at all. However, the second interpretation causes problems when considering the international scope of the disqualification order. It means that the scope of the disqualification order will fluctuate in all cases where the connection between a foreign company and the jurisdiction is dynamic in nature. In such cases, the scope of the order will ebb and flow as the foreign company in question acquires and loses its connections with England.

Further, the second interpretation is wholly uncertain and unpredictable in application. The occurrence or otherwise of a breach of the disqualification order will depend on an English court's assessment of sufficiency of connection and probability of benefit to creditors. Experience shows that the decisions of judges cannot be predicted with certainty. For these reasons it may be possible to challenge the current assumption that the second interpretation is correct.

The court may grant permission to serve disqualification proceedings on defendants out of the jurisdiction.[22] Foreign nationals may also be made the subject of disqualification proceedings. This is necessary to ensure that the CDDA 1986 is not a partially blunt tool in the context of today's cross-border business deals and communications. In *Re Seagull Manufacturing Co. Ltd (No. 2)*,[23] it was said that modern communications enabled companies to be controlled across frontiers, and Parliament must be presumed to have intended that Section 6 CDDA 1986 would extend both to foreigners who were out of the jurisdiction and to conduct which occurred out of the jurisdiction. In exercising its discretion to order

---

[21] [2001] EWCA Civ 111 (unreported, 25 January 2001).
[22] Rule 5(2) of the Disqualification Rules and paragraph 7.3 of the Practice Direction.
[23] [1994] 1 BCLC 273.

service out of the jurisdiction, the court will need to be satisfied that the claimant has a good arguable case against the defendant.

13.5 Procedure

The vast majority of applications for disqualification are brought under Section 7 CDDA 1986 for an order under Section 6 CDDA 1986. Proceedings under Section 7 CDDA 1986 can be commenced by the Secretary of State or, in circumstances where the company is being wound up by the court, by the Official Receiver at the Secretary of State's direction.[24] The court to which the application is to be made is determined by Section 6(3) CDDA 1986.[25] Where proceedings are to be commenced in a county court, it being the court in which the company is being wound up at the time the disqualification proceedings are commenced, its jurisdiction to hear the disqualification proceedings will subsist after the company is dissolved.[26] However, where the company has been dissolved prior to the commencement of disqualification proceedings, the only court in which disqualification proceedings may be commenced is the High Court.[27] In circumstances where the proceedings have been commenced in the wrong court, the proceedings may be transferred to the correct court in accordance with CPR Part 30 and the Practice Direction thereto, or the court may strike out the proceedings.[28]

Factors which the court will take into consideration when deciding whether to order the transfer of the proceedings include:

(a) whether they are frivolous or vexatious;
(b) whether the proceedings were commenced within two years of the company's insolvency;
(c) the public interest in the disqualification of errant directors;
(d) whether a fair trial is still possible due to the delay caused.

---

[24] Section 7(1) CDDA 1986.
[25] The date when the application is brought is the relevant date for determining which court has jurisdiction: *Re Lichfield Freight Terminal Ltd* [1997] 2 BCLC 109. Section 117 IA 1986 defines which courts have jurisdiction to wind up a company.
[26] *Re Working Project Ltd* [1995] 1 BCLC 226.
[27] *Re N P Engineering & Security Products Ltd* [1998] 1 BCLC 208. Such proceedings must be brought by the Secretary of State.
[28] *Re N P Engineering & Security Products Ltd* [1998] 1 BCLC 208 CA.

It is not the function of the court on applications for a transfer to punish the claimant.

13.5.1 The relevant procedural rules

The relevant procedural rules for an application for a disqualification order will be determined by the section under which the application for disqualification is made. The sources of the procedural rules for disqualification proceedings are the Practice Direction: Directors' Disqualification Proceedings ("the Practice Direction"), the Insolvent Companies (Disqualification of Unfit Directors) Proceedings Rules 1987,[29] as amended by the Insolvent Companies (Disqualification of Unfit Directors) (Amendment Rules) 1999[30] ("the Disqualification Rules") and the Civil Procedure Rules ("the CPR"). The procedure for disqualification proceedings for orders under Sections 6 and 8 CDDA 1986 is provided for by both the Disqualification Rules and the Practice Direction.[31] The Disqualification Rules apply the provisions of the CPR to proceedings except where the provisions of the Disqualification Rules are inconsistent with the CPR,[32] and the application of the CPR is also subject to the application of the appeal and review procedure under Rules 7.47 and 7.49 IA 1986.[33]

13.5.2 Pre-action prima facie case recommendations to the Secretary of State under Section 7(3) CDDA 1986

In cases where the company is insolvent, it is the insolvency practitioner office holder who is likely to discover grounds capable of supporting a finding of unfitness. He is the person who will discover the information which the Secretary of State will need to consider when determining whether to commence disqualification proceedings. Section 7(3) CDDA 1986 requires the office holder[34] of an insolvent company who is of the

---

[29] SI 1987/2023.
[30] SI 1999/1023.
[31] Paragraph 1.3(1)(d)(e) of the Practice Direction.
[32] Rule 2(1) of the Disqualification Rules; CPR 2.1(2).
[33] Rule 2.4 of the Disqualification Rules.
[34] The office holder will be the official receiver in relation to all companies being wound up by the court. The obligation remains on the official receiver even when his appointment as liquidator is superseded by the appointment of another liquidator. The officer holder will be the liquidator in creditors' voluntary liquidations. In administration and administrative receivership, the office holder will be the administrator and the administrative receiver respectively.

opinion that a director, past or present, of the company is unfit to act as such, to report his view to the Secretary of State.[35] The failure of the office holder to perform this duty may lead to professional sanctions against the office holder.[36]

Section 7(3) CDDA 1986 is supplemented by Section 7(4) CDDA 1986 which enables both the Secretary of State and the Official Receiver, where he is not the office holder, to require the office holder to provide such information or documents as the Secretary of State reasonably requires in order to determine whether to bring proceedings for a disqualification order. The Secretary of State has no absolute right to production of the documents. The court exercises its discretion when determining whether to order the office holder to comply with the request of the Secretary of State, as can be seen from *Re Lombard Shipping and Forwarding Ltd*.[37] An application to the court for the disclosure of the documents may be made pursuant to Rule 6 of the Insolvent Companies (Reports on Conduct of Directors) Rules 1996, which will be made by a CPR Part 8 claim where there are no pending disqualification proceedings, or by application notice under CPR Part 23 where such a claim is pending (paragraph 18 of the Practice Direction).

The purposes of liquidation, administration and administrative receivership include obtaining information on the conduct of the affairs of the company and of those responsible for it during its trading history, with the consequence that the duty to report such information to the Secretary of State under Section 7(3) should be readily complied with. In *Re Polly Peck International plc*,[38] interviews of officers of the company had been conducted under Section 236 IA 1986 on the basis that the joint administrators had assured the interviewees that the information would only be used for the purposes of the administration. It was held that disclosure of the transcripts of the interviews to the Secretary of State would be in accordance with the undertaking, as it would be in furtherance of the purposes of the administrations.

---

[35] The reporting obligation placed upon office holders is governed by the Insolvent Companies (Reports on Conduct of Directors) Rules 1996. These rules also require the office holder to provide returns detailing the identities of all directors and shadow directors.

[36] These may include proceedings under Rule 4(7) of the Insolvent Companies (Reports on Conduct of Directors) Rules 1996 or a disqualification under Section 4 CDDA 1986.

[37] [1993] BCLC 238, at 245.

[38] [1994] BCC 15.

In *Re Westminster Property Management Ltd*,[39] it was held that the use of statements obtained under Section 235 IA 1986 in disqualification proceedings did not necessarily involve a breach of Article 6 of the European Convention on Human Rights. In *Re Pantmaenog Timber Co Ltd*,[40] however, it was held that the court has no power to make an order under Section 236 IA 1986 requiring third parties to disclose documents and provide information to the Official Receiver where the Official Receiver's sole purpose is to obtain evidence for use in the disqualification proceedings.

A report compiled by the office holder will not be subject to legal professional privilege, with the consequence that the court can order disclosure of the report to a defendant to disqualification proceedings.[41] In contrast, the working papers of the office holder or inspector will not be admissible or disclosable.[42]

It should be noted that the Secretary of State is perfectly entitled to use information which has come into his possession by means other than the report of the office holder when determining whether an application for a disqualification order should be made. The Secretary of State will form his own view on the relevant report and is under no obligation to act in accordance with the opinion of the office holder. The Secretary of State will commence proceedings where he believes that it is in the public interest to do so. The decision of the Secretary of State to commence proceedings is one which, in theory at least, is susceptible to judicial review. The prospects of succeeding in such an application are, however, very poor.[43]

13.5.3 Procedure on an application for a disqualification order

Section 16(1) of CDDA 1986 provides that:

> "a person intending to apply for the making of a disqualification order by the court having jurisdiction to wind up a company shall

---

[39] [2001] BCC 121.
[40] [2002] 2 WLR 20.
[41] In *Re Barings plc* [1998] Ch 356, Scott V-C held that disclosure of the report was necessary in the interests of fairness and to save costs.
[42] *Re Astra Holdings plc* [1998] 2 BCLC 44.
[43] As displayed by the decision in *Secretary of State v Davies (No. 2)* [1997] 2 BCLC 317.

give not less than 10 days' notice of his intention to the person against whom the order is sought".[44]

The courts have had to consider whether this provision is intended to be mandatory or directory. In the event that it were held to be mandatory, the failure to comply with the 10-day notice period would render the proceedings a nullity, whereas the failure to comply with a directory provision would merely constitute a procedural irregularity which the court has a discretion to excuse. In *Re Cedac Ltd*,[45] the Court of Appeal held that failure to give notice was a procedural irregularity, and therefore did not render the proceedings a nullity.

The notice does not need to contain any indication of the grounds upon which a disqualification order will be sought; it needs only to state the intention to make an application for a disqualification order.[46] In fact, the notice is unlikely to be of any practical use to the director unless he can show that it is a case of mistaken identity. The respondent should attempt to use this period to obtain legal representation.

Applications for disqualification orders are to be made by the issue of a claim form and the use of Part 8 of the Civil Procedure Rules.[47] All disqualification proceedings are to be allocated to the multi-track (the CPR relating to allocation questionnaires and track allocation shall not apply).[48]

Upon issuing the claim form, the claimant will be given a date for the first hearing of the application before a registrar (a district judge in a county court), such date to be at least eight weeks after the date of issue.[49] At the time of issuing the claim form, the claimant shall file his evidence

---

[44] The requisite 10 days' notice is calculated excluding both the date on which the notice is given and the date on which the proceedings are issued. This provision is only applicable to those cases where the application is made to the court with jurisdiction to wind up a company, and is not applicable where the court is empowered of its own motion to make a disqualification order, or where the application is before a court which does not have jurisdiction to wind up a company (*Re Cedac* [1991] Ch 402).

[45] [1991] Ch 402 CA.

[46] *Re Surrey Leisure* [1999] 1 BCLC 731.

[47] Paragraph 4.2 of the Practice Direction; Rule 2(2) of the Disqualification Rules. Part 8 of the Civil Procedure Rules is to apply to disqualification applications, subject to the provisions of the Practice Direction and the Disqualification Rules.

[48] Paragraph 2 of the Practice Direction.

[49] Paragraph 4.3 of the Practice Direction.

Disqualification of Directors

in support of the application. It is for the claimant to effect service of the claim form and the affidavit evidence upon which he relies,[50] which shall be accompanied by an acknowledgment of service. Service of the claim form by first class post shall be deemed to be effective on the seventh day after posting, unless the contrary is shown.[51]

Upon receipt of the claim form, the defendant should ensure that he files and serves the acknowledgment of service form within 14 days after service of the claim form. This acknowledgment of service form shall state whether:

(a) he contests the application on the grounds that he was not a director or shadow director of a named company at the time of the conduct which forms the basis of the application; or that he disputes that his conduct was as alleged by the claimant;
(b) in the case of any conduct which he admits, he disputes that such conduct renders him unfit; and
(c) while not intending to defend the application for his disqualification, he intends to adduce mitigating factors with a view to reducing the period of disqualification which is to be imposed.[52]

Where a defendant fails to file and serve an acknowledgment of service form within the prescribed period, he is entitled to attend the hearing of the application but is not entitled to take part in the proceedings unless the court gives him permission to do so.[53]

Within 28 days of service of the claim form upon him, the defendant must file and serve any evidence in opposition to the application upon which he wishes to rely. In the event that the claimant wishes to submit evidence in reply, such evidence must be filed and served within 14 days after receiving the defendant's evidence. At all times before the first hearing of the application, it is open to the parties to extend the time for service of evidence by written agreement.[54]

---

[50] All evidence in disqualification proceedings is to be by affidavit, subject to the exception that when the official receiver is a party, his evidence may be in the form of a written report.
[51] Rule 5(1) of the Disqualification Rules; paragraph 7.2 of the Practice Direction.
[52] Rule 5(4) of the Disqualification Rules; paragraph 8.2 of the Practice Direction.
[53] Paragraph 8.4 of the Practice Direction.
[54] Paragraph 9.7 of the Practice Direction.

At the first hearing of the application the registrar will either determine the case or give directions and adjourn the application. It is advisable to seek all necessary directions at this first hearing, as it is intended that disqualification applications should be determined at the earliest possible date. Furthermore, it will be in the defendant's interests to do so in order to keep the cost of the proceedings down.

On applications under Section 7 or 8 CDDA 1986, the court may hear and determine the application summarily on the first hearing of the application without further notice to the defendant. In the event that this approach is taken by the court, the maximum period of disqualification which may be imposed by the court is five years. In circumstances where the court is of the view that a period in excess of five years would be appropriate, it will adjourn the application to be heard at a later date that will be notified to the defendant.[55] The registrar will also take the course of adjourning the application where he is of the view that there are questions of law or fact which are not appropriate for summary determination.[56]

Where the registrar adjourns the application, he will direct whether the application is to be heard by a registrar or a judge and give any further directions for the case management of the application.[57] In contested applications, such directions are likely to include fixing of a pre-trial review of the case after the close of evidence.

13.5.4 Applications under Section 7CDDA 1986 to commence proceedings for an order under Section 6 CDDA 1986 out of time

Pursuant to paragraph 17 of the Practice Direction, an application for permission to bring Section 6 proceedings out of time is made by Application Notice under Part 23 of the Civil Procedure Rules to the court that would ordinarily have jurisdiction had the proceedings been issued in time. Applications under Section 7 CDDA 1986 should be brought within two years of the company becoming "insolvent" within

---

[55] Rule 7(4)(a) of the Disqualification Rules; paragraphs 6.1(4) and 10.5 of the Practice Direction.

[56] Rule 7(4)(b) of the Disqualification Rules; paragraph 10.5(2).

[57] Rule 7(5) of the Disqualification Rules; paragraph 11 of the Practice Direction. In *Lewis* v *Secretary of State for Trade & Industry* [2001] 2 BCLC 597, the court established guidelines for the factors to be taken into account when considering whether a disqualification application should be tried before a registrar or a judge.

Disqualification of Directors

the meaning ascribed to the term by Section 6(2) CDDA 1986.[58] When the application is made outside this period, the permission of the court is needed. The application for permission should be made to the court which would have jurisdiction over the disqualification proceedings under Section 6(3) CDDA 1986 if permission were to be given, and the proposed respondent must be made a party. The Secretary of State will bear the burden of showing a good reason for the extension of the period. When permission is not obtained prior to the issue of a claim form outside this time limit, the defendant will be entitled to have the proceedings struck out, as the permission must be obtained prospectively rather than retrospectively.

The case law reveals that the imposition of a two-year period for the issue of proceedings by Section 7(2) CDDA 1986 has two main objectives:

(a) to give those who have been directors of insolvent companies the ability to organise their affairs once the two-year period has passed free of the risk of future disqualification; and
(b) to protect the public interest, as it is obviously wrong that a person whom the Secretary of State considers to be unfit to act as a director should be left free to act as one any longer than is necessary.[59]

In *Re Probe Data Systems Ltd (No. 3)*,[60] Scott LJ stated that factors which the court will take into account when considering an application to commence proceedings out of time include the length of the delay,[61] the reasons for the delay,[62] the prejudice caused to the director by the

---

[58] Where more than one event of insolvency occurs, the two-year period runs begins to run from the time of the first event: *Re Tasbian* [1989] BCLC 720. The case law supports the proposition that the day on which the company became insolvent, within Section 6(2), is to be included when calculating the relevant period of two years. There is no time limit in relation to applications for orders under Sections 2–5, 8 and 10.
[59] *Re Blackspur Group plc (No.2)* [1998] 1 WLR 422; *Re Noble Trees Ltd* [1993] BCLC 1185, at 1190; *Re Polly Peck International plc (No. 2)* [1994] 1 BCLC 574, at 590.
[60] [1992] BCLC 405, at 416.
[61] *Re Manlon Trading* [1995] 4 All ER 14, at 23: the public interest in the disqualification of unfit directors does not diminish with the passage of time, but it must be balanced against the right of the director to carry on without the threat of disqualification proceedings for an unreasonable period.
[62] *Re Copecrest Ltd* [1994] 2 BCLC 284: permission was given where the delay was attributable to the conduct of the directors. Where the delay is not due to the conduct of the director, the reasons for such delay should be explained by the Secretary of State.

delay[63] and the strength and seriousness of the case against the director (the public protection factor).[64] These factors, although important, are not exhaustive, and all relevant factors will be taken into account. The court will then carry out a balancing exercise to determine whether the grant of permission is appropriate on the facts of the case, and in doing so its discretion is unfettered. This is shown by the decision in *Re Stormont Ltd*.[65] The court was of the view that it would be appropriate to give permission in relation to the claim against one of the directors, but exercised its discretion to stay the proceedings on the basis of undertakings offered by the director. It is likely that the course adopted by the court is an exceptional one in the light of the undertaking that the director would not act in accordance with Section 1 CDDA 1986 for an unlimited time with the prospect of permission to act being excluded by the undertaking.

It should be noted that Article 6(1) of the European Convention on Human Rights ("ECHR") incorporated into English law by the Human Rights Act 1998 provides the right to a fair trial within a reasonable time. This has not had any impact on the way in which the judicial discretion is exercised, as the guidelines set out in the case law do require judges to take both the factors of delay and prejudice to the director into account. Where judges take into account the relevant considerations, their decisions will be upheld. Where they fail to carry out the necessary balancing act, their decisions will be overturned. A similar approach has been adopted in relation to the length of time for which proceedings have been under way. In *EDC v UK*,[66] on one hand, the court held that where proceedings brought against a director under CDDA 1986 had been pending for over four years and four months, the length of the proceedings exceeded the "reasonable time" requirement referred to in Article 6(1) of the ECHR. In *Re Blackspur Group Ltd*,[67] on the other hand, the court held that there had been no breach of the defendant's right to a hearing "within a reasonable time" even though proceedings against him under Section 6 CDDA 1986 had been under way for over eight years.

---

[63] *Re Polly Peck International plc (No. 2)* [1994] 1 BCLC 574: illness of the director may, on suitable facts, be taken to represent so serious a prejudice as to bar an extension. The prejudice caused by disqualification proceedings on the director's livelihood may be taken into account. The weakening of the director's evidence with the passage of time may also be taken into account as a form of prejudice.
[64] *Re Stormont Ltd* [1997] 1 BCLC 437; *Re Packaging Direct Ltd* [1994] BCC 213.
[65] [1997] 1 BCLC 437.
[66] [1998] BCC 370.
[67] [2001] 1 BCLC 653.

13.6 Determining unfitness

There are three factors which must be present in order for the court to make an order under Section 6, namely:

(a) the defendant must have been a director of the company;
(b) the company must have become "insolvent"; and
(c) unfitness must be proved.

13.6.1 Who is a director?

The reach of the CDDA 1986 extends to apply to:

(a) directors properly appointed in accordance with the articles of association of the company;
(b) shadow directors as defined in Section 22(5) CDDA 1986; and
(c) de facto directors.

The first category is straightforward and requires no comment. The second category has proved more troublesome in its application. The statutory definition in Section 22(5) CDDA 1986 provides that a shadow director is someone on whose directions and instructions the company's board is accustomed to act. In *Secretary of State for Trade & Industry* v *Deverell*,[68] the Court of Appeal held that the statutory definition must not be narrowly construed. The directions or instructions do not have to extend over all or most of the corporate activities of the company. The Court of Appeal said that the purpose of the legislation is to identify those with real influence in the company's affairs. Such a person does not have to be hidden in the shadows. It is not necessary to prove the state of mind of the giver or receiver of the instructions or directions nor to show that the board was subservient to or surrendered its discretion to the shadow director to any greater extent than was implicit in the statutory definition.

The third category derives from Section 22(4) CDDA 1986, which provides that the definition of the word "director" includes "any person occupying the position of director". In *Re Kaytech International plc*,[69] the Court of Appeal made clear that a de facto director is a person who assumes to act as a director. He is held out as a director by the company,

---

[68] [2000] 2 All ER 365.
[69] [1999] BCC at 390.

and claims and purports to be a director, although never actually or validly appointed as such. To establish that a person was a de facto director of a company it is necessary to plead and prove that he undertook functions in relation to the company which could properly be discharged only by a director. It is not sufficient to show that he was concerned in the management of the company's affairs or undertook tasks in relation to its business which can properly be performed by a manager below board level.

13.6.2 When does a company become insolvent?

A company becomes "insolvent" for the purposes of Section 7 CDDA 1986 on the happening of any of the events mentioned in Section 6(2) CDDA 1986, namely the company goes into liquidation (within Section 22(3) CDDA 1986 and Section 247 IA 1986) at a time when its assets are insufficient for the payment of its debts, other liabilities and the expenses of the winding-up, an administration order is made, or an administrative receiver is appointed. It should be noted that the event of insolvency may occur "whether while he was a director or subsequently" (Section 6(1)(a) CDDA 1986). In *Re Gower Enterprises Ltd*,[70] Evans-Lombe J held for the purposes of determining whether a liquidation was insolvent:

(a) the assets and liabilities should be valued as at the date of liquidation, and not according to what is realised subsequently;
(b) interest accruing on debts after the liquidation and statutory interest under Section 189 IA 1986 is not to be taken into account; and
(c) the "expenses of the winding-up" must be construed as if the word "reasonable" were included immediately before the phrase.

It will not be open to the director to challenge the validity of the insolvency proceedings, by reason of which the company is deemed to be insolvent, within the disqualification proceedings. The validity of the insolvency proceedings must be determined in other proceedings, pending the outcome of which the disqualification proceedings may be adjourned or stayed.[71]

---

[70] [1995] BCC 293.
[71] *Secretary of State for Trade and Industry v Jabble* [1998] 1 BCLC 598, at 601.

13.6.3 What does "unfitness" mean?

In *Secretary of State* v *Baker*,[72] the Court of Appeal considered the meaning of the word "unfitness" in the context of CDDA 1986 and made the following points:

(a) The court must consider the question of "unfitness" by reference to the conduct relied on by the Secretary of State and decide whether viewed cumulatively and taking into account any extenuating circumstances it has fallen below the standards of competence appropriate for persons fit to be directors of companies. Thus it is no answer to the allegations of the Secretary of State that separately and individually none of them is sufficiently serious to demonstrate the requisite unfitness.

(b) The director's responsibility for the causes of the company becoming insolvent requires a broad approach and is not to be assessed by reference to nice legal concepts of causation. Thus it matters not that others may also have been responsible for the causes of the insolvency whether more or less proximately.

(c) Where the allegation is incompetence without dishonesty, it is to be demonstrated to a high degree. This follows from the nature of the penalty. Nevertheless the degree of incompetence should not be exaggerated given the ability of the court to grant leave, notwithstanding the making of such an order.

(d) It is not necessary for the Secretary of State to show that the person in question is unfit to be concerned in the management of any company in any role. This "lowest common denominator" approach is not what the Act enjoins. The court is concerned only with the respondent's conduct in respect of which complaint is made set in the context of his actual management role in that company. If his conduct in that role shows incompetence to the requisite degree then a finding of unfitness and a consequential disqualification order should be made.

(e) A finding of breach of duty is neither necessary nor of itself sufficient for a finding of unfitness. A person may be unfit even though no breach of duty is proved against him or may remain fit notwithstanding the proof of various breaches of duty.

Section 9 and Schedule 1 CDDA 1986 provide a non-exhaustive list of guidance on the matters to which the court may "have regard in

---

[72] [2000] 1 BCLC 523.

particular"[73] when assessing whether a respondent is unfit.[74] The matters listed in Schedule 1 CDDA 1986 to which the court will have regard include:

(a) any breach of fiduciary duty;
(b) misapplication of the company's assets;
(c) failure to comply with the obligations in the Companies Act 1985 in relation to keeping proper records;
(d) extent of responsibility for the insolvency of the company;
(e) extent of responsibility for the company entering into transactions liable to be set aside as preferences or transactions at an undervalue;[75] and
(f) a failure to comply with the obligations placed on a director by the IA 1986.

In each case it will be a question of fact for the court whether the conduct amounts to unfitness.[76] Although the determination of whether a director's conduct was such as to render him unfit will always be a question of fact, an analysis of the case law reveals that certain types of conduct usually result in the making of a disqualification order:

(a) Misconduct by the director which has the consequence of conferring a benefit upon him personally to the detriment of the company is likely to lead to a finding of unfitness. An obvious example is where a director causes a company to enter into a transaction which constitutes a preference within Section 239 IA 1986 or a transaction at an undervalue within Section 238 IA 1986, the beneficiary of which is the director. In *Re Funtime*,[77] for example, a company director who knowingly entered transactions that were improper preferences in favour of himself and his associates was declared to be unfit to be a director. This case should be contrasted with the

---

[73] Section 9(1) CDDA 1986. These words and the phrase "conduct in relation to any matter connected with or arising out of the insolvency of that company" in Section 6(2) CDDA 1986, show that the court may take any misconduct into account: *Re Landhurst Leasing plc* [1999] 1 BCLC 286.
[74] Only the factors listed in Part I of Schedule 1 will be relevant on an application for a disqualification order under Section 8 CDDA 1986. On an application for an order under Section 6 CDDA 1986 both Part I and Part II of Schedule 1 will be applicable. Schedule 1 will not be applicable in applications under Section 9A.
[75] Sections 238–240 of the IA 1986.
[76] *Re Sevenoaks Stationers (Retail) Ltd* [1991] Ch 164.
[77] [2000] 1 BCLC 247.

case of *Re Deaduck Ltd*,[78] in which it was held that the fact that a director had caused an insolvent company to make a payment which was detrimental to the general body of creditors did not justify a finding that the director was unfit.

(b) A history of repeated failure, whether ignorant or intentional, to comply with the statutory obligations to prepare and file financial statements, annual returns and other statutory documents will usually lead to a finding of unfitness. The principal reason behind the attitude of the court to this type of misconduct is that compliance with the statutory provisions should enable the company to detect and address financial difficulties at an early juncture. The failure to detect such matters at an early stage is likely to have the consequence of increasing losses sustained by creditors.[79]

(c) Directors should be careful before seeking to transfer the assets and goodwill of an ailing company to a new company prior to the ailing company entering into a formal insolvency procedure. Apart from the personal liabilities which can arise out of such facts, it is very likely that the director will be found to be unfit if the transferee company subsequently becomes insolvent.[80]

(d) A director of a company which becomes insolvent is obliged, under IA 1986, to cooperate with and give assistance to the office holder appointed over the insolvent company's affairs. This cooperation is essential in order for the office holder to be able to identify and recover the company's assets. A repeated failure on the part of a former director to comply with his duty to cooperate is likely to result in a finding of unfitness.[81]

It will not be a sufficient answer for a respondent to disqualification proceedings to merely assert that they did not have any direct involvement in the affairs of the company with the consequence that he is not responsible for the failure of the company. A director will, at the very least, be under a continuing duty to inform himself about the company's affairs in order to properly discharge his duty as a director. This will not be satisfied where the director only maintains a negligible actual involvement in the affairs of the company.[82] As long as an individual continues to hold office as a director, and in particular to receive remuneration from it, he is under a duty to inform himself as to the financial affairs of the

---

[78] [2000] 1 BCLC 148.
[79] *Re Swift 736 Ltd* [1993] BCLC 896.
[80] *Re Keypak Homecare Ltd (No. 2)* [1990] BCLC 440.
[81] *Secretary of State v McTighe (No. 2)* [1996] 2 BCLC 477.
[82] *Re Wimbledon Village Restaurant Ltd* [1994] BCC 753.

company and to play an appropriate role in the management of its business. In the event that a director is not prepared to discharge these responsibilities properly, the appropriate course is for him to resign his directorship.[83] There are several cases where a director has, in effect, been disqualified on grounds of complete non-participation.

The case of *Re Continental Assurance Co. of London plc*[84] makes it clear that a non-executive director will also be under an obligation to inform himself of the affairs of the company, and that an experienced non-executive director, in this case an experienced corporate financier, will be expected to read and understand the company's accounts and inquire as to any difficulties. It is suggested that this approach is necessary to ensure that the practice of appointing respected city figures as directors to improve investor confidence has appropriate safeguards.

Under Schedule 1 CDDA 1986 the court is required to consider the relative responsibility of the respondent for the defaults of the company. In practice, this will involve both the consideration of each director's involvement in the particular acts relied upon to establish unfitness, and an investigation of the division of work within the company, and the experience and particular expertise of each board member.

In *Re Bradcrown*,[85] it was held that the fact that a director has professional advisers who fail to draw attention to the impropriety of transactions might negative a finding of unfitness or be a mitigating factor in the period of disqualification to be imposed. However, any reliance on such advice had to be reasonable. The delegation of certain functions is a necessary element of the affairs of most companies, and directors are clearly entitled to order the company's affairs in this manner. While this is a perfectly reasonable act, the mere act of delegation will not absolve a director from any responsibility for that particular part of the business. When delegating the functions a director will be entitled to trust the competence and integrity of the person to a reasonable extent, in the absence of any facts putting him on inquiry, but he and the other members of the board of directors, will remain responsible for supervising the conduct of the person in fulfilling the

---

[83] *Re Galeforce Pleating Co Ltd* [1999] 2 BCLC 686.
[84] [1997] 1 BCLC 48.
[85] [2001] BCLC 547.

delegated duties.[86] The extent of supervision which is necessary will be dependent on the facts of the particular case, and it is likely to be a different standard for executive and non-executive directors.

There are certain duties, however, which cannot be delegated to others. For example, statutory duties such as maintaining proper financial statements, and fiduciary duties cannot be delegated to others. Furthermore, all directors, including non-executive directors, need to keep themselves informed of the company's financial position.

A director will not be able simply to assert that another director had responsibility for the area of the business which led to the failure of the company. The board of directors as a whole remains collectively responsible for the supervision of the conduct of the individual director in carrying out the delegated functions.[87] A non-executive director will be able to rely on what he is told by the executive directors, but must ensure that he evaluates in a critical and objective manner the information given.[88]

The effect of the decision in Re Landhurst Leasing plc is that it is imperative for the less senior directors to question the actions of those more senior to them, and not simply be led blindly by an autocratic chairman. As Hart J stated, the duties to which directors are subject "require them to act with independence and courage".[89] An employee who has been promoted to the board of directors must ensure that he satisfies his responsibility for supervising the conduct of the more

---

[86] Re Barings (No. 5) [1999] 1 BCLC 433, at 586E–F:

"from time to time the question whether the system that has been put in place and over which the individual is presiding is operating efficiently, and whether the individuals to whom duties, in accordance with the system, have been delegated are discharging those duties efficiently."

Re Polly Peck International plc (No. 2) [1994] 1 BCLC 574; Re Westmid Packing Services [1998] 2 All ER 124.

[87] Re Landhurst Leasing plc [1999] 1 BCLC 286, at 346F:

"even where there are no reasons to think reliance [on an individual director] is misplaced, a director may still be in breach of duty if he leaves to others matters for which the board as a whole must take responsibility".

[88] Re TLL Realisations Ltd unreported, 27 November 1998.
[89] [1999] 1 BCLC 286, at 353G.

senior members of the board. In the event that he is not consulted on, for example, financial matters and the other members of the board refuse to consider the matter at his request, the appropriate course may be to resign unless he remains in office to continue to challenge the conduct of the other directors. If the other directors continue to pay insufficient attention to financial matters, the director may have a duty to inform the non-executive directors, or even the company's auditors, of the misconduct.

Regardless of the size or structure of the company in relation to which the conduct alleged to render the director unfit is said to have occurred, the court must decide whether that conduct is such to render the respondent unfit to be concerned in the management of companies in general, regardless of size or structure.[90]

The court is also able to consider the defendant's conduct in relation to other companies when determining whether the defendant is unfit, and such companies need not be insolvent.[91] There is no need for the conduct relied upon in relation to the collateral companies to be the same as or similar to that adduced in relation to the "lead company". The only connection necessary is that the defendant had been a director of the collateral companies and that his conduct as a director of the collateral company tended to show unfitness.[92] The conduct of the defendant in relation to collateral companies will only be looked at cumulatively with those matters in relation to the insolvent company for the purpose of finding additional matters of complaint. The respondent will not be able to set up his conduct as a director in relation to other companies which have been successful in the period running up to his trial in order to prevent a disqualification order being made.[93]

In *Re Surrey Leisure Ltd*,[94] the Court of Appeal rejected the argument that there could be only one "lead company" in an application for an order under Section 6 CDDA 1986. The decision was based upon there being no provision in CDDA 1986 which imposed a limit on the number of lead companies on which the applicant for a disqualification order

---

[90] *Re Polly Peck International plc (No. 2)* [1994] 1 BCLC 574.
[91] Where a collateral company is solvent, the factors listed in Part II of Schedule 1 CDDA 1986 will not be relevant.
[92] *Secretary of State for Trade and Industry v Ivens* [1997] 2 BCLC 334.
[93] *Re Bath Glass* [1988] BCLC 329; *Re Grayan Building Services Ltd* [1995] Ch 241.
[94] [1999] 2 BCLC 457.

could rely. It was held that it would be inappropriate for the court to impose a maximum on the number of lead companies in these circumstances as it would not advance the cause of public protection, and permitting more than one lead company would not give rise to any unfair procedure.

13.7 Period of disqualification

In the event that the court finds a director unfit on an application made under Section 6 CDDA 1986, it must impose a disqualification period of at least two years. In contrast, where a director is found unfit on an application brought under Section 8 CDDA 1986, the court can exercise its discretion against making a disqualification order in an appropriate case.

In the leading case of *Re Sevenoaks Stationers (Retail) Ltd* ,[95] the Court of Appeal laid down certain guidelines, since adopted by the courts, which divide the possible 15-year period into three brackets:

(a) the minimum bracket of two to five years was for those cases where, though disqualification was mandatory, the case was not very serious;
(b) the middle bracket of six to 10 years was for those cases which were serious but did not fall within the top bracket;
(c) the top bracket of over 10 years was for particularly serious cases. An example given was a case where a director who had already been disqualified was disqualified again.

The Court of Appeal has recently stated that it is not appropriate or necessary to perform a detailed comparison with the facts of other cases when determining the period of disqualification.[96]

When determining the appropriate period of disqualification the court will take into account any mitigating factors which are present. These factors can be either extenuating circumstances accompanying the misconduct, such as reliance on professional advice or an absence of personal gain, or factors which are unconnected to the misconduct such as a low likelihood of reoffending or personal loss in the failure

---

[95] [1991] Ch 164.
[96] *Re Westmid Packaging Services Ltd* [1998] 2 All ER 124.

of the company (the former type of mitigating factor will have more weight).

13.8 Disqualification undertakings

The Insolvency Act 2000 ("IA 2000") came into force on 2 April 2001. One of the main changes effected by this Act was the amendment of CDDA 1986 so as to permit the Secretary of State for Trade and Industry to accept disqualification undertakings from directors without the need for a court hearing. This new procedure avoids the need for the costly *Carecraft* procedure that the courts had developed previously.[97]

Section 1A CDDA 1986 as amended provides that the circumstances specified in Sections 7 and 8 CDDA 1986 the Secretary of State may accept a disqualification undertaking, that is to say an undertaking by any person that, for a period specified in the undertaking, the person will not be a director of a company, act as receiver of a company's property, or in any way, whether directly or indirectly, be concerned or take part in the promotion, formation or management of a company unless (in each case) he has the leave of a court, and will not act as an insolvency practitioner.

The maximum period which may be specified in a disqualification undertaking is 15 years, and the minimum period which may be specified in a disqualification undertaking under Section 7 is two years (Section 1A(2) CDDA 1986). Where a disqualification undertaking by a person who is already subject to such an undertaking or to a disqualification order is accepted, the periods specified in those undertakings or (as the case may be) the undertaking and the order shall run concurrently (Section 1A(3) CDDA 1986).

In determining whether to accept a disqualification undertaking by any person, the Secretary of State may take account of matters other than criminal convictions notwithstanding that the person may be criminally liable in respect of those matters (Section 1A(4) CDDA 1986).

A disqualification undertaking therefore corresponds in terms to the order which the court may make under Section 6 CDDA 1986 and has the same consequences. The director will be prohibited by the undertaking from acting as a director or as a receiver of a company's property

---

[97] *Re Carecraft Construction Co Ltd* [1994] 1 WLR 172.

Disqualification of Directors

or as an insolvency practitioner for the period stated in the undertaking, and any breach of the undertaking during the period of disqualification would constitute a criminal offence under Section 13 of CDDA 1986.

The preliminary considerations are also the same. Section 7(1) CDDA 1986 requires the Secretary of State to form the view that it is expedient in the public interest that a disqualification order should be made against a person under Section 6 before initiating proceedings for such an order. Section 7(2A) CDDA 1986 now provides as follows:

> "If it appears to the Secretary of State that the conditions mentioned in Section 6(1) are satisfied as respects any person who has offered to give him a disqualification undertaking, he may accept the undertaking if it appears to him that it is expedient in the public interest that he should do so (instead of applying, or proceeding with an application, for a disqualification order)."

The Secretary of State must form the opinion that the conditions specified in Section 6(1) are satisfied before becoming entitled to accept a disqualification undertaking. He must therefore apply his mind to the evidence of conduct and unfitness in precisely the same way as the court is required to do when considering an application for a disqualification order. In considering the issue of conduct the court is required to have regard to the matters specified in Schedule 1 to the 1986 Act which include such things as:

(a) misfeasance and breach of any fiduciary or other duty by the director;
(b) any misapplication or retention by the director or any conduct by the director giving rise to an obligation to account for any money or other property of the company; and
(c) the extent of the director's responsibility for the company entering into any transaction liable to be set aside under Part XVI IA 1986.

In cases where the company has become insolvent the court is required to have regard to the extent of the director's responsibility for the causes of the company's insolvency and his responsibility for any failure by the company to supply any goods or services which have been paid for whether in whole or in part. These provisions now also apply in relation to the acceptance of a disqualification undertaking. Section 9(1A) CDDA 1986 provides that in determining whether he may accept a disqualification undertaking from any person, the Secretary of State shall, as respects the person's conduct as a director of any company concerned, have regard in particular to the matters mentioned in Part 1, Schedule 1 CDDA 1986 and, where the company has become insolvent, to the matters mentioned in Part II of Schedule 1.

It is therefore clear that before the Secretary of State can determine whether it is expedient in the public interest that he should accept the undertaking which is offered, he must first satisfy himself that the necessary basis for disqualification is made out.

CDDA 1986 as amended also contains provisions for the release or modification of any disqualification undertakings that are accepted. Section 1A CDDA 1986 quoted above makes the prohibition contained in the undertaking subject to the leave of the court and Section 17 CDDA 1986 sets out the procedure to be followed in cases where leave is applied for. On the hearing of an application for leave for the purposes of Section 1(1)(a) or 1A(1)(a), the Secretary of State must appear and call the attention of the court to any matters which seem to him to be relevant, and may himself give evidence or call witnesses (Section 17(5) CDDA 1986).

A director who has given a disqualification undertaking may also apply to the court under Section 8A CDDA 1986 for the period of disqualification to be reduced or for the undertaking to cease to be in force. On the hearing of an application under Subsection (1), the Secretary of State shall appear and call the attention of the court to any matters which seem to him to be relevant, and may himself give evidence or call witnesses (Section 8A(2) CDDA 1986).

Section 18(2) CDDA 1986 requires the Secretary of State to maintain a register of disqualification orders and of cases in which leave has been granted to vary an order or a disqualification undertaking or for the undertaking to cease to be in force. In addition Section 18(2A) now provides that the Secretary of State shall include in the register such particulars as he considers appropriate for disqualification undertakings accepted by him under Section 7 or 8 and of cases in which leave has been granted as mentioned in Subsection (1)(d).

Sections 1A and 17 CDDA 1986, as amended, are deemed by Section 21(2) of the Act to be included in Parts I–VII IA 1986 for the purposes of various Sections of that Act. These include Section 411 which contains the power to make insolvency rules. Section 411(4) IA 1986 provides that rules made under that Section must be made by statutory instrument subject to annulment in pursuance of a resolution of either House of Parliament.

In *Re Blackspur Group plc*,[98] the court was asked to consider whether the Secretary of State was entitled to refuse to accept a disqualification undertaking without an accompanying statement of unfit conduct. It was held that the Secretary of State did have power to require such a statement and was entitled to refuse to accept a disqualification undertaking unless such a statement was provided. This decision means that the *Carecraft* procedure may continue to be utilised in limited circumstances. For this reason, it is necessary to outline the details of the *Carecraft* procedure.

In cases where the director determines that he does not wish to contest the proceedings, the parties may enter into negotiations to reach a statement of facts which are either agreed or uncontested. The statement will also include the period of disqualification or a range of a period of disqualification that the parties accept the facts to justify. The adoption of the procedure is dependent upon the parties being able to draft an agreed statement. This statement will be placed before the court, and the court will be requested to exercise its discretion to make an order based only upon the facts in the statement. The use of the procedure is now enshrined in paragraph 13 of the Practice Direction. The Practice Direction further provides that where the court makes a disqualification order under the *Carecraft* procedure, the *Carecraft* statement should be annexed to the order.

The ultimate discretion of whether to make an order on a *Carecraft* basis lies with the court, and this gives rise to a need for the statement to provide for its status in the event that the court refuses to deal with the application on this basis. This should ensure that any admissions of fact made by the director in the statement cannot be used at the full hearing of the application.

There is no critical time by which a director must agree to the use of the *Carecraft* procedure or otherwise face a full trial of the application for his disqualification. In the interest of costs, however, it will be prudent for the director to determine whether he is amenable to compromising the proceedings by use of the *Carecraft* procedure at the earliest opportunity. To this end the defendant should prepare his evidence at the earliest

---

[98] [2001] 1 BCLC 653.

possible stage in order to evaluate the relative strengths and weaknesses of the case against him. The Secretary of State will not usually be prepared to enter into negotiations until after he has received the director's affidavit evidence in opposition to his application. It is advisable that all negotiations which are focused upon agreeing a *Carecraft* statement should be conducted on a without prejudice basis. This will ensure that in the event that the parties are unable to reach an agreement, the negotiations will not be available to the court at the full trial of the application.

In addition to setting out those admitted or undisputed facts which are said to justify a finding of unfitness, the *Carecraft* statement should also set out any mitigating circumstances relied upon by the parties. The willingness of the director to adopt the *Carecraft* procedure may, in itself, constitute a mitigating factor.

The law relating to disqualification undertakings will be modified when the new competition provisions of the CDDA 1986 come into force. Section 9B CDDA 1986 was inserted by Section 204(2) of the Enterprise Act 2002 to create "competition disqualification undertakings". At the time of writing, it is not yet in force. When it comes into force, it will apply where:

(a) the OFT thinks that a company has committed or is committing a breach of competition law; and
(b) the OFT also thinks that a director of that company is unfit to be concerned in the management of a company; and
(c) the director in question offers to give the OFT a disqualification undertaking.

The OFT will have a discretion to accept a disqualification undertaking from the director instead of applying for or proceeding with an application for a disqualification order. The maximum period that may be specified in a disqualification undertaking will be 15 years.

13.9 Discontinuance of proceedings and applications for a stay of the proceedings by the defendant

The Secretary of State may discontinue disqualification proceedings at any time by filing and serving a notice of discontinuance on each defendant specifying against which defendants the claim is discontinued.[99] When the director wishes to set aside the notice he must make an application to do so within 28 days of the notice of discontinuance being served on him. When the director has filed a defence prior to the discontinuance of the proceedings and the Secretary of State seeks to make another claim arising out of the same or substantially the same facts, the Secretary of State will need the permission of the court to make the claim.[100] The costs incurred by the director in defending the proceedings up to the date of service of the notice will, unless the court otherwise orders, be paid by the Secretary of State.[101]

The decision of the Court of Appeal in *Re Barings plc (No. 3)*[102] shows that the fact that a defendant to disqualification proceedings has previously successfully resisted disciplinary proceedings brought against him by the Securities and Futures Authority ("the SFA") will not necessarily be a bar to the commencement of subsequent disqualification proceedings against him. The defendant applied for a stay of the disqualification proceedings on the ground that the prosecution of the proceedings against him would infringe the principle of double jeopardy (or the collateral attack principle), since he had already successfully resisted much the same, or substantially the same, charges as were made by the Secretary of State in the disqualification proceedings, or on the alternative ground that, in the circumstances, the prosecution of the proceedings against him would be unfair, unjust and oppressive.

The Court of Appeal held that the court would stay proceedings on the ground of abuse of process where to allow them to continue would bring the administration of justice into disrepute among right-thinking people. On the facts, however, the issues on which the court would need to adjudicate in the disqualification proceedings were not the same as those which had already been investigated and adjudicated on in the SFA proceedings. The charges in the SFA proceedings were that the defendant had failed to act with the due care and skill of a prudent manager. In the disqualification proceedings, the relevant question was whether his conduct as a director had fallen so far short of the competence required of a director that the court ought to reach the conclusion that he was unfit

---

[99] Under CPR Part 38. In circumstances where any party to the disqualification proceedings has given an undertaking to the court, the Secretary of State will need the permission of the court to discontinue the proceedings.
[100] CPR 38.7.
[101] CPR 38.6.
[102] [1999] 1 BCLC 226.

to be concerned in the management of any company, and the proceedings would involve an investigation into what responsibility he had as a director for his company's insolvency.

13.10 Appeals

A defendant may appeal a disqualification order on the ground that it should not have been made or on the ground that the period imposed was excessive. An appeal may also be made by the Secretary of State on the ground that the period imposed was too lenient. An appeal from an order made by a County Court Judge, or a District Judge, or a Registrar of the High Court will lie to a single judge of the High Court. Appeals from a High Court Judge will lie to the Court of Appeal, but permission is required.

The appeal will be a true appeal, rather than a hearing *de novo*, with the result that the appellate court will not depart from the trial judge's findings of primary fact on the oral evidence of the witnesses unless such finding was perverse. Similarly, the actual order or period of disqualification will not be interfered with unless the trial judge can be shown to have erred in principle.

It is possible for a disqualified person to seek a stay of the order pending his appeal. The presence of a provision within the CDDA 1986 enabling the court to grant permission to act as a director notwithstanding a disqualification order will lead to an application for such permission being the more appropriate course, rather than an application for a stay of the disqualification order.

13.11 The effect of a disqualification order

All disqualification orders are recorded in a register kept by the Secretary of State, which also includes details of any relevant permission to act granted by the courts. On the making of a disqualification order the person disqualified should ensure that he resigns from any offices which he is now prohibited from holding by Section 1(1) CDDA 1986.[103]

---

[103] In the event that the company has adopted Article 81(a) of Table A of the Companies (Tables A to F) Regulations 1985, the articles will provide that he will vacate the office of director upon becoming "prohibited by law from being a director". The effect of this provision will be to terminate the person's office on the making of the disqualification order.

Section 1(1) CDDA 1986 provides that a disqualification order is one that prevents the person subject to the order from acting as a director,[104] liquidator or administrator,[105] a receiver or manager of a company's property,[106] or being directly or indirectly concerned or taking part in the promotion, formation or management of a company.[107] Section 1 CDDA 1986 was amended by IA 2000 to prevent disqualified directors from acting as insolvency practitioners.

The range of activities prohibited by a disqualification order is very wide. The court does not have jurisdiction to order that the disqualified person is only prohibited from doing certain of the acts specified in Section 1(1), it is an all or nothing situation.[108] In *R v Ward*,[109] the court held that there was no jurisdiction to limit a disqualification order to the holding of directorships in a public company. Furthermore, the court does not have jurisdiction to impose additional prohibitions upon the disqualified person.

A company for the purposes of Section 1(1) CDDA 1986 includes any company which may be wound up under Part V IA 1986, which has the effect of extending the prohibition extends to foreign companies which could be wound up in the UK as unregistered companies. *See* 13.4 above for a discussion of the extraterritorial scope of the disqualification prohibition.[110] The disqualification period takes effect from the date of the order, but unless the court otherwise directs, the prohibition imposed by the order begins on the twenty-first day after the day on which the order is made.[111] The prohibition will apply to companies limited by guarantee and unlimited companies, as well as private and public companies limited by shares.[112] However, the prohibition does not extend to preventing the disqualified person from carrying on business as a partner

---

[104] Section 1(1)(a) CDDA 1986.
[105] Section 1(1)(b) CDDA 1986.
[106] Section 1(1)(a) CDDA 1986.
[107] Section 1(1)(a) CDDA 1986.
[108] *Re Gower Enterprises Ltd (No. 2)* [1995] 2 BCLC 201.
[109] *The Times*, 10 August 2001.
[110] The prohibition imposed upon an undischarged bankrupt is rather more narrow in scope, as the foreign company must have an established place of business in Great Britain (Section 22(2) CDDA 1986).
[111] Rule 9 of the Disqualification Rules, paragraph 16 of the Practice Direction.
[112] This is the effect of Section 22(9) CDDA 1986.

in a partnership.[113] It is suggested that this is the case because carrying on business as a partnership does not allow those concerned to take advantage of the concept of limited liability.

The disqualified person will be prohibited from acting as a director regardless of the title he uses, with the result that he will be in breach of the order if he is acting as a director even if the title he uses is, for example, "trustee".[114] It is also irrelevant whether the person is a *de jure* director or a *de facto* director. Furthermore, a disqualification order on the grounds of unfitness will result in the person being prohibited from acting as a shadow director in relation to a company.[115] A disqualification order will also prevent the person from acting as a director of a building society,[116] and as a member of the committee of management or officer of an incorporated friendly society.[117]

The other prohibition in Section 1(1) CDDA 1986 which merits further consideration is that of being directly or indirectly concerned or taking part in the promotion, formation or management of a company. There is no statutory definition for the terms "promotion", "formation" or "management", with the result that interpretation of these vital terms is left to the courts. The concepts of "taking part in" promotion, formation

---

[113] This conclusion is supported by the references in the authorities to a disqualification order leading to the loss of limited liability (e.g. *Re Probe Data Systems (No. 3) Ltd* [1991] BCLC 586, at 593), and the fact that the Insolvent Partnerships Order 1994 fails to make any provision for disqualification from acting as a partner, although it specifically extends the CDDA 1986 so that an order under Sections 6–10 CDDA 1986 may be based upon conduct in relation to an insolvent partnership.

[114] Section 22(4) CDDA 1986.

[115] Section 22(4) CDDA 1986. The term "shadow director" is defined in Section 22(5) CDDA 1986 as:

"a person in accordance with whose directions or instructions the directors of the company are accustomed to act (but so that a person is not deemed a shadow director by reason only that the directors act on advice given by him in a professional capacity."

Although CDDA 1986 does not provide expressly that persons who are disqualified on grounds other than unfitness are prohibited from acting as shadow directors, it is suggested that such conduct would fall within the prohibition being concerned in or taking part in the management of the company.

[116] Section 22A CDDA 1986.

[117] Section 22B CDDA 1986.

Disqualification of Directors

and management, and being "concerned in" promotion, formation and management are distinct[118] and may either be satisfied by direct or indirect conduct.

It is suggested that the courts approach the task of construction by bearing in mind the protective purpose of the making of a disqualification order and will, therefore, give the words a liberal interpretation.[119] It is likely that any involvement in the internal or external management of a company will constitute a breach of the disqualification order. In these circumstances, a person who is unsure whether his proposed conduct would be in breach of his disqualification should seriously consider applying to the court for permission to act in such a manner.

Section 390(4) IA 1986 provides that an insolvency practitioner who is subject to a disqualification order is automatically disqualified from acting as an insolvency practitioner. The effect of this provision is that the impact of the order will be wider than that envisaged by Section 1(1) CDDA 1986. The prohibition will extend to acting, for example, as a provisional liquidator, administrative receiver, trustee in bankruptcy and supervisor of a corporate or individual voluntary arrangement. It is an offence under IA 1986 to act as an insolvency practitioner without the relevant qualifications.

A person subject to a disqualification order is also unable to act as a charity trustee[120] or as a trustee of an occupational pension scheme established under a trust.[121]

In the event that a person acts in breach of a disqualification order he is liable to both civil and criminal sanctions. He is liable on conviction on indictment to imprisonment for not more than two years or a fine or both;[122] and on summary conviction to imprisonment for not more than six months or a fine not exceeding the statutory maximum or both.[123]

Where a body corporate which is subject to a disqualification order acts in contravention of the order and it is proved that the offence occurred

---

[118] *R v Campbell* (1984) 78 Cr App Rep 95.
[119] *R v Campbell* (1984) 78 Cr App Rep 95, at 98.
[120] Section 72(1)(f) Charities Act 1993.
[121] Section 29(1)(f) Pensions Act 1995.
[122] Section 13(a) CDDA 1986.
[123] Section 13(b) CDDA 1986.

with the consent or connivance of, or was attributable to any neglect on the part of any director, manager, secretary or other similar officer, or any person purporting to act in such a capacity, he is also guilty of the offence.

The offence committed by acting in breach of a disqualification order is one of strict liability, with the consequence that an honest belief that the acts did not breach the order will not be a sustainable defence.[124]

Section 15 CDDA 1986 provides for civil liability in circumstances where a disqualified person acts and is involved in the management of a company.[125] By virtue of Section 15(1)(a) CDDA 1986 the person will be personally liable for all the debts and other liabilities of the company which are incurred at a time when he was involved in the management of the company.[126] Section 15(1)(b) imposes civil liability on others involved in the management of the company who act, or are willing to act, on instructions given by a disqualified person without permission of the court if they know the person to be disqualified. The liability imposed is personal liability for all the debts and other liabilities of the company which are incurred at a time when the person was acting or was willing to act on instructions given by the disqualified person.[127] For this purpose, once it is shown that the person acted, or was willing to act, on the instructions of a person whom he knew to be subject to a disqualification order, there is a rebuttable presumption that he was willing at any time thereafter to act on any instructions given by the disqualified person.[128]

The liability imposed by Section 15 is joint and several liability with the company and any other person who may be personally liable for the company's debts. Those who are appointed directors in place of the disqualified person should be particularly aware of this potential liability. They must ensure that they do not merely act as the nominee for the disqualified person, or act in any way which enables the disqualified person to play a role in the management of the company.

---

[124] *R v Brockley* [1994] 1 BCLC 606.
[125] "Management" is defined as: "a director of the company or if he is concerned, whether directly or indirectly, or takes part, in the management of the company" (Section 15(4) CDDA 1986).
[126] Section 15(3)(a) CDDA 1986.
[127] Section 15(3)(b) CDDA 1986.
[128] Section 15(5) CDDA 1986.

13.12 Applications for permission to act by a disqualified director

Although the making of a disqualification order prohibits the disqualified director from engaging in any of the conduct specified in Section 1(1) CDDA 1986, such prohibition is specifically stated to subsist "without the leave of the court".[129] This ensures that in deserving cases, a person will not be prevented from acting as a director for the entirety of the period of his disqualification.

The procedure which governs an application for permission to act is found in Section 17 CDDA 1986. The Practice Direction provides that the application will be made by a Part 8 claim form,[130] or by an application notice in existing disqualification proceedings.[131] If possible the application should be made immediately upon the making of the order, or at least within the 21-day period before the disqualification order commences, as this will enable the applicant to request permission to continue to act in the proposed capacity pending the hearing of his application.[132] The respondent to an application for permission will be the person who made the application for the disqualification order.[133]

When considering an application for permission, the court will be mindful not to grant permission too freely for fear of undermining either the protection of the public[134] or the deterrent effect served by the making of a disqualification order.[135] The case law dealing with applications by disqualified directors for permission to act reveals that the court will not usually entertain an application for the prohibition simply to be lifted.

---

[129] The disqualification imposed upon an undischarged bankrupt by Section 11(1) CDDA 1986 and under Section 12(2) CDDA 1986 is also expressed to take effect "except with leave of the court".

[130] A claim form issued pursuant to Part 8 of the Civil Procedure Rules.

[131] Paragraph 20 of the Practice Direction.

[132] The evidence in support of the application must be by affidavit (paragraph 22 of the Practice Direction).

[133] In circumstances where the applicant for the disqualification order was not the Secretary of State, the Secretary of State for Trade and Industry should also be made a respondent to the application. For the avoidance of doubt, paragraph 23 of the Practice Direction provides that in all applications the claim form or application notice and supporting evidence must be served on the Secretary of State.

[134] *Re Barings plc (No. 4)* [1999] 1 All ER 262.

[135] *Re Tech Textiles Ltd* [1998] 1 BCLC 259.

Rather, the court will normally only grant permission in relation to a specific company or companies.

The applicant will bear the burden of proof in establishing that the case is one in which it is appropriate for the court to give permission. In cases where the court is prepared to give permission, it will only do so subject to conditions which it believes are necessary to give the public sufficient protection.[136] The court is likely, on balance, to be less ready to grant permission to the applicant to act if the disqualification order made against him was in the "higher bracket". The adoption of this approach by the courts reflects the need to protect the public from the conduct of the individual which is evidenced by the making of the disqualification order by the court in the first place. The cases show that the chances of the application being successful are enhanced where the application relates to a company with which the applicant was involved at the time of the disqualification order, but his conduct in relation to the company did not form part of the disqualification proceedings.

The court will look to all of the circumstances of the case when determining whether to give permission, and its discretion is not fettered in any way.[137] The case law reveals that two factors will have an important bearing on the exercise of the court's discretion:

(a) whether there is a need for the applicant to act contrary to the prohibition imposed by Section 1(1) CDDA 1986; and
(b) whether the public would be adequately protected in the event that the court gives permission.

The applicant will need to address the grounds upon which his original disqualification was based to show that there are sufficient controls in place at the company in respect of which he seeks permission to act as a director, to convince the court that the misconduct is unlikely to occur again. The court will wish to be informed of the financial position of the company in order to be:

---

[136] Although there is no provision in CDDA 1986 which gives the court power to attach conditions to the grant of permission, the case law reveals that the courts have consistently adopted such a course. Conditions commonly ordered include the imposition of controls at board level, for example by the appointment of an independent accountant as a finance director, an obligation to hold board meetings at monthly intervals, and an obligation to have the monthly management accounts inspected by the auditors.

[137] *Re Dawes & Henderson (Agencies) Ltd (No. 2)* [1999] 2 BCLC 317.

(a) satisfied that it is trading successfully;
(b) satisfied that the company has adequate financial controls;
(c) informed of the risks inherent in the company's business; and
(d) satisfied that the company is being managed in accordance with the standards prescribed by the relevant legislation and the courts.[138]

In *Re Barings plc (No. 3)*,[139] Scott V-C heard an application by the former Chief Executive Officer of Barings for permission to act as a non-executive director in respect of three private companies. The application was made before the disqualification order made against Mr Norris (it should be noted that there were no allegations of dishonesty or fraudulent impropriety against him, only ones of incompetence). Scott V-C granted permission as he held that there was no risk of the recurrence of the defects apparent in Mr Norris' previous conduct. This was especially so in a case where the applicant was not seeking to be given permission to exercise any executive responsibilities in relation to the companies. Permission was therefore given on the condition that Mr Norris remained an unpaid non-executive director and that he be barred from entering into a service contract with the companies. Scott V-C stated:

> "The improprieties which have led to and required the making of a disqualification order must be kept clearly in mind when considering whether a grant of s 17 leave should be made. If the conduct of a director has been tainted by any dishonesty, if the company in question has been allowed to continue trading while obviously hopelessly insolvent, if a director has been withdrawing from a struggling company excessive amounts by way of remuneration in anticipation of the company's collapse and, in effect, living off the company's creditors, and if a disqualification order were then made, these circumstances would loom very large on any s 17 application. The court would, I am sure, have in mind the need to protect the public from any repetition of the conduct in question. That conduct, and the protection of the public from it, would have been the major factor requiring the imposition of the disqualification."[140]

He rejected the submission that the applicant had to show a "need" to act as a prerequisite for success, and held that the balancing exercise was

---

[138] For example the obligations in Part VII of the Companies Act 1985.
[139] [1999] 1 BCLC 262.
[140] At 265 c–e.

between the protection of the public and the desire of the applicant to act as a director.

In *Re Britannia Homes Centres Ltd*,[141] the registrar's decision to grant leave was overturned on appeal on the grounds that it undermined the effect of the disqualification order. Leave would have meant that the disqualification order had no practical effect whatsoever because the respondent would have been trading in the same way having previously managed a series of one-man companies, all of which had gone into liquidation.

In the event that the applicant is successful, the order of the court granting permission to act, along with any conditions imposed, must be notified to the Secretary of State for entry on the register of disqualification orders. Conditions which will commonly be attached to the grant of permission include the appointment of an independent accountant as a finance director, an obligation to hold regular board meetings, the auditing of monthly management accounts and the removal of the applicant from the company's bank mandate.

13.13 Conclusion

The brief analysis of the law of disqualification which has been afforded by this Chapter demonstrates that the imposition of disqualification orders is an essential part of preventing the abuse of the status afforded by a limited liability company. Directors of companies must ensure that they are fully aware of their duties, whether statutory or common law, and that they act in accordance with such duties. In the event that directors fail to conduct themselves in the required manner, the imposition of a disqualification order is vitally important for the protection of the creditors of limited liability companies and for deterring from similar conduct others who hold the office of director.

---

[141] [2001] 2 BCLC 63.

Index

NB: All references are to chapter number followed by paragraph number, e.g. 6.5.2.1 refers to Chapter 6, paragraph 5.2.1.

ABI (Association of British Insurers)
  Institutional Shareholders'
    Committee, representation on
    2.1
  remuneration of directors
    Combined Code requirements
    6.5.2.1
    new Guidelines 6.3.3
  service contracts, limits on term
    length 6.3.3
  termination payments statement *see*
    **Best Practice on Executive
    Contracts and Severance
    (ABI/NAPF joint statement)**
accounting/reporting
  Companies Bill 9.4.3.4
acquisitions
  appointment of directors 2.2.3
**Action Plan on Modernising Company
  Law (European Commission)**
  3.4.2.3
administrative receivers
  company books, access to 8.3.2.1
ADR (Alternative Dispute Resolution)
  10.5.2
age qualifications
  Companies Bill 2.9.1.7
  statutory 2.3.1
  termination of office 2.4.3
AGM (annual general meeting)
  criticisms 9.3.5
  opting in (Companies Bill) 2.9.1.2
  principles as to best practice 9.3.5
  proxies, rights of 9.4.3.3
  retirement of directors 2.4.2
Alternative Dispute Resolution (ADR)
  10.5.2
anti-avoidance provisions
  fair dealing 5.3, 5.8.5

  holding company transactions
    5.8.6.5
  minor transactions 5.8.6.4
  small loans 5.8.6.3
**Anti-Terrorism, Crime and Security Act
  2001** *see* **ATCSA (Anti-Terrorism,
  Crime and Security Act) 2001**
appeals
  disqualification of directors 13.10
appointment of directors
  by court 2.2.5
  by directors 2.1, 2.2.2
  entrenchment 2.2.6
  invalid, effect 2.3.9
  method
    appointment by court 2.2.5
    appointment by directors 2.1, 2.2.2
    appointment by shareholders 2.1,
      2.2.3
    appointment by third parties 2.2.4
    entrenchment 2.2.6
    first director(s) 2.2.1
  new companies 2.2.1
  notification
    company stationery 2.5.4
    to company 2.5.1
    to Registrar of Companies 2.5.2
    to UK Listing Authority 2.5.3
  retirement and reappointment 2.2.2,
    2.4.2
  by shareholders 2.1, 2.2.3, 9.1
  by third parties 2.2.4
  see also **removal of directors**
articles of association
  alternate directors 2.6
  amendments (disputes) 10.2.1.4
  appointment of directors
    retirement/re-election 2.4.2
    by shareholders 2.2.3

431

by third parties 2.2.4
fair dealing, disclosure of interests 5.4
governance systems 9.2
memorandum, contradicting 8.1.1
notification of board meetings
  10.1.1.1
qualification of directors 2.3.5
replacement, Companies Bill 2.9.1.1
service contracts, authorisation 6.2
ultra vires acts, beyond directors'
  authority 4.1.2
vacation of office 2.4.4
assets
  misappropriation 10.4.1.7
  non-cash, approval of transfers 5.6
associate
  defined 7.6.2
Association of British Insurers (ABI)
  see **ABI (Association of British Insurers)**
Association of Investment Trust Companies
  Institutional Shareholders'
  Committee, representation on
  2.1
ATCSA (Anti-Terrorism, Crime and Security Act) 2001
  criminal liability 3.4.3.2
audit committees
  Combined Code 9.3.4
  Smith report *see* **Smith Report**
Australia
  directors' duties 1.2
  economic analysis 1.2.1

back-to-back arrangements
  anti-avoidance provisions 5.8.5
balance of probabilities
  market abuse 7.2.5
Bank of England
  investigations 12.6
Barings **case**
  care, skill and diligence 3.3
  delegation of powers 8.2.5
  disqualification proceedings 13.12
BCCI
  corporate failure 9.2
Beckett, Margaret 9.2

Beherrschungsvertrag (domination
  agreement) 3.6
Belgian Companies Code
  changes to 3.6
Best Practice on Executive Contracts and Severance (ABI/NAPF joint statement)
  compensation for loss of office
    early termination of service contract
    6.7.1
  golden parachutes/handshakes
    6.7.3
  fair dealing 5.2
  Higgs Review and 6.7.5.1
  service contracts, limits on length
    6.3.3
betting duty
  Crown debts 4.5.1.2
beyond reasonable doubt
  market abuse 7.2.5
Bills of Exchange Act (1882)
  company liability 4.4.4
boards of directors
  appointments 2.9.2.3
  shareholder rights 2.2.3
  composition 2.9.2.2
  corporate governance, defined 9.1
  disputes with members
    Foss v *Harbottle see Foss* v
    Harbottle, **rule in**
    shareholder agreements 10.2.1.5
    shareholders' personal rights
    10.2.1.1
    statutory rights 10.2.1.6
    transactions outside company's
    powers 10.2.1.3
  disputes within
    deadlock 10.1.3
    exclusion from proceedings
    10.1.1.1
    majority standpoint 10.1.1
    minority standpoint 10.1.2
    removal of directors 10.1.1.2
    notification of meetings 10.1.1.1
  role 2.9.2.1
  shareholders' role distinguished 9.2
  size 2.9.2.2
  structure 9.3.1, 9.4.2

Index

body corporate, dealings with
  connected persons 5.12
Bullock Report
  industrial democracy 1.2
burden of proof
  market abuse 7.2.5
business judgment rule
  duties of directors 1.2, 3.2.2.7

Cadbury Report
  accountability/audit requirement
    9.3.2
  background 9.2
  chairman, role of 9.3.1
  Code of Best Practice 9.2
  corporate governance
    meaning 9.1
    shareholder/board relationship 9.2
  delegation of authority
    general 8.2.1
    to committees 8.2.2
    to individual executives 8.2.3
  non-executive directors 3.3
  objective of Committee 9.2
care, skill and diligence
  Barings case 3.3
  case law 3.3
    chairman, special duties required of
      3.3.1
    codes 3.3
    experts, reliance on 3.3
    general principles, proposed
      statement 3.5.2.4
    Higgs Review 3.3.2
    regulatory background 1.2.2
    standards 1.2.2, 3.3
Carecraft **procedure**
  disqualification of directors 13.8
certificate of incorporation 2.2.1
chairman
  ostensible authority 8.2.6
  role of 9.3.1
  special duties required of 3.3.1
charities
  fiduciary duties 3.2.2.3
chartered directors 2.3.8
circulars to shareholders
  takeovers 4.6.3

City Code on Takeovers and Mergers
  see **Takeover Code**
civil liability
  fraudulent trading 4.7.2.2
Civil Procedure Rules (CPR)
  derivative actions, procedure 10.3.7
  disqualification proceedings
    commencement out of time 13.5.4
    procedure on application 13.5.3
    relevant rules 13.5.1
  unfair prejudice
    claims 10.5.2
    procedure 10.4.4
civil proceedings
  self-incrimination, privilege against
    12.10
**Co-ordinating Group on Audit and
    Accounting Issues**
  financial statements 3.4.2.1
Code of Best Practice
  Cadbury Committee 9.2
**Combined Code of Corporate
    Governance**
  accountability 9.3.2
  appointment of directors, public
    companies 2.2.2
  audit 9.3.2
  audit committee 9.3.4
  background 9.2
  board structure 9.3.1
  compensation, loss of office 6.7.4
  delegation of authority
    general 8.2.1
    to committees 8.2.2
  disclosure requirements 9.3.5
  financial statements 3.4.2.1
  going concern requirement 9.3.2
  Hampel Committee 9.3
  and Higgs Review 3.3.2, 9.3
  internal control 8.2.5, 9.3.3
  listed companies 2.3.7
  non-executive directors 3.3, 9.4.2
  remuneration of directors
    content requirements 6.5.2
    disclosure requirements 6.5.4.1,
      6.5.4.3
    performance related 6.5.2
    remuneration committee, role 6.5.3

433

salary 6.5.1.1
retirement and re-election of directors 2.4.2, 9.3.1
service contracts, limits on term length 6.3.2
Shareholder Activism, ISC Code 2.9.2.6
shareholders 9.3.5
Committee on Corporate Governance
Combined Code 2.2.2
Companies Act 1985
compensation, loss of office 6.7.2
disclosure requirements
circumstances where obligation not discharged 7.6.1.5
Exchange, duty to notify 7.6.1.7
existing/subsequent interests 7.6.1.1
false statements 7.6.1.3
'interest', meaning 7.6.1.2
period for making notification 7.6.1.4
register of directors' interests 7.6.1.6
remuneration of directors 6.5.4.1
spouses/children 7.6.1.3
fair dealing, remedies for breach (s 330) 5.10
Part X
company, defined 5.1
connected persons, Law Commission Consultation Paper 5.12
director, defined 5.1
duties of directors 1.2.2
economic analysis 1.2.1
holding company, defined 5.1
reform proposals 1.4
subsidiary, defined 5.1
remuneration of directors, disclosure requirements 6.5.4.1
Table A *see* **Table A (Companies Act 1985)**
Companies Bill, draft (2002)
accounting 9.4.3.4
age of requirements 2.9.1.7
AGM requirement, opting in 2.9.1.2
background 9.2, 9.4.3.1

company stationery 2.9.1.8
corporate directors 2.9.1.4
disclosure of relationships 2.9.1.5
memorandum and articles, replacement 2.9.1.1
position of directors 9.4.3.2
position of shareholders 9.4.3.3
qualifications of directors 2.9.1.7
reporting 9.4.3.4
service contracts 2.9.1.6
shareholder resolutions 2.9.1.3
training of directors 2.9.1.7
company accounts
access to 8.3.2.1
see also **accounting/reporting; financial statements**
company books, access to
company accounts 8.3.2.1
by directors 8.3.1
inspection, rights of 8.3.1
liquidators 8.3.2.1
register of charges 8.3.2.1
register of directors' interests in shares/debentures 8.3.2.1
register of directors/secretaries 8.3.2.1
by third parties 8.3.2
general viewing 8.3.2.1
company debts
costs, unsuccessful litigation 4.5.3
Crown debts *see* **Crown debts**
disqualified directors 4.5.2
person 'involved in management' 4.7.4
phoenix companies 4.7.4
'relevant' 4.7.4
see also **personal liability of directors**
Company Law Review
AGM requirements, opting in 2.9.1.2
company stationery information 2.9.1.8
de facto directors 2.9.1.5
reform 1.4
service contracts 2.9.1.6
shadow directors 2.9.1.5
shareholders' resolutions 2.9.1.3
third parties, benefits from 3.5.2.7
training and experience requirements 2.9.1.7

Company Law Review Steering Group
  accounting/reporting 9.4.3.4
  background 2.9
  business judgment rule 1.2
  company law recommendations
    9.4.3.1
  corporate governance, present system
    9.4.3.1
  directors' duties 9.4.3.2
  fair dealing provisions 5.1
    connected persons 5.12
  'Long Term' issue 3.2.2.4
  proxies, rights of 9.4.3.3
  reporting/accounting 9.4.3.4
  shareholders 9.4.3.3
  stakeholder debate 1.1, 9.4.1
company liability
  contracts *see* **contracts, liability for**
  crimes *see* **criminal liability**
  debts *see* **company debts**
  indemnity 4.8
  insurance against 4.8
  reasonableness standard 4.9
  securities issues *see* **securities issues**
  statutory relief 4.9
  torts *see* **torts**
  ultra vires acts
    beyond director's authority 4.1.2
    company, acts ultra vires the 4.1.1
    company constitution 3.2.3.1, 8.1.1
  winding up *see* **winding up**
    proceedings
  see also **directors' liability**
company powers
  constitution 8.1.1
  delegation *see* **delegation of powers**
  directors' personal liability *see*
    directors' liability
  inspect, right to 8.3.1
  objects clauses 8.1.2
  statutory provisions 8.1.1
company secretary
  ostensible authority 8.2.6
company stationery
  Companies Bill 2.9.1.8
  directors' names 2.5.4
compensation, loss of office
  Combined Code 6.7.6

  Companies Act 1985 requirements
    6.7.2
  damages 6.7.1
    see also **damages**
  golden parachutes/handshakes 6.7.3
  payment in lieu of notice 6.7.3
  'PILON' clauses 6.7.3
  reform proposals
    DTI consultation 6.7.5.3
    Higgs review 6.7.5.1
    Modernising Company Law
      (Government White Paper)
      6.7.5.2
  wrongful dismissal 6.7.3
competition provisions
  breaches, disqualified directors 2.3.6,
    13.2
  Enterprise Act (2002) 3.4.3.2
confidentiality
  breaches as misapplication of
    property 3.2.4
  investigations 12.4, 12.5
confidentiality orders
  appointment of directors 2.2.1
conflict of interests
  directors' duties 3.5.2.5
  fiduciary duties 3.2.6
  General Principles, proposed
    statement 3.5.2.5
  indemnity against liability 4.8
  investigations 12.14.1
connected persons
  fair dealing 5.12
  Model Code (share dealing) 7.3.2
contracts (company liability)
  Bills of Exchange Act (1882) 4.4.4
  non-disclosure, company details
    4.4.3
  pre-incorporation 4.4.1
  public company business, prior CA s
    117 certificate 4.4.2
contracts (fair dealing)
  disclosure of interests 5.4
  sole members, directors as 5.5
Cork Committee
  wrongful trading 4.7.3
corporate directors
  Companies Bill 2.9.1.4

corporate failures
  causes 9.1
  listed companies 2.3.7
  reform of company law 2.9
  Cadbury Committee 9.2
corporate governance
  accountability of directors 2.1
  background 9.2
  Combined Code *see* **Combined Code of Corporate Governance**
  failures, corporate *see* **corporate failures**
  meaning 9.1
  present system
    board structure 9.4.2
    monitoring of directors 9.4.2
    stakeholder debate 9.4.1
  see also **Committee on Corporate Governance**
corporate manslaughter
  criminal liability 3.4.3.3
costs
  derivative actions 10.3.6
  directors' expenditure, funding 5.8.6.6
  unfair prejudice 10.4.2
  unsuccessful litigation 4.5.3
CPR (Civil Procedure Rules) *see* **Civil Procedure Rules (CPR)**
credit transactions
  fair dealing 5.8.3
creditors
  interests of 1.1
    fiduciary duties 3.2.2.1
  secured, wrongful trading 11.2.1.1
  transactions defrauding 11.2.3.6
    intention to defraud, fraudulent trading 4.7.2.2
  unsecured, wrongful trading 11.2.1.1
CREST system 9.3.5
criminal liability
  breaches of injunctions/undertakings 4.2.2
  case law 4.2.2
  Companies Act requirements 3.4.3.1
  contempt of court 4.2.2
  corporate manslaughter 3.4.3.3

fair dealing, remedies for breach (Companies Act, s 330) 5.10
  fraudulent trading 4.7.2.1
  legislation 3.4.3.2
  mens rea 4.2
  offences of 'consent or connivance' 4.2.1
  relevant areas 3.4.3
Crown debts
  betting duty 4.5.1.2
  national insurance 4.5.1.4
  social security contributions 4.5.1.1
  VAT 4.5.1.3

D&O (directors' and officers') liability insurance 8.1.4.2, 12.14.4
damages
  early termination of service contract 6.7.1
  fraudulent misrepresentation 4.6.4
  misfeasance 4.7.1
  wrongful dismissal 6.7.3
de facto **directors**
  Company Law Review 2.9.1.5
  disclosure requirements, Companies Bill 2.9.1.5
  statutory provisions 2.7
  wrongful trading 4.7.3
debts, company *see* **company debts**
default rules
  directors' duties, economic analysis 1.2.1
delegation of powers
  Barings case 8.2.5
  care, skill and diligence requirements 3.3
  case law 8.2.3, 8.2.4
  continuing duties of directors 8.2.5
  general 8.2.1
  General Principles, proposed statement 3.5.2.3
  ostensible authority 8.2.6
  revocation of authority 8.2.2
  Table A 8.2.3
  to committees 8.2.2
  to individual executives 8.2.3
  to non-officer employees/other parties 8.2.4

where no official delegation of authority 8.2.6
Department of Trade and Industry (DTI)
  investigations, scope 12.2
  working group consultation exercise 9.3.5
derivative actions
  case law 19.3.6
  'clean hands' test 10.3.5
  costs 10.3.6
  defined 10.2, 10.3
  Foss v *Harbottle*, rule in 10.3.1
  fraud on the minority 10.3.2, 10.4.1
  independent organ 10.3.2
  obstacles 10.3.5
  preliminary hearings 10.3.7
  procedure 10.3.7
  ratification 10.3.5
  reform proposals 10.5.1
  special/extraordinary resolutions required 10.3.4
  ultra vires transactions 10.3.3
directors
  alternate 2.6
  appointment *see* **appointment of directors**
  de facto see **de facto directors**
  de jure 2.9.1.5
  decision-making process 9.4.3.2
  definition 2.1, 2.3
  disqualified *see* **disqualification of directors**
  duties *see* **duties of directors**
  loans to *see* **loans to directors (fair dealing)**
  monitoring of performance
    board structure 9.4.2
    by shareholders 2.1
  nominee 2.1, 2.8
  non-executive *see* **non-executive directors, role**
  number, maximum 2.3.2
  qualifications *see* **qualification of directors**
  remuneration *see* **remuneration of directors**
  resignation 2.4.1
  retirement 2.4.2
  'shadow' *see* **shadow directors**
  shareholders
    monitor of performance by 2.1
    role in appointment of 2.1
  role distinguished 2.1
directors' liability
  breach of trust 8.1.3
  fair dealing 5.11
  limiting
    court order 8.1.4.3
    indemnity agreements 8.1.4.1
    insurance policies 8.1.4.2
  misappropriation of property 8.1.3
  negligent misrepresentations 4.3.2
  'phoenix companies' 4.7.4
  statutory provisions 8.1.3
  see also **company debts**
disclosure requirements
  Combined Code of Corporate Governance 9.3.5
  Companies Act 1985
    circumstances where obligation not discharged 7.6.1.5
    Exchange, duty to notify 7.6.1.7
    existing/subsequent interests 7.6.1.1
    false statements 7.6.1.3
    'interest', meaning 7.6.1.2
    period for making notification 7.6.1.4
    register of directors' interests 7.6.1.6
    remuneration of directors 6.5.4.1
    spouses/children 7.6.1.3
  conflict of interest 3.2.6
  fair dealing 5.4
  insider dealing 7.2.1.3
    defences 7.2.2.2
  investigations 12.13
  remuneration of directors
    audited information 6.5.4.1
    Combined Code 6.5.4.3
    Companies Act 1985 6.5.4.1
    Listing Rules 6.5.4.2
    non-audited information 6.5.4.1
    quoted companies 6.5.4.1
    Report Regulations 2.1, 2.4.2, 6.5.4.1, 9.2

service contracts
   information requirements 6.4.2
   Listing Rules 6.4.2
   persons entitled to inspect 6.4.4
   Quotations Committee 6.4.2
   statutory requirements 6.4.1
   Takeover Code 6.4.3
   Takeover Code 7.6.2
dishonesty
   fraudulent trading 4.7.2.1
   indemnity against liability 4.8
disputes
   between board and members
      articles, amendments to 10.2.1.4
      case law 10.2.1.4
      Foss v *Harbottle see* **Foss** v **Harbottle, rule in**
      personal actions 10.2.1
      shareholders' agreements 10.2.1.5
      shareholders' personal rights 10.2.1.1
      statutory rights 10.2.1.6
      transactions outside company powers 10.2.1.3
   derivative actions *see* **derivative actions**
   reform proposals
      derivative actions 10.5.1
      unfair prejudice claims 10.5.2
   unfair prejudice remedy *see* **unfair prejudice**
   within board
      deadlock 10.1.3
      exclusion from proceedings 10.1.1.1
      majority standpoint 10.1.1
      minority standpoint 10.1.2
      removal of directors 10.1.1.2
disqualification of directors
   appeals 13.10
   applications for stay by defendant 13.9
   arising when 2.3.6
   Barings case 13.12
   Carecraft procedure 13.8
   case law
      discontinuance of proceedings 13.9
      disqualification order, application procedure 13.5.3
   grounds 13.2
   period of disqualification 13.7
   Secretary of State, recommendations to 13.5.2
   territorial limits 13.4
   CDDA 1986, territorial limits 13.4
   company debts 4.5.2
   discontinuance of proceedings 13.9
   grounds 13.2
   period of disqualification 13.2, 13.7
   permission to act, applications for 13.12
   persistent default 13.2
   procedure
      applications to commence proceedings out of time 13.5.4
      disqualification order application 13.5.3
      pre-action prima facie case recommendation to Secretary of State 13.5.2
      relevant factors 13.5
      relevant rules 13.5.1
      statutory 13.5
   public interest considerations 13.2
   purpose 13.1, 13.3
   undertakings 13.8
   unfitness, determining
      becoming insolvent when 13.6.2
      case law 13.6.3
      categories of directors 13.6.1
      meaning of 'unfitness' 13.6.3
   wrongful trading 4.7.3
disqualification orders
   appeals 13.10
   applications to commence proceedings out of time 13.5.4
   effect 13.11
   insolvent companies 13.1
   procedure on application for 13.5.3
duties of directors
   business judgment rule 1.2
   care, skill and diligence *see* **care, skill and diligence**
   case law 1.2.2, 3.1
   company law 1.2.1
   Company Law Review Steering Group 9.4.3.2

criminal liability *see* **criminal liability**
default rules 1.2.1
direct, to shareholders 3.4.1
economic analysis 1.2.1
EU countries, other 3.6
financial affairs of company, knowledge of 11.2.1.1
financial statements *see* **financial statements**
'fit and prudent' criteria 1.2.3
General Principles, proposed statement *see* **General Principles, proposed statutory statement**
insolvency, relating to *see* **insolvency**
mandatory rules 1.2.1
Modernising Company Law (White Paper) 3.5.1
penalties, non-compliance 1.2.1
penalty default rules 1.2.1
reform 1.4
regulatory background 1.2.2
sanctions for non-compliance 1.2.3, 1.4
statutory 1.2.1
United States 3.6
voluntary codes 1.2.2

ECHR (European Convention on Human Rights)
disqualification of directors, applications out of time 13.5.4
investigations 12.1
civil proceedings 12.12.2
criminal proceedings 12.12.1
EGM (extraordinary general meeting)
insolvency 11.4.1
EMI (enterprise management incentive) schemes 6.6.2.2
employees
interests of, fiduciary duties 3.2.2.2
Enhancing Corporate Governance (European Commission) 3.4.2.3
Enron, failure of
corporate governance, role 9.1
Higgs Review 9.2
qualification of directors 2.3.7
reform and 2.9

Enterprise Act 2002
criminal liability 3.4.3.2
enterprise management incentive (EMI) schemes 6.6.2.2
Equitable Life
former directors, action against 8.1.4.2
European Commission
Company Law Reform 3.4.2.3
Market Abuse Directive 7.2.6
European Company Law
reform 3.4.2.3
European Convention on Human Rights *see* **ECHR (European Convention on Human Rights)**
European Union (EU)
directors' duties 3.6
reform of company law 2.9, 2.9.3, 3.4.2.3
evidence
case law 12.14.7
computer records 12.14.6.3
documents 12.14.6.1
production 12.14.7
telephones 12.14.6.2
extraordinary resolutions
derivative actions 10.3.4

facilitation payments
anti-bribery rules 3.4.3.2
fair dealing
anti-avoidance provisions 5.3, 5.8.5
case law
disclosure of interests in contracts 5.4
payments company previously agreed to make 5.3
Companies Act 1985 (Part X), definitions 5.1
connected persons 5.12
credit transactions 5.8.3
disclosure of interests 5.4
exceptions to prohibitions
intra-group loans 5.8.6.2
minor business transactions 5.8.6.4
short-term quasi-loans 5.8.6.1
small loans 5.8.6.3
Law Commission review (1998) 5.1

loans to directors *see* **loans to directors (fair dealing)**
loss of office 5.2
payments company previously agreed to make 5.3
related party transactions 5.7
remedies for breach (Companies Act 1985, s 330) 5.10
retirement from office 5.2
sole member directors, contracts with 5.5
substantial property transactions 5.6
transactions involving directors, liability for 5.11
transactions/arrangements on behalf of another 5.8.4
see also **securities issues; share dealing**
fiduciary duties
case law
Aberdeen Railway Co v *Blaikie Brothers* 3.2.4
Bristol and West Building Society v *Mothew* 3.2.1, 3.2.2
Colin Gwyer & Associates Ltd v *London Wharf (Limehouse) Ltd* 3.2.2.1
Fulham Football Club v *Cabra Estates* 3.2.5
Guinness v *Saunders* 3.2.4
Harkness v *CBA* 3.2.2.6
Hirsche v *Sims* 3.2.3.2
Howard Smith v *Ampol Petroleum* 3.2.3.2
J J Harrison (Properties) Ltd v *Harrison* 3.2.6
Mutual Life Insurance v *Rank Organisation Ltd* 3.2.6
Parke v *Daily News* 3.2.2.2
Regal (Hastings) Ltd v *Gulliver* 3.2.4
Secretary of State v *McTighe & Another* 3.2.2.1
company's interests, acting in *see* **interests of company, acting in**
conflict of interest 3.2.6
director-shareholder relationship 1.1
economic analysis 1.2.1
fairness between shareholders 3.2.7

general 3.2.1
independence 3.2.5
insolvency
 case law 11.3.2, 11.3.3
 insolvent companies 11.3.2
 nature of duties 11.3.1
 prospectively insolvent companies 11.3.3
'Long Term' issue 3.2.2.4
loyalty *see* **interests of company, acting in**
misapplication of property 3.2.4
nature, insolvency 11.3.1
no secret profits 3.2.4
obedience
 acting for proper purpose only 3.2.3.2
 compliance with constitution 3.2.3.1
penalties for breach 3.2.1
regulatory background 1.2.2
ultra vires acts 4.1.1
Final Report on Modern Company Law Company Law Review Steering Group 5.1
finance director
ostensible authority 8.2.6
Financial Reporting Council (FRC)
delegation of authority 8.2.2
financial statements 3.4.2.1
Higgs Review 2.9.2, 3.3.2
Financial Services Authority *see* **FSA (Financial Services Authority)**
Financial Services and Markets Act 2000 *see* **FSMA (Financial Services and Markets Act) 2000**
financial statements
European Company law reform (Winter Report, 2002) 3.4.2.1, 3.4.2.3
responsibility for 3.4.2.1
Sarbanes-Oxley Act (2002) 3.4.2.1, 3.4.2.2, 3.6
Winter Report (2002) 3.4.2.1, 3.4.2.3
Foss v *Harbottle*, **rule in**
derivative actions 10.3.1
exceptions to 10.3.5
 unfair prejudice 10.4.1
impact 10.2.1.2

Index

'majority rule' principle 10.2.1.2
'proper claimant' principle 10.2.1.2
reform proposals 10.5.1
restated 10.3.1
special/extraordinary resolution required when 10.3.4
ultra vires acts 10.2.1.3
France
  board structure 9.4.2
fraud on the minority
  derivative actions 10.3.2, 10.4.1
fraudulent misrepresentation
  company liability 4.6.4
fraudulent trading
  carrying on of company business 4.7.2.2
  case law 4.7.2.2
  civil liability 4.7.2.2
  criminal liability 4.7.2.1, 11.2.2
  defined 11.2.2
  disqualification of directors 13.2
  intention to defraud 4.7.2.2, 11.2.2
  'party to' 4.7.2.2
  statutory duties (IA 1986) 11.2.2
  wrongful trading distinguished 4.7.3, 11.2.2
FRC (Financial Reporting Council) *see* Financial Reporting Council (FRC)
FSA (Financial Services Authority)
  company liability 4.6.1
  fit and proper person requirement 2.3.3
  Higgs Review recommendations 3.3.2
  investigations
    autonomy of investigators 12.6
    confidentiality 12.5
  market abuse 7.2.5
  Smith report 9.2
  Supervision Manual, investigations 12.14.5
FSMA (Financial Services and Markets Act) 2000
  criminal liability 3.4.3.2
  market abuse 7.2.5
FURBS (funded unapproved retirement benefit schemes) 6.6.1.1

gateways
  defined 12.13
General Principles
  directors' duties
    care, skill and diligence 3.5.2.4
    company objectives, promotion of 3.5.2.2
    conflicts of interest 3.5.2.5
    delegation 3.5.2.3
    independence of judgment 3.5.2.3
    obeying constitution 3.5.2.1
    personal use, company property, information or opportunity 3.5.2.6
    reform proposals 1.4
    third party benefits 3.5.2.7
    regulatory background 1.2.2
Germany
  board structure 9.4.2
  domination agreement 3.6
going concern requirement
  Combined Code of Corporate Governance 9.3.2
good faith, dealing in 8.1.1
Greenbury Committee
  background 9.2
  Code of Best Practice 9.2
  Report on Corporate Governance, delegation of authority 8.2.3
group company directors 1.3.2
Guinness v *Saunders* **case**
  fiduciary duties 3.2.4
  investigations 12.10
  service contracts 6.2.1

Hampel Committee
  AGM recommendations 9.3.5
  background/purpose 9.2
  board structure 9.3.1
  Combined Code 9.3
  Report on Corporate Governance
    board structure 9.4.2
    chairman, role of 9.3.1
    delegation of authority 8.2.3
    and regulatory background 1.2.2
    stakeholder debate 9.4.1
Hedley Byrne **principle**
  negligent misrepresentations 4.3.2

A Practitioner's Guide to Directors' Duties and Responsibilities

Higgs Review
appointment of directors 2.2.2
background/purpose 2.9, 9.2
board
  appointments 2.9.2.3
  composition 2.9.2.2
  role 2.9.2.1
  size 2.9.2.2
  structure 9.3.1, 9.4.2
care, skill and diligence 3.3.2
chairman, role of 9.3.1
Combined Code and 9.3
compensation, loss of office 6.7.5.1
criticism of 2.9.2
D&O insurance 8.1.4.2
delegation, to committees 8.2.2
duties of directors 1.3.1, 3.3
  fiduciary 3.2.1
ISC activism code 9.3.5
non-executive directors
  induction 2.3.8
  role 2.9.2.4, 9.4.3.2
  shareholders, availability to 9.3.1
  see also **non-executive directors**
performance evaluation 2.9.2.5
purpose 2.3.7
self-regulation 1.2.2
service contracts 2.9.1.6
shareholder activism 2.9.2.6
training of directors 2.3.8, 2.9.2.5
High Level Group of Company Law Experts
duties of directors 1.2, 1.2.1
European company law reform 2.9.3
non-executive directors, role 1.3.1
recommendations 2.9.3
Winter Report, financial statements 3.4.2.3
holding companies
fair dealing provisions 5.8.6.5
Human Rights Convention *see* **ECHR (European Convention on Human Rights)**

ICSA (Institute of Chartered Secretaries & Administrators)
service contract Guidance Note 6.7.5.1

incentive schemes
directors' remuneration 6.5.1.3
indemnity agreements
liability of directors, limiting 8.1.4.1
potential liabilities 4.8
independence
fiduciary duties 3.2.5
insider dealing
CJA 1993 provisions 7.2.1
  defences 7.2.2.1
defences
  CJA 1993 provisions 7.2.2.1
  dealing 7.2.2.1
  disclosing 7.2.2.2
  encouraging another to deal 7.2.2.1
  'equality of information' 7.2.2.1
disclosure of information 7.2.1.3
encouraging another to deal 7.2.1.2
'inside information', defined 7.2.1
  'unpublished price-sensitive information' and 7.3.2
'inside sources', defined 7.2.1
liability, establishing 7.2.1
'market information', defined 7.2.2.1
offences outlined 7.2.1
price-affected securities 7.2.1.1
'professional intermediary', defined 7.2.1.1
'requisite knowledge', defined 7.2.1
'securities', defined 7.2.1
'significant', defined 7.2.1
'specific or precise', defined 7.2.1
insiders
defined 8.1.1
insolvency
company 'insolvent' when 13.6.2
disqualification of directors 13.1
Enterprise Act (2002) 3.4.3.2
fiduciary duties, breach of 3.2.1
fiduciary duties of directors
  case law 11.3.2, 11.3.3
  insolvent companies 11.3.2
  nature 11.3.1
  prospectively insolvent companies 11.3.3
fraudulent trading *see* **fraudulent trading**
'insolvent liquidation', defined 11.2.1

Index

misfeasance 4.7.1
officer, director as 4.7.1
onset 11.2.3.4
practical matters 11.5
preferences *see* **preferences**
shareholders, duties to
   Listing Rules 11.4.2
   serious loss of capital 11.4.1
statutory duties (IA 1986), wrongful trading *see* **wrongful trading**
statutory provisions 11.1
transactions at an undervalue *see* **transactions at an undervalue**
transactions defrauding creditors 11.2.3.6
see also **winding up proceedings**
insolvent liquidation
   phoenix companies 4.7.4
   wrongful trading 4.7.3
inspect, right to
   access to company books 8.3.1
Institute of Chartered Accountants
   internal control requirements 8.2.5
Institute of Chartered Secretaries and Administrators
   on AGMs 9.3.5
Institute of Directors (IoD)
   stakeholder debate 9.4.1
Institutional Shareholders' Committee (ISC)
   fiduciary duties, statement of principles 3.2.1
   memorandum on shareholder activism 2.1, 9.3.5
   numbers of directors 2.3.2
insurance
   company liability 4.8
   directors' liability 8.1.4.2
interests of company, acting in
   appointing shareholders 3.2.2.6
   business judgment rule 3.2.2.7
   creditors' interests 1.1, 3.2.2.1
   employees' interests 3.2.2.2
   not-for-profit companies 3.2.2.3
   other companies in same group 3.2.2.5
   other stakeholders 3.2.2.4
   shareholders' interests 1.1

stakeholders' interests 1.1
internal control requirements
   Combined Code of Corporate Governance 9.3.3
   Institute of Chartered Accountants 8.2.5
investigations
   autonomy of investigators 12.6
   case law 12.2
   categories 12.6
   centralisation of management 12.14.2
   'civil'/'criminal' matters 12.12.1
   common law right to remain silent 12.1
   confidentiality 12.4, 12.5
   conflicts of interest 12.14.1
   Directors and Officers (D&O) liability insurance 12.14.4
   disclosure requirements 12.13
   evidence
      case law 12.14.7
      computer records 12.14.6.3
      documents 12.14.6.1
      production 12.14.7
      telephones 12.14.6.2
   external advisers 12.14.3
   false/misleading information 12.8.2
   information, use of
      civil proceedings 12.12.2
      criminal proceedings 12.12.1
   insurance 12.14.4
   investigators, categories 12.11
   limits on powers
      duty to act fairly 12.9.1
      duty to act within reference terms 12.9.2
      legal professional privilege 12.9.3
      obligations, other 12.9.4
   material gathered during 12.14.9
   methods 12.1
   notice of investigator's appointment 12.3
      effect 12.4
   notification 12.14.5
   powers of investigators 12.7
   product 12.11
   regulators 12.1

sanctions
  for failure 12.8.1
  for obstruction 12.8.2
Saunders case 12.10
scope 12.2
self-incrimination, privilege against 12.10
'statutory' 12.1
warrants 12.7
witnesses 12.14.8
Investment Management Association
  Institutional Shareholders'
    Committee, representation on 2.1
ISC (Institutional Shareholders'
    Committee) *see* **Institutional**
    Shareholders' Committee (ISC)
Italy
  reform of company law 3.6

Konzernrecht (codified law of
    corporate groups) 3.6

Laing, Sir Hector 1.1
large companies
  small distinguished 1.3
Law Commission
  alternate directors 2.6
  Alternative Dispute Resolution 10.5.2
  anti-avoidance provisions 5.8.5
  business judgment rule 1.2
  conflict of interest 3.2.6
  derivative actions 10.3
    reforms 10.5.1
  directors' duties, economic
    considerations 1.2.1
  disputes
    Alternative Dispute Resolution 10.5.2
    unfair prejudice 10.4.2, 10.4.1.7, 10.5.2
  fair dealing review 5.1
  connected persons 5.12
  shareholder remedies, reform 1.4
  stakeholders' interests, concept of 1.1
  unfair prejudice
    claims 10.5.2
    obstacles 10.4.2
    terminology 10.4.1.7

Law Society
  Company Law Committee 3.5.2.7, 9.4.1
legal advice privilege 12.9.3
legal professional privilege 12.9.3
liability of directors *see* **directors' liability**
liquidators
  company books, access to 8.3.2.1
listed companies
  insolvent, duties to shareholders
    Listing Rules 11.4.2
    serious loss of capital 11.4.1
  qualification requirements 2.3.7
Listing Authority
  notification of board changes 2.5.3
Listing Rules
  appointment of directors 2.2.2
  company liability 4.6.1
  disclosure
    remuneration of directors 6.5.4.2
    service contracts 6.4.2
  duties of directors, self-regulation 1.2.2
  election of directors 9.3.1
  insurance, directors' liability 8.1.4.2
  related party transactions 5.7
  share schemes 6.6.2
litigation privilege 12.9.3
loans to directors (fair dealing) 5.8.1
  definition of 'loan' 5.8.1
  directors' expenditure, funding 5.8.6.6
  holding company transactions 5.8.6.5
  house purchases 5.9
  intra-group 5.8.6.2
  minor business transactions 5.8.6.4
  money-lending companies 5.8.6.7
  prohibition exceptions
    directors' expenditure, funding 5.8.6.6
    holding company transactions 5.8.6.5
    intra-group loans 5.8.6.2
    minor business transactions 5.8.6.4
    money-lending companies 5.8.6.7
    short-term quasi-loans 5.8.6.1
    small loans 5.8.6.3

444

quasi-loans
  definitions 5.8.2
  money-lending companies 5.8.6.7
  short-term 5.8.6.1
relevant amounts 5.9
'relevant companies' 5.8.1
small 5.8.6.3
London Stock Exchange
Principles of Good Governance 9.2
loss of office
compensation
  Combined Code 6.7.4
  Companies Act 1985 requirements 6.7.2
  damages 6.7.1
  DTI Consultation 6.7.5.3
  golden parachutes/handshakes 6.7.3
  Higgs Review 6.7.5.1
  Modernising Company Law (White Paper) 6.7.5.2
  payment in lieu of notice 6.7.3
  'PILON' clauses 6.7.3
  wrongful dismissal 6.7.3
fair dealing 5.2
loyalty *see* **interests of company, acting in**

managing director
ostensible authority 8.2.6
mandatory rules
directors' duties, economic analysis 1.2.1
market abuse
Directive 7.2.6
Model Code and 7.3.3
offences 7.2.5
market information
defined 7.2.2.1
Maxwell, Kevin 12.9.1
Maxwell, Robert 12.11
'Maxwell syndrome'
corporate failures 9.1, 9.2
memorandum of association
appointment of directors, by third parties 2.2.4
governance systems 9.2
replacement, Companies Bill 2.9.1.1

ultra vires acts
  beyond directors' authority 4.1.2
  company, acts ultra vires the 4.1.1
  company constitution 8.1.1
  unclear, when 8.1.1
  see also **articles of association**
misapplication of property
fiduciary duties 3.2.4
misappropriation of assets
unfair prejudice 10.4.1.7
misfeasance
winding up proceedings 4.7.1
mismanagement
unfair prejudice 10.4.1.7
misrepresentation
fraudulent 4.6.4
negligent 4.3.2
misuse of information
market abuse 7.2.5
Model Code (share dealing)
'close periods' 7.3.2
connected persons 7.3.2
dealing restrictions 7.3.2
employee share schemes 7.3.2
'exceptional circumstances' 7.3.2
future developments 7.3.4
Listing Rules, located in 7.3.1
market abuse regime, interaction with 7.3.3
scope 7.3.2
'unpublished price-sensitive information' 7.3.2
Modern Company Law
Consultation Document 5.1
connected persons 5.12
Modernising Company Law **(White Paper)**
accounting 9.4.3.4
background 3.5.1, 9.2, 9.4.3.1
care and skill, statutory standard 1.2.2
Companies Bill 2.9.1
compensation, loss of office 6.7.5.2
duties of directors 3.5.1
  reform 1.4
financial statements 3.4.2.1
'hard law', legislative reform 3.3.2
position of directors 9.4.3.2

position of shareholders 9.4.3.3
provisions 3.5.1
purpose 2.9.1
reform proposals 1.4
reporting 9.4.3.4
service contracts 2.9.1.6
shareholders, communication with 9.3.5
small and large companies, distinguished 1.3
stakeholder debate 3.2.2.4, 9.4.1
third parties, benefits from 3.5.2.7
money-lending companies
fair dealing provisions 5.8.6.7
multiple jeopardy
market abuse 7.2.5
Myners review
institutional investment 9.2
shareholder activism 9.3.5

NAPF (National Association of Pension Funds) *see* **National Association of Pension Funds (NAPF)**
NASDAQ
remuneration disclosure requirements 6.5.4.1
National Association of Pension Funds (NAPF)
Institutional Shareholders' Committee, represented on 2.1
termination payments statement *see* Best Practice on Executive Contracts and Severance (ABI/NAPF joint statement)
national insurance
Crown Debts 4.5.1.4
negligence
acts/omissions 4.3.1
misrepresentations 4.3.2
misstatements 3.4.1
New York Stock Exchange
remuneration disclosure requirements 6.5.4.1

New Zealand
directors' duties 1.2
economic analysis 1.2.1

nominee directors 2.1, 2.8
non-cash asset
defined 5.6
non-executive directors, role
Barings case 8.2.5
board structure 9.3.1, 9.4.2
codes of conduct 3.3
Combined Code 3.3, 9.4.2
EU countries 3.6
Higgs Review *see* **Higgs Review**: non-executive directors
independence issues 9.3.1
induction requirements 2.3.8
nature of companies 1.3.1
nominees 2.8
non-for-profit companies
fiduciary duties 3.2.2.3
notification
of appointments
company stationery 2.5.4
to company 2.5.1
to Listing Authority 2.5.3
to Registrar of Company 2.2.1, 2.5.2
board meetings 10.1.1.1
investigations 12.14.5

objects clauses
drafting/interpretation 8.1.2
officer
director as 4.7.1
OFR (Operating and Financial Review)
financial statements 3.4.2.1, 9.4.3.4
options, prohibition on dealing in 7.5
ordinary directors
ostensible authority 8.2.6

Panel on Takeovers and Mergers
Takeover Code 4.6.3, 7.4
pension arrangements
'earnings cap' 6.6.1
funded unapproved retirement benefit schemes (FURBS) 6.6.1.1
Inland Revenue Consultation Paper 6.6.1
share schemes
discretionary share option 6.6.2.1
enterprise management incentive (EMI) 6.6.2.2

Index

Listing Rules 6.6.2
'phantom' 6.6.2.3
unfunded unapproved retirement schemes (UURBS) 6.6.1.2
Pensions Investment Research Consultants Limited (PIRC) 9.3.1
performance evaluation
Higgs Review 2.9.2.5
Pergamon Press
investigations 12.11
'phantom' share schemes
pension arrangements 6.6.2.3
'phoenix companies'
winding up 4.7.4
PIRC (Pensions Investment Research Consultants Limited) 9.3.1
Polly Peck
corporate failure 9.2
POS (Public Offers of Securities) Regulations (1995) 4.6.2
powers of directors
see also **company books, access to; company powers; delegation of powers**
pre-emption rights
unfair prejudice 10.4.2
pre-incorporation contracts
vliability for 4.4.1
preferences
case law 11.2.3.3
'clawback' provisions 11.2.3.5
defined 11.2.3.3
desire to prefer 11.2.3.3
order, effect of 11.2.3.5
see also **transactions at an undervalue**
Principles of Good Governance
London Stock Exchange 9.2
private companies
owner-managed 1.3
private equity-backed companies
directors
appointment by shareholders 2.2.3
nominee 2.1
vacation of office 2.4.6
professional intermediary
defined 7.2.1.1

proxies
rights of 9.4.3.3
public companies
appointment of directors, Combined Code 2.2.2
board structure 9.4.2
insolvent, duties to shareholders
Listing Rules 11.4.2
serious loss of capital 11.4.1
mandatory share scheme 9.4.3.3
shareholders' power 9.1
Public Offers of Securities (POS) Regulations 1995
company liability 4.6.2

qualification of directors
age limit 2.3.1
Companies Bill 2.9.1.7
articles, within 2.3.5
bankruptcy 13.2
chartered directors 2.3.8
Companies Bill 2.9.1.7
and disqualification 2.3.6
Higgs review 2.3.8
invalid appointment, effect 2.3.9
listed companies 2.3.7
number of directors 2.3.2
qualification shares 2.3.4
safeguards 2.3
shareholding 2.3.4
resignation of director 2.4.1
specific to certain types of company 2.3.3
training 2.3.8
qualification shares 2.3.4
resignation of director 2.4.1
quasi-partnership
unfair prejudice 10.4.1.6, 10.4.1.7

reform
care, skill and diligence, 'hard law' 3.3.2
compensation, loss of office
DTI consultation 6.7.5.3
Higgs review 6.7.5.1
White Paper 6.7.5.2
directors' duties 1.4

447

financial statements, Winter Report 3.4.2.3
register of charges
  access to 8.3.2.1
register of directors' interests in shares/debentures
  access to 8.3.2
  disclosure requirements, Companies Act 1985 7.6.1.6
register of directors/secretaries
  access to 8.3.2.1
Registrar of Companies
  notification to 2.2.1, 2.5.2
Regulatory Information Service
  notification of board changes 2.5.3
  unpublished information notified to 7.3.2
related party transactions
  fair dealing 5.7
removal of directors
  age 2.4.3
  case law 2.4.5
  company articles 2.4.4
  court order 2.4.7
  disputes 10.1.1.2
  fair dealing 5.2
  retirement by rotation/potential re-election 2.4.2, 9.3.1
  service contract provision 2.4.6
  shareholder's right, ordinary resolution 2.2.6, 10.1.1.2
  statutory (CA 1985, s 303) 2.4.5, 10.1.1.2
  voluntary resignation 2.4.1
remuneration committees
  ABI guidelines 6.5.2.1
  role 6.5.3
remuneration of directors
  ABI Guidelines on Executive Remuneration 6.5.2.1
  bonus 6.5.1.2
  case law 3.3
  Combined Code requirements
    ABI Guidelines 6.5.2.1
    content 6.5.2
    disclosure 6.5.4.3
    performance related payments 6.5.2

remuneration committee, role 6.5.3
disclosure requirements
  audited information 6.5.4.1
  Combined Code 6.5.4.1, 6.5.4.3
  Companies Act 1985 6.5.4.1
  Listing Rules 6.5.4.2
  non-audited information 6.5.4.1
  quoted companies 6.5.4.1
  Report Regulations 2.1, 2.4.2, 6.5.4.1, 9.2
excessive, unfair prejudice 10.4.1.7
golden hellos 6.5.1.4
long-term incentive schemes 6.5.1.3
pre-contractual statements 6.5.1.2
Remuneration Committee, role 6.5.3
salary 6.5.1.1
see also **pension arrangements**
retirement from office
  fair dealing 5.2
  by rotation 2.4.2
Review of the Role and Effectiveness of Non-Executive Directors see **Higgs Review**
rules against profiting
  indemnity against liability 4.8

Sarbanes-Oxley Act (2002)
  company law reforms 2.9
  directors' duties 3.4.2.1, 3.4.2.2, 3.6
Scotland
  age limits, qualification as director 2.3.1
Securities and Exchange Commission (SEC) (US) 3.4.2.2
Securities and Futures Authority 12.12.1
securities issues
  definitions, insider dealing 7.2.1
  fraudulent misrepresentation 4.6.4
  FSA 4.6.1
  Listing Rules 4.6.1
  loss, liability for 4.6.1
  Public Offers of Securities (POS) Regulations 1995 4.6.2
  Takeover Code 4.6.3
  see also **fair dealing**
self-incrimination
  privilege against 12.10

Index

self-regulation
  duties of directors 1.2.2
separate corporate personality doctrine
  torts, liability for 4.3.1
service contracts
  authorisation, case law 6.2.1, 6.2.2
  case law
    Charterbridge Corporation Ltd v
      Lloyds 3.2.2.5
    Guinness v *Saunders* 6.2.1
    Runciman v *Walter Runciman plc*
      6.2.2
  Companies Bill 2.9.1.6
  compliance with company
    constitution, case law 6.2.1, 6.2.2
  disclosure
    'appropriate place' 6.4.1
    information requirements 6.4.2
    Listing Rules 6.4.2
    persons entitled to inspect 6.4.4
    Quotations Committee 6.4.2
    statutory requirements 6.4.1
    Takeover Code 6.4.3
  early termination, damages for 6.7.1
  limits on term length
    ABI Guidelines 6.3.3
    change-of-control clauses
      (remuneration) 6.3.3
    Combined Code 6.3.2
    current practice 6.3.4
    executive remuneration 6.3.3
    statutory 6.3.1
  reform, Companies Bill 2.9.1.6
  vacation of office 2.4.6
  see also **pension arrangements**;
    remuneration of directors
SFO (Serious Fraud Office) 12.1
shadow directors
  case law 2.7
  Company Law Review 2.9.1.5
  defined 5.4
  disclosure requirements, Companies
    Bill 2.9.1.5
  statutory provisions 2.7
share dealing
  case law 7.1
  CJA 1993 provisions
    insider dealing 7.2.1, 7.2.2.1

  penalties 7.2.4
  common law 7.1
  disclosure of interests *see* **disclosure
    requirements**: Companies Act
    1985; **disclosure requirements**:
    Takeover Code
  Model Code *see* **Model Code (share
    dealing)**
  options, prohibition on dealing 7.5
  privilege of directors 7.1
  restrictions
    future developments 7.2.6
    insider dealing *see* **insider dealing**
    jurisdiction 7.2.3
    market abuse 7.2.5
    Model Code 7.3.2
    penalties 7.2.4
  statutory provisions, need for 7.1
  Takeover Code 7.4
  see also **fair dealing**
share schemes
  discretionary option 6.6.2.1
  enterprise management incentive
    (EMI) 6.6.2.2
  Listing Rules 6.6.2
  'phantom' 6.6.2.3
shareholder directors 1.3
shareholders
  activism
    Higgs Review 2.9.2.6
    Institutional Shareholders'
      Committee (ISC) memorandum
      on 2.1
    Myners review 9.3.5
  agreements 10.2.1.5
  appointing 3.2.2.6
  board role distinguished 9.2
  circulars to, takeovers 4.6.3
  as class 11.3.1
  Combined Code recommendations,
    corporate governance 9.3.5
  Company Law Review Steering
    Group 9.4.3.3
  direct duties to 3.4.1
  directors
    appointment of, role in 2.1, 2.2.3,
      9.1
    monitor of performance 2.1

449

removing 2.2.6, 10.1.1.2
role distinguished 2.1
disputes with board, personal actions 10.2.1
fairness between 3.2.7
insolvent companies, public/listed
  Listing Rules 11.4.2
  serious loss of capital 11.4.1
interests of 1.1
locus standi 10.2.1.3
personal actions
  arising when 10.2.1
  articles, amendments to 10.2.1.4
  case law 10.2.1.4
  Foss v *Harbottle*, rule in 10.2.1.2
  insider/outsider rights 10.2.1.1
  rights 10.2.1.1
  shareholders' agreements 10.2.1.5
  statutory rights 10.2.1.6
  ultra vires acts 10.2.1.3
powers 9.1
remedies, reform 1.4
remuneration policy changes, ABI guidelines 6.5.2.1
resolutions of, Companies Bill 2.9.1.3
statutory rights 10.2.1.6
unfair prejudice remedy, 'company's affairs', meaning 10.4.1.5
voidable transactions, powers relating to 8.1.1
see also **ISC (Institutional Shareholders' Committee)**
shares
  qualification 2.3.4
    resignation of director 2.4.1
small companies
  large distinguished 1.3
Smith Report
  audit committee, role 9.3.4
  background/purpose 9.2
  care, skill and diligence 3.3
  delegation of authority 8.2.2
  fiduciary duties 3.2.1
  financial statements 3.4.2.1
social security contributions
  Crown debts 4.5.1.1
special resolutions
  derivative actions 10.3.4

stakeholder debate
  corporate governance 9.4.1
stakeholders' interests 1.1, 3.2.2.4
substantial property transactions
  fair dealing 5.6

Table A (Companies Act 1985)
  appointment of directors
    alternate directors 2.6
    by directors 2.2.2
    first director(s) 2.2.1
    by shareholders 2.2.3
    by third parties 2.2.4
  delegation of powers 8.2.3
  numbers of directors 2.3.2
  retirement by rotation 2.4.2
  vacation of office 2.4.4
Takeover Code
  'acting in concert' 7.4
  'associate', meaning 7.6.2
  background 7.4
  company liability 4.6.3
  disclosure requirements 7.6.2
  discretionary clients, dealings for 7.6.2
  documents, production standards 1.3
  duties of directors, self-regulation 1.2.2
  loss of office, compensation 5.2
  residence requirements 7.4
  scope 7.4
  service contracts, disclosure 6.4.3
  share dealing 7.4
takeovers
  circulars to shareholders 4.6.3
third parties
  access to company books 8.3.2
    general viewing 8.3.2.1
  appointment of directors 2.2.4
  general principles, proposed statement 3.5.2.7
  legal obligations, company constitution 8.1.1
torts
  case law 4.3.1
  negligent acts/omissions 4.3.1
  negligent misrepresentations 4.3.2
  negligent misstatements 3.4.1

training of directors
  Companies Bill 2.9.1.7
  Higgs review 2.3.8, 2.9.2.5
  voluntary 2.3.8
transactions at an undervalue
  case law 11.2.3.1
  'clawback' provisions 11.2.3.5
  creditors, transactions defrauding 11.2.3.6
  defined 11.2.3.1
  group company directors 1.3.2
  order, effect of 11.2.3.5
  relevant time 11.2.3.2
  see also **preferences**
Turnbull Committee
  background and purpose 9.2
  internal control 9.3.3
Turnbull Guidance
  non-executive directors 3.3

UKLA (UK Listing Authority)
  Listing Rules *see* **Listing Rules**
ultra vires acts
  beyond directors' authority 4.1.2
  company, acts ultra vires the 4.1.1
  company constitution, compliance with 3.2.3.1, 8.1.1
  derivative actions 10.3.3
  personal actions 10.2.1.3
unfair prejudice
  'company's affairs', meaning 10.4.1.5
  'interests', meaning 10.4.1.6
  'legitimate expectation' 10.4.1.6
  obstacles 10.4.2
  procedure 10.4.4
  quasi-partnerships 10.4.1.6
  reform proposals, claims 10.5.2
  remedies available 10.4.3
  removal of directors, court order 2.4.7
  statutory requirements
    complainant must be member 10.4.1.1
    complaint must be made in petitioner's capacity as member 10.4.1.2
    conduct of company's affairs 10.4.1.4
    effect on other members 10.4.1.3
    'interests' 10.4.1.2
    'just and equitable' grounds 10.4.1.6
    'legitimate expectation' 10.4.1.6
    meaning of 'company's affairs' 10.4.1.5
    meaning of 'interests' 10.4.1.6
    meaning of 'unfairly prejudicial' 10.4.1.7
    'quasi-partnerships' 10.4.1.6
    shareholders 10.4.1.5
    'strict legal rights' 10.4.1.2
    'unfairly prejudicial', meaning 10.4.1.7
unfitness, determining
  becoming insolvent when 13.6.2
  case law 13.6.3
  categories of directors 13.6.1
  definition of 'unfitness' 13.6.3
United States
  board structure 9.4.2
  business judgment rule 1.2
  Corporations Law 1.2.1
  directors' duties 3.6
  Sarbanes-Oxley Act (2002)
    company law reforms 2.9
    directors' duties 3.4.2.1, 3.4.2.2, 3.6
UURBS (unfunded unapproved retirement benefit schemes) 6.6.1.2

vacation of office *see* **removal of directors**
Value Added Tax (VAT)
  Crown debts 4.5.1.3
voidable transactions
  memorandum, non-compliance with 8.1.1

Wednesbury principles
  business judgment rule 3.2.2.7
White Paper (Modernising Company Law) *see* ***Modernising Company Law*** **(White Paper)**
'wilful default'
  indemnity against liability 4.8

winding up proceedings
  fraudulent trading
    civil liability 4.7.2.2
    criminal liability 4.7.2.1
  insolvent liquidation, company in
    'phoenix companies' 4.7.4
    wrongful trading 4.7.3
  misfeasance 4.7.1
  'Phoenix companies' 4.7.4
  wrongful trading 4.7.3
Winter Report
  European Company Law reform 3.4.2.1, 3.4.2.3

witnesses
  investigations 12.14.8
wrongful trading
  case law 11.2.1.1
  continuing to trade 11.2.1.1
  defence to proceedings 11.2.1
  fraudulent trading distinguished 4.7.3, 11.2.2
  liquidator's powers 11.2.1
  options available 11.2.1.1
  practical problems 11.2.1.1
  winding up proceedings 4.7.3